# BRIAN MICHAEL BENDIS



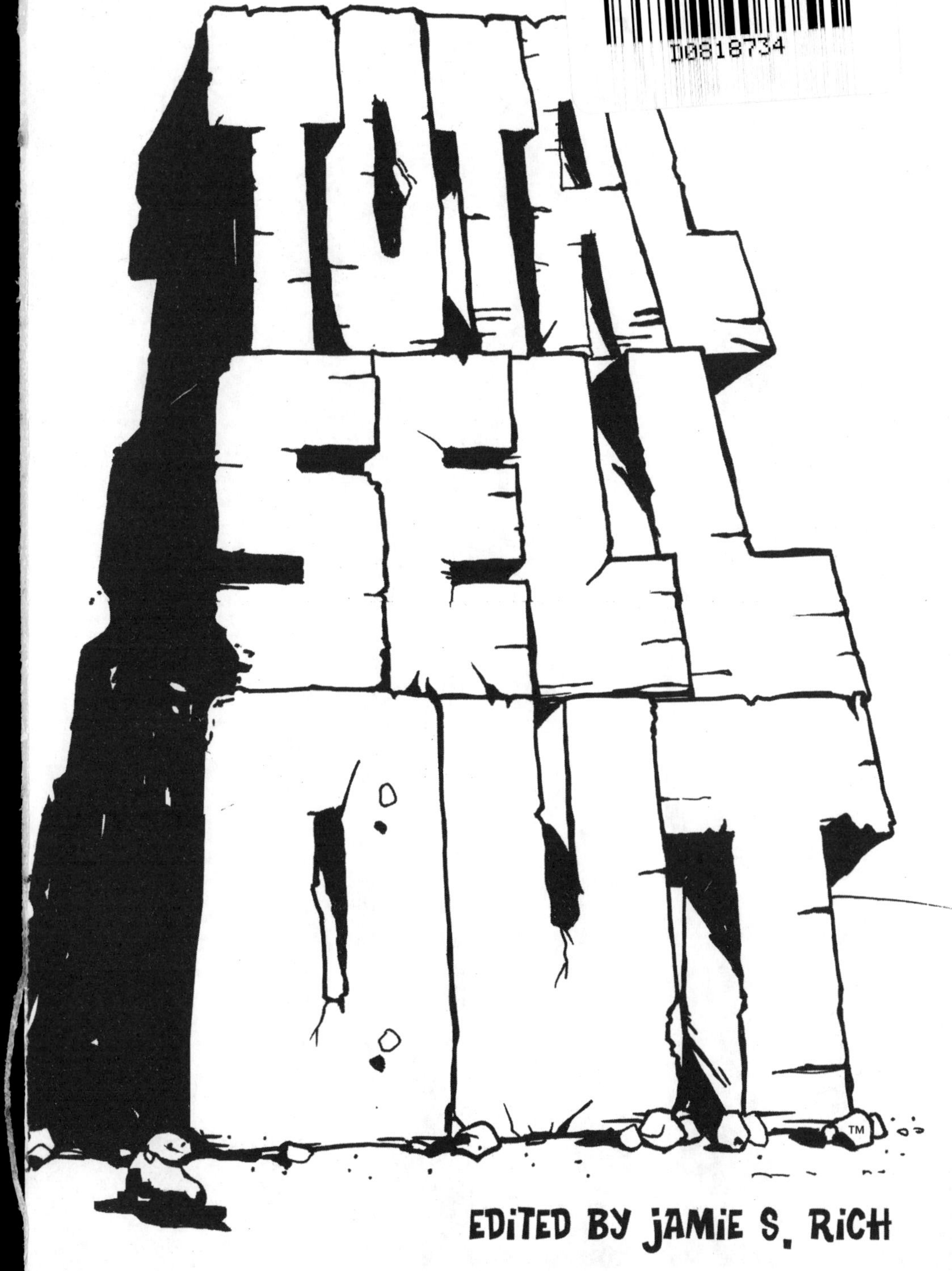
TOTAL SELL OUT
TM

EDITED BY JAMIE S. RICH

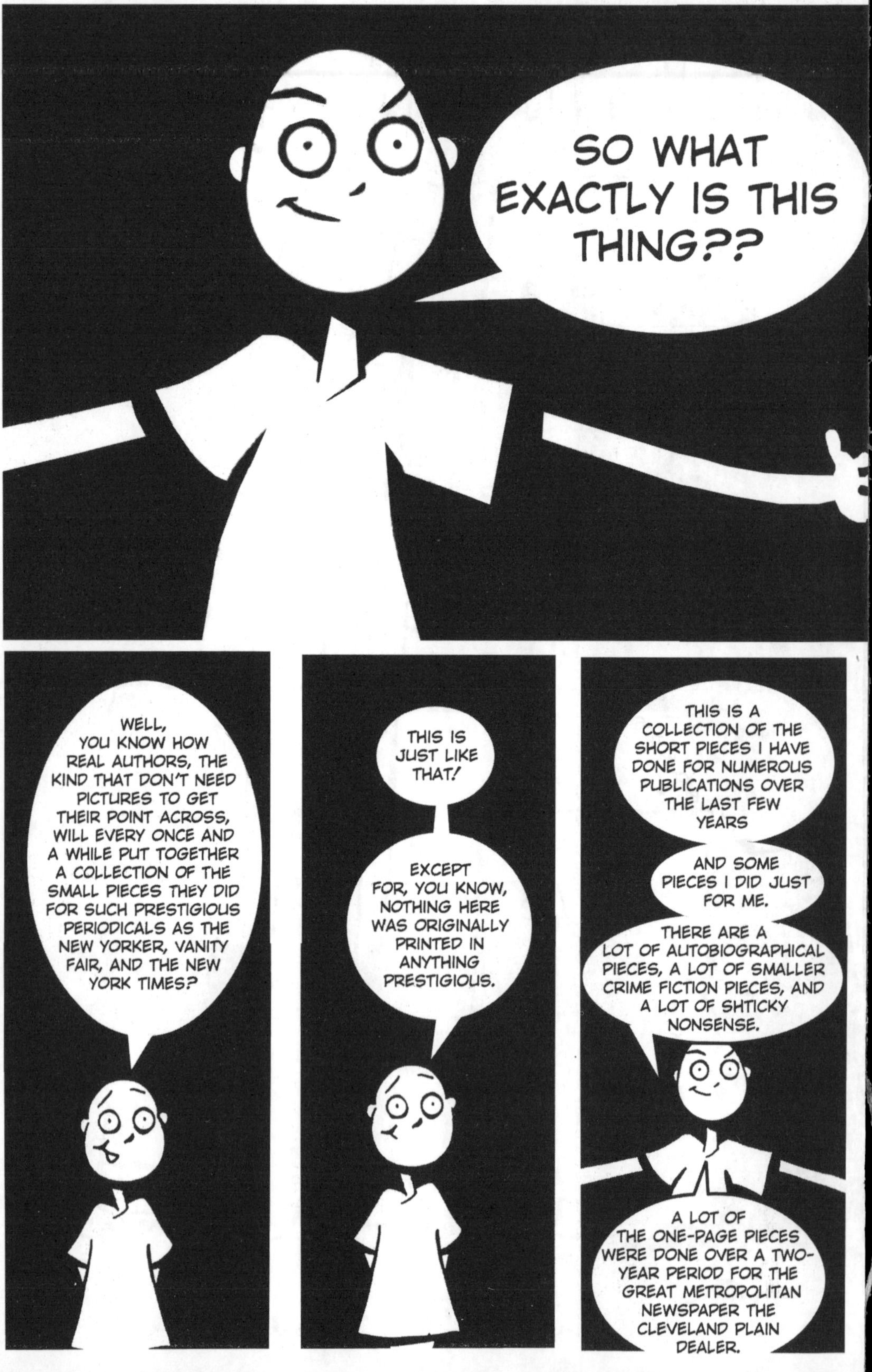
SO WHAT EXACTLY IS THIS THING??
WELL, YOU KNOW HOW REAL AUTHORS, THE KIND THAT DON'T NEED PICTURES TO GET THEIR POINT ACROSS, WILL EVERY ONCE AND A WHILE PUT TOGETHER A COLLECTION OF THE SMALL PIECES THEY DID FOR SUCH PRESTIGIOUS PERIODICALS AS THE NEW YORKER, VANITY FAIR, AND THE NEW YORK TIMES?
THIS IS JUST LIKE THAT!
EXCEPT FOR, YOU KNOW, NOTHING HERE WAS ORIGINALLY PRINTED IN ANYTHING PRESTIGIOUS.
THIS IS A COLLECTION OF THE SHORT PIECES I HAVE DONE FOR NUMEROUS PUBLICATIONS OVER THE LAST FEW YEARS
AND SOME PIECES I DID JUST FOR ME.
THERE ARE A LOT OF AUTOBIOGRAPHICAL PIECES, A LOT OF SMALLER CRIME FICTION PIECES, AND A LOT OF SHTICKY NONSENSE.
A LOT OF THE ONE-PAGE PIECES WERE DONE OVER A TWO-YEAR PERIOD FOR THE GREAT METROPOLITAN NEWSPAPER THE CLEVELAND PLAIN DEALER.

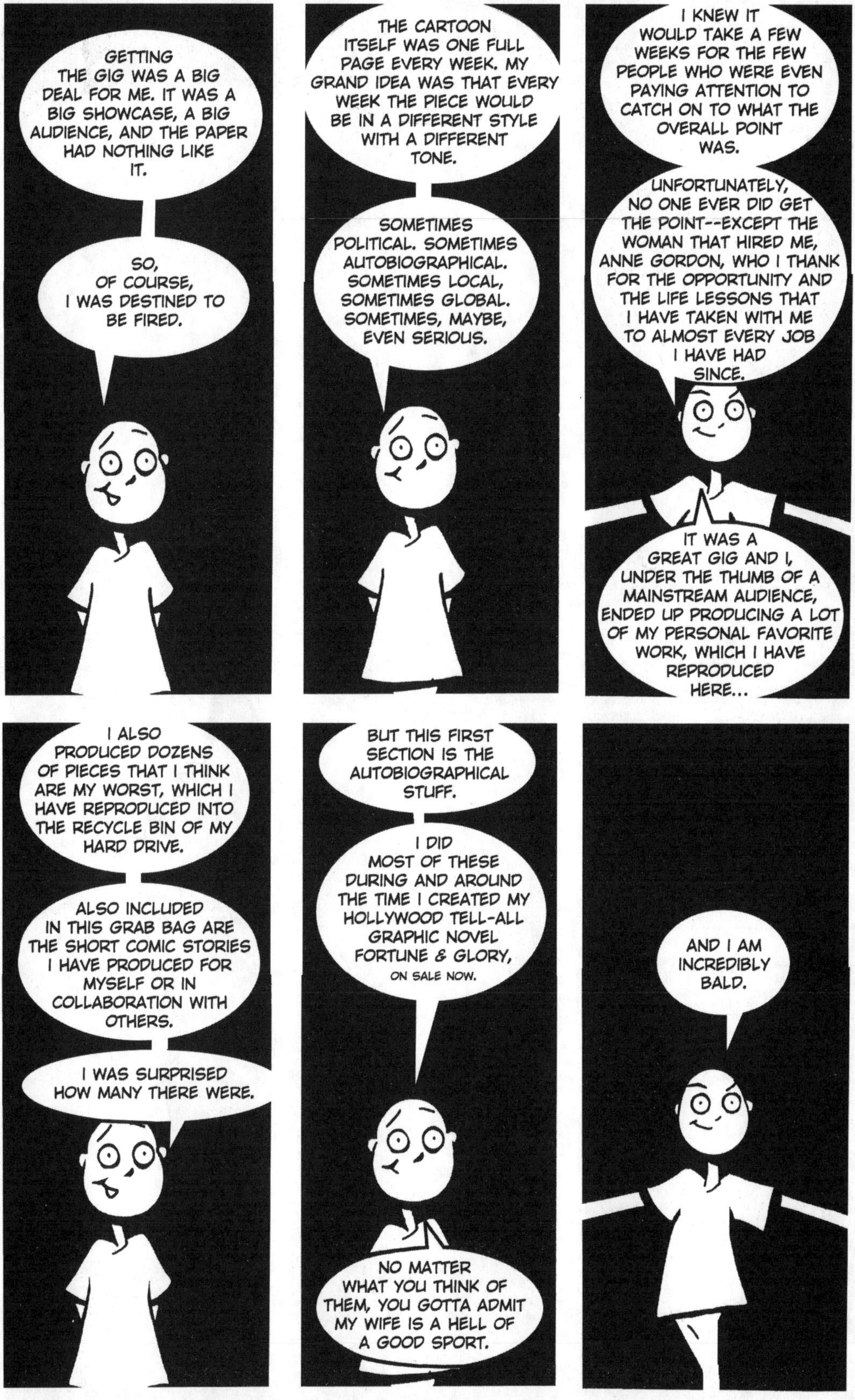
GETTING THE GIG WAS A BIG DEAL FOR ME. IT WAS A BIG SHOWCASE, A BIG AUDIENCE, AND THE PAPER HAD NOTHING LIKE IT.
SO, OF COURSE, I WAS DESTINED TO BE FIRED.
THE CARTOON ITSELF WAS ONE FULL PAGE EVERY WEEK. MY GRAND IDEA WAS THAT EVERY WEEK THE PIECE WOULD BE IN A DIFFERENT STYLE WITH A DIFFERENT TONE.
SOMETIMES POLITICAL. SOMETIMES AUTOBIOGRAPHICAL. SOMETIMES LOCAL, SOMETIMES GLOBAL. SOMETIMES, MAYBE, EVEN SERIOUS.
I KNEW IT WOULD TAKE A FEW WEEKS FOR THE FEW PEOPLE WHO WERE EVEN PAYING ATTENTION TO CATCH ON TO WHAT THE OVERALL POINT WAS.
UNFORTUNATELY, NO ONE EVER DID GET THE POINT--EXCEPT THE WOMAN THAT HIRED ME, ANNE GORDON, WHO I THANK FOR THE OPPORTUNITY AND THE LIFE LESSONS THAT I HAVE TAKEN WITH ME TO ALMOST EVERY JOB I HAVE HAD SINCE.
IT WAS A GREAT GIG AND I, UNDER THE THUMB OF A MAINSTREAM AUDIENCE, ENDED UP PRODUCING A LOT OF MY PERSONAL FAVORITE WORK, WHICH I HAVE REPRODUCED HERE...
I ALSO PRODUCED DOZENS OF PIECES THAT I THINK ARE MY WORST, WHICH I HAVE REPRODUCED INTO THE RECYCLE BIN OF MY HARD DRIVE.
ALSO INCLUDED IN THIS GRAB BAG ARE THE SHORT COMIC STORIES I HAVE PRODUCED FOR MYSELF OR IN COLLABORATION WITH OTHERS.
I WAS SURPRISED HOW MANY THERE WERE.
BUT THIS FIRST SECTION IS THE AUTOBIOGRAPHICAL STUFF.
I DID MOST OF THESE DURING AND AROUND THE TIME I CREATED MY HOLLYWOOD TELL-ALL GRAPHIC NOVEL FORTUNE & GLORY, ON SALE NOW.
NO MATTER WHAT YOU THINK OF THEM, YOU GOTTA ADMIT MY WIFE IS A HELL OF A GOOD SPORT.
AND I AM INCREDIBLY BALD.

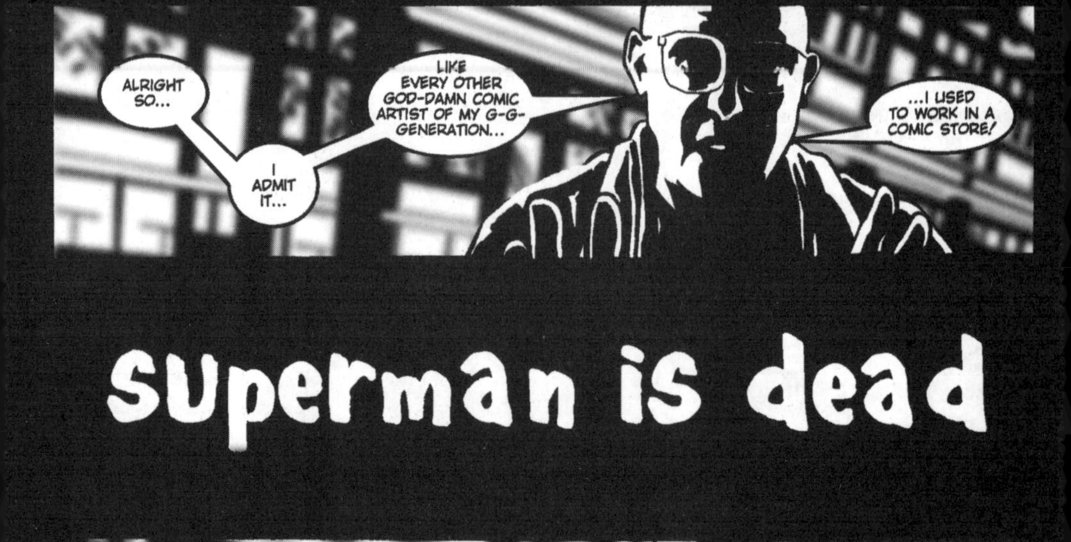
ALRIGHT SO...
I ADMIT IT...
LIKE EVERY OTHER GOD-DAMN COMIC ARTIST OF MY G-G-GENERATION...
...I USED TO WORK IN A COMIC STORE!

# superman is dead

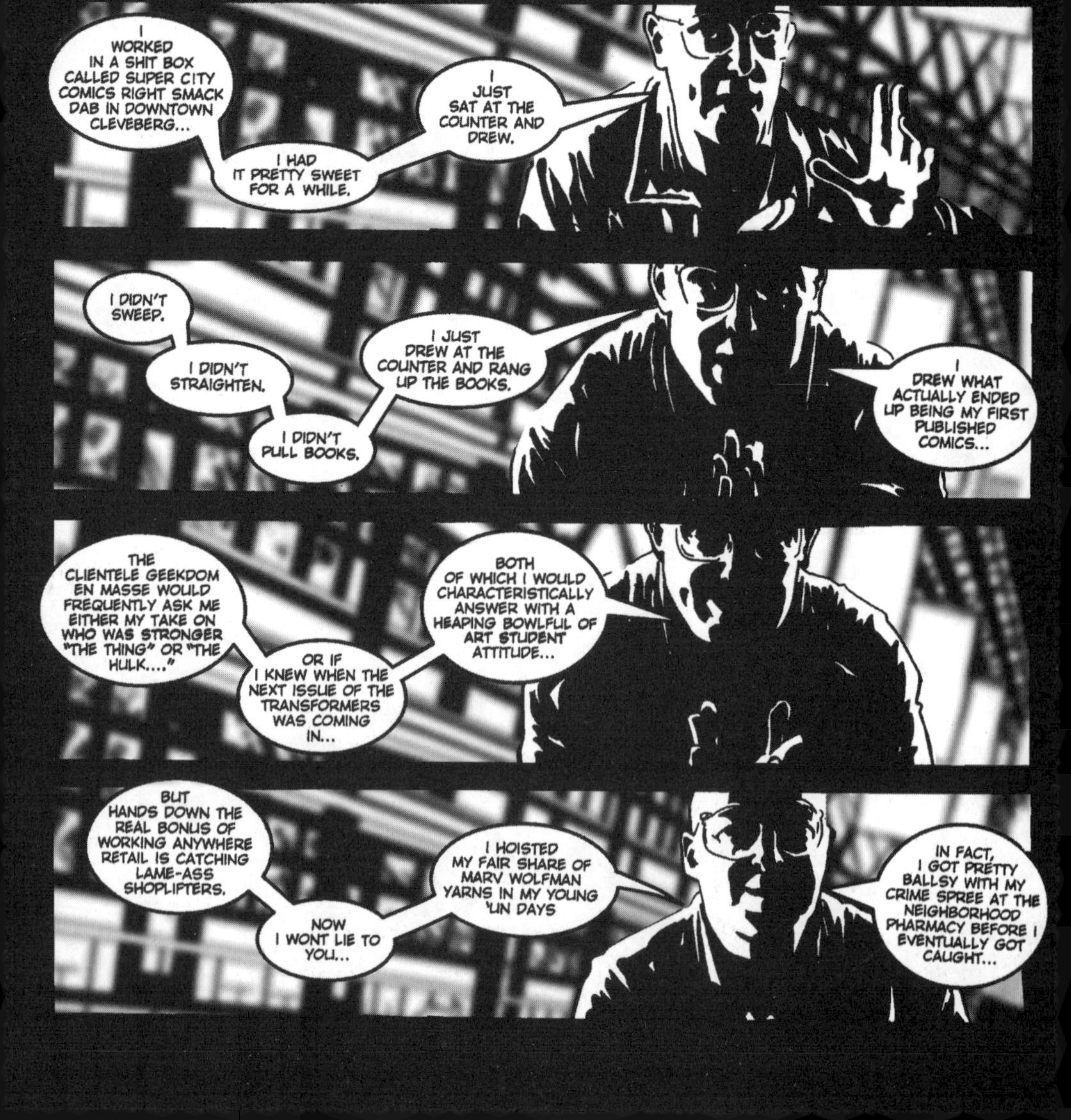
I WORKED IN A SHIT BOX CALLED SUPER CITY COMICS RIGHT SMACK DAB IN DOWNTOWN CLEVEBERG...
I HAD IT PRETTY SWEET FOR A WHILE.
I JUST SAT AT THE COUNTER AND DREW.
I DIDN'T SWEEP.
I DIDN'T STRAIGHTEN.
I DIDN'T PULL BOOKS.
I JUST DREW AT THE COUNTER AND RANG UP THE BOOKS.
I DREW WHAT ACTUALLY ENDED UP BEING MY FIRST PUBLISHED COMICS...
THE CLIENTELE GEEKDOM EN MASSE WOULD FREQUENTLY ASK ME EITHER MY TAKE ON WHO WAS STRONGER "THE THING" OR "THE HULK...."
OR IF I KNEW WHEN THE NEXT ISSUE OF THE TRANSFORMERS WAS COMING IN...
BOTH OF WHICH I WOULD CHARACTERISTICALLY ANSWER WITH A HEAPING BOWLFUL OF ART STUDENT ATTITUDE...
BUT HANDS DOWN THE REAL BONUS OF WORKING ANYWHERE RETAIL IS CATCHING LAME-ASS SHOPLIFTERS.
NOW I WONT LIE TO YOU...
I HOISTED MY FAIR SHARE OF MARV WOLFMAN YARNS IN MY YOUNG 'UN DAYS
IN FACT, I GOT PRETTY BALLSY WITH MY CRIME SPREE AT THE NEIGHBORHOOD PHARMACY BEFORE I EVENTUALLY GOT CAUGHT...

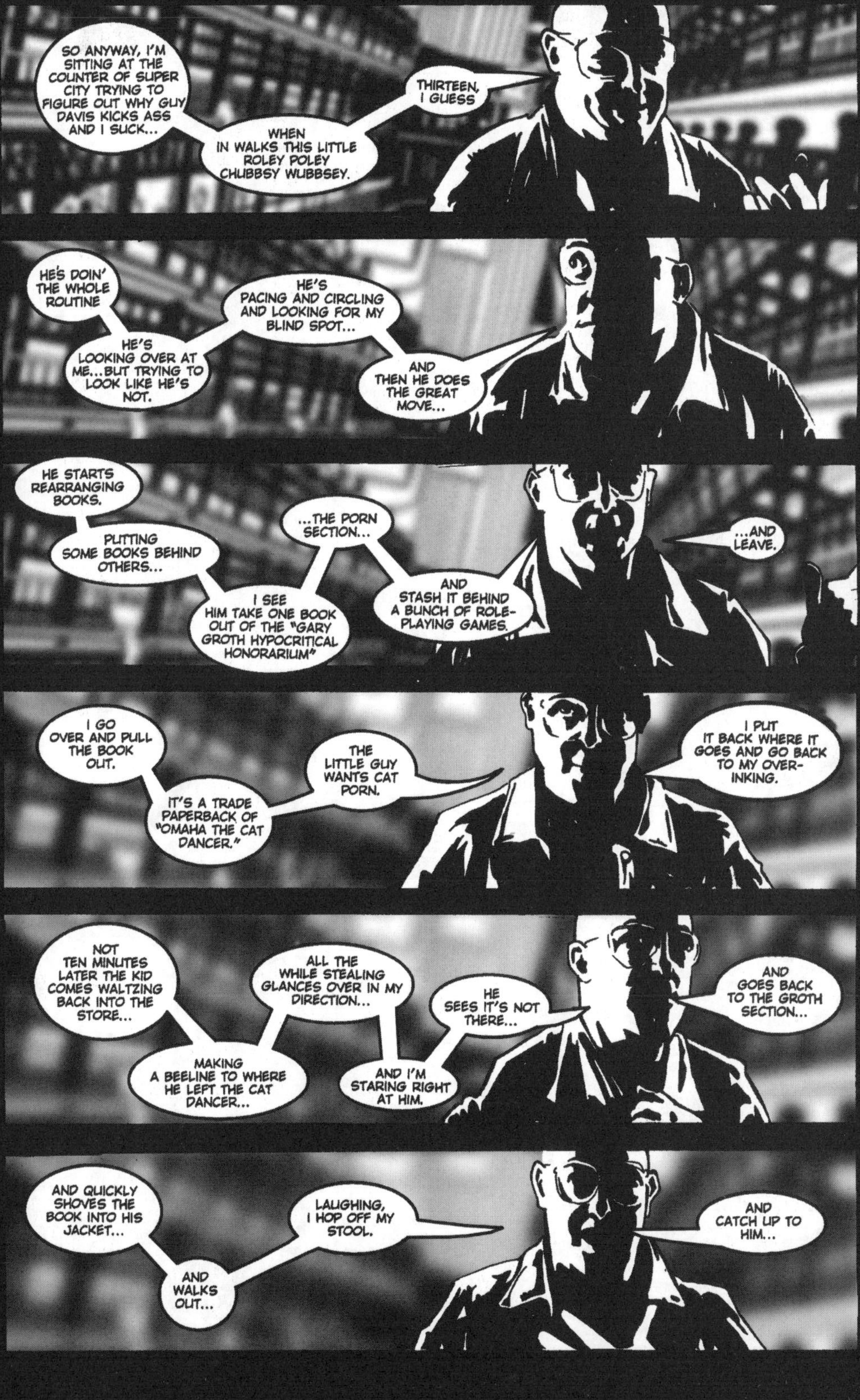
SO ANYWAY, I'M SITTING AT THE COUNTER OF SUPER CITY TRYING TO FIGURE OUT WHY GUY DAVIS KICKS ASS AND I SUCK...
WHEN IN WALKS THIS LITTLE ROLEY POLEY CHUBBSY WUBBSEY.
THIRTEEN, I GUESS
HE'S DOIN' THE WHOLE ROUTINE
HE'S LOOKING OVER AT ME...BUT TRYING TO LOOK LIKE HE'S NOT.
HE'S PACING AND CIRCLING AND LOOKING FOR MY BLIND SPOT...
AND THEN HE DOES THE GREAT MOVE...
HE STARTS REARRANGING BOOKS.
PUTTING SOME BOOKS BEHIND OTHERS...
I SEE HIM TAKE ONE BOOK OUT OF THE "GARY GROTH HYPOCRITICAL HONORARIUM"
...THE PORN SECTION...
AND STASH IT BEHIND A BUNCH OF ROLE-PLAYING GAMES.
...AND LEAVE.
I GO OVER AND PULL THE BOOK OUT.
IT'S A TRADE PAPERBACK OF "OMAHA THE CAT DANCER."
THE LITTLE GUY WANTS CAT PORN.
I PUT IT BACK WHERE IT GOES AND GO BACK TO MY OVER-INKING.
NOT TEN MINUTES LATER THE KID COMES WALTZING BACK INTO THE STORE...
MAKING A BEELINE TO WHERE HE LEFT THE CAT DANCER...
ALL THE WHILE STEALING GLANCES OVER IN MY DIRECTION...
AND I'M STARING RIGHT AT HIM.
HE SEES IT'S NOT THERE...
AND GOES BACK TO THE GROTH SECTION...
AND QUICKLY SHOVES THE BOOK INTO HIS JACKET...
AND WALKS OUT...
LAUGHING, I HOP OFF MY STOOL.
AND CATCH UP TO HIM...

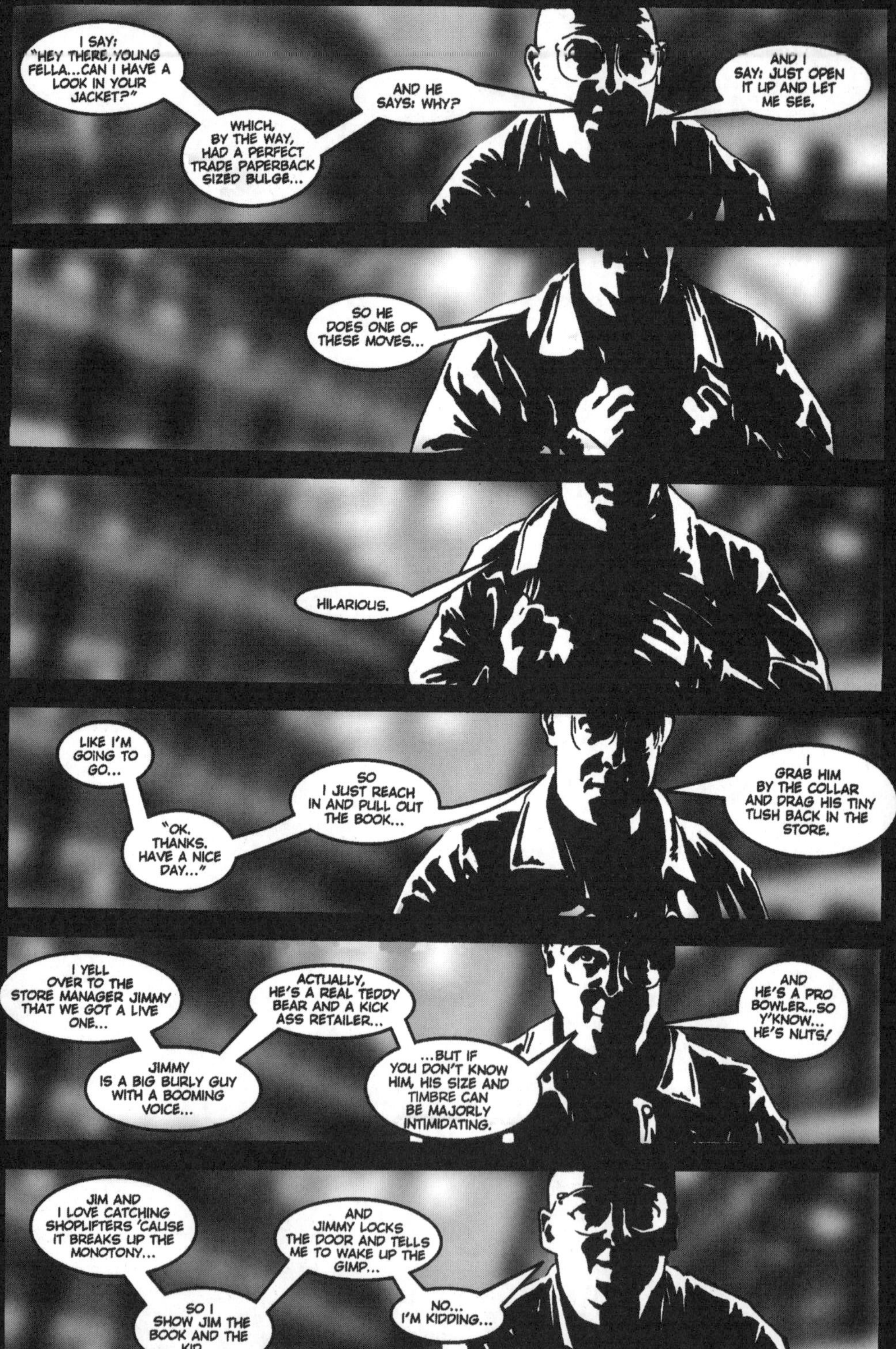
I SAY: "HEY THERE, YOUNG FELLA...CAN I HAVE A LOOK IN YOUR JACKET?"
WHICH, BY THE WAY, HAD A PERFECT TRADE PAPERBACK SIZED BULGE...
AND HE SAYS: WHY?
AND I SAY: JUST OPEN IT UP AND LET ME SEE.
SO HE DOES ONE OF THESE MOVES...
HILARIOUS.
LIKE I'M GOING TO GO...
"OK. THANKS. HAVE A NICE DAY..."
SO I JUST REACH IN AND PULL OUT THE BOOK...
I GRAB HIM BY THE COLLAR AND DRAG HIS TINY TUSH BACK IN THE STORE.
I YELL OVER TO THE STORE MANAGER JIMMY THAT WE GOT A LIVE ONE...
JIMMY IS A BIG BURLY GUY WITH A BOOMING VOICE...
ACTUALLY, HE'S A REAL TEDDY BEAR AND A KICK ASS RETAILER...
...BUT IF YOU DON'T KNOW HIM, HIS SIZE AND TIMBRE CAN BE MAJORLY INTIMIDATING.
AND HE'S A PRO BOWLER...SO Y'KNOW... HE'S NUTS!
JIM AND I LOVE CATCHING SHOPLIFTERS 'CAUSE IT BREAKS UP THE MONOTONY...
SO I SHOW JIM THE BOOK AND THE KID...
AND JIMMY LOCKS THE DOOR AND TELLS ME TO WAKE UP THE GIMP...
NO... I'M KIDDING...

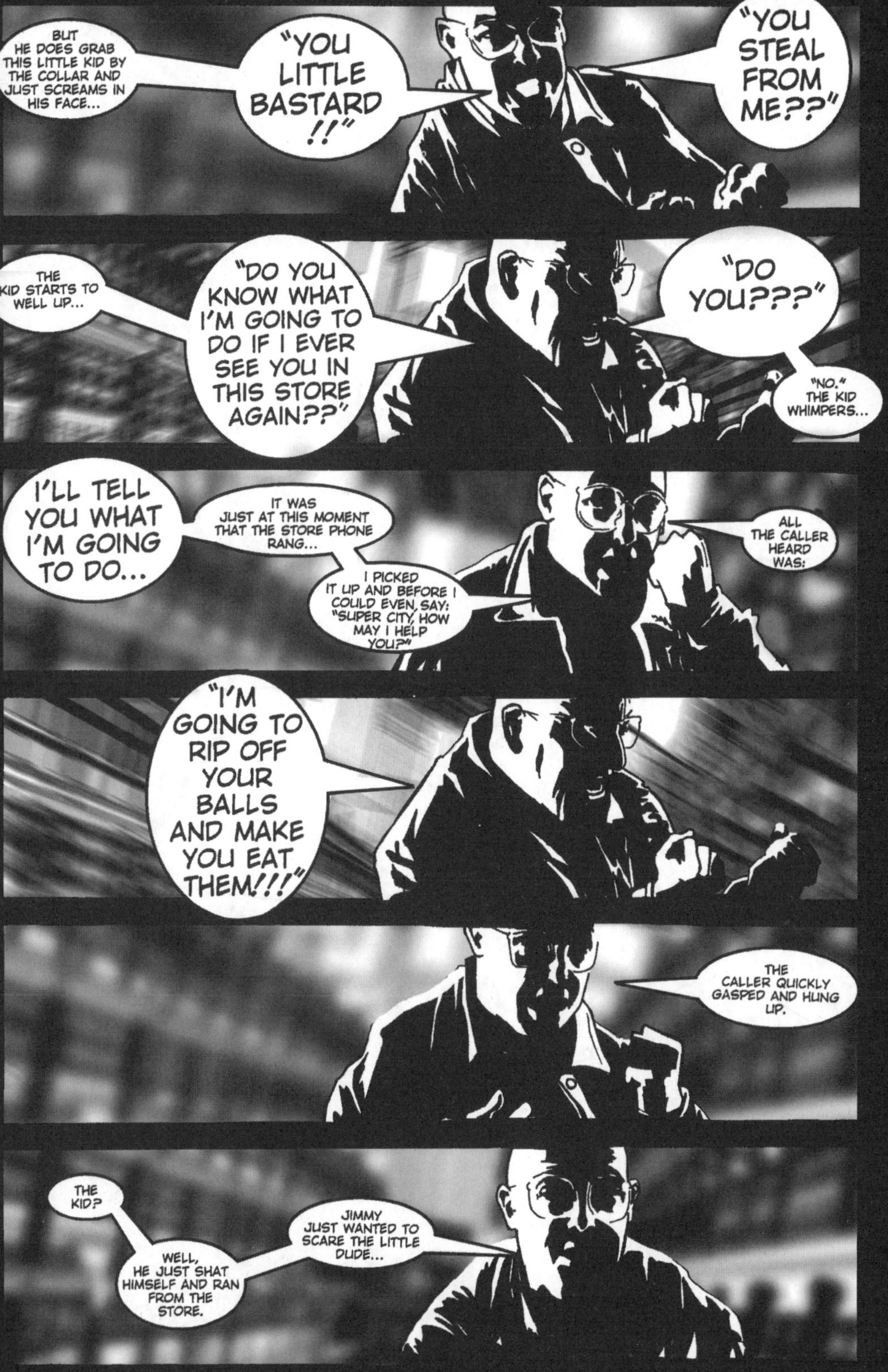
BUT HE DOES GRAB THIS LITTLE KID BY THE COLLAR AND JUST SCREAMS IN HIS FACE...
"YOU LITTLE BASTARD !!"
"YOU STEAL FROM ME??"
THE KID STARTS TO WELL UP...
"DO YOU KNOW WHAT I'M GOING TO DO IF I EVER SEE YOU IN THIS STORE AGAIN??"
"DO YOU???"
"NO." THE KID WHIMPERS...
I'LL TELL YOU WHAT I'M GOING TO DO...
IT WAS JUST AT THIS MOMENT THAT THE STORE PHONE RANG...
I PICKED IT UP AND BEFORE I COULD EVEN SAY: "SUPER CITY, HOW MAY I HELP YOU?"
ALL THE CALLER HEARD WAS:
"I'M GOING TO RIP OFF YOUR BALLS AND MAKE YOU EAT THEM!!!"
THE CALLER QUICKLY GASPED AND HUNG UP.
THE KID?
WELL, HE JUST SHAT HIMSELF AND RAN FROM THE STORE.
JIMMY JUST WANTED TO SCARE THE LITTLE DUDE...

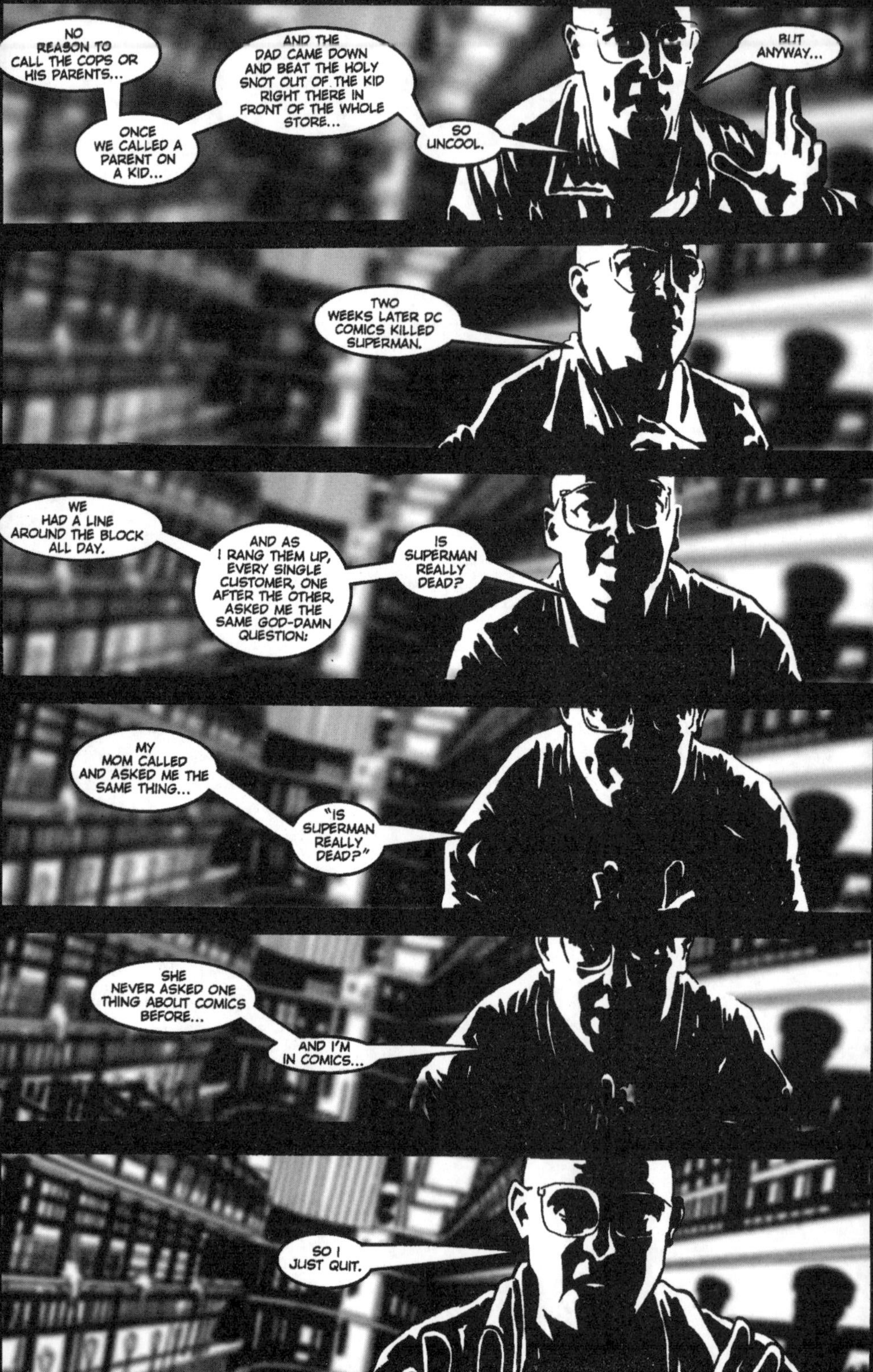
NO REASON TO CALL THE COPS OR HIS PARENTS...
ONCE WE CALLED A PARENT ON A KID...
AND THE DAD CAME DOWN AND BEAT THE HOLY SNOT OUT OF THE KID RIGHT THERE IN FRONT OF THE WHOLE STORE...
SO UNCOOL.
BUT ANYWAY...
TWO WEEKS LATER DC COMICS KILLED SUPERMAN.
WE HAD A LINE AROUND THE BLOCK ALL DAY.
AND AS I RANG THEM UP, EVERY SINGLE CUSTOMER, ONE AFTER THE OTHER, ASKED ME THE SAME GOD-DAMN QUESTION:
IS SUPERMAN REALLY DEAD?
MY MOM CALLED AND ASKED ME THE SAME THING...
"IS SUPERMAN REALLY DEAD?"
SHE NEVER ASKED ONE THING ABOUT COMICS BEFORE...
AND I'M IN COMICS...
SO I JUST QUIT.

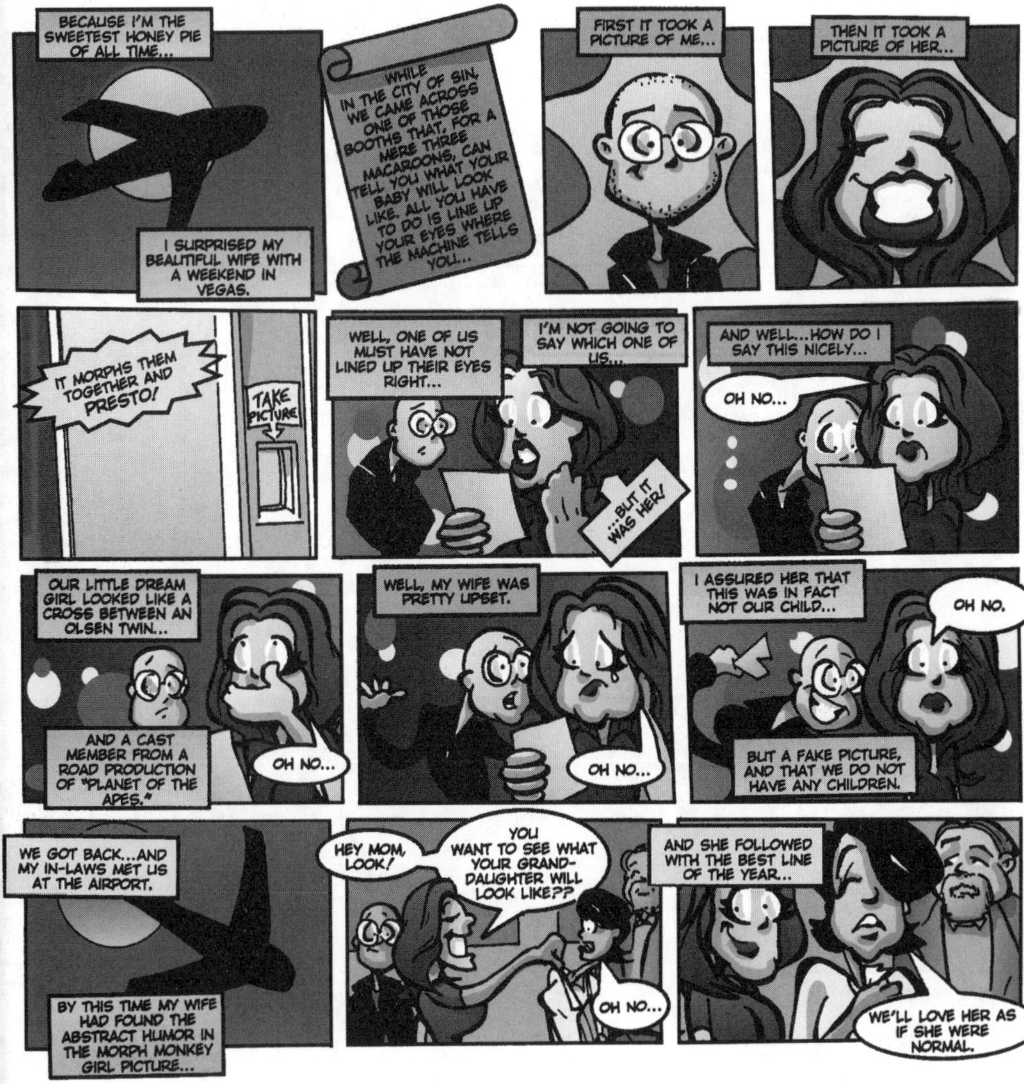

BECAUSE I'M THE SWEETEST HONEY PIE OF ALL TIME...
I SURPRISED MY BEAUTIFUL WIFE WITH A WEEKEND IN VEGAS.
WHILE IN THE CITY OF SIN, WE CAME ACROSS ONE OF THOSE BOOTHS THAT, FOR A MERE THREE MACAROONS, CAN TELL YOU WHAT YOUR BABY WILL LOOK LIKE. ALL YOU HAVE TO DO IS LINE UP YOUR EYES WHERE THE MACHINE TELLS YOU...
FIRST IT TOOK A PICTURE OF ME...
THEN IT TOOK A PICTURE OF HER...
IT MORPHS THEM TOGETHER AND PRESTO!
TAKE PICTURE
WELL, ONE OF US MUST HAVE NOT LINED UP THEIR EYES RIGHT...
I'M NOT GOING TO SAY WHICH ONE OF US...
...BUT IT WAS HER!
AND WELL...HOW DO I SAY THIS NICELY...
OH NO...
OUR LITTLE DREAM GIRL LOOKED LIKE A CROSS BETWEEN AN OLSEN TWIN...
AND A CAST MEMBER FROM A ROAD PRODUCTION OF "PLANET OF THE APES."
OH NO...
WELL, MY WIFE WAS PRETTY UPSET.
OH NO...
I ASSURED HER THAT THIS WAS IN FACT NOT OUR CHILD...
OH NO.
BUT A FAKE PICTURE, AND THAT WE DO NOT HAVE ANY CHILDREN.
WE GOT BACK...AND MY IN-LAWS MET US AT THE AIRPORT.
BY THIS TIME MY WIFE HAD FOUND THE ABSTRACT HUMOR IN THE MORPH MONKEY GIRL PICTURE...
HEY MOM, LOOK!
YOU WANT TO SEE WHAT YOUR GRAND-DAUGHTER WILL LOOK LIKE??
OH NO...
AND SHE FOLLOWED WITH THE BEST LINE OF THE YEAR...
WE'LL LOVE HER AS IF SHE WERE NORMAL.

# MOVIE STAR PART 1

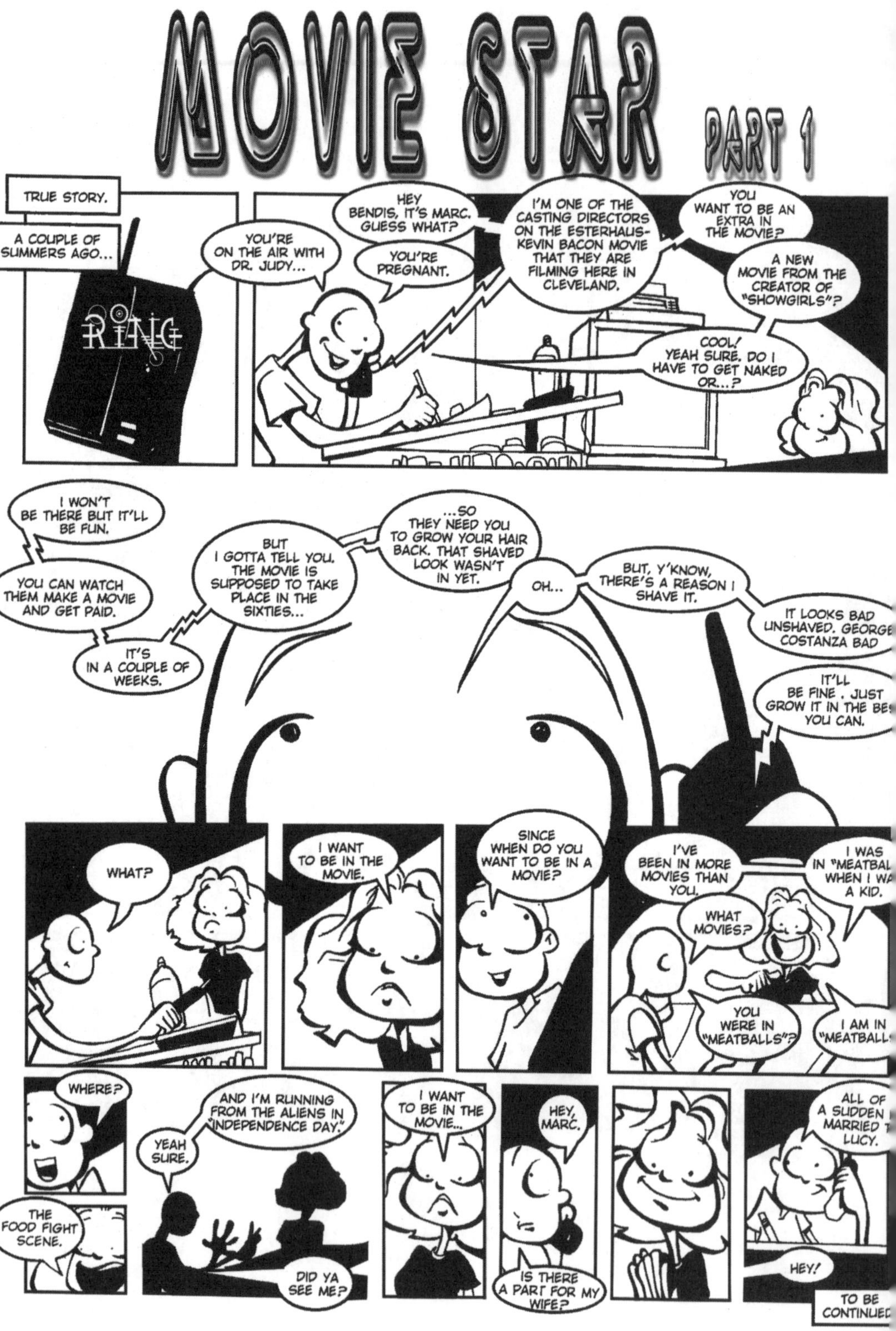

TRUE STORY.
A COUPLE OF SUMMERS AGO...
RING
YOU'RE ON THE AIR WITH DR. JUDY...
HEY BENDIS, IT'S MARC. GUESS WHAT?
YOU'RE PREGNANT.
I'M ONE OF THE CASTING DIRECTORS ON THE ESTERHAUS-KEVIN BACON MOVIE THAT THEY ARE FILMING HERE IN CLEVELAND.
YOU WANT TO BE AN EXTRA IN THE MOVIE?
A NEW MOVIE FROM THE CREATOR OF "SHOWGIRLS"?
COOL! YEAH SURE. DO I HAVE TO GET NAKED OR...?
I WON'T BE THERE BUT IT'LL BE FUN.
YOU CAN WATCH THEM MAKE A MOVIE AND GET PAID.
IT'S IN A COUPLE OF WEEKS.
BUT I GOTTA TELL YOU. THE MOVIE IS SUPPOSED TO TAKE PLACE IN THE SIXTIES...
...SO THEY NEED YOU TO GROW YOUR HAIR BACK. THAT SHAVED LOOK WASN'T IN YET.
OH...
BUT, Y'KNOW, THERE'S A REASON I SHAVE IT.
IT LOOKS BAD UNSHAVED. GEORGE COSTANZA BAD
IT'LL BE FINE . JUST GROW IT IN THE BE YOU CAN.
WHAT?
I WANT TO BE IN THE MOVIE.
SINCE WHEN DO YOU WANT TO BE IN A MOVIE?
I'VE BEEN IN MORE MOVIES THAN YOU.
I WAS IN "MEATBAL WHEN I WA A KID.
WHAT MOVIES?
YOU WERE IN "MEATBALLS"?
I AM IN "MEATBALL
WHERE?
THE FOOD FIGHT SCENE.
YEAH SURE.
AND I'M RUNNING FROM THE ALIENS IN "INDEPENDENCE DAY."
DID YA SEE ME?
I WANT TO BE IN THE MOVIE...
HEY, MARC.
IS THERE A PART FOR MY WIFE?
ALL OF A SUDDEN MARRIED T LUCY.
HEY!
TO BE CONTINUEI

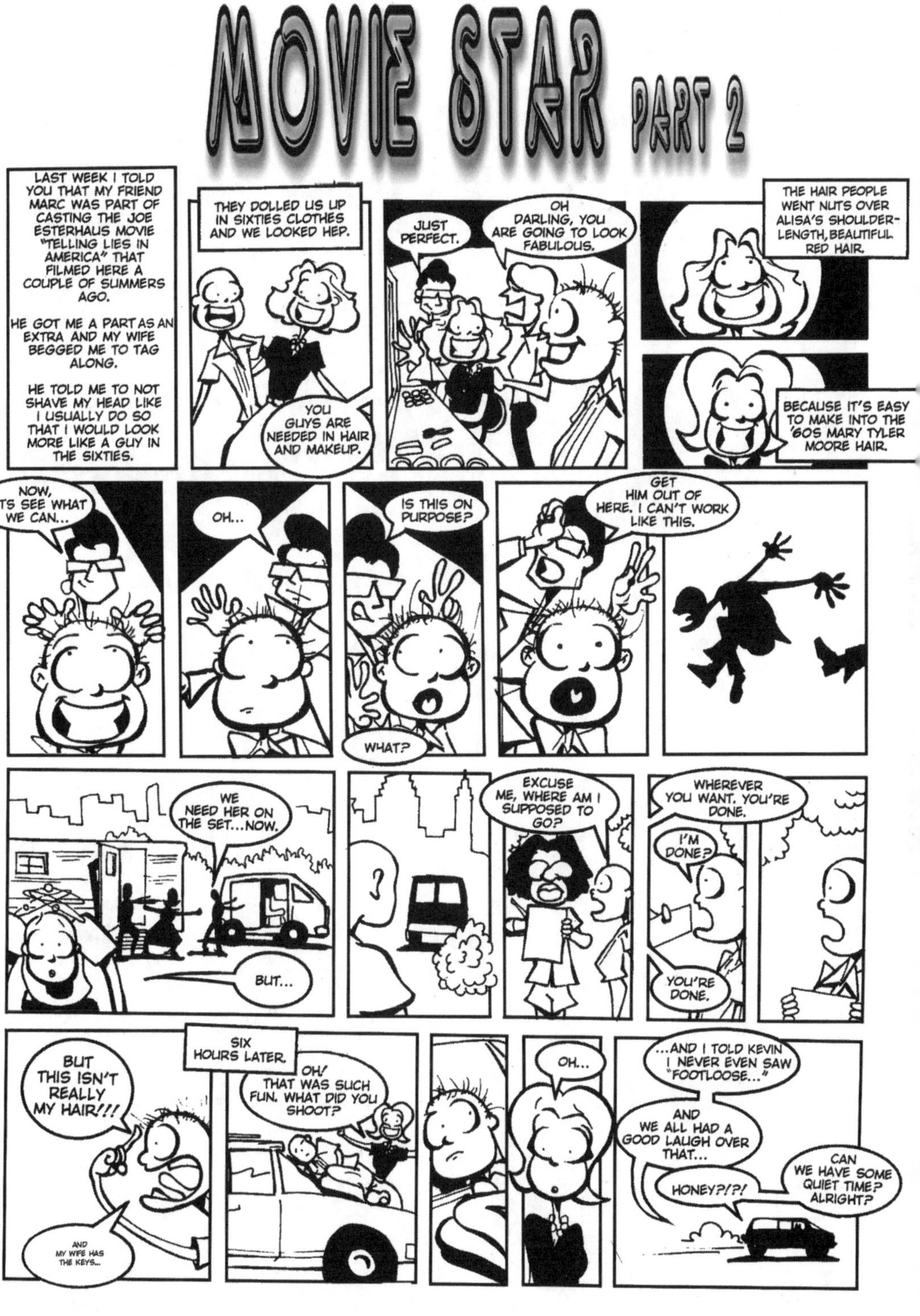
MOVIE STAR PART 2
LAST WEEK I TOLD YOU THAT MY FRIEND MARC WAS PART OF CASTING THE JOE ESTERHAUS MOVIE "TELLING LIES IN AMERICA" THAT FILMED HERE A COUPLE OF SUMMERS AGO.
HE GOT ME A PART AS AN EXTRA AND MY WIFE BEGGED ME TO TAG ALONG.
HE TOLD ME TO NOT SHAVE MY HEAD LIKE I USUALLY DO SO THAT I WOULD LOOK MORE LIKE A GUY IN THE SIXTIES.
THEY DOLLED US UP IN SIXTIES CLOTHES AND WE LOOKED HEP.
YOU GUYS ARE NEEDED IN HAIR AND MAKEUP.
JUST PERFECT.
OH DARLING, YOU ARE GOING TO LOOK FABULOUS.
THE HAIR PEOPLE WENT NUTS OVER ALISA'S SHOULDER-LENGTH, BEAUTIFUL RED HAIR.
BECAUSE IT'S EASY TO MAKE INTO THE '60S MARY TYLER MOORE HAIR.
NOW, LETS SEE WHAT WE CAN...
OH...
IS THIS ON PURPOSE?
WHAT?
GET HIM OUT OF HERE. I CAN'T WORK LIKE THIS.
WE NEED HER ON THE SET...NOW.
BUT...
EXCUSE ME, WHERE AM I SUPPOSED TO GO?
WHEREVER YOU WANT. YOU'RE DONE.
I'M DONE?
YOU'RE DONE.
SIX HOURS LATER.
BUT THIS ISN'T REALLY MY HAIR!!!
AND MY WIFE HAS THE KEYS...
OH! THAT WAS SUCH FUN. WHAT DID YOU SHOOT?
OH...
...AND I TOLD KEVIN I NEVER EVEN SAW "FOOTLOOSE..."
AND WE ALL HAD A GOOD LAUGH OVER THAT...
HONEY?!?!
CAN WE HAVE SOME QUIET TIME? ALRIGHT?

# SUPERDAY PART 1

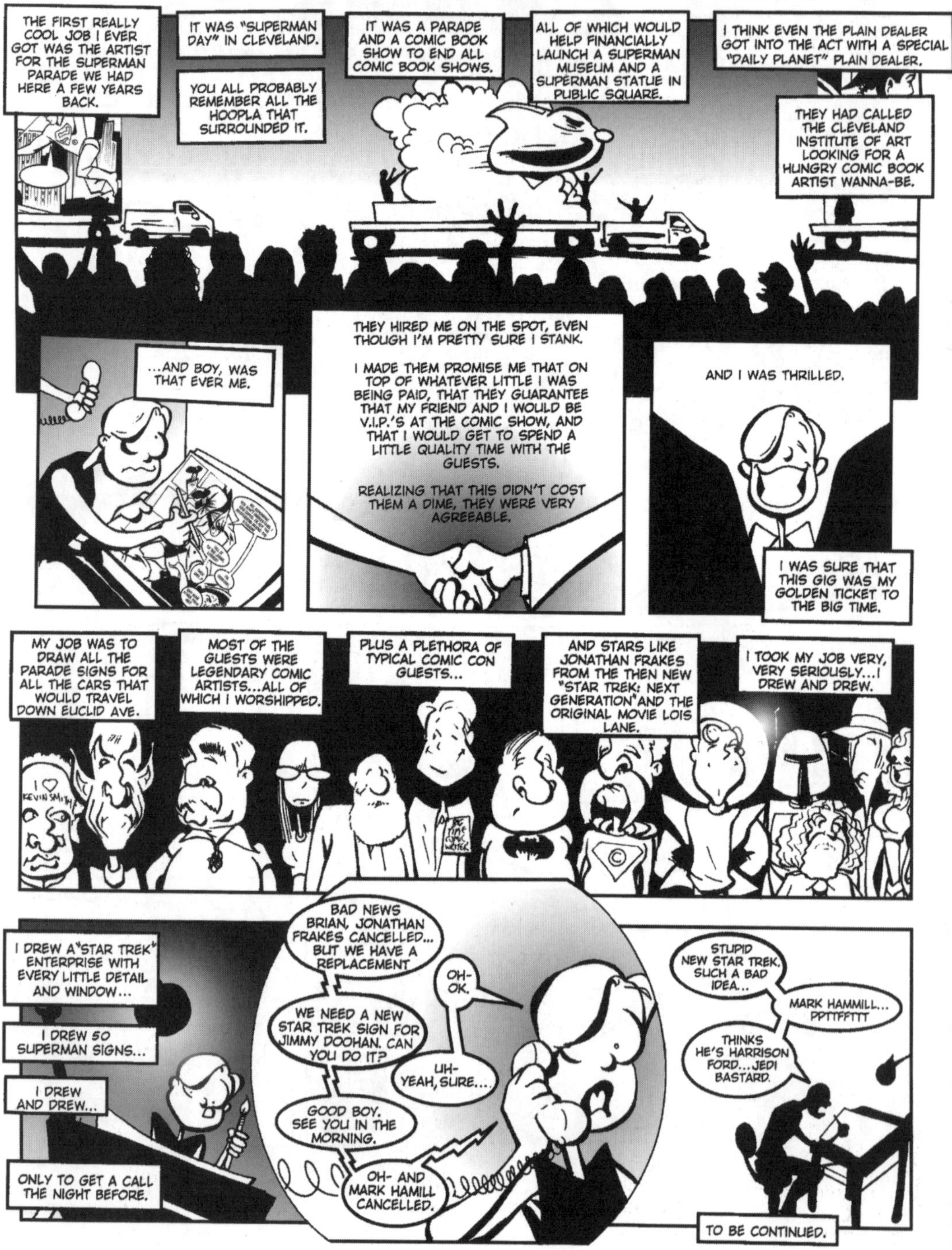

THE FIRST REALLY COOL JOB I EVER GOT WAS THE ARTIST FOR THE SUPERMAN PARADE WE HAD HERE A FEW YEARS BACK.
IT WAS "SUPERMAN DAY" IN CLEVELAND.
YOU ALL PROBABLY REMEMBER ALL THE HOOPLA THAT SURROUNDED IT.
IT WAS A PARADE AND A COMIC BOOK SHOW TO END ALL COMIC BOOK SHOWS.
ALL OF WHICH WOULD HELP FINANCIALLY LAUNCH A SUPERMAN MUSEUM AND A SUPERMAN STATUE IN PUBLIC SQUARE.
I THINK EVEN THE PLAIN DEALER GOT INTO THE ACT WITH A SPECIAL "DAILY PLANET" PLAIN DEALER.
THEY HAD CALLED THE CLEVELAND INSTITUTE OF ART LOOKING FOR A HUNGRY COMIC BOOK ARTIST WANNA-BE.
...AND BOY, WAS THAT EVER ME.
THEY HIRED ME ON THE SPOT, EVEN THOUGH I'M PRETTY SURE I STANK.
I MADE THEM PROMISE ME THAT ON TOP OF WHATEVER LITTLE I WAS BEING PAID, THAT THEY GUARANTEE THAT MY FRIEND AND I WOULD BE V.I.P.'S AT THE COMIC SHOW, AND THAT I WOULD GET TO SPEND A LITTLE QUALITY TIME WITH THE GUESTS.
REALIZING THAT THIS DIDN'T COST THEM A DIME, THEY WERE VERY AGREEABLE.
AND I WAS THRILLED.
I WAS SURE THAT THIS GIG WAS MY GOLDEN TICKET TO THE BIG TIME.
MY JOB WAS TO DRAW ALL THE PARADE SIGNS FOR ALL THE CARS THAT WOULD TRAVEL DOWN EUCLID AVE.
MOST OF THE GUESTS WERE LEGENDARY COMIC ARTISTS...ALL OF WHICH I WORSHIPPED.
PLUS A PLETHORA OF TYPICAL COMIC CON GUESTS...
AND STARS LIKE JONATHAN FRAKES FROM THE THEN NEW "STAR TREK: NEXT GENERATION" AND THE ORIGINAL MOVIE LOIS LANE.
I TOOK MY JOB VERY, VERY SERIOUSLY...I DREW AND DREW.
I ♡ KEVIN SMITH
I DREW A "STAR TREK" ENTERPRISE WITH EVERY LITTLE DETAIL AND WINDOW...
I DREW 50 SUPERMAN SIGNS...
I DREW AND DREW...
ONLY TO GET A CALL THE NIGHT BEFORE.
BAD NEWS BRIAN, JONATHAN FRAKES CANCELLED... BUT WE HAVE A REPLACEMENT
OH-OK.
WE NEED A NEW STAR TREK SIGN FOR JIMMY DOOHAN. CAN YOU DO IT?
UH-YEAH, SURE....
GOOD BOY. SEE YOU IN THE MORNING.
OH- AND MARK HAMILL CANCELLED.
STUPID NEW STAR TREK. SUCH A BAD IDEA...
MARK HAMMILL... PPTTFFTTT
THINKS HE'S HARRISON FORD...JEDI BASTARD.
TO BE CONTINUED.

# SUPERDAY PART 2

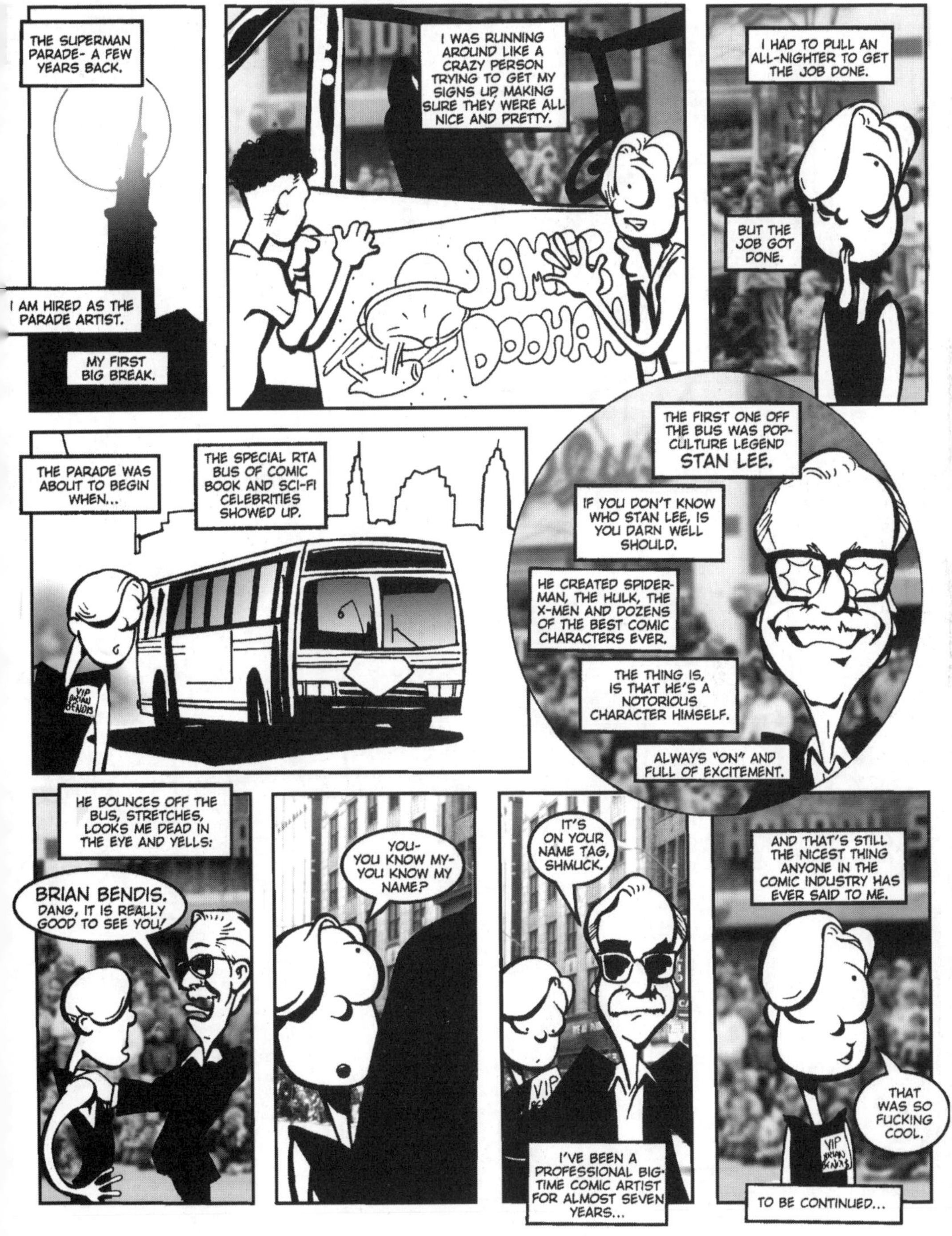

THE SUPERMAN PARADE- A FEW YEARS BACK.
I AM HIRED AS THE PARADE ARTIST.
MY FIRST BIG BREAK.
I WAS RUNNING AROUND LIKE A CRAZY PERSON TRYING TO GET MY SIGNS UP, MAKING SURE THEY WERE ALL NICE AND PRETTY.
JAMES DOOHAN
I HAD TO PULL AN ALL-NIGHTER TO GET THE JOB DONE.
BUT THE JOB GOT DONE.
THE PARADE WAS ABOUT TO BEGIN WHEN...
THE SPECIAL RTA BUS OF COMIC BOOK AND SCI-FI CELEBRITIES SHOWED UP.
VIP BRIAN BENDIS
THE FIRST ONE OFF THE BUS WAS POP-CULTURE LEGEND STAN LEE.
IF YOU DON'T KNOW WHO STAN LEE, IS YOU DARN WELL SHOULD.
HE CREATED SPIDER-MAN, THE HULK, THE X-MEN AND DOZENS OF THE BEST COMIC CHARACTERS EVER.
THE THING IS, IS THAT HE'S A NOTORIOUS CHARACTER HIMSELF.
ALWAYS "ON" AND FULL OF EXCITEMENT.
HE BOUNCES OFF THE BUS, STRETCHES, LOOKS ME DEAD IN THE EYE AND YELLS:
BRIAN BENDIS. DANG, IT IS REALLY GOOD TO SEE YOU!
YOU- YOU KNOW MY- YOU KNOW MY NAME?
IT'S ON YOUR NAME TAG, SHMUCK.
I'VE BEEN A PROFESSIONAL BIG-TIME COMIC ARTIST FOR ALMOST SEVEN YEARS...
AND THAT'S STILL THE NICEST THING ANYONE IN THE COMIC INDUSTRY HAS EVER SAID TO ME.
THAT WAS SO FUCKING COOL.
VIP BRIAN BENDIS
TO BE CONTINUED...

# SUPERDAY PART 3

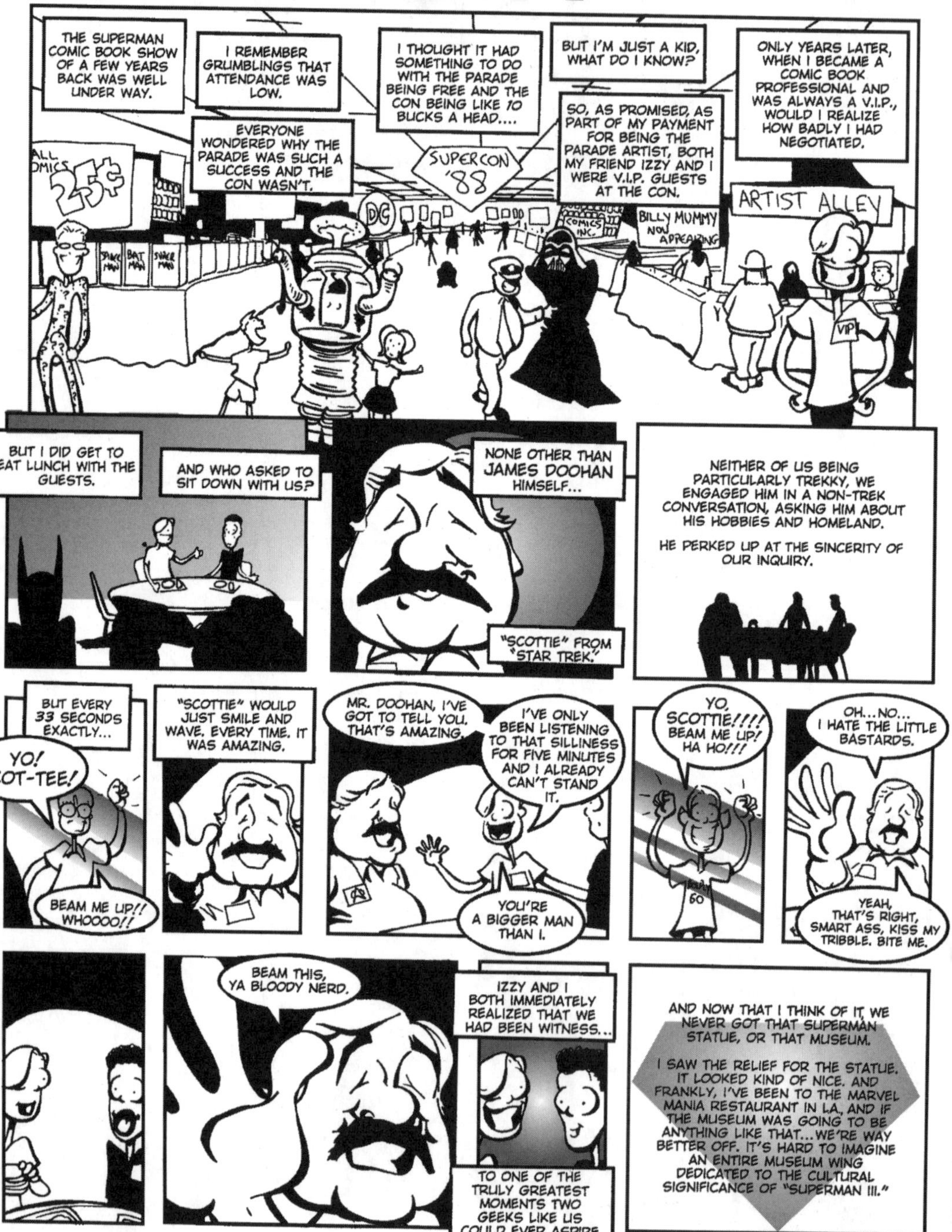

THE SUPERMAN COMIC BOOK SHOW OF A FEW YEARS BACK WAS WELL UNDER WAY.
I REMEMBER GRUMBLINGS THAT ATTENDANCE WAS LOW.
EVERYONE WONDERED WHY THE PARADE WAS SUCH A SUCCESS AND THE CON WASN'T.
I THOUGHT IT HAD SOMETHING TO DO WITH THE PARADE BEING FREE AND THE CON BEING LIKE 10 BUCKS A HEAD....
BUT I'M JUST A KID, WHAT DO I KNOW?
SO, AS PROMISED, AS PART OF MY PAYMENT FOR BEING THE PARADE ARTIST, BOTH MY FRIEND IZZY AND I WERE V.I.P. GUESTS AT THE CON.
ONLY YEARS LATER, WHEN I BECAME A COMIC BOOK PROFESSIONAL AND WAS ALWAYS A V.I.P., WOULD I REALIZE HOW BADLY I HAD NEGOTIATED.
ALL COMICS 25¢
SUPERCON '88
DC
COMICS INC.
BILLY MUMMY NOW APPEARING
ARTIST ALLEY
VIP
BUT I DID GET TO EAT LUNCH WITH THE GUESTS.
AND WHO ASKED TO SIT DOWN WITH US?
NONE OTHER THAN JAMES DOOHAN HIMSELF...
"SCOTTIE" FROM "STAR TREK."
NEITHER OF US BEING PARTICULARLY TREKKY, WE ENGAGED HIM IN A NON-TREK CONVERSATION, ASKING HIM ABOUT HIS HOBBIES AND HOMELAND.
HE PERKED UP AT THE SINCERITY OF OUR INQUIRY.
BUT EVERY 33 SECONDS EXACTLY...
YO! COT-TEE!
BEAM ME UP!! WHOOOO!!
"SCOTTIE" WOULD JUST SMILE AND WAVE. EVERY TIME. IT WAS AMAZING.
MR. DOOHAN, I'VE GOT TO TELL YOU. THAT'S AMAZING.
I'VE ONLY BEEN LISTENING TO THAT SILLINESS FOR FIVE MINUTES AND I ALREADY CAN'T STAND IT.
YOU'RE A BIGGER MAN THAN I.
YO, SCOTTIE!!!! BEAM ME UP! HA HO!!!
OH...NO... I HATE THE LITTLE BASTARDS.
YEAH, THAT'S RIGHT, SMART ASS, KISS MY TRIBBLE. BITE ME.
BEAM THIS, YA BLOODY NERD.
IZZY AND I BOTH IMMEDIATELY REALIZED THAT WE HAD BEEN WITNESS...
TO ONE OF THE TRULY GREATEST MOMENTS TWO GEEKS LIKE US COULD EVER ASPIRE TO.
AND NOW THAT I THINK OF IT, WE NEVER GOT THAT SUPERMAN STATUE, OR THAT MUSEUM.
I SAW THE RELIEF FOR THE STATUE. IT LOOKED KIND OF NICE. AND FRANKLY, I'VE BEEN TO THE MARVEL MANIA RESTAURANT IN LA, AND IF THE MUSEUM WAS GOING TO BE ANYTHING LIKE THAT...WE'RE WAY BETTER OFF. IT'S HARD TO IMAGINE AN ENTIRE MUSEUM WING DEDICATED TO THE CULTURAL SIGNIFICANCE OF "SUPERMAN III."

# mclife lessons

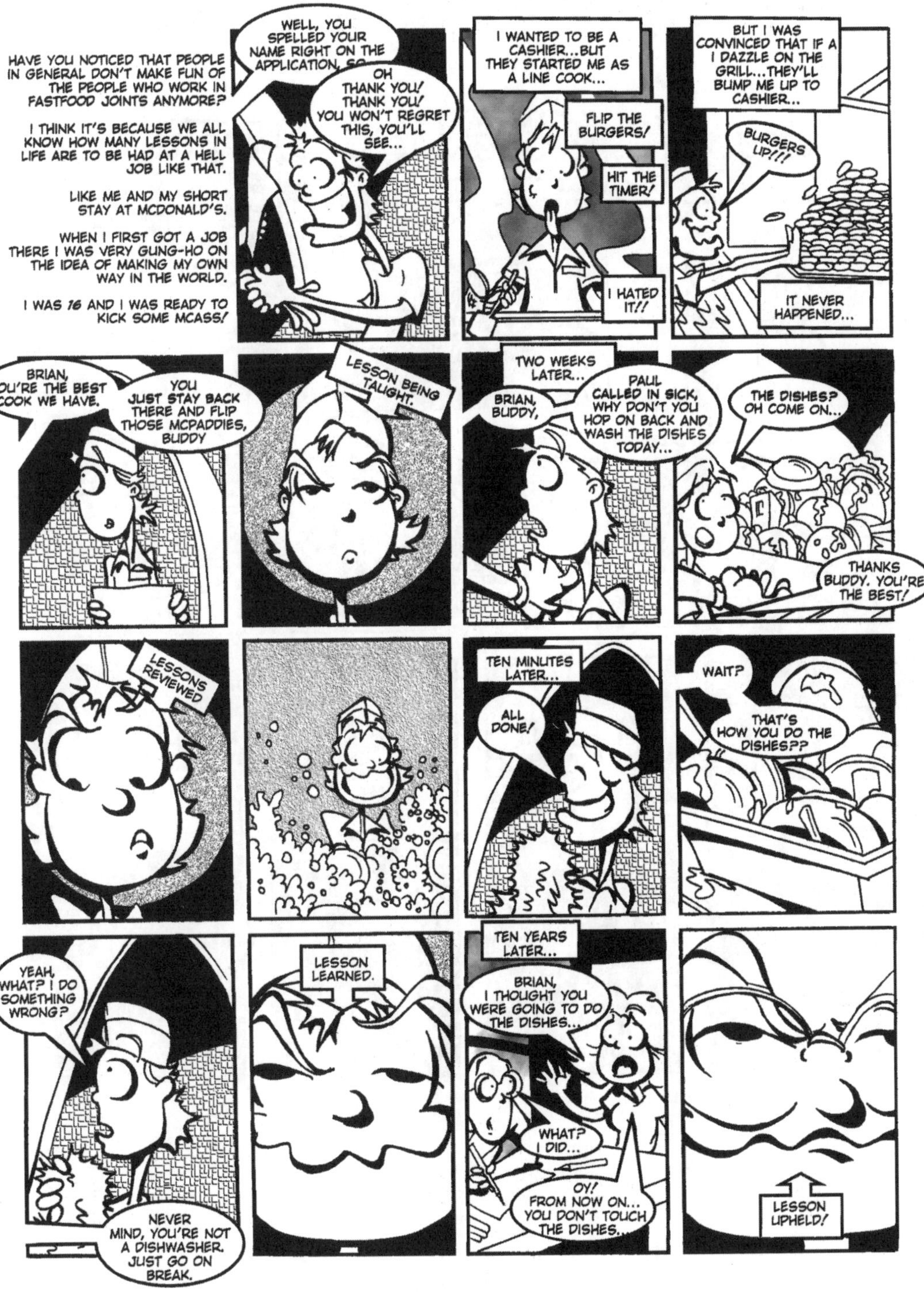

HAVE YOU NOTICED THAT PEOPLE IN GENERAL DON'T MAKE FUN OF THE PEOPLE WHO WORK IN FASTFOOD JOINTS ANYMORE?
I THINK IT'S BECAUSE WE ALL KNOW HOW MANY LESSONS IN LIFE ARE TO BE HAD AT A HELL JOB LIKE THAT.
LIKE ME AND MY SHORT STAY AT MCDONALD'S.
WHEN I FIRST GOT A JOB THERE I WAS VERY GUNG-HO ON THE IDEA OF MAKING MY OWN WAY IN THE WORLD.
I WAS 16 AND I WAS READY TO KICK SOME MCASS!
WELL, YOU SPELLED YOUR NAME RIGHT ON THE APPLICATION, SO...
OH THANK YOU! THANK YOU! YOU WON'T REGRET THIS, YOU'LL SEE...
I WANTED TO BE A CASHIER...BUT THEY STARTED ME AS A LINE COOK...
FLIP THE BURGERS!
HIT THE TIMER!
I HATED IT!!
BUT I WAS CONVINCED THAT IF A I DAZZLE ON THE GRILL...THEY'LL BUMP ME UP TO CASHIER...
BURGERS UP!!!
IT NEVER HAPPENED...
BRIAN, YOU'RE THE BEST COOK WE HAVE.
YOU JUST STAY BACK THERE AND FLIP THOSE MCPADDIES, BUDDY
LESSON BEING TAUGHT.
TWO WEEKS LATER...
BRIAN, BUDDY,
PAUL CALLED IN SICK, WHY DON'T YOU HOP ON BACK AND WASH THE DISHES TODAY...
THE DISHES? OH COME ON...
THANKS BUDDY. YOU'RE THE BEST!
LESSONS REVIEWED
TEN MINUTES LATER...
ALL DONE!
WAIT?
THAT'S HOW YOU DO THE DISHES??
YEAH, WHAT? I DO SOMETHING WRONG?
NEVER MIND, YOU'RE NOT A DISHWASHER. JUST GO ON BREAK.
LESSON LEARNED.
TEN YEARS LATER...
BRIAN, I THOUGHT YOU WERE GOING TO DO THE DISHES...
WHAT? I DID...
OY! FROM NOW ON... YOU DON'T TOUCH THE DISHES...
LESSON UPHELD!

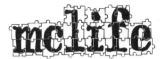

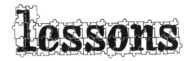

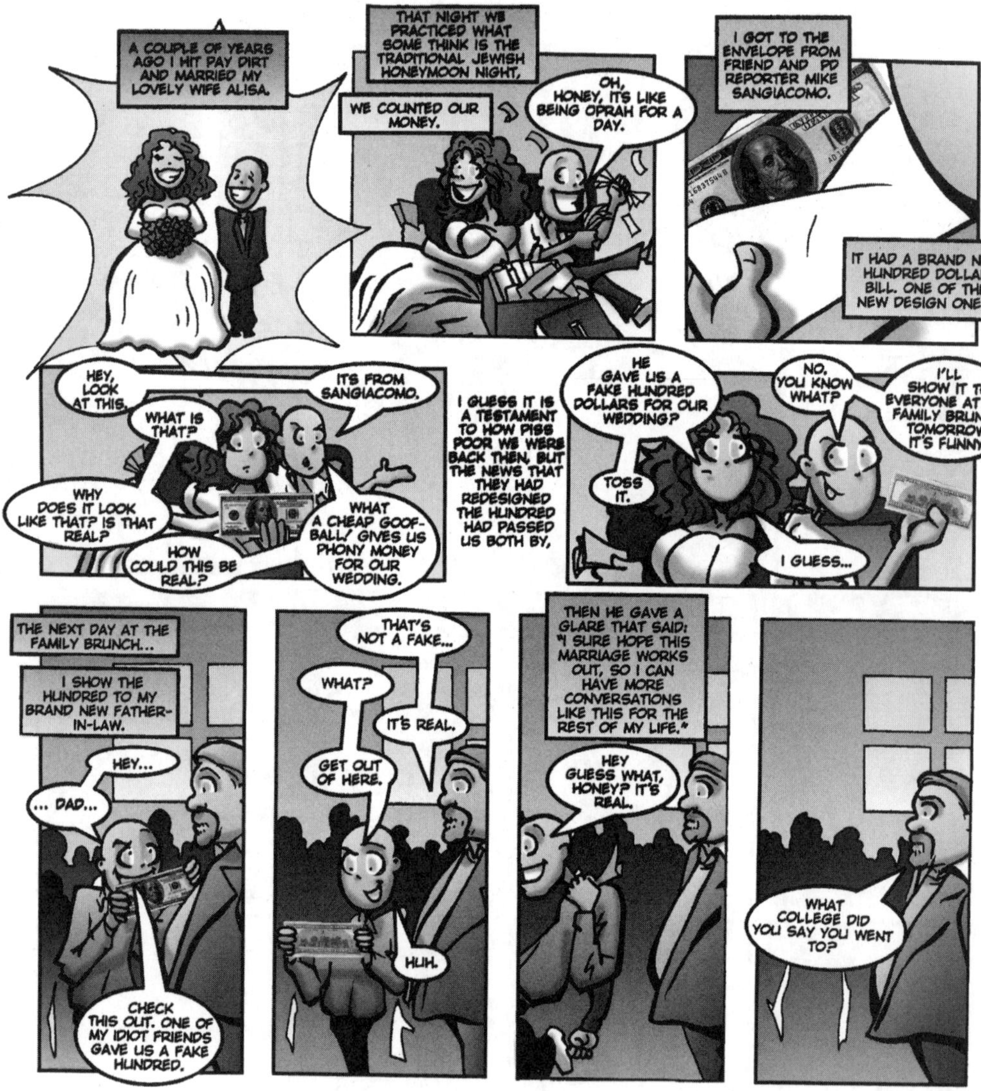
A COUPLE OF YEARS AGO I HIT PAY DIRT AND MARRIED MY LOVELY WIFE ALISA.
THAT NIGHT WE PRACTICED WHAT SOME THINK IS THE TRADITIONAL JEWISH HONEYMOON NIGHT,
WE COUNTED OUR MONEY.
OH, HONEY, IT'S LIKE BEING OPRAH FOR A DAY.
I GOT TO THE ENVELOPE FROM FRIEND AND PD REPORTER MIKE SANGIACOMO.
IT HAD A BRAND NEW HUNDRED DOLLAR BILL. ONE OF THE NEW DESIGN ONES.
HEY, LOOK AT THIS.
ITS FROM SANGIACOMO.
WHAT IS THAT?
WHY DOES IT LOOK LIKE THAT? IS THAT REAL?
HOW COULD THIS BE REAL?
WHAT A CHEAP GOOF-BALL! GIVES US PHONY MONEY FOR OUR WEDDING.
I GUESS IT IS A TESTAMENT TO HOW PISS POOR WE WERE BACK THEN, BUT THE NEWS THAT THEY HAD REDESIGNED THE HUNDRED HAD PASSED US BOTH BY.
HE GAVE US A FAKE HUNDRED DOLLARS FOR OUR WEDDING?
TOSS IT.
NO, YOU KNOW WHAT?
I'LL SHOW IT TO EVERYONE AT THE FAMILY BRUNCH TOMORROW, IT'S FUNNY.
I GUESS...
THE NEXT DAY AT THE FAMILY BRUNCH...
I SHOW THE HUNDRED TO MY BRAND NEW FATHER-IN-LAW.
HEY...
... DAD...
CHECK THIS OUT. ONE OF MY IDIOT FRIENDS GAVE US A FAKE HUNDRED.
THAT'S NOT A FAKE...
WHAT?
IT'S REAL.
GET OUT OF HERE.
HUH.
THEN HE GAVE A GLARE THAT SAID: "I SURE HOPE THIS MARRIAGE WORKS OUT, SO I CAN HAVE MORE CONVERSATIONS LIKE THIS FOR THE REST OF MY LIFE."
HEY GUESS WHAT, HONEY? IT'S REAL.
WHAT COLLEGE DID YOU SAY YOU WENT TO?

# CHRISTMAS REFUNDS

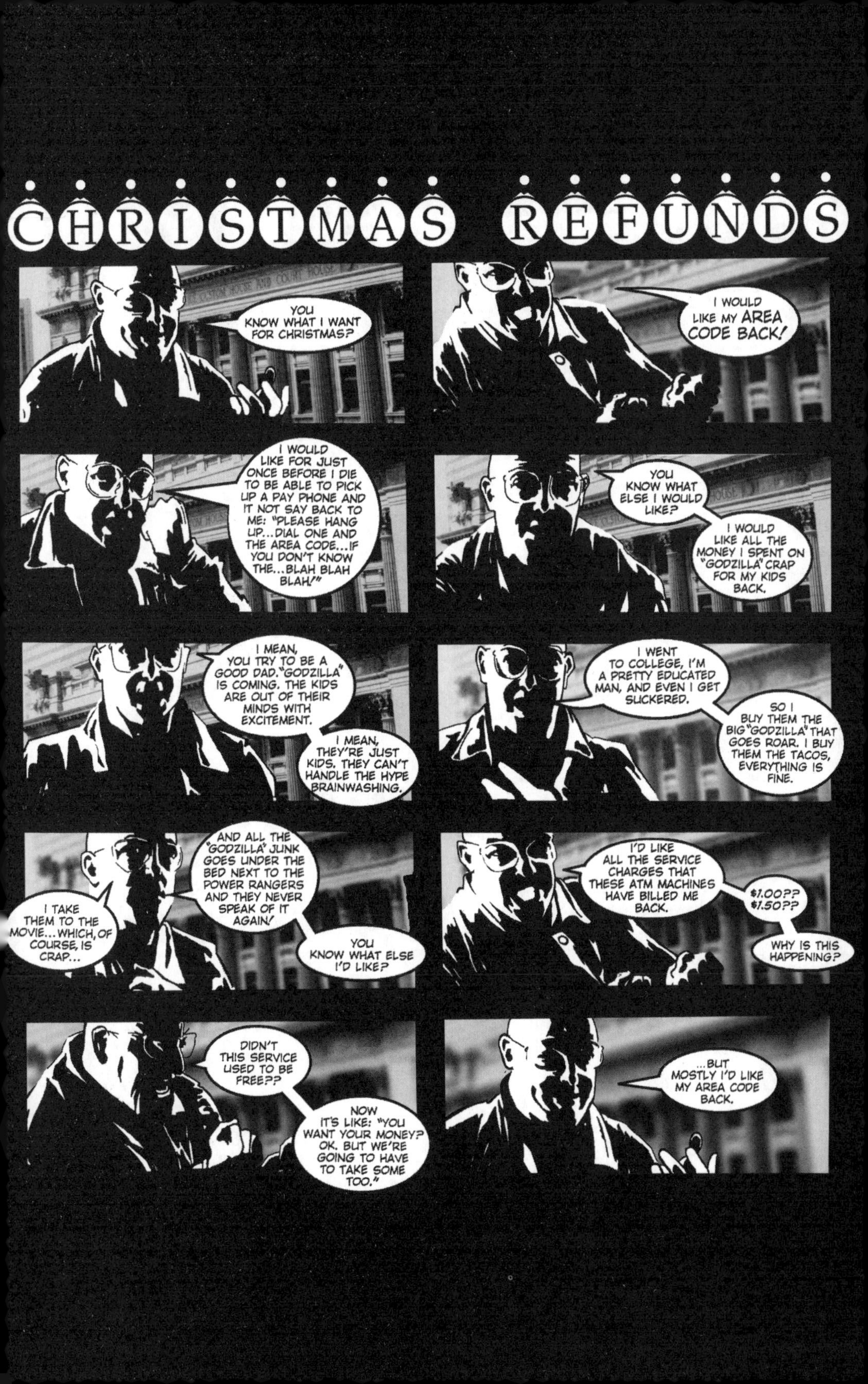
YOU KNOW WHAT I WANT FOR CHRISTMAS?
I WOULD LIKE MY AREA CODE BACK!
I WOULD LIKE FOR JUST ONCE BEFORE I DIE TO BE ABLE TO PICK UP A PAY PHONE AND IT NOT SAY BACK TO ME: "PLEASE HANG UP...DIAL ONE AND THE AREA CODE...IF YOU DON'T KNOW THE...BLAH BLAH BLAH!"
YOU KNOW WHAT ELSE I WOULD LIKE?
I WOULD LIKE ALL THE MONEY I SPENT ON "GODZILLA" CRAP FOR MY KIDS BACK.
I MEAN, YOU TRY TO BE A GOOD DAD. "GODZILLA" IS COMING. THE KIDS ARE OUT OF THEIR MINDS WITH EXCITEMENT.
I MEAN, THEY'RE JUST KIDS. THEY CAN'T HANDLE THE HYPE BRAINWASHING.
I WENT TO COLLEGE, I'M A PRETTY EDUCATED MAN, AND EVEN I GET SUCKERED.
SO I BUY THEM THE BIG "GODZILLA" THAT GOES ROAR. I BUY THEM THE TACOS, EVERYTHING IS FINE.
I TAKE THEM TO THE MOVIE...WHICH, OF COURSE, IS CRAP...
AND ALL THE "GODZILLA" JUNK GOES UNDER THE BED NEXT TO THE POWER RANGERS AND THEY NEVER SPEAK OF IT AGAIN!
YOU KNOW WHAT ELSE I'D LIKE?
I'D LIKE ALL THE SERVICE CHARGES THAT THESE ATM MACHINES HAVE BILLED ME BACK.
$1.00?? $1.50??
WHY IS THIS HAPPENING?
DIDN'T THIS SERVICE USED TO BE FREE??
NOW IT'S LIKE: "YOU WANT YOUR MONEY? OK. BUT WE'RE GOING TO HAVE TO TAKE SOME TOO."
...BUT MOSTLY I'D LIKE MY AREA CODE BACK.

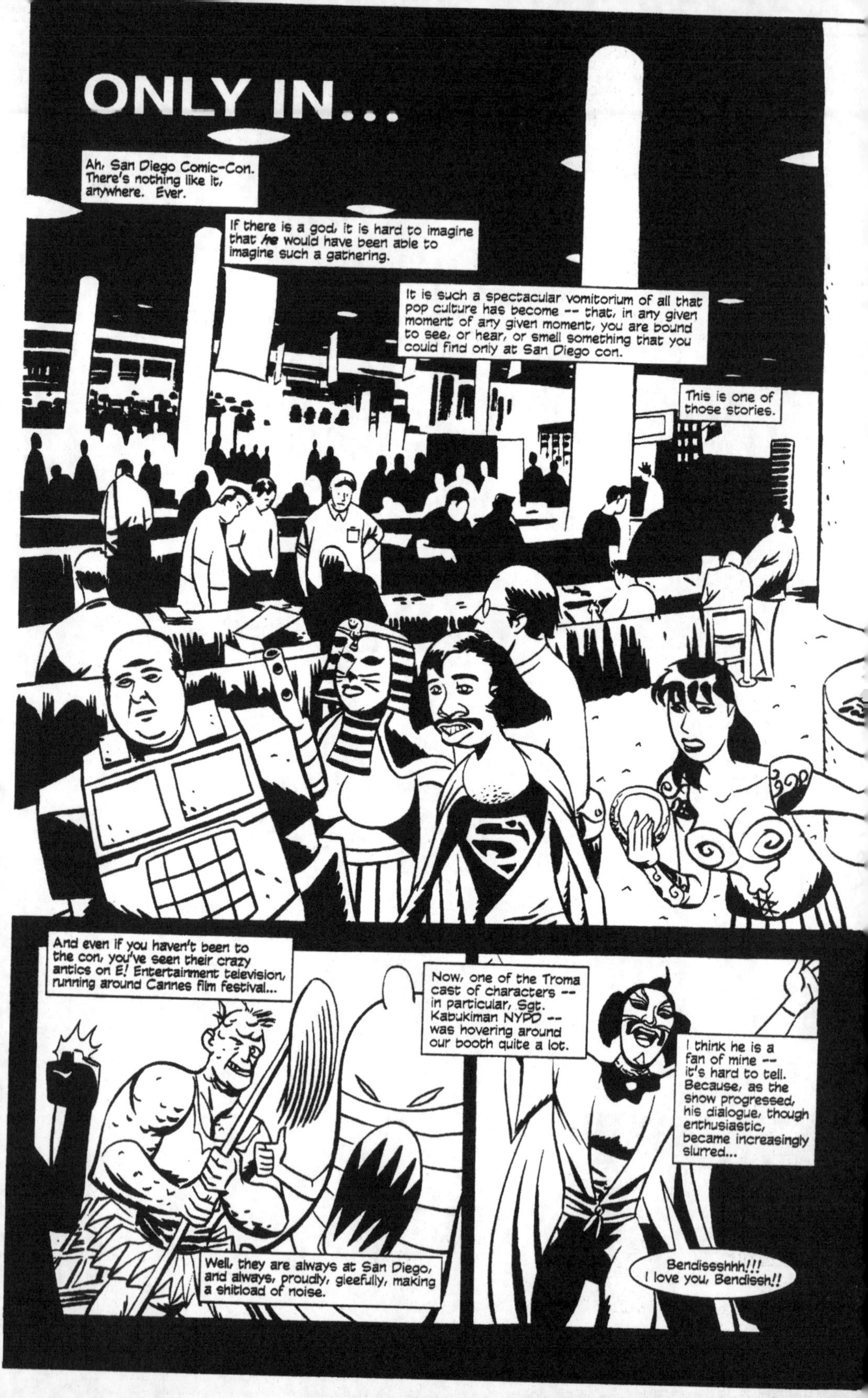
ONLY IN...
Ah, San Diego Comic-Con. There's nothing like it, anywhere. Ever.
If there is a god, it is hard to imagine that *he* would have been able to imagine such a gathering.
It is such a spectacular vomitorium of all that pop culture has become -- that, in any given moment of any given moment, you are bound to see, or hear, or smell something that you could find only at San Diego con.
This is one of those stories.
And even if you haven't been to the con, you've seen their crazy antics on E! Entertainment television, running around Cannes film festival...
Well, they are always at San Diego, and always, proudly, gleefully, making a shitload of noise.
Now, one of the Troma cast of characters -- in particular, Sgt. Kabukiman NYPD -- was hovering around our booth quite a lot.
I think he is a fan of mine -- it's hard to tell. Because, as the show progressed, his dialogue, though enthusiastic, became increasingly slurred...
Bendissshhh!!! I love you, Bendissh!!

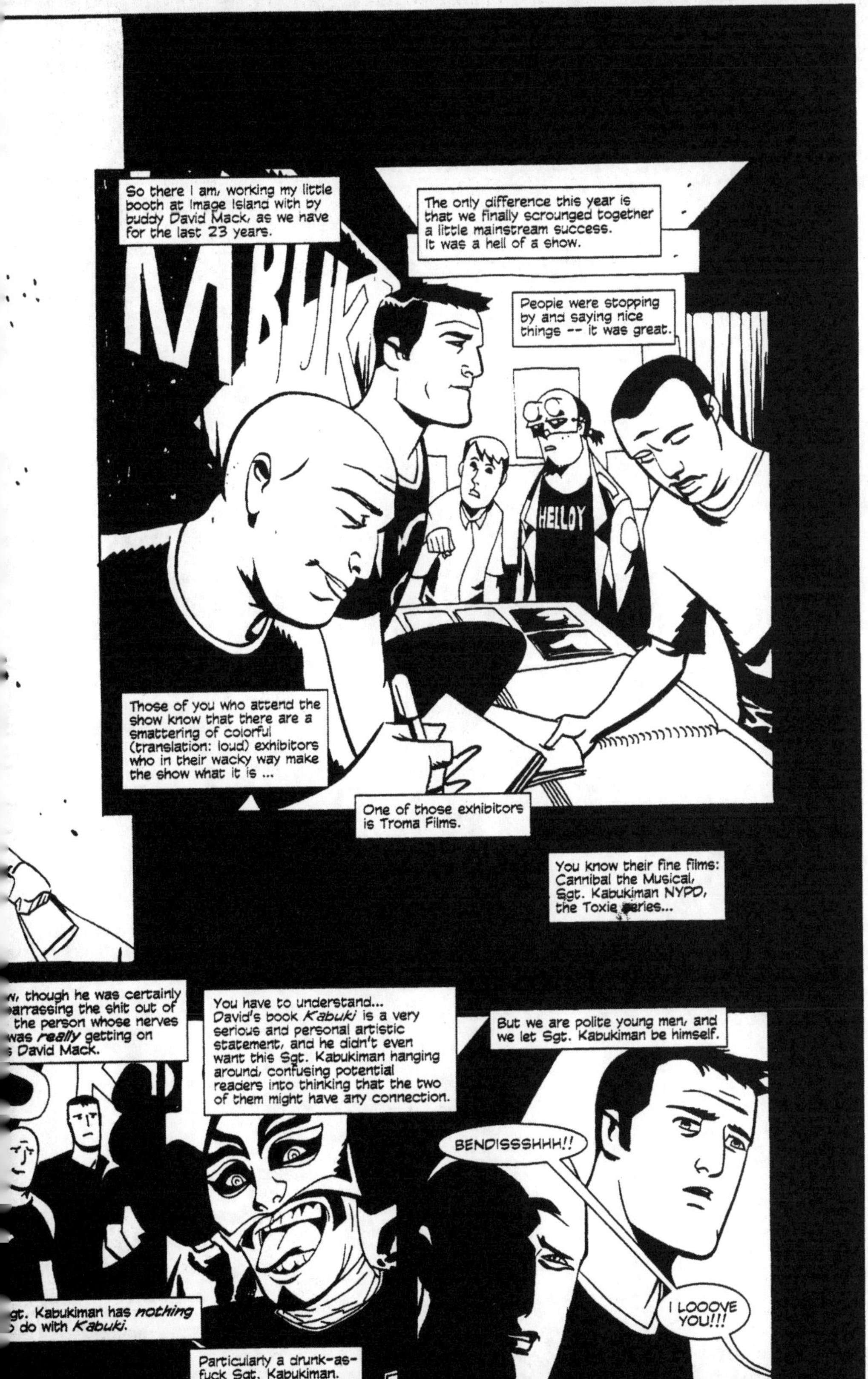

So there I am, working my little booth at Image Island with by buddy David Mack, as we have for the last 23 years.
The only difference this year is that we finally scrounged together a little mainstream success. It was a hell of a show.
People were stopping by and saying nice things -- it was great.
HELLOY
Those of you who attend the show know that there are a smattering of colorful (translation: loud) exhibitors who in their wacky way make the show what it is ...
One of those exhibitors is Troma Films.
You know their fine films: Cannibal the Musical, Sgt. Kabukiman NYPD, the Toxie series...
w, though he was certainly barrassing the shit out of the person whose nerves was *really* getting on s David Mack.
You have to understand... David's book *Kabuki* is a very serious and personal artistic statement, and he didn't even want this Sgt. Kabukiman hanging around, confusing potential readers into thinking that the two of them might have any connection.
But we are polite young men, and we let Sgt. Kabukiman be himself.
BENDISSSHHH!!
I LOOOVE YOU!!!
gt. Kabukiman has *nothing* o do with *Kabuki*.
Particularly a drunk-as-fuck Sgt. Kabukiman.

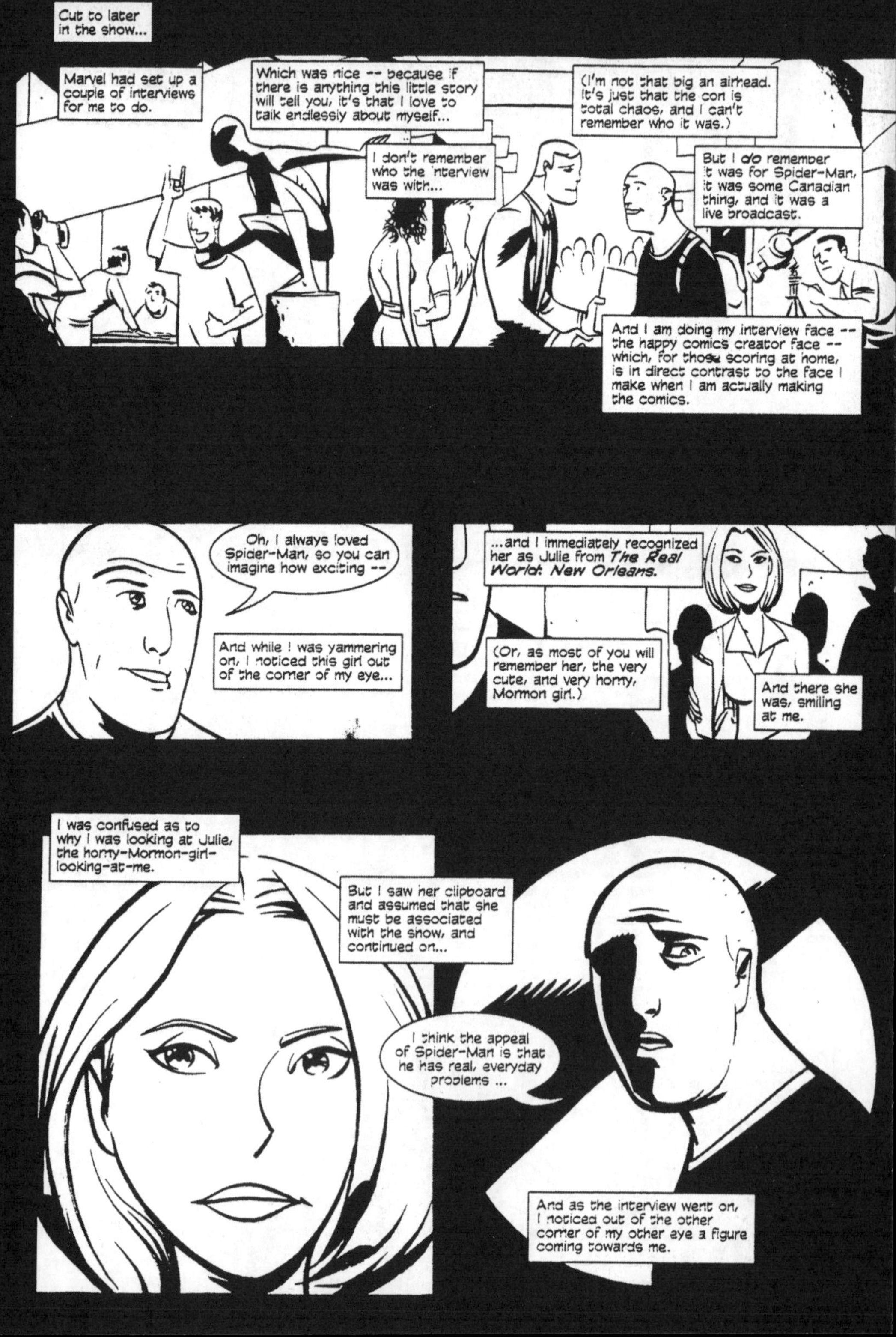

Cut to later in the show...
Marvel had set up a couple of interviews for me to do.
Which was nice -- because if there is anything this little story will tell you, it's that I love to talk endlessly about myself...
I don't remember who the interview was with...
(I'm not that big an airhead. It's just that the con is total chaos, and I can't remember who it was.)
But I *do* remember it was for Spider-Man, it was some Canadian thing, and it was a live broadcast.
And I am doing my interview face -- the happy comics creator face -- which, for those scoring at home, is in direct contrast to the face I make when I am actually making the comics.
Oh, I always loved Spider-Man, so you can imagine how exciting --
And while I was yammering on, I noticed this girl out of the corner of my eye...
...and I immediately recognized her as Julie from *The Real World: New Orleans.*
(Or, as most of you will remember her, the very cute, and very horny, Mormon girl.)
And there she was, smiling at me.
I was confused as to why I was looking at Julie, the horny-Mormon-girl-looking-at-me.
But I saw her clipboard and assumed that she must be associated with the show, and continued on...
I think the appeal of Spider-Man is that he has real, everyday problems ...
And as the interview went on, I noticed out of the other corner of my other eye a figure coming towards me.

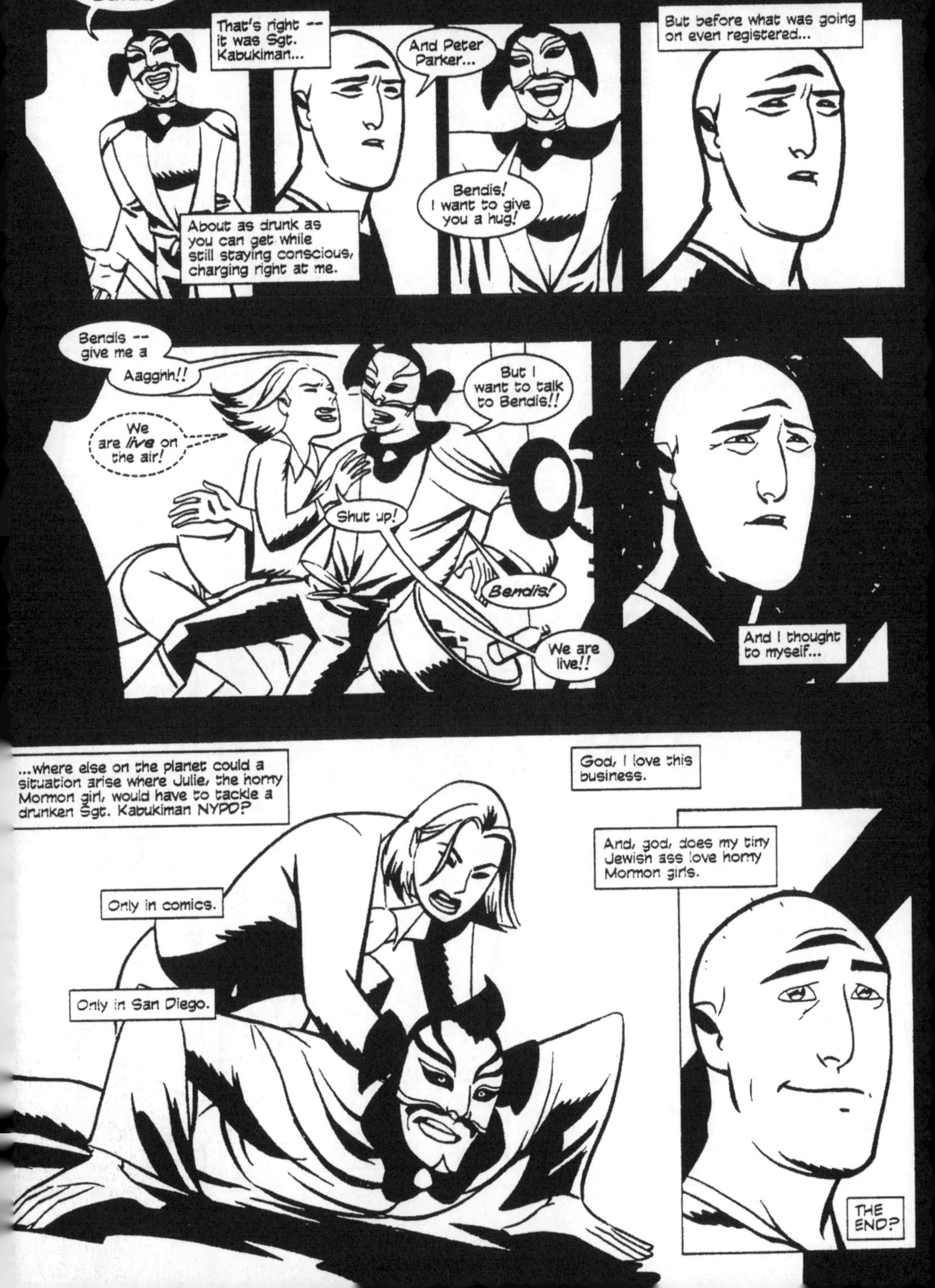

Hey, Bendis! *Bendis!*
That's right -- it was Sgt. Kabukiman...
About as drunk as you can get while still staying conscious, charging right at me.
And Peter Parker...
Bendis! I want to give you a hug!
But before what was going on even registered...
Bendis -- give me a Aaggh!!
We are *live* on the air!
But I want to talk to Bendis!!
Shut up!
*Bendis!*
We are live!!
And I thought to myself...
...where else on the planet could a situation arise where Julie, the horny Mormon girl, would have to tackle a drunken Sgt. Kabukiman NYPD?
Only in comics.
Only in San Diego.
God, I love this business.
And, god, does my tiny Jewish ass love horny Mormon girls.
THE END?

# I MARRIED A FOOD CHANNEL ADDIC

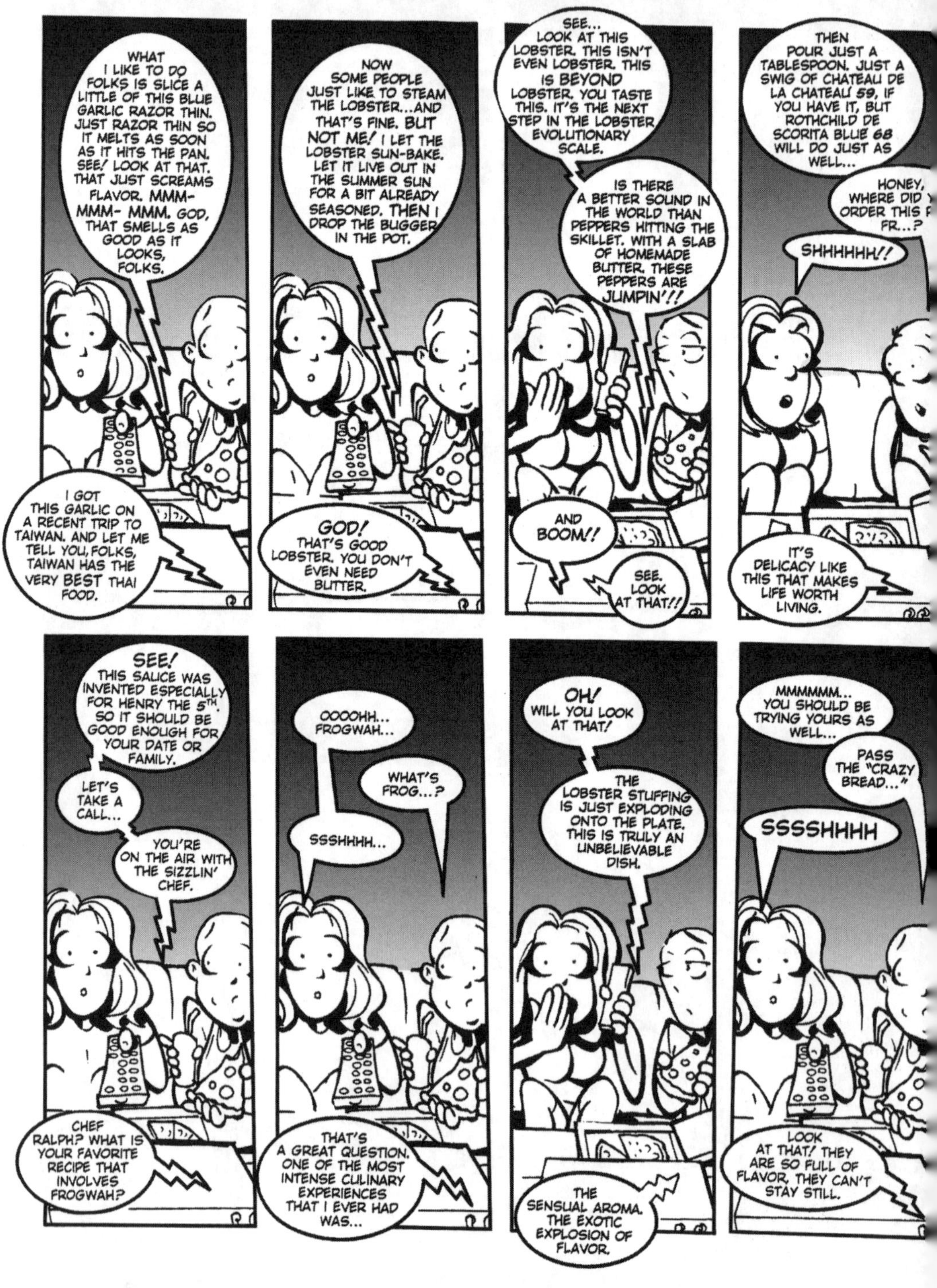
WHAT I LIKE TO DO FOLKS IS SLICE A LITTLE OF THIS BLUE GARLIC RAZOR THIN. JUST RAZOR THIN SO IT MELTS AS SOON AS IT HITS THE PAN. SEE! LOOK AT THAT. THAT JUST SCREAMS FLAVOR. MMM-MMM- MMM. GOD, THAT SMELLS AS GOOD AS IT LOOKS, FOLKS.
I GOT THIS GARLIC ON A RECENT TRIP TO TAIWAN. AND LET ME TELL YOU, FOLKS, TAIWAN HAS THE VERY BEST THAI FOOD.
NOW SOME PEOPLE JUST LIKE TO STEAM THE LOBSTER...AND THAT'S FINE. BUT NOT ME! I LET THE LOBSTER SUN-BAKE. LET IT LIVE OUT IN THE SUMMER SUN FOR A BIT ALREADY SEASONED. THEN I DROP THE BUGGER IN THE POT.
GOD! THAT'S GOOD LOBSTER. YOU DON'T EVEN NEED BUTTER.
SEE... LOOK AT THIS LOBSTER. THIS ISN'T EVEN LOBSTER. THIS IS BEYOND LOBSTER. YOU TASTE THIS. IT'S THE NEXT STEP IN THE LOBSTER EVOLUTIONARY SCALE.
IS THERE A BETTER SOUND IN THE WORLD THAN PEPPERS HITTING THE SKILLET. WITH A SLAB OF HOMEMADE BUTTER. THESE PEPPERS ARE JUMPIN'!!
AND BOOM!!
SEE. LOOK AT THAT!!
THEN POUR JUST A TABLESPOON. JUST A SWIG OF CHATEAU DE LA CHATEAU 59, IF YOU HAVE IT, BUT ROTHCHILD DE SCORITA BLUE 68 WILL DO JUST AS WELL...
HONEY, WHERE DID ORDER THIS FR...?
SHHHHHH!!
IT'S DELICACY LIKE THIS THAT MAKES LIFE WORTH LIVING.
SEE! THIS SAUCE WAS INVENTED ESPECIALLY FOR HENRY THE 5TH. SO IT SHOULD BE GOOD ENOUGH FOR YOUR DATE OR FAMILY.
LET'S TAKE A CALL...
YOU'RE ON THE AIR WITH THE SIZZLIN' CHEF.
CHEF RALPH? WHAT IS YOUR FAVORITE RECIPE THAT INVOLVES FROGWAH?
OOOOHH... FROGWAH...
WHAT'S FROG...?
SSSHHHH...
THAT'S A GREAT QUESTION. ONE OF THE MOST INTENSE CULINARY EXPERIENCES THAT I EVER HAD WAS...
OH! WILL YOU LOOK AT THAT!
THE LOBSTER STUFFING IS JUST EXPLODING ONTO THE PLATE. THIS IS TRULY AN UNBELIEVABLE DISH.
THE SENSUAL AROMA. THE EXOTIC EXPLOSION OF FLAVOR.
MMMMMM... YOU SHOULD BE TRYING YOURS AS WELL...
PASS THE "CRAZY BREAD..."
SSSSHHHH
LOOK AT THAT! THEY ARE SO FULL OF FLAVOR, THEY CAN'T STAY STILL.

# T.V. STAR

This is a totally true story!

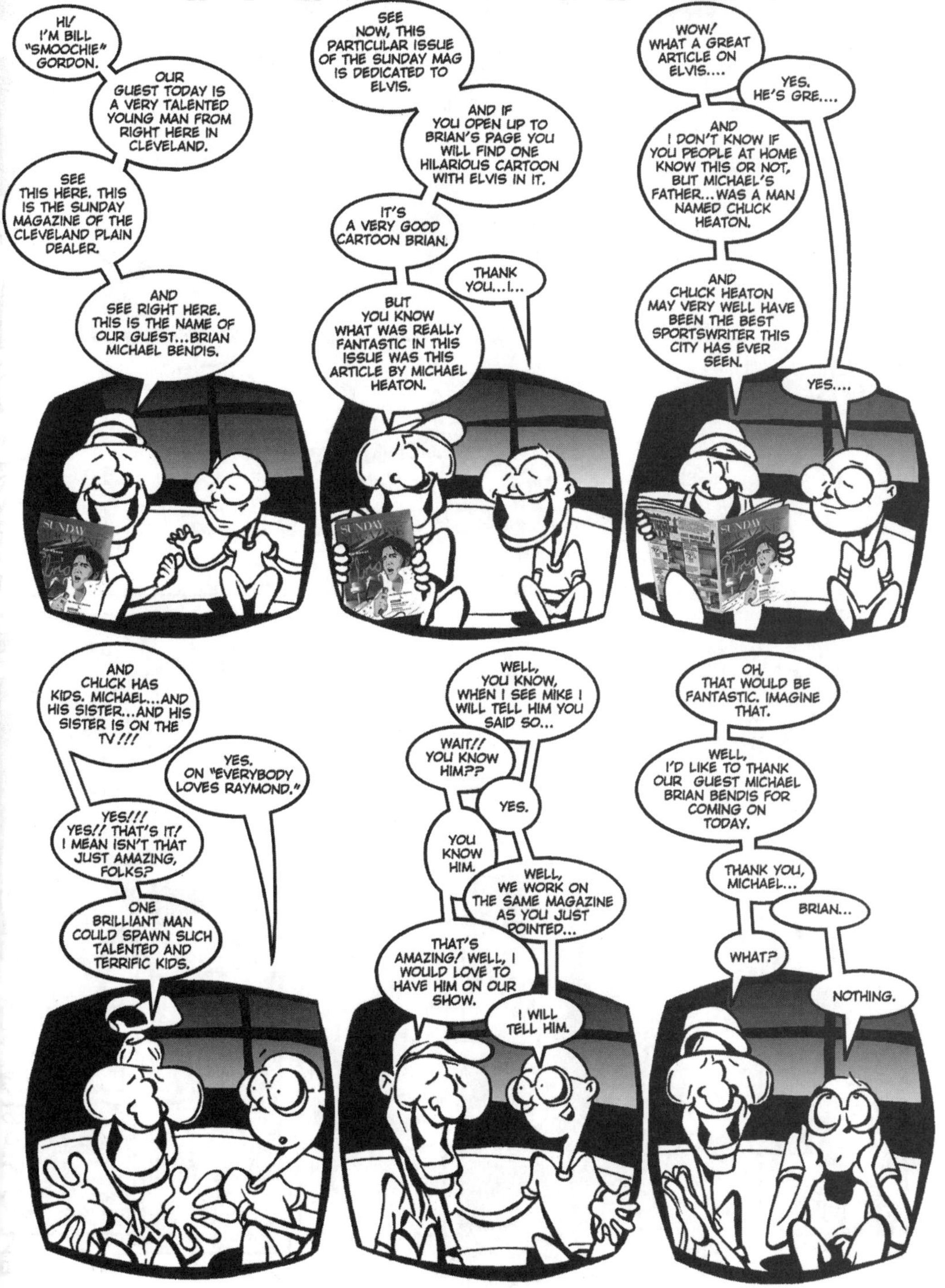

HI! I'M BILL "SMOOCHIE" GORDON.
OUR GUEST TODAY IS A VERY TALENTED YOUNG MAN FROM RIGHT HERE IN CLEVELAND.
SEE THIS HERE. THIS IS THE SUNDAY MAGAZINE OF THE CLEVELAND PLAIN DEALER.
AND SEE RIGHT HERE. THIS IS THE NAME OF OUR GUEST...BRIAN MICHAEL BENDIS.
SEE NOW, THIS PARTICULAR ISSUE OF THE SUNDAY MAG IS DEDICATED TO ELVIS.
AND IF YOU OPEN UP TO BRIAN'S PAGE YOU WILL FIND ONE HILARIOUS CARTOON WITH ELVIS IN IT.
IT'S A VERY GOOD CARTOON BRIAN.
THANK YOU...I...
BUT YOU KNOW WHAT WAS REALLY FANTASTIC IN THIS ISSUE WAS THIS ARTICLE BY MICHAEL HEATON.
WOW! WHAT A GREAT ARTICLE ON ELVIS....
YES. HE'S GRE....
AND I DON'T KNOW IF YOU PEOPLE AT HOME KNOW THIS OR NOT, BUT MICHAEL'S FATHER...WAS A MAN NAMED CHUCK HEATON.
AND CHUCK HEATON MAY VERY WELL HAVE BEEN THE BEST SPORTSWRITER THIS CITY HAS EVER SEEN.
YES....
AND CHUCK HAS KIDS. MICHAEL...AND HIS SISTER...AND HIS SISTER IS ON THE TV!!!
YES. ON "EVERYBODY LOVES RAYMOND."
YES!!! YES!! THAT'S IT! I MEAN ISN'T THAT JUST AMAZING, FOLKS?
ONE BRILLIANT MAN COULD SPAWN SUCH TALENTED AND TERRIFIC KIDS.
WELL, YOU KNOW, WHEN I SEE MIKE I WILL TELL HIM YOU SAID SO...
WAIT!! YOU KNOW HIM??
YES.
YOU KNOW HIM.
WELL, WE WORK ON THE SAME MAGAZINE AS YOU JUST POINTED...
THAT'S AMAZING! WELL, I WOULD LOVE TO HAVE HIM ON OUR SHOW.
I WILL TELL HIM.
OH, THAT WOULD BE FANTASTIC. IMAGINE THAT.
WELL, I'D LIKE TO THANK OUR GUEST MICHAEL BRIAN BENDIS FOR COMING ON TODAY.
THANK YOU, MICHAEL...
BRIAN...
WHAT?
NOTHING.

# THE MOST GHOULISH HALLOWEEN STORY YOU'VE EVER HEARD

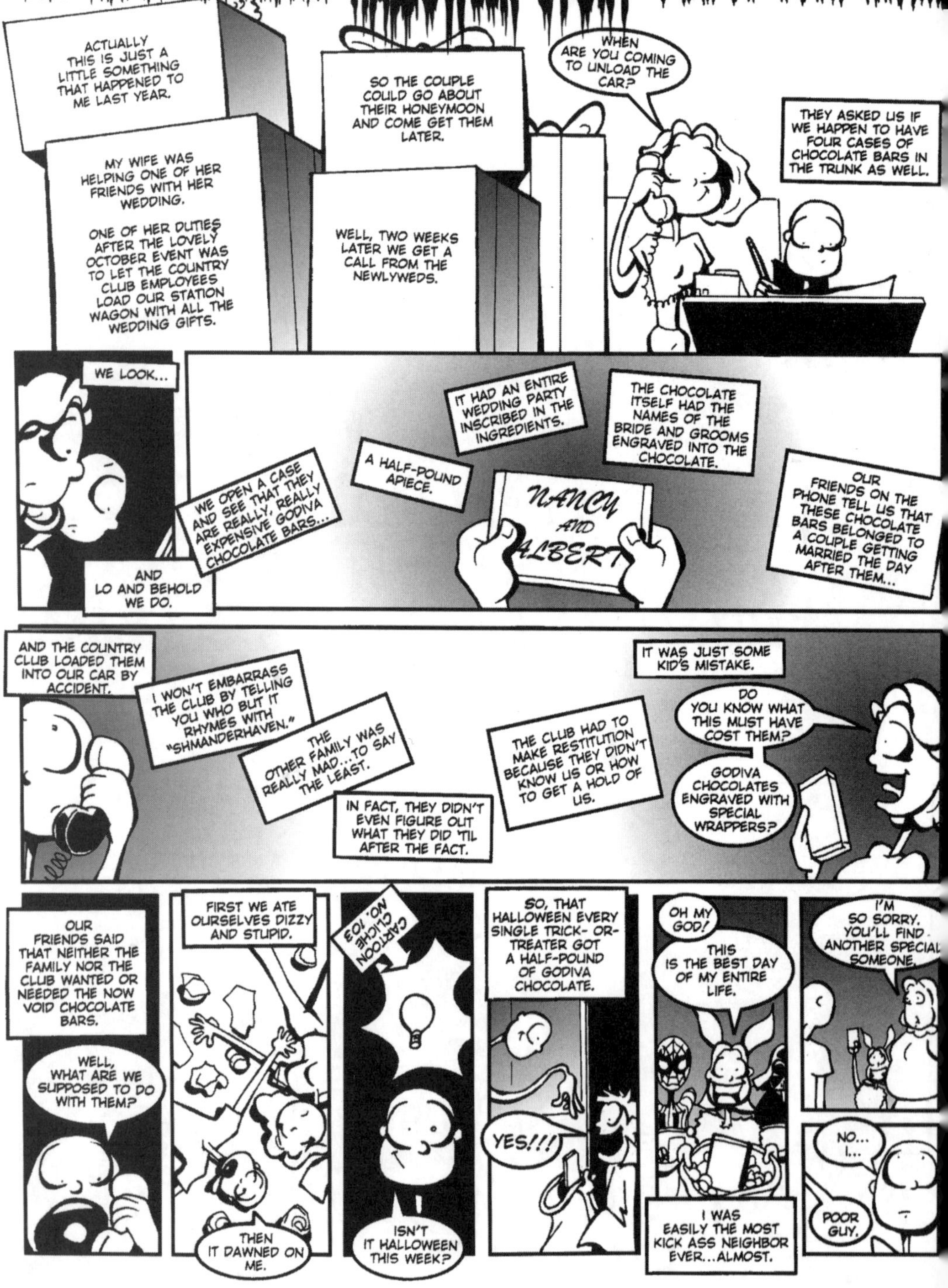
ACTUALLY THIS IS JUST A LITTLE SOMETHING THAT HAPPENED TO ME LAST YEAR.
MY WIFE WAS HELPING ONE OF HER FRIENDS WITH HER WEDDING.
ONE OF HER DUTIES AFTER THE LOVELY OCTOBER EVENT WAS TO LET THE COUNTRY CLUB EMPLOYEES LOAD OUR STATION WAGON WITH ALL THE WEDDING GIFTS.
SO THE COUPLE COULD GO ABOUT THEIR HONEYMOON AND COME GET THEM LATER.
WELL, TWO WEEKS LATER WE GET A CALL FROM THE NEWLYWEDS.
WHEN ARE YOU COMING TO UNLOAD THE CAR?
THEY ASKED US IF WE HAPPEN TO HAVE FOUR CASES OF CHOCOLATE BARS IN THE TRUNK AS WELL.
WE LOOK...
AND LO AND BEHOLD WE DO.
WE OPEN A CASE AND SEE THAT THEY ARE REALLY, REALLY EXPENSIVE GODIVA CHOCOLATE BARS...
A HALF-POUND APIECE.
IT HAD AN ENTIRE WEDDING PARTY INSCRIBED IN THE INGREDIENTS.
THE CHOCOLATE ITSELF HAD THE NAMES OF THE BRIDE AND GROOMS ENGRAVED INTO THE CHOCOLATE.
NANCY AND ALBERT
OUR FRIENDS ON THE PHONE TELL US THAT THESE CHOCOLATE BARS BELONGED TO A COUPLE GETTING MARRIED THE DAY AFTER THEM...
AND THE COUNTRY CLUB LOADED THEM INTO OUR CAR BY ACCIDENT.
I WON'T EMBARRASS THE CLUB BY TELLING YOU WHO BUT IT RHYMES WITH "SHMANDERHAVEN."
THE OTHER FAMILY WAS REALLY MAD...TO SAY THE LEAST.
IN FACT, THEY DIDN'T EVEN FIGURE OUT WHAT THEY DID 'TIL AFTER THE FACT.
THE CLUB HAD TO MAKE RESTITUTION BECAUSE THEY DIDN'T KNOW US OR HOW TO GET A HOLD OF US.
IT WAS JUST SOME KID'S MISTAKE.
DO YOU KNOW WHAT THIS MUST HAVE COST THEM?
GODIVA CHOCOLATES ENGRAVED WITH SPECIAL WRAPPERS?
OUR FRIENDS SAID THAT NEITHER THE FAMILY NOR THE CLUB WANTED OR NEEDED THE NOW VOID CHOCOLATE BARS.
WELL, WHAT ARE WE SUPPOSED TO DO WITH THEM?
FIRST WE ATE OURSELVES DIZZY AND STUPID.
THEN IT DAWNED ON ME.
CARTOON CLICHE NO. 103
ISN'T IT HALLOWEEN THIS WEEK?
SO, THAT HALLOWEEN EVERY SINGLE TRICK- OR-TREATER GOT A HALF-POUND OF GODIVA CHOCOLATE.
YES!!!
OH MY GOD!
THIS IS THE BEST DAY OF MY ENTIRE LIFE.
I WAS EASILY THE MOST KICK ASS NEIGHBOR EVER...ALMOST.
I'M SO SORRY. YOU'LL FIND ANOTHER SPECIAL SOMEONE.
NO... I...
POOR GUY.

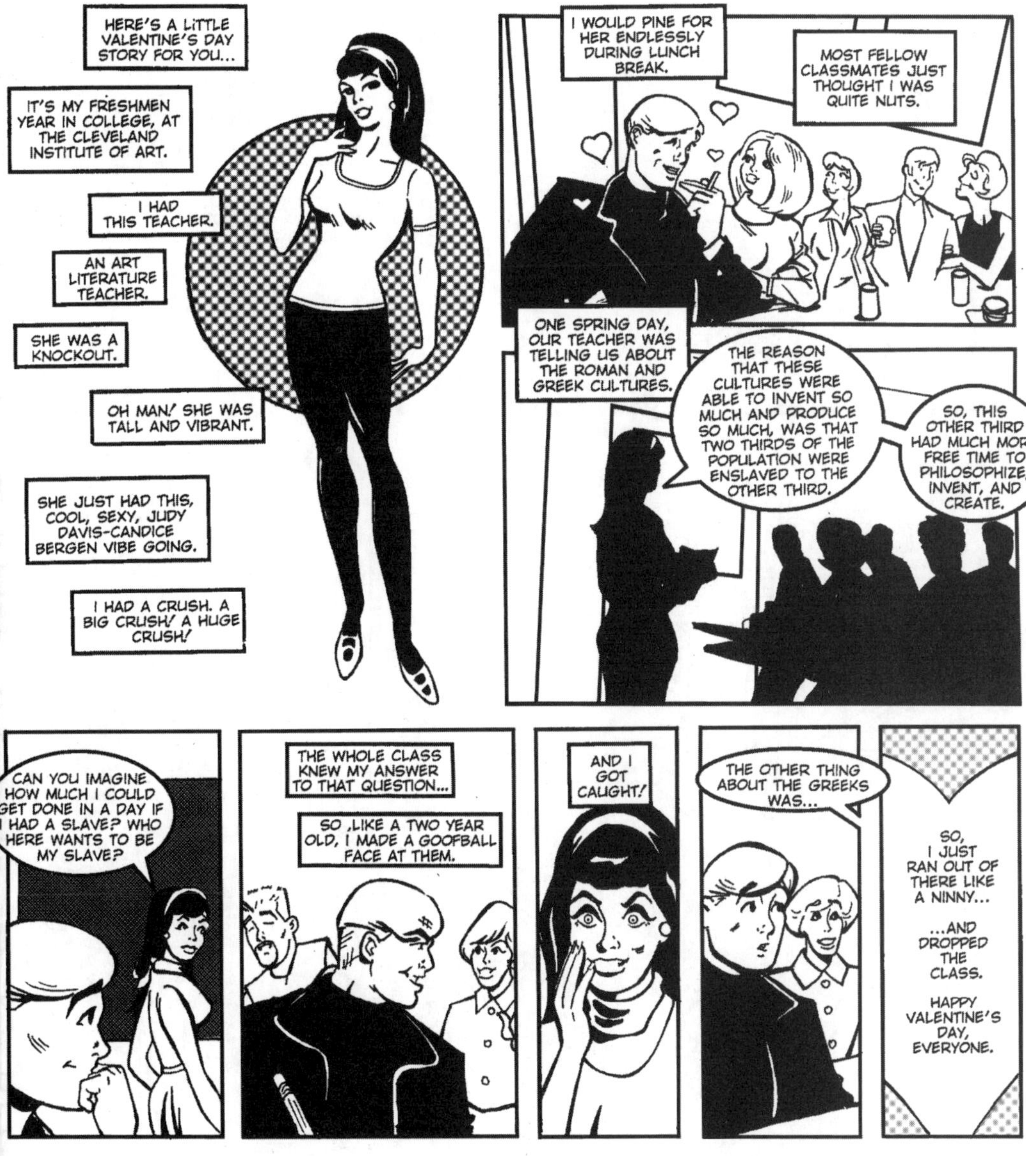
HERE'S A LITTLE VALENTINE'S DAY STORY FOR YOU...
IT'S MY FRESHMEN YEAR IN COLLEGE, AT THE CLEVELAND INSTITUTE OF ART.
I HAD THIS TEACHER.
AN ART LITERATURE TEACHER.
SHE WAS A KNOCKOUT.
OH MAN! SHE WAS TALL AND VIBRANT.
SHE JUST HAD THIS, COOL, SEXY, JUDY DAVIS-CANDICE BERGEN VIBE GOING.
I HAD A CRUSH. A BIG CRUSH! A HUGE CRUSH!
I WOULD PINE FOR HER ENDLESSLY DURING LUNCH BREAK.
MOST FELLOW CLASSMATES JUST THOUGHT I WAS QUITE NUTS.
ONE SPRING DAY, OUR TEACHER WAS TELLING US ABOUT THE ROMAN AND GREEK CULTURES.
THE REASON THAT THESE CULTURES WERE ABLE TO INVENT SO MUCH AND PRODUCE SO MUCH, WAS THAT TWO THIRDS OF THE POPULATION WERE ENSLAVED TO THE OTHER THIRD.
SO, THIS OTHER THIRD HAD MUCH MORE FREE TIME TO PHILOSOPHIZE, INVENT, AND CREATE.
CAN YOU IMAGINE HOW MUCH I COULD GET DONE IN A DAY IF I HAD A SLAVE? WHO HERE WANTS TO BE MY SLAVE?
THE WHOLE CLASS KNEW MY ANSWER TO THAT QUESTION...
SO ,LIKE A TWO YEAR OLD, I MADE A GOOFBALL FACE AT THEM.
AND I GOT CAUGHT!
THE OTHER THING ABOUT THE GREEKS WAS...
SO, I JUST RAN OUT OF THERE LIKE A NINNY...
...AND DROPPED THE CLASS.
HAPPY VALENTINE'S DAY, EVERYONE.

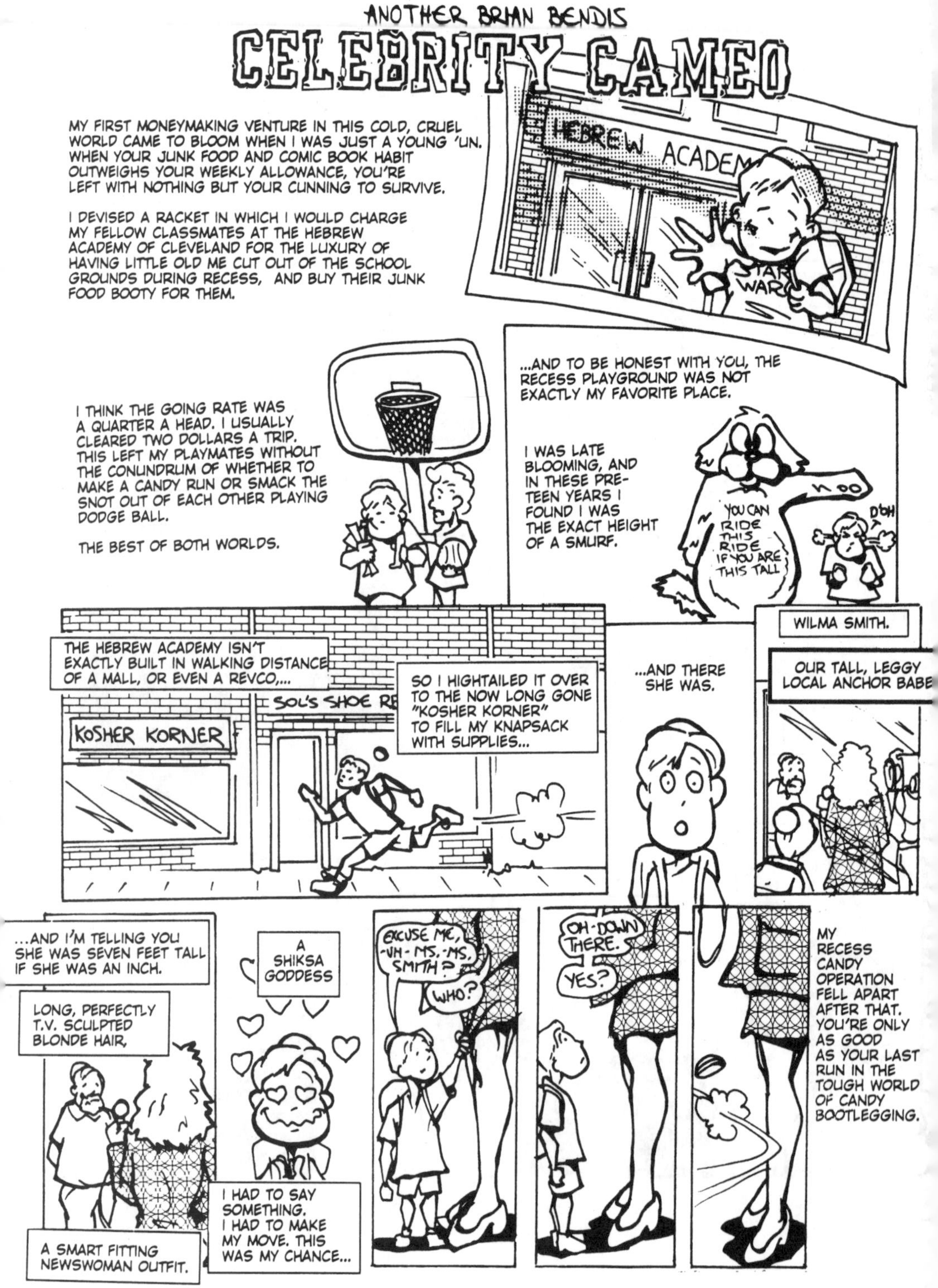

ANOTHER BRIAN BENDIS
CELEBRITY CAMEO
MY FIRST MONEYMAKING VENTURE IN THIS COLD, CRUEL WORLD CAME TO BLOOM WHEN I WAS JUST A YOUNG 'UN. WHEN YOUR JUNK FOOD AND COMIC BOOK HABIT OUTWEIGHS YOUR WEEKLY ALLOWANCE, YOU'RE LEFT WITH NOTHING BUT YOUR CUNNING TO SURVIVE.
I DEVISED A RACKET IN WHICH I WOULD CHARGE MY FELLOW CLASSMATES AT THE HEBREW ACADEMY OF CLEVELAND FOR THE LUXURY OF HAVING LITTLE OLD ME CUT OUT OF THE SCHOOL GROUNDS DURING RECESS, AND BUY THEIR JUNK FOOD BOOTY FOR THEM.
HEBREW ACADEM
I THINK THE GOING RATE WAS A QUARTER A HEAD. I USUALLY CLEARED TWO DOLLARS A TRIP. THIS LEFT MY PLAYMATES WITHOUT THE CONUNDRUM OF WHETHER TO MAKE A CANDY RUN OR SMACK THE SNOT OUT OF EACH OTHER PLAYING DODGE BALL.
THE BEST OF BOTH WORLDS.
...AND TO BE HONEST WITH YOU, THE RECESS PLAYGROUND WAS NOT EXACTLY MY FAVORITE PLACE.
I WAS LATE BLOOMING, AND IN THESE PRE-TEEN YEARS I FOUND I WAS THE EXACT HEIGHT OF A SMURF.
YOU CAN RIDE THIS RIDE IF YOU ARE THIS TALL
D'OH
THE HEBREW ACADEMY ISN'T EXACTLY BUILT IN WALKING DISTANCE OF A MALL, OR EVEN A REVCO,...
SO I HIGHTAILED IT OVER TO THE NOW LONG GONE "KOSHER KORNER" TO FILL MY KNAPSACK WITH SUPPLIES...
SOL'S SHOE RE
KOSHER KORNER
...AND THERE SHE WAS.
WILMA SMITH.
OUR TALL, LEGGY LOCAL ANCHOR BABE
...AND I'M TELLING YOU SHE WAS SEVEN FEET TALL IF SHE WAS AN INCH.
LONG, PERFECTLY T.V. SCULPTED BLONDE HAIR,
A SMART FITTING NEWSWOMAN OUTFIT.
A SHIKSA GODDESS
I HAD TO SAY SOMETHING. I HAD TO MAKE MY MOVE. THIS WAS MY CHANCE...
EXCUSE ME, -UH- MS. MS. SMITH?
WHO?
OH- DOWN THERE.
YES?
MY RECESS CANDY OPERATION FELL APART AFTER THAT. YOU'RE ONLY AS GOOD AS YOUR LAST RUN IN THE TOUGH WORLD OF CANDY BOOTLEGGING.

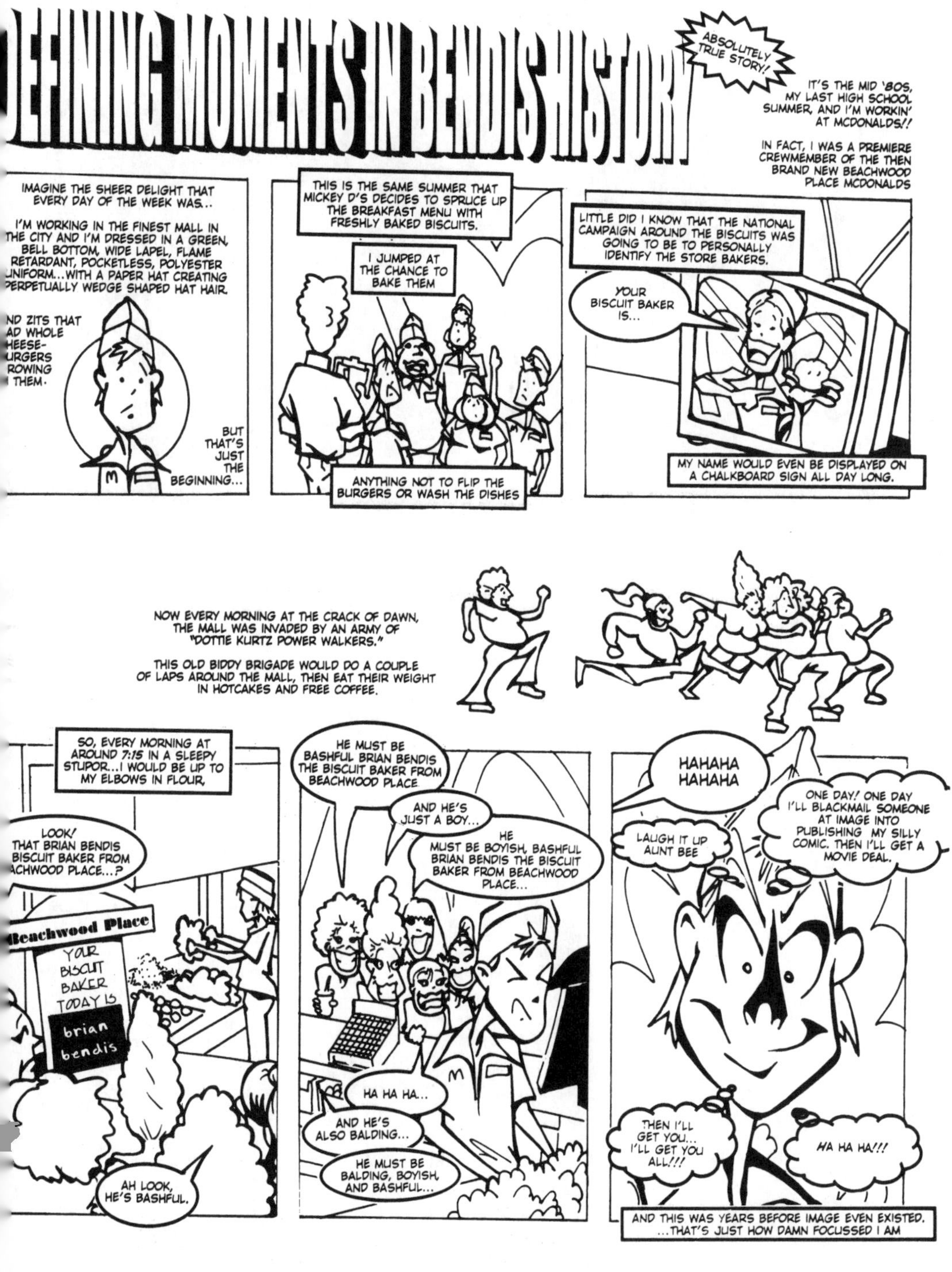
DEFINING MOMENTS IN BENDIS HISTORY
ABSOLUTELY TRUE STORY!
IT'S THE MID '80S, MY LAST HIGH SCHOOL SUMMER, AND I'M WORKIN' AT MCDONALDS!!
IN FACT, I WAS A PREMIERE CREWMEMBER OF THE THEN BRAND NEW BEACHWOOD PLACE MCDONALDS
IMAGINE THE SHEER DELIGHT THAT EVERY DAY OF THE WEEK WAS...
I'M WORKING IN THE FINEST MALL IN THE CITY AND I'M DRESSED IN A GREEN, BELL BOTTOM, WIDE LAPEL, FLAME RETARDANT, POCKETLESS, POLYESTER UNIFORM...WITH A PAPER HAT CREATING PERPETUALLY WEDGE SHAPED HAT HAIR.
ND ZITS THAT AD WHOLE HEESE- URGERS ROWING THEM.
BUT THAT'S JUST THE BEGINNING...
THIS IS THE SAME SUMMER THAT MICKEY D'S DECIDES TO SPRUCE UP THE BREAKFAST MENU WITH FRESHLY BAKED BISCUITS.
I JUMPED AT THE CHANCE TO BAKE THEM
ANYTHING NOT TO FLIP THE BURGERS OR WASH THE DISHES
LITTLE DID I KNOW THAT THE NATIONAL CAMPAIGN AROUND THE BISCUITS WAS GOING TO BE TO PERSONALLY IDENTIFY THE STORE BAKERS.
YOUR BISCUIT BAKER IS...
MY NAME WOULD EVEN BE DISPLAYED ON A CHALKBOARD SIGN ALL DAY LONG.
NOW EVERY MORNING AT THE CRACK OF DAWN, THE MALL WAS INVADED BY AN ARMY OF "DOTTIE KURTZ POWER WALKERS."
THIS OLD BIDDY BRIGADE WOULD DO A COUPLE OF LAPS AROUND THE MALL, THEN EAT THEIR WEIGHT IN HOTCAKES AND FREE COFFEE.
SO, EVERY MORNING AT AROUND 7:15 IN A SLEEPY STUPOR...I WOULD BE UP TO MY ELBOWS IN FLOUR.
LOOK! THAT BRIAN BENDIS BISCUIT BAKER FROM ACHWOOD PLACE...?
Beachwood Place
YOUR BISCUIT BAKER TODAY IS
brian bendis
AH LOOK, HE'S BASHFUL.
HE MUST BE BASHFUL BRIAN BENDIS THE BISCUIT BAKER FROM BEACHWOOD PLACE.
AND HE'S JUST A BOY...
HE MUST BE BOYISH, BASHFUL BRIAN BENDIS THE BISCUIT BAKER FROM BEACHWOOD PLACE...
HA HA HA...
AND HE'S ALSO BALDING...
HE MUST BE BALDING, BOYISH, AND BASHFUL...
HAHAHA HAHAHA
LAUGH IT UP AUNT BEE
ONE DAY! ONE DAY I'LL BLACKMAIL SOMEONE AT IMAGE INTO PUBLISHING MY SILLY COMIC. THEN I'LL GET A MOVIE DEAL.
THEN I'LL GET YOU... I'LL GET YOU ALL!!!
HA HA HA!!!
AND THIS WAS YEARS BEFORE IMAGE EVEN EXISTED. ...THAT'S JUST HOW DAMN FOCUSSED I AM

# MY BLUE HEAVEN

A PRETTY CLOSE TO TRUE TALE TOLD IN MONOTONOUS MONOLOGUE
BY BRIAN MICHAEL BENDIS

O.K., SO I'M HOME FROM SCHOOL OVER PASSOVER VACATION.

THIS WOULD BE AROUND 1982, I GUESS. OR SOMEWHERE AROUND THERE.

PASSOVER VACATION IS ONE OF THE VERY FEW PERKS THAT COMES WITH THE SOCIOLOGICAL TERROR OF ATTENDING A PRIVATE HEBREW SCHOOL. YOU GET A GOOD SOLID TWO FULL WEEKS OFF OF SCHOOL IN EARLY SPRING.

BY THIS PERIOD IN MY LIFE I HAD PRETTY MUCH DECIDED THAT I HAD FOUND MY CALLING.

I KNEW AS SURE AS I KNEW ANYTHING THAT I WAS GOING TO BE A COMIC ARTIST.

A GREAT COMIC ARTIST.

A LEGEND COMIC ARTIST.

I WAS GOING TO BE GEORGE PEREZ.

I WAS GOING TO BE RICH AND ADMIRED, REVERED AND ADORED.

AND I WOULD HAVE THIS BY MY 17TH BIRTHDAY,

EASY.

SO, ON THIS RELATIVELY QUIET VACATION FROM SCHOOL, I EMBARKED ON A SINGULAR QUEST.

I DECIDED THAT IT WAS MY DUTY TO THE WORLD AS A BUDDING SEQUENTIAL ARTIST TO SINGLE HANDILY PRODUCE A COMPREHENSIVE AND FAITHFUL ADAPTATION OF "RAIDERS OF THE LOST ARK."

I HAD, AND MAYBE STILL HAVE, SOME SORT OF UNHEALTHY ATTACHMENT TO THIS MOVIE, AND WAS PERSONALLY OFFENDED BY THE SLACKJAWED MARVEL COMICS SO-CALLED ADAPTATION.

MARVEL WAS PRODUCING QUIET A FEW ANTISEPTIC MOVIE ADAPTATIONS AROUND THIS TIME, WITH NO OBVIOUS RHYME OR REASON TO WHICH MOVIES THEY LICENSED.

(ANYBODY REMEMBER VINCE COLLETTA'S GROUND-BREAKING WORK ON THE FEEL GOOD HIT "ANNIE"?)

ANYWOO, I DECIDED MY BEST COURSE OF ACTION WAS TO SIT MYSELF DOWN, POP IN MY OWN VIDEO CASSETTE COPY OF THE MOVIE, AND DRAW

MY ADAPTATION RIGHT OFF THE SCREEN.

I WOULD DO THIS BY SIMPLY PAUSING THE TAPE AFTER EACH EDIT AND DRAW THE STILL IMAGE.

I'LL DRAW THE ENTIRE MOVIE SHOT FOR SHOT! EVER FAITHFUL TO THE VISION OF THE MASTER FILMMAKER.

I WOULD THEN HAND THIS IN TO MARVEL. THEY WOULD THEN RECALL THEIR MISGUIDED EFFORT, APOLOGIZE TO THE PUBLIC AT LARGE AND MAKE IT UP TO THEM BY PRESENTING MY ADAPTATION.

I WAS DOING OUR CULTURE AND MANKIND A GREAT SERVICE.

NOW HERE COMES THE GOOD STUFF.

MY SEASONAL JUNK FOOD DE JOUR THAT SPRING WAS CHOCOLATE PUDDING.

NOT JUST ANY CHOCOLATE PUDDING. I'M TALKING ABOUT THE REAL CHEAP CRAP. THE PUDDING THAT IS PACKED IN NONDESCRIPT SOUP CANS WITH PLASTIC CAPS.

THE KIND THAT LEAVES THAT FEROCIOUS SACCHARINE AFTERTASTE IN YOUR MOUTH.

THE PLUS SIDE IS THAT IT IS VERY AFFORDABLE AND VERY AVAILABLE IN LARGE QUANTITIES. PERFECT FOR A LIMITED BUDGET PRETEEN WITH A COMIC JONES.

( A LITTLE CONSUMER TIP, FOR ALL YOU UP AND COMERS.)

SO, ARMED WITH MY WEIGHT IN PUDDING, A ZESTY CHIP CHASER, MY TRUSTY VCR, AND ALTOGETHER THE WRONG ART SUPPLIES, I EMBARKED ON MY QUEST.

FULL SPEED!

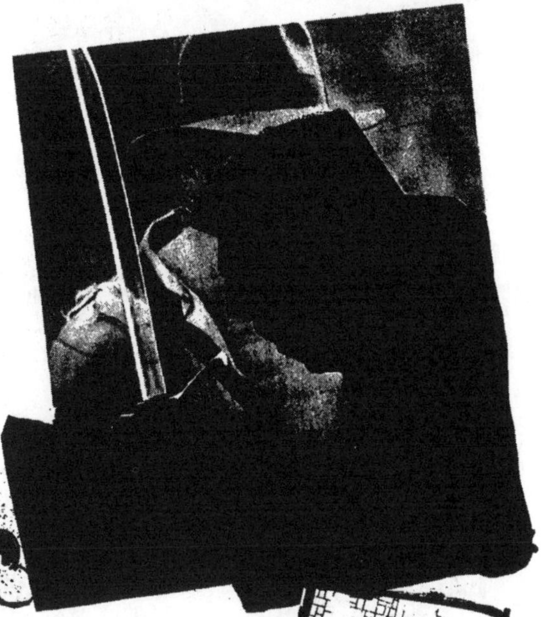

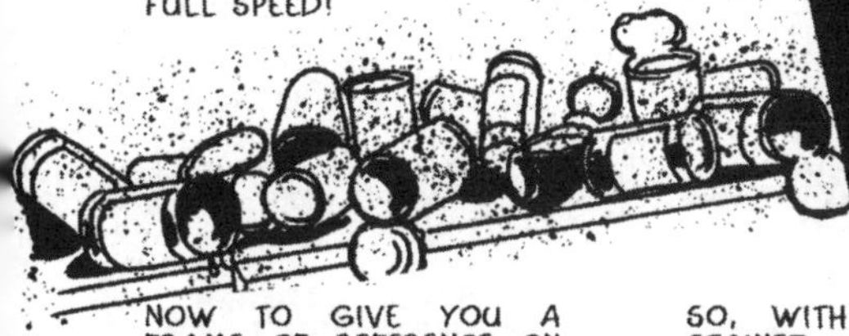

NOW TO GIVE YOU A FRAME OF REFERENCE ON HOW LONG I PURSUED THIS TRIVIAL NONSENSE, I CREATED NO LESS THAN A WHOPPING FORTY PAGES OF FINISHED, OR AS FINISHED AS I GOT IN THOSE DAYS, ARTWORK.

FORTY FREAKIN' PAGES OF FULL COMIC ART.

NOW TO SHOW YOU HOW WHACKED I WAS ON THE BASIC PRINCIPALS OF SEQUENTIAL STORYTELLING AND PACING, I HAD YET TO PASS THE POINT IN THE MOVIE WHERE INDY ENTERED THE CAVE OF DOOM IN THE FIRST SCENES IN THE MOVIE.

IF FACT, I'M PRETTY SURE I JUST SQUEAKED PAST THE 'DIRECTED BY STEVEN SPEILBERG' CREDIT.

FORTY PAGES FOR TWO MINUTES OF FILM.

WELL, YOU CAN DO YOUR OWN MATH ON HOW MUCH PUDDING I HAD POUNDED DOWN.

WHATEVER YOUR GUESS IS,..- I'D MULTIPLY IT BY THREE,

I WAS AT THAT AGE. Y'KNOW, THAT AGE WHERE YOU CAN CONSUME ANYTHING YOU WANT IN ANY CONCEIVABLE VOLUME, AS EVERY BLOATED ADULT CURSES AT YOU THAT IT'LL CATCH UP TO YOU.

SO, WITH MY GRAPHITE STAINED PALMS,... I SHOVELED IT ALL IN,

(NOW, IT'S GOING TO GET A LITTLE UGLY HERE, SO TREAD LIGHTLY.)

CUT TO A BATHROOM BREAK.

NOW, I AM THE KING OF CHRONIC BATHROOM READERS. I GET SO LOST IN WHATEVER I READ IN THERE THAT I USUALLY GET ONE OF THOSE TOILET SEAT INDENTATIONS ON MY ASS FROM PROLONGED SITTING.

I DON'T KNOW WHAT IT IS, THE SEAT, THE ANGLE, THE CALM.

IT'S JUST THE PERFECT PLACE FOR ME TO READ.

I MEAN IT.

I DO SO MUCH READING IN THERE THAT ONE OF MY EX-GIRLFRIENDS BOUGHT ME THIS LITTLE DESK TO PUT IN FRONT OF THE TOILET.

I STILL HAVE IT AND USE IT. IT'S THE BEST PRESENT I'VE EVER GOTTEN.

SO AFTER AN EXTENDED TOILET READ. I CASUALLY ROSE UP, AS I'M PRONE TO DO.

AND I DON'T KNOW IF I ALWAYS DO THIS, BUT I HAPPENED TO GLANCE DOWN IN THE BOWL TO ASSESS THE DAMAGE... AND... AND...

WHAT I SAW ...

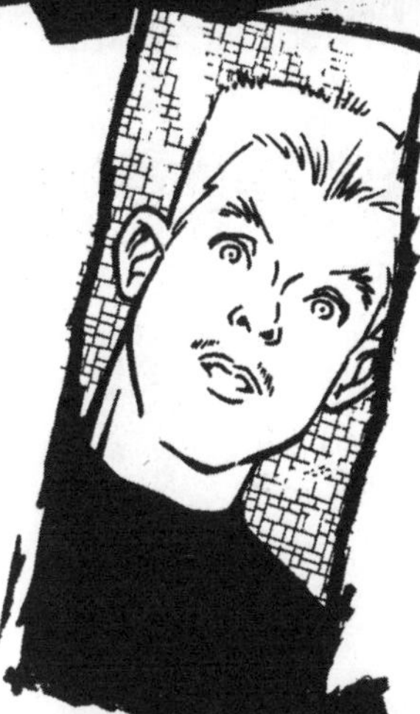

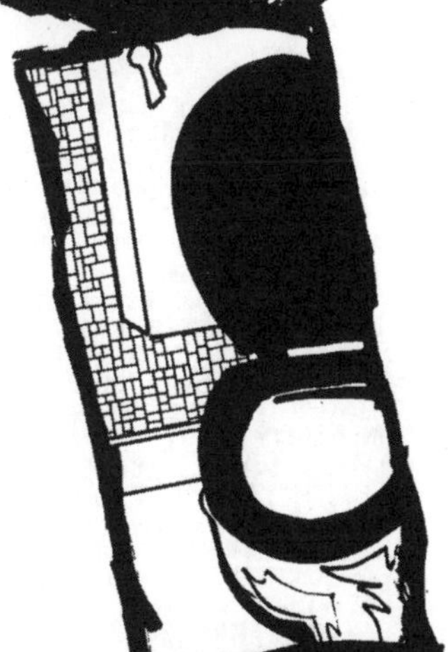

I DON'T KNOW HOW ELSE TO SAY IT. I DON'T KNOW HOW ELSE TO DESCRIBE IT, SO I GUESS I'LL COME RIGHT OUT AND SAY IT.

MY SHIT WAS BLUE.

AND I DON'T MEAN BLUE-ISH, OR A BROWN BLUE.

I MEAN...BLUE.

THE CLOSEST THING I CAN COME UP WITH TO DES-CRIBE IT...IS SMURF BLUE.

I REMEMBER FRANTICALLY YELLING OUT TO MY MOM TO COME AND TAKE A LOOK. SHE YELLED BACK, OR I SHOULD SAY SHRIL-LED BACK: "THERE'S NOTH-ING IN THERE THAT I HAVE TO SEE!"

MOM, BURNED MORE THAN ONCE FROM ADOLESCENT INSIPIDNESS ON MY PART, HAD OBVIOUSLY LEARNED BETTER.

BUT, AFTER A CALL FOR FAMILY UNITY, MY MOM DID COME IN AND DID CONFIRM MY FINDING.

ACTUALLY, MOM FREAKED.

ACTING WITH THE DEX-TERITY AND EXPERTISE THAT ONLY A JEWISH MOM WITH A FEW YEARS UNDER HER BELT CAN, SHE EMBARKED ON A FIT OF HYSTERICS THAT CON-CLUDED WITH HER HAND-ING ME A BAGGIE, COMMANDING ME TO ACTUALLY PICK UP THE UNHOLY SPECIMEN, SO THAT WE COULD TAKE IT TO THE DOCTOR:

"IMMEDIATELY, IF NOT SOONER." (A TRADEMARK MA BENDIS PHRASE.)

AND AS I DIPPED MY HAND INTO THE COLD, RANCID WATERS OF MY OWN MAKING, I REMEMBER THINKING THAT IT DOESN'T MATTER WHERE YOU LIVE, IT DOESN'T MATTER WHAT YOU'RE SOCIAL STANDING IN THE COMMUNITY IS, IT DOESN'T MATTER WHAT RELIGION OR FAITH YOU ADHERE TO, UNIVERSALLY, THE TEXT BOOK DEFINITION OF A DAY TURNED BAD IS IF SOMEWHERE WITH IN THAT DAY YOU FIND YOURSELF MANHANDLING YOUR OWN BLUE TURD.

SO OFF TO THE PED-IATRICIAN WE GO, (STILL THE ONLY MAN TO TOUCH MY GENITALS OTHER THAN ME.)

MY DOCTOR, OBVIOUSLY INTRIGUED BY MY MOT-HER'S DELIRIOUSLY FRAN-TIC CALL AGREED TO SEE US RIGHT AWAY.

MY DOCTOR WAS ONE OF THOSE "HIP FUNKY" DOCTORS. A WACKY PED-IATRICIAN WHO FILLED HIS OFFICE WITH GADGETS AND GAGS, UNDER THE GUISE OF MAKING THE KIDS FEEL MORE AT HOME AND RELAXED, BUT YOU JUST KNEW THEY WERE REALLY FOR HIM.

HE HAD THIS GORGEOUS DISPLAY OF ALL THE STAR WARS ACTION FIGURES ON THEIR OFFICIAL STAR WARS DISPLAY STAND. I REALLY WANTED IT.

(I HAD A LAME DARTH VADER COLLECTOR'S CASE, AND THE DAMN FIGURES WOULD NEVER STAY IN THEIR LITTLE COMPART-MENTS. FUCKERS!!)

NOW, I DON'T REMEMBER IF WE HAD TO WAIT A DAY OR WHAT, BUT LOGIC DICTATES THAT WE PROB-ABLY DID.

MY MOM AND I BOTH SAT QUIETLY IN THE DOCTOR'S OFFICE, ANXIOUSLY AWAITING THE DOCTOR'S STANDARD CAVALIER ENTRANCE.

"GET YOUR HANDS OFF MY PET ROCK, BRIAN." HE MUTTERED AS HE FLIPPED OPEN MY FILE.

"WELL..." SAID MY MOM WITH TYPICAL 'CUT THE BULLSHIT DOC AND GIVE IT TO ME STRAIGHTNESS.'

"YES. JUNK FOOD."

"JUNK FOOD?" I CRACKED.

"EAT A LOT OF JUNK-FOOD?"

"WELL, WHAT'S, LIKE, A LOT?"

"HE DOES." SHE BLURTS. "I TRY TO STOP HIM, BUT YOU CAN'T BE WITH HIM TWENTY FOUR HOURS A DAY.I...."

"DOES THIS JUNK HAVE A LOT OF ARTIFICIAL FLAV-ORING?"

"NO..." I DENIED WITH THE BULLET SPEED OF A GUIL-TY TEEN.

"NO?"

"NO..."

"REALLY? NO...?"

"DOES, UH, DOES CHOC-OLATE PUDDING HAVE ARTIFICIAL FLAVORING IN IT?" I ASKED WITH THAT PITIFUL LOOK THAT I CARRIED WITH ME WELL INTO COLLEGE.

"NO." EXCLAIMED THE DOC

"OH GOOD" I GRINNED "CAUSE I REALLY..."

"NO SON, CHOCOLATE PUD-DING COMES FROM CANDY LAND," DR. SARCASM QUIPPED. "OF COURSE IT HAS ARTIFICIAL FLAV-ORING IN IT. CHOCOLATE PUDDING IS ARTIFICIAL FLAVORING. NOW LISTEN UP, ALL THE DYES AND ARTIFICIAL CRAP IN THIS SO-CALLED PUDDING OF YOURS HAS ACTUALLY STAINED YOUR DIGESTIVE TRACK."

"OH NO!! OH GOD!!. WHAT ARE WE GOING TO DO, DOCTOR?" PLEADED MY MOTHER, HEADING TOW-ARDS HER NERVOUS BREAKDOWN AT WARP FACTOR EIGHT.

"YOU WANT TO KNOW WHAT TO DO? O.K. BUT I NEED YOU TWO TO FOLLOW THESE INSTRUC-TIONS TO THE T."

"YES..?"

"DON'T- EAT- CHOCOLATE-PUDDING!!!" HE SMILED AND SLAMMED MY FILE SHUT.

I WASN'T EXACTLY SOLD ON THE SCIENTIFIC SIDE OF THIS DIAGNOSIS. I OF-FERED MY OPINION THAT MAYBE, JUST MAYBE, THE HUE OF MY BILE WAS THE RESULT OF MY V.C.R. BEING ON PAUSE FOR SUCH A LENGTHY PERIOD OF TIME.

MAYBE, JUST MAYBE, THE V.C.R. WAS EMANATING SOME SORT OF WEIRD, FREAKISH X-RAY OR RADIATION.

LAME? YES. BUT THIS WAS THE BEST THING MY COMIC BOOK ADDLED BRAIN COULD MUSTER.

"WHAT'S WRONG WITH YOU?" MY MOTHER SNEERED AT ME WITH THAT "HOW DID THIS COME OUT OF ME" LOOK.

MY DOCTOR JUST CHORTLED IN SUPERIORITY: "HEY! KEEP THE DOCTORIN' TO THE DOCTOR"

NOT YET HAVING FASHIONED THE LARGE WELL TO STUFF ALL MY REJECTION IN, I STARED AT HIM WITH A PITIFUL LOOK OF ABANDONMENT.

SEEING MY DISTRAUGHT PUPPY FACE. HE MAGNANIMOUSLY INVITED ME TO MOSEY OVER TO THE FAR WALL WHERE HUNG AN ODDLY SCULPTED FRONT OF A HEAD(OR BUST) OF A GYPSY. IT WAS SORT OF A NORMAN ROCKWELL CHARACTER IN 3-D. FROM HIS HEAD HUNG A SIMILARLY SCULPTED TIE.

MY DOCTOR TOLD ME TO PULL THE TIE.

I DID.

WELL, MY MOM AND DOCTOR ROARED WITH THAT HYSTERICAL HYENA LAUGH YOU ALWAYS HEAR ON OLD T.V. KINESCOPES LIKE "YOUR SHOW OF SHOWS." THE KIND OF WHOOPING LAUGHTER THAT MAKES YOU THINK: "O.K. IT'S FUNNY, BUT ITS NOT THAT FUNNY."

NOW, I DON'T KNOW ABOUT YOU, BUT IT'S MOMENTS LIKE THESE THAT GIVE ME INTENSE ALMOST SURREAL CLARITY.

AS I STOOD THERE WET AND MOCKED, STARING AHEAD LIKE A PIG BLOOD COVERED CARRIE, I FOUND THAT MY VIRGIN MUSTACHED LIP HAD CURLED INTO A LITTLE SMILE.

SURE, I WAS NEVER, EVER GOING TO BE GEORGE PEREZ.

SURE, THE ORGASM THAT IS CHOCOLATE PUDDING WOULD FOREVER BE DENIED ME.

SURE, MY MOM AND DOCTOR ARE LAUGHING AT MY EXPENSE.

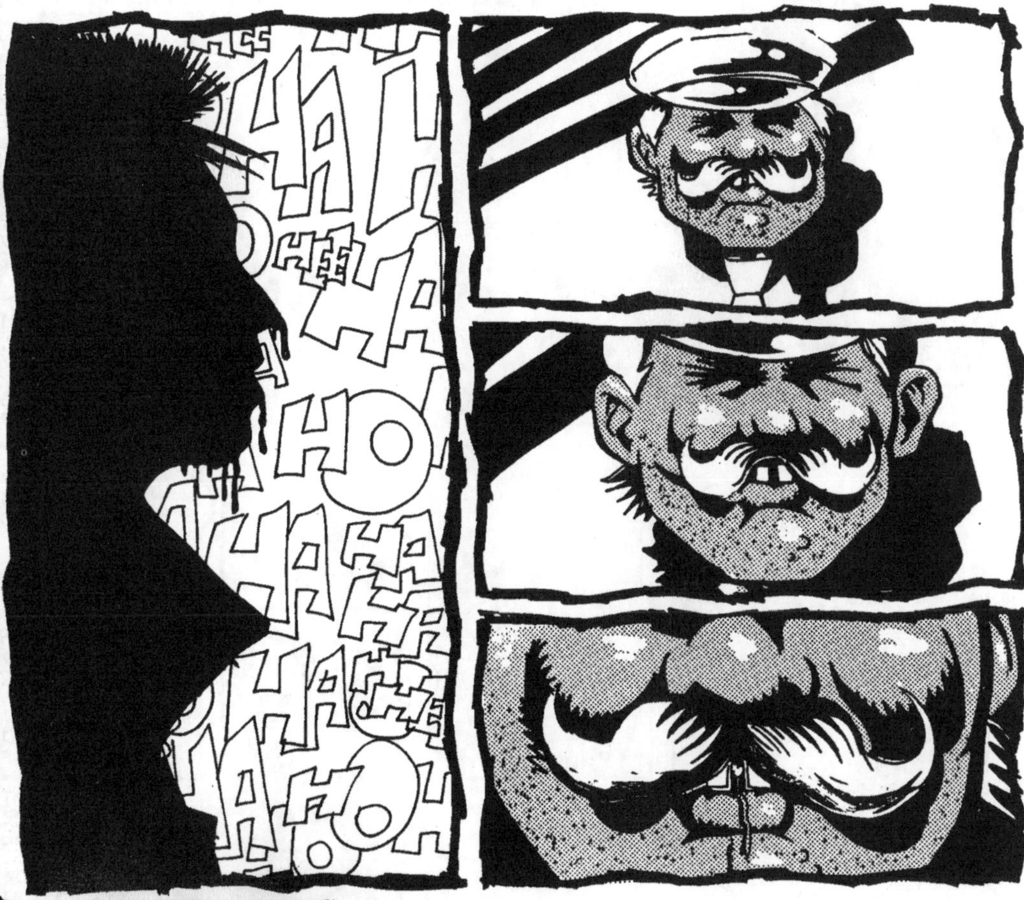
HA
HEE
HO
HA HA
HEE
HO

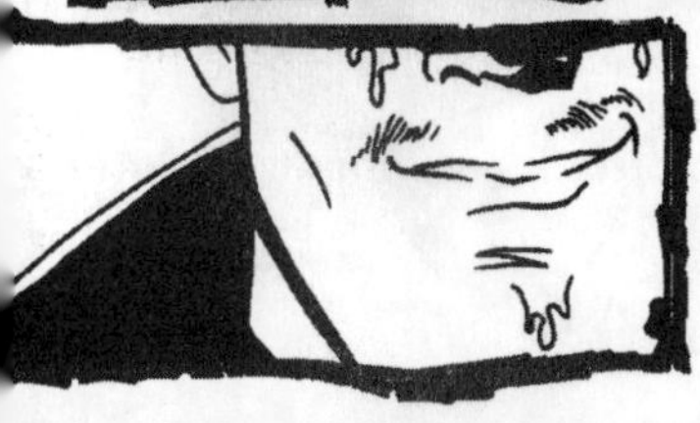

BUT...BUT!! I HAD THIS MAN ACTUALLY EXAMINE MY FREAKISH SHIT.

AND I HAD MY MOM PAY MONEY TO THIS GUY TO DO THIS.

HA!

LISTEN I KNOW IT'S NOT A LOT, BUT IT'S WHAT I HAD.

SCREW MY BAR-MITZVAH. THIS DAY I WAS A MAN.

I WAS INDIANA JONES.

# ANOTHER BRIAN BENDIS CELEBRITY CAMEO

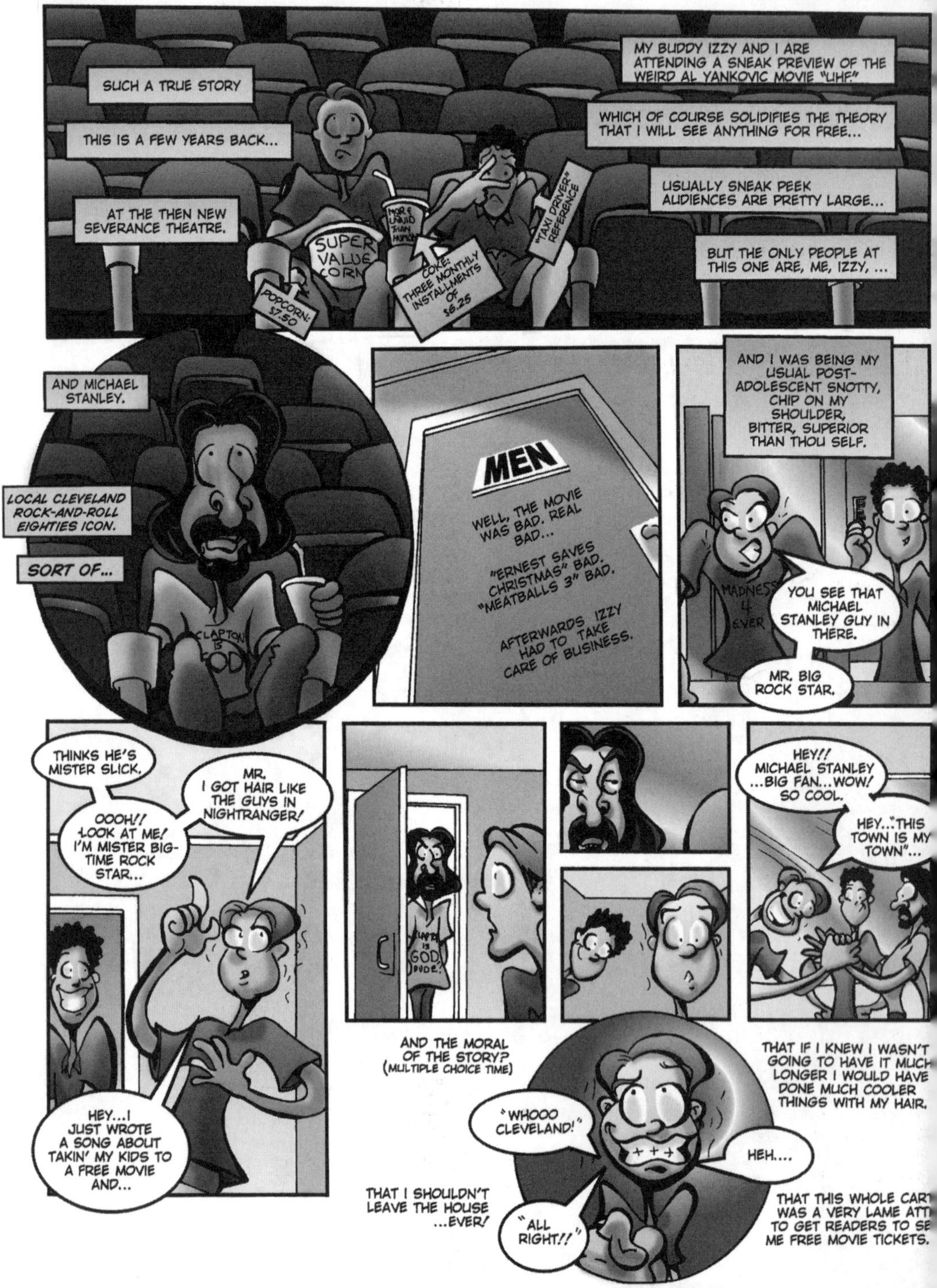

SUCH A TRUE STORY
THIS IS A FEW YEARS BACK...
AT THE THEN NEW SEVERANCE THEATRE.
MY BUDDY IZZY AND I ARE ATTENDING A SNEAK PREVIEW OF THE WEIRD AL YANKOVIC MOVIE "UHF"
WHICH OF COURSE SOLIDIFIES THE THEORY THAT I WILL SEE ANYTHING FOR FREE...
USUALLY SNEAK PEEK AUDIENCES ARE PRETTY LARGE...
BUT THE ONLY PEOPLE AT THIS ONE ARE, ME, IZZY, ...
SUPER VALUE CORN
POPCORN: $7.50
COKE: THREE MONTHLY INSTALLMENTS OF $6.25
"TAXI DRIVER" REFERENCE
AND MICHAEL STANLEY.
LOCAL CLEVELAND ROCK-AND-ROLL EIGHTIES ICON.
SORT OF...
CLAPTON IS GOD
MEN
WELL, THE MOVIE WAS BAD. REAL BAD...
"ERNEST SAVES CHRISTMAS" BAD. "MEATBALLS 3" BAD.
AFTERWARDS IZZY HAD TO TAKE CARE OF BUSINESS.
AND I WAS BEING MY USUAL POST-ADOLESCENT SNOTTY, CHIP ON MY SHOULDER, BITTER, SUPERIOR THAN THOU SELF.
MADNESS 4 EVER
YOU SEE THAT MICHAEL STANLEY GUY IN THERE.
MR. BIG ROCK STAR.
THINKS HE'S MISTER SLICK.
OOOH!! LOOK AT ME! I'M MISTER BIG-TIME ROCK STAR...
MR. I GOT HAIR LIKE THE GUYS IN NIGHTRANGER!
HEY...I JUST WROTE A SONG ABOUT TAKIN' MY KIDS TO A FREE MOVIE AND...
CLAPTON IS GOD DUDE
HEY!! MICHAEL STANLEY ...BIG FAN...WOW! SO COOL.
HEY..."THIS TOWN IS MY TOWN"...
AND THE MORAL OF THE STORY? (MULTIPLE CHOICE TIME)
THAT I SHOULDN'T LEAVE THE HOUSE ...EVER!
"WHOOO CLEVELAND!"
"ALL RIGHT!!"
THAT IF I KNEW I WASN'T GOING TO HAVE IT MUCH LONGER I WOULD HAVE DONE MUCH COOLER THINGS WITH MY HAIR.
HEH....
THAT THIS WHOLE CAR
WAS A VERY LAME AT
TO GET READERS TO S
ME FREE MOVIE TICKETS.

# EVERYTHING YOU WANTED TO KNOW ABOUT POISON ELVES CREATOR DREW HAYES BUT ...

It all started when I thought I had come up with a totally revolutionary idea: Wouldn't it be cool if a comic book letter column was actually entertaining and reflected the tone of the book, rather than being the usual public masturbation for the comic creators involved?

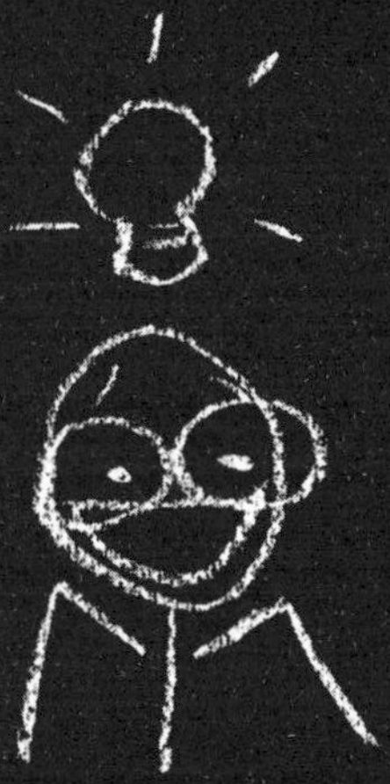

I realized that though I personally enjoyed nothing more than total strangers lauding me with praise, gifts, and sexual favors, that this might not be that interesting to the average comic reader. So by the time I had renamed my flagship series from Goldfish to Jinx, (published bi-monthly by Image comics, on sale now, I know you know. Sorry, habit.) the letter columns in my book had become a huge hit.

And I was glad. Cause these comics that are wall to wall house ads...man, the people behind them should be taken out and whipped like the guy in High Plains Drifter. These comics are so fucking expensive as it is! Fill the comic with cartoon entertainment. At least try. Am I right people!?!?!?!?! (Sorry, just watched Dennis Miller).

Anyway. So the letter column was a hit, and my audience had quickly seen the trick to getting their letters published. If you write something outlandish. Or give me an easy target in which to comeback on you, then you're as good as in.

You're the next Olav Beemer.

So a couple of years back as I waded through what ol' Dave letterman refers to as the voluminous viewer mail, I came across a letter that read as follows:

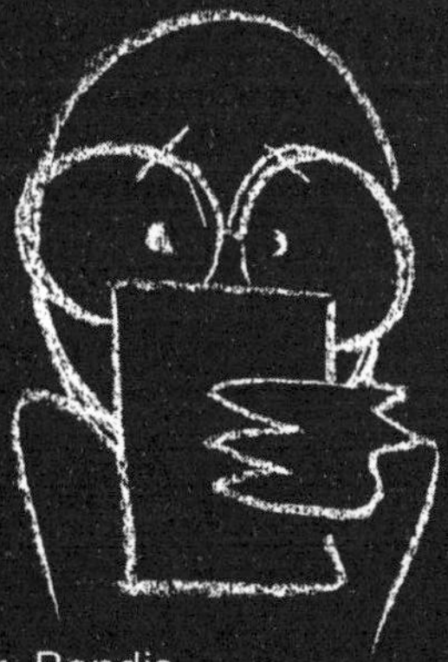

Dear Mr. Bendis,

I probably shouldn't ask you this, but well, do you think you could take Drew Hayes of "Poison Elves" in a fight? I'm not saying you should, its more form a rhetorical perspective. He's about the only other creator I can think of who's consistently willing to say his mind, and risk having people think he's a jerk. Actually what would be really interesting would be you two versus some 'big two" zombie creators in a sort of " battle royale cage match to the Finish!" Yeah, I watched wrestling as a kid.
So, beyond the fact that we all know

he wrote that while watching wrestling, I had to come up with a clever answer. Now, I had never heard of Drew Hayes, and had avoided his book because as a person who is only four foot six, I don't need to be picking up anything with the word elf in the title.

So, I scribbled: "It's public knowledge that Drew Hayes is my bitch, and I remain 'undefeated and still champion' the biggest jerk in comics."

Followed by the chickening out of: "See me next issue for the forced apology to Drew Hayes, after he beats the living crap out of me at the bar at Chicago con with a rolled up copy of this book."

Now one of my oldest and best friends in comics is David Mack, the award winning creator of Kabuki.

The letter columns quickly became and still are created solely to make David laugh. I fax them, and if he laughs, I print it.

So, I fax over the latest batch. He immediately calls me up and says: "Oh my god, this is hilarious! Do you know Drew Hayes?"

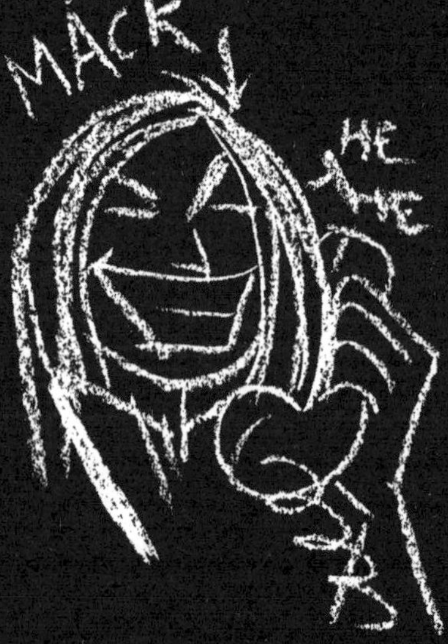
MACK
HE HE

And I said: " I didn't even think he was a real person, have you met him?

He says: " Yeah: I just met him at a show. So you've never seen him?"

And I said: " No, why?"

He says: "Oh, nothing. No, you should print this. This is funny!!!!"

"You sure."

"Definitely."

And as he hung up, I thought I caught just a split second of maniacal laughter from his end. I thought: he does live in Kentucky. He's probably all whacked out on that Woody Harrelson pot.

So, I publish it. I get much feedback. In fact, no one talked about the actual issue to me, just the letter.

So a couple of months later. I am set up at Chicago con with my usual clique of comic buds. Herr Mackaroni, Marc "Nowheresville" Ricketts, Jay "the Lost" Geldhof, Galen "Big Books" Showman, Marc "Dr. Strange" Andreyko. And my good friend Alan Moore who has told me a thousand times: "Don't ever name drop."

When a fan comes up to me and says: "Mr. Bendis. Hi. Can you sign this letter column for me?"

And I said: "Do you see me talking here?!?!?!!"

(No, that wasn't me, that was John Byrne.)

No, what I said was: "Thank you. You like me. You really like me."

And then I ask him why I'm signing the letter column instead of the cover.

He said: "Oh, I wrote this letter about Drew, and now I'm going to have Drew Hayes sign it too."

Well, as I do to all my fans, I gave him his deep tissue massage, his big kiss full on the lips, and sent him on his way.

Then as I began my mid-afternoon two hour draught of fanless staring at Fransesco con mania, I heard a thundering rumble. It grew louder and louder. I slowly turn my head to see this huge freakish Goth-like monster barreling his way down my alley in artist alley. It locked on to my shiny head and bellowed: "BENDIS!! You bitch!! Come here!! You're my bitch now, Bendis!"

Now if you have never actually met Drew in person before, he is the one person in comics who actually looks like what you expect him to look like. I mean I can't tell you how many people have come up to Mack for instance, shocked by how young he is. And how many have come up to me mesmerized by my model-like good looks.

With a shock of black dreds and a gleam of satanic ritual gone array in his eye. And as soon as I saw him coming for me like "The Thing" on a low blood sugar tirade. Well, I shit my pants, then shit them again.
I didn't know this guy, but he knew me. And I knew enough life and my place in it to know that I had coming to me whatever was coming.

But on the bright side. If I were about to be fisted publicly, at least I'd finally make the cover of the Comics Journal.

Well, it was Drew Hayes. Who was just razzin' my chain? He'd never seen the letter before but heard about it and it turns out he thought it was hilarious.

We talked for a bit. I don't remember about what, because I was trying to shift comfortably in my now packed underos. He told me the letter was great.

Then told me to keep a lookout for issue 8 of PE He told me I was going to ove it.

Well, a couple months go by and PE ssue 18 debuts. I popped it open right here in the store and HOLY SHIT!!

Did Drew rip me an asshole!!

OH!! It was brutal.

He made a reference that I was a shit Sin City. That I'd invented a new comic genre…instead of bad girl, ugly girl. It vas awful. But surprisingly it had not even a slight inkling that it was a joke. t was just brutal. It did make me laugh and I showed it to everyone. But man, it vas harsh and uncompromising.

Well, lo and behold, I got hate e-mail rom PEers the next day. There were some gruesome public postings.

So, I retaliated with a couple of nasty quips in my next issue. I think the lowest blow was that Barry Blair wanted his career back and that Drew was the bastard baby of Meat Loaf and Chrissie Hyndes. Now I knew that the last bit vas opening up a can of worms. Personal appearance attacks were a fight no one could win. Especially a bald Jewish beanie baby like myself.

The next issue of PE ?? Yikes!! The funny thing about the next round was that Drew actually called me up and read me what was to come. He, as I was, vas beginning to wonder if we were crossing the line with our fake public feud. He read them to me. We both had a real good laugh. But when the issue

came out, even though it was word for word the way he read it, I was like, Yeeeeoooouuccch!!

Man, what a zing.

Both of us were accosted by each other's fans at shows. Of course his fans were huge guys in Ebola Zaire shirts ready to die for Drew, while mine are admittedly, in comparison, something more out of "Gullliver's Travels."

(No offense. I'm not talking about you, I'm talking about the other fan.)

Most people got the joke, or just enjoyed the ride. But many thought it was a for real thing that would inevitably end up as a very special episode of Jerry Springer.

We kept it going for as long as our egos could take it. And over the period of time actually became strong admirers of each other's work and fans. Drew did a piece for my book, and I promised to do a cover to Poison Elves, but got a movie deal and blew him off.

My point? Well, I have none. Except, that it takes a special kind of lunatic to embrace a public fake feud that comes out of nowhere from a total stranger with just balls and style.

I wish there were more like him in this biz. A little less ass kissing, and a little more Drew Hayes style maniacally fearless honesty.

That's just the kind of guy Drew is. I mean he is so out of his fucking mind he might have actually written this.

# I MARRIED A SCI-FI-GEEK

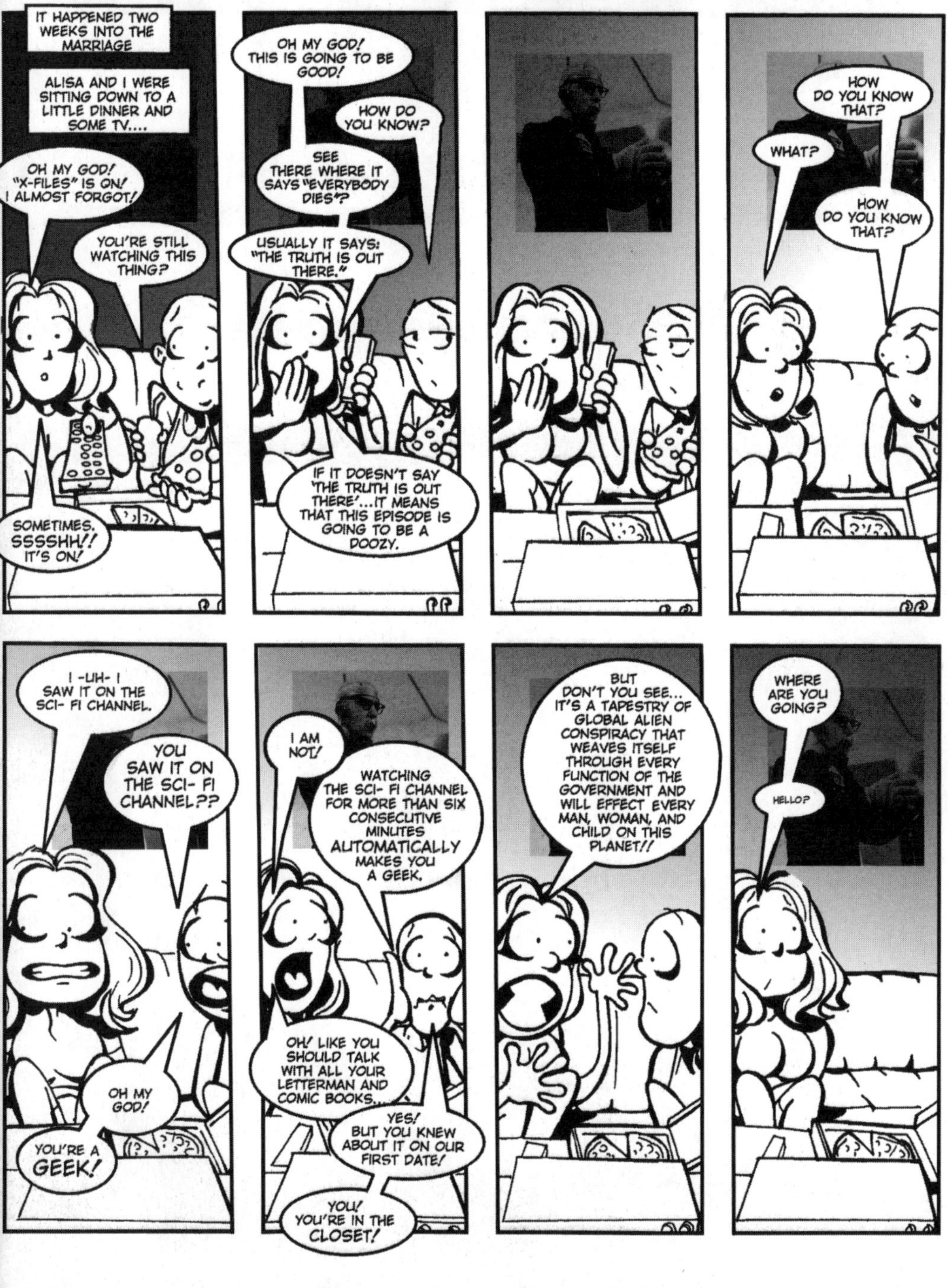
IT HAPPENED TWO WEEKS INTO THE MARRIAGE
ALISA AND I WERE SITTING DOWN TO A LITTLE DINNER AND SOME TV....
OH MY GOD! "X-FILES" IS ON! I ALMOST FORGOT!
YOU'RE STILL WATCHING THIS THING?
SOMETIMES. SSSSHH!! IT'S ON!
OH MY GOD! THIS IS GOING TO BE GOOD!
HOW DO YOU KNOW?
SEE THERE WHERE IT SAYS "EVERYBODY DIES"?
USUALLY IT SAYS: "THE TRUTH IS OUT THERE."
IF IT DOESN'T SAY 'THE TRUTH IS OUT THERE'...IT MEANS THAT THIS EPISODE IS GOING TO BE A DOOZY.
HOW DO YOU KNOW THAT?
WHAT?
HOW DO YOU KNOW THAT?
I -UH- I SAW IT ON THE SCI- FI CHANNEL.
YOU SAW IT ON THE SCI- FI CHANNEL??
OH MY GOD!
YOU'RE A GEEK!
I AM NOT!
WATCHING THE SCI- FI CHANNEL FOR MORE THAN SIX CONSECUTIVE MINUTES AUTOMATICALLY MAKES YOU A GEEK.
OH! LIKE YOU SHOULD TALK WITH ALL YOUR LETTERMAN AND COMIC BOOKS...
YES! BUT YOU KNEW ABOUT IT ON OUR FIRST DATE!
YOU! YOU'RE IN THE CLOSET!
BUT DON'T YOU SEE... IT'S A TAPESTRY OF GLOBAL ALIEN CONSPIRACY THAT WEAVES ITSELF THROUGH EVERY FUNCTION OF THE GOVERNMENT AND WILL EFFECT EVERY MAN, WOMAN, AND CHILD ON THIS PLANET!!
WHERE ARE YOU GOING?
HELLO?

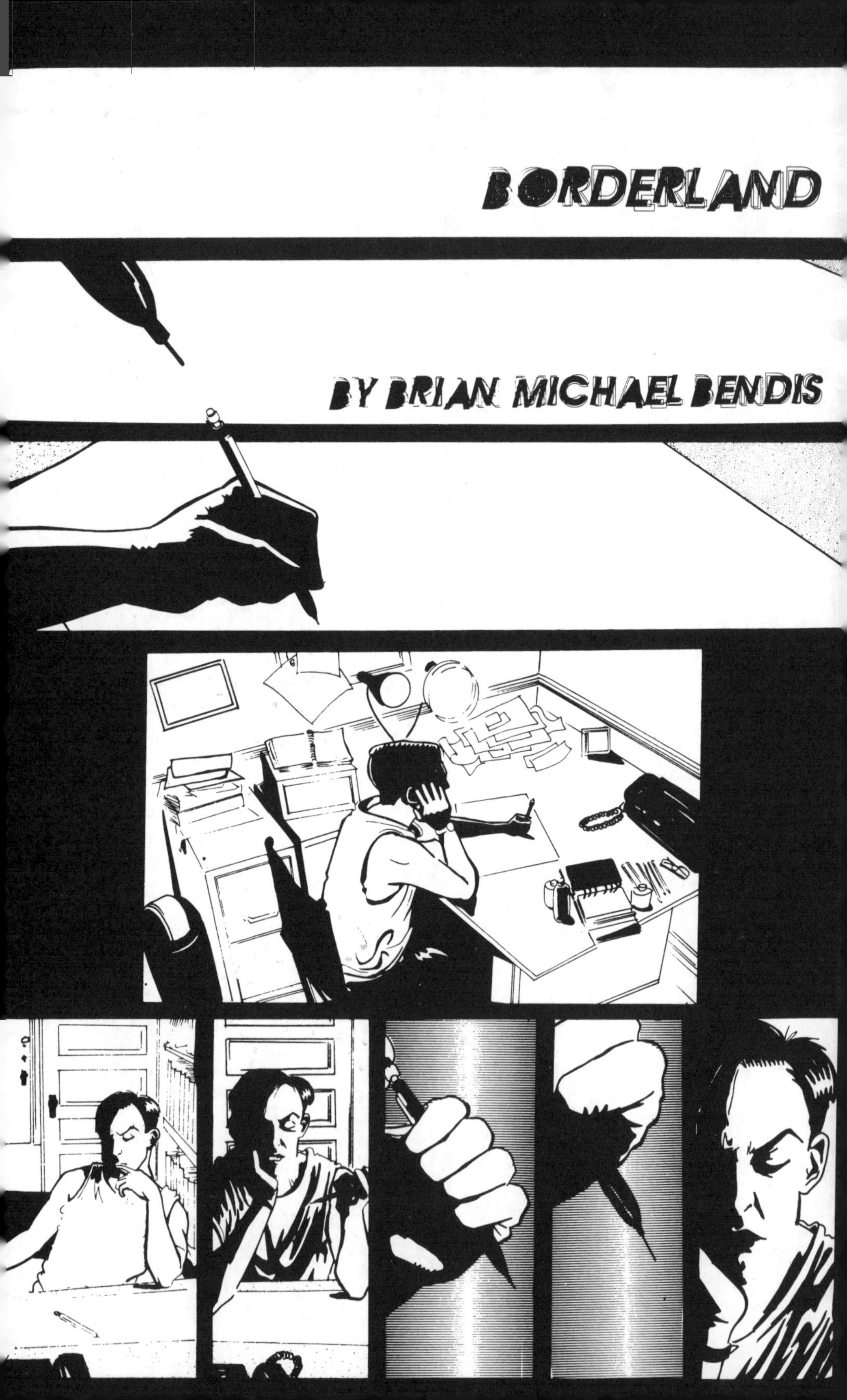
BORDERLAND
BY BRIAN MICHAEL BENDIS

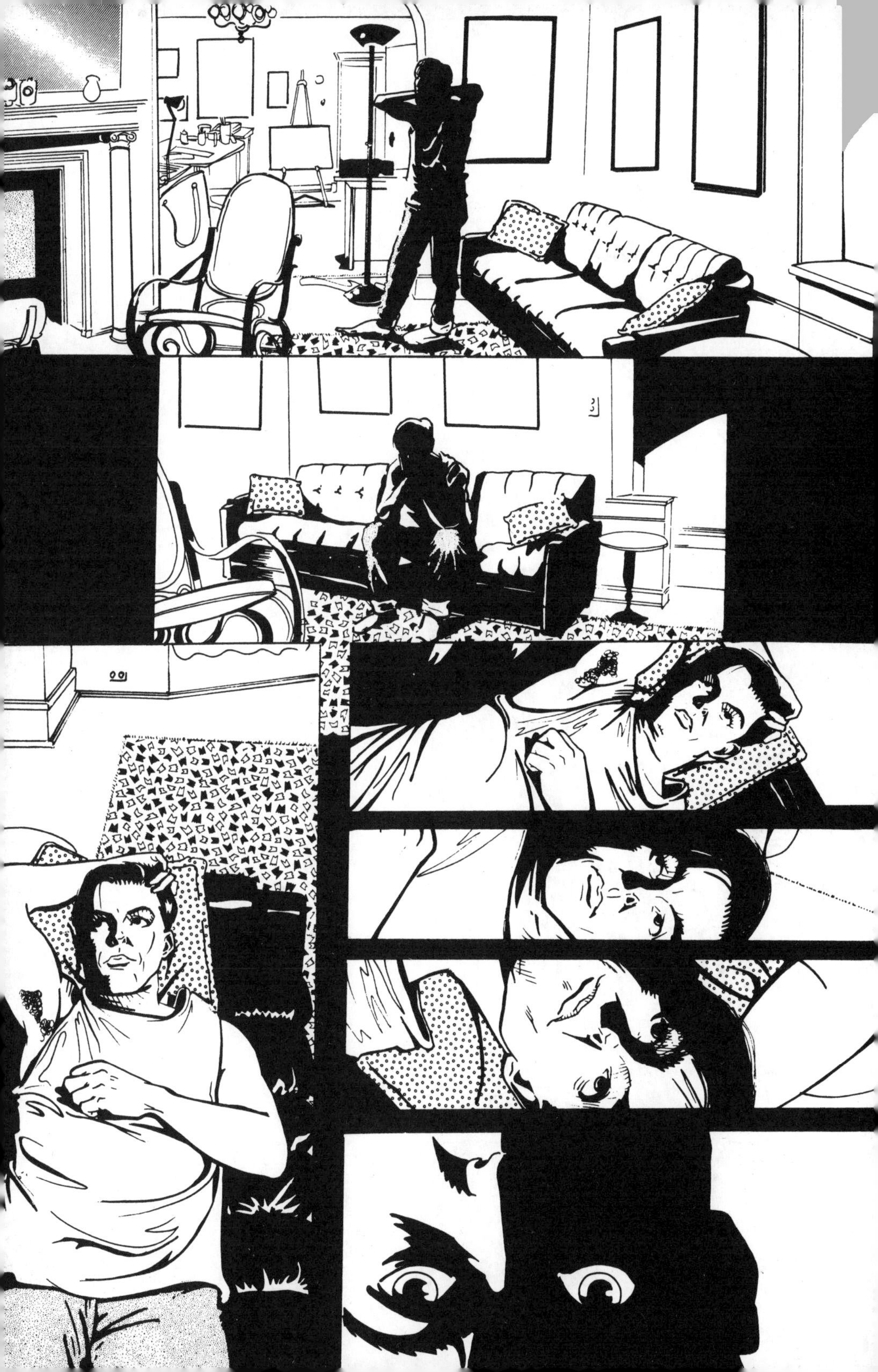

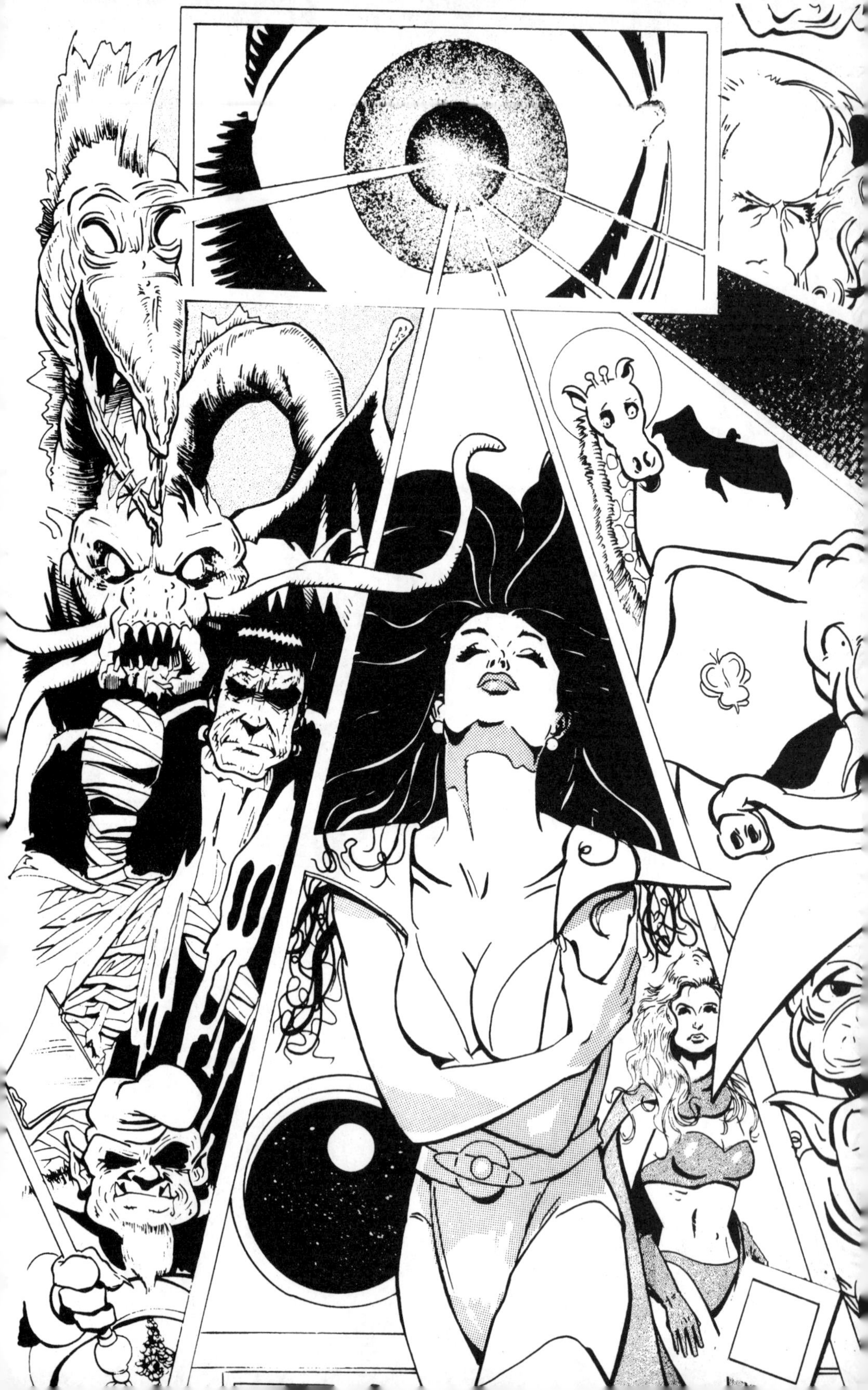

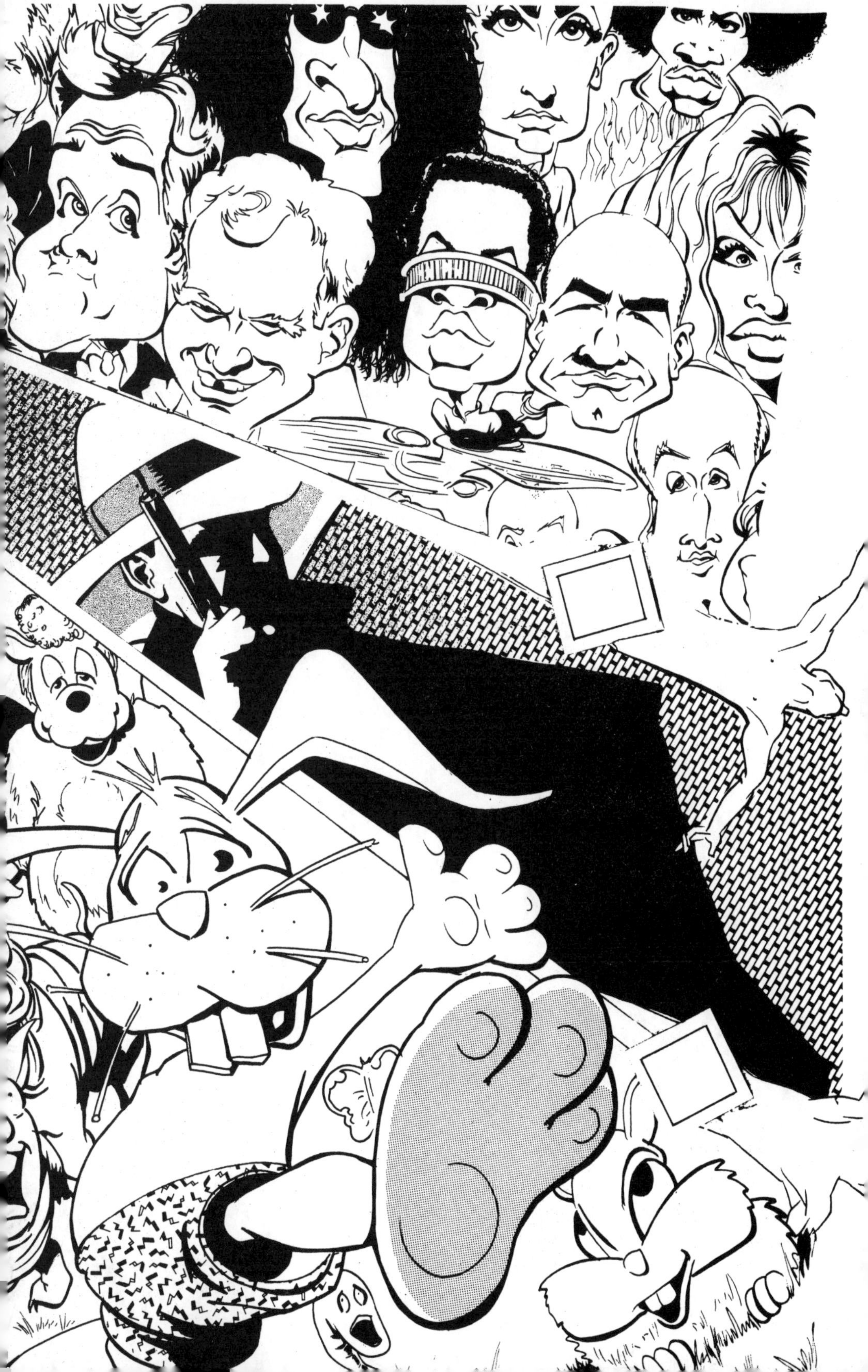

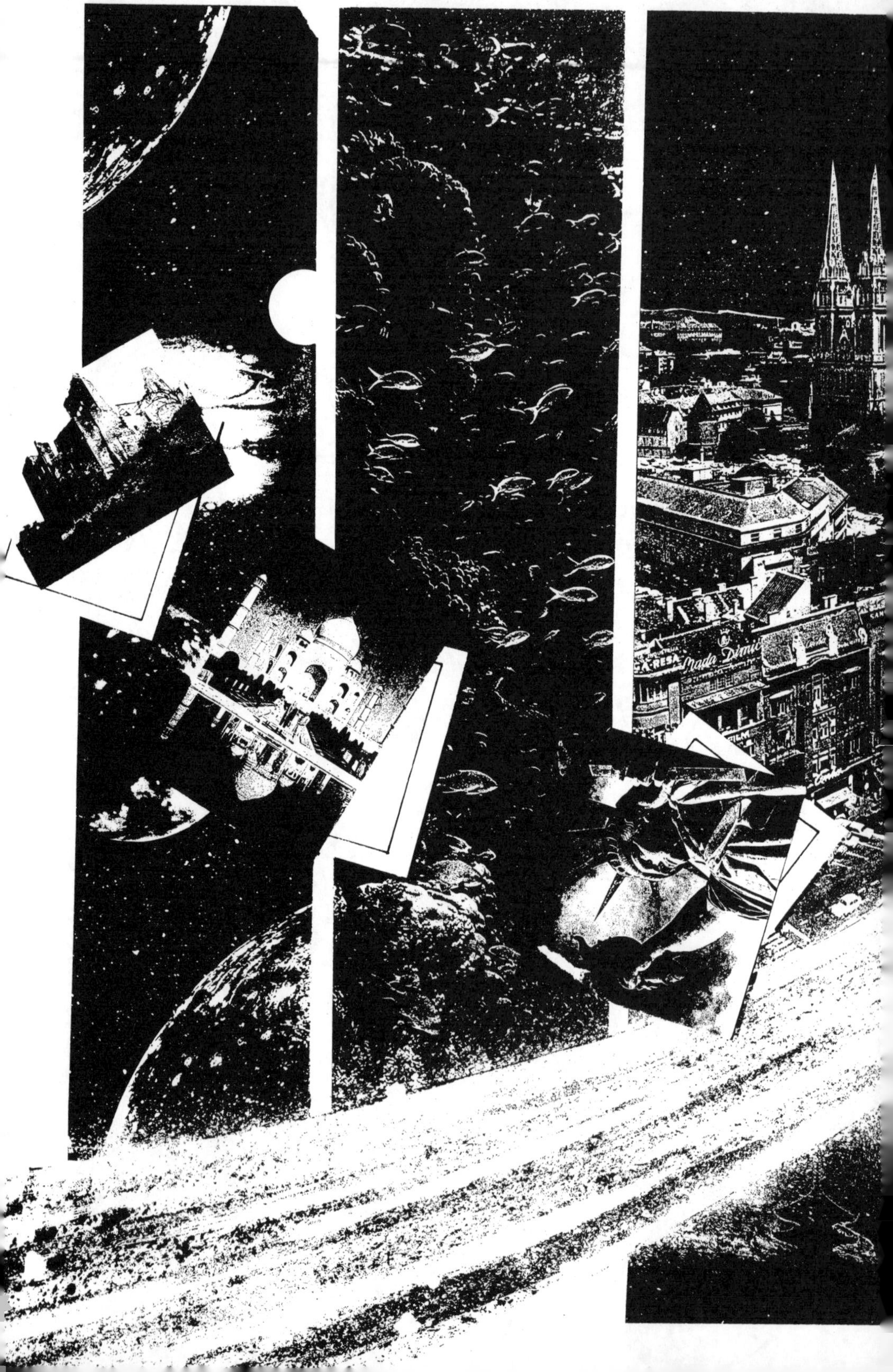

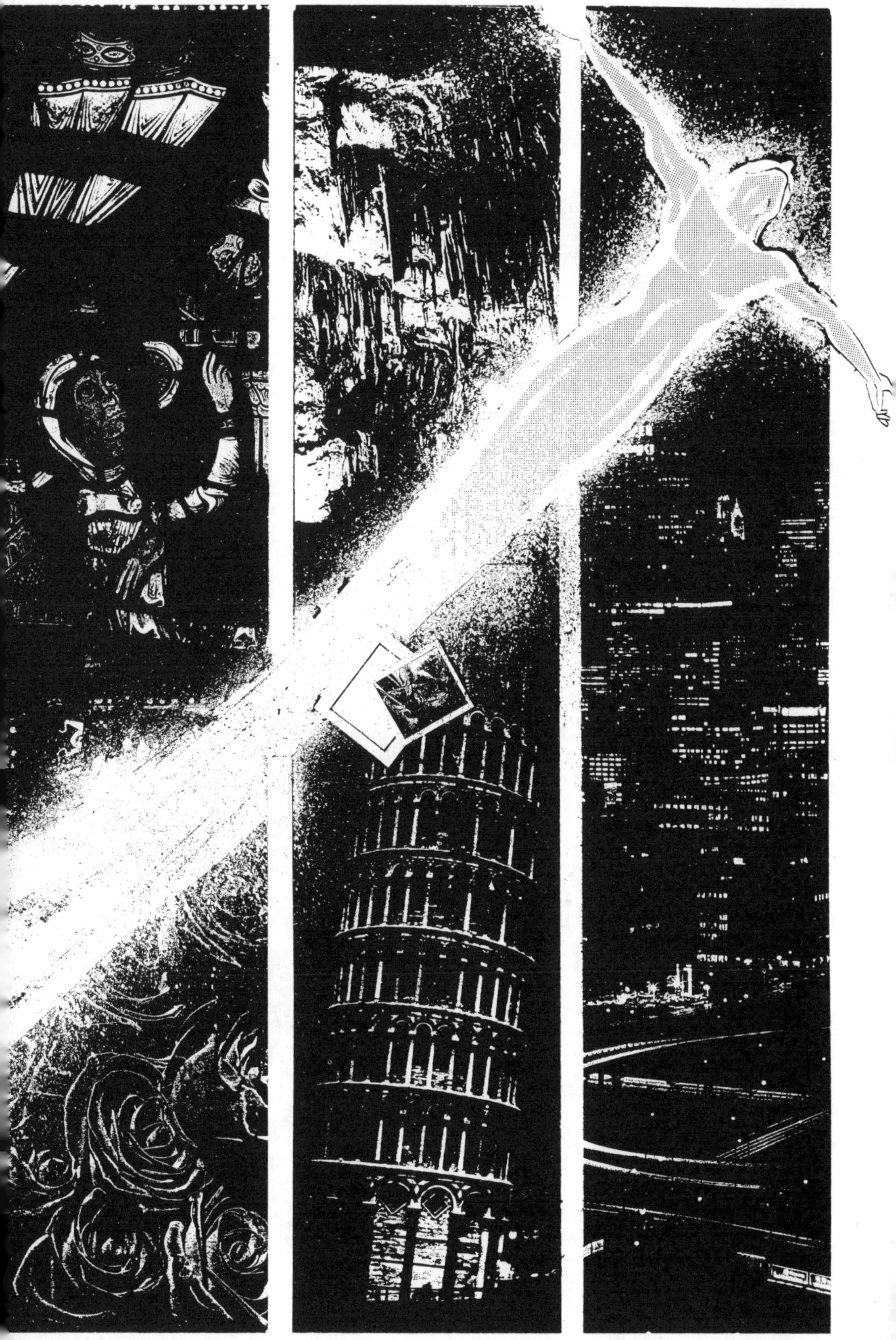

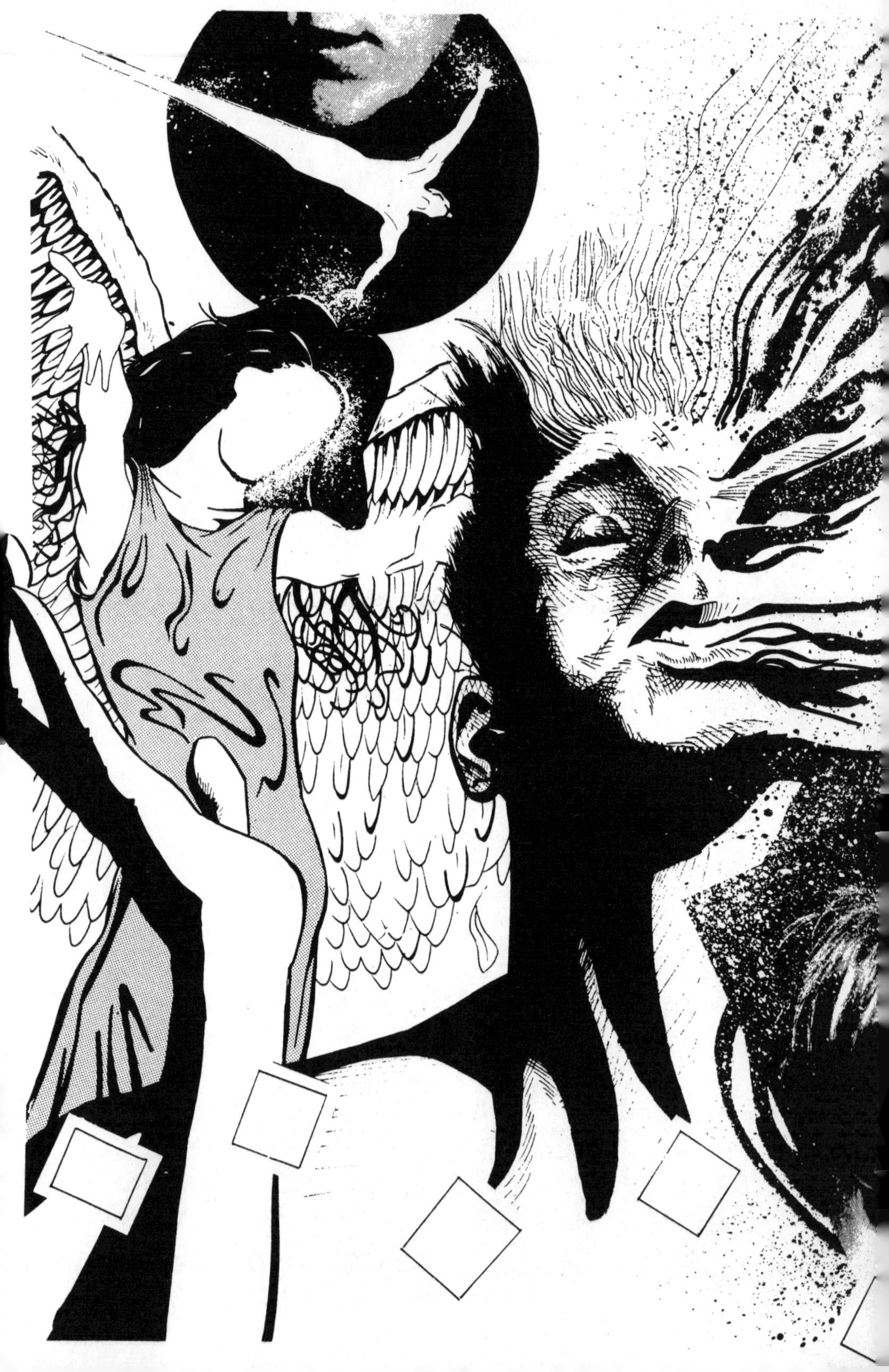

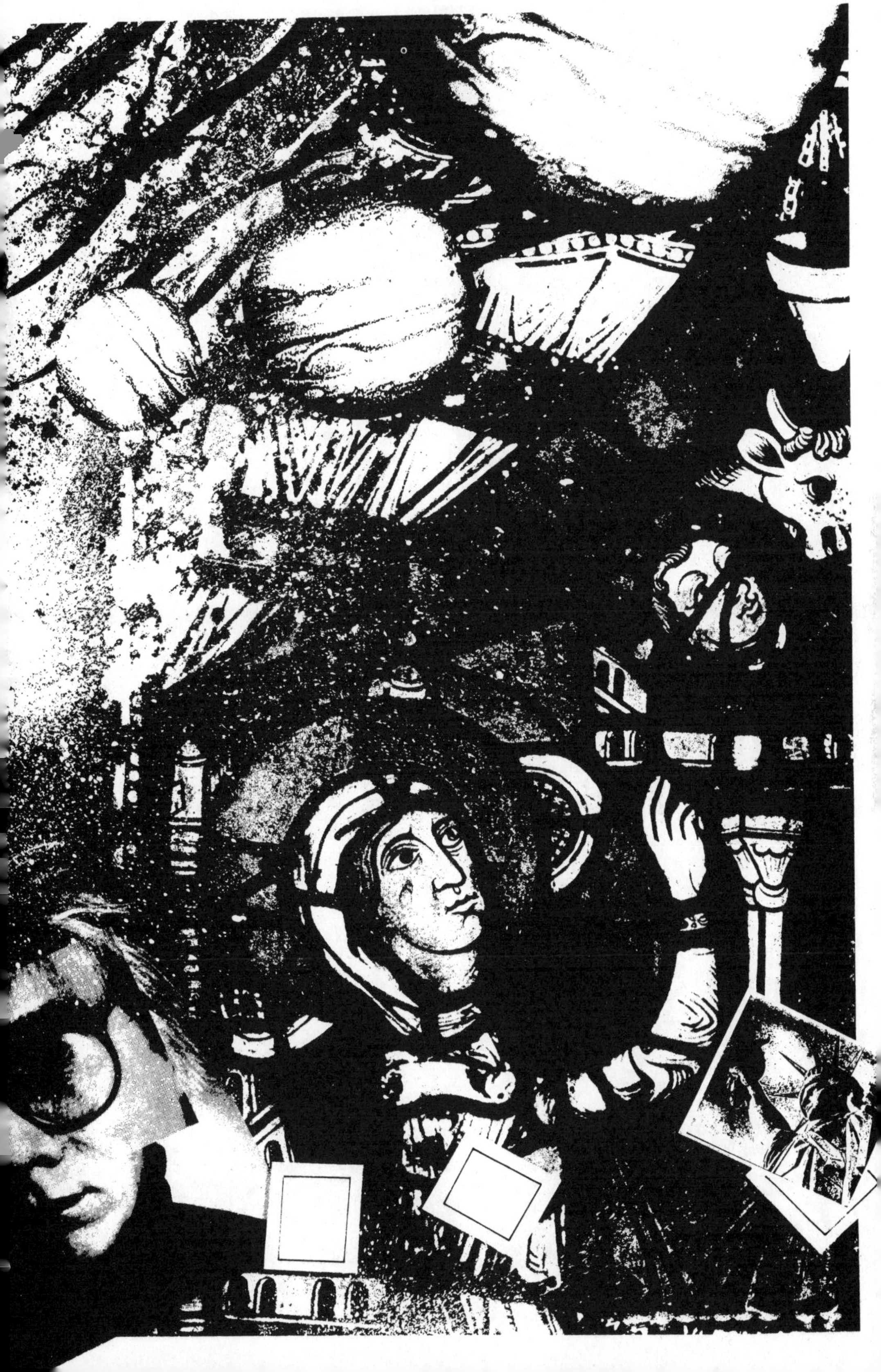

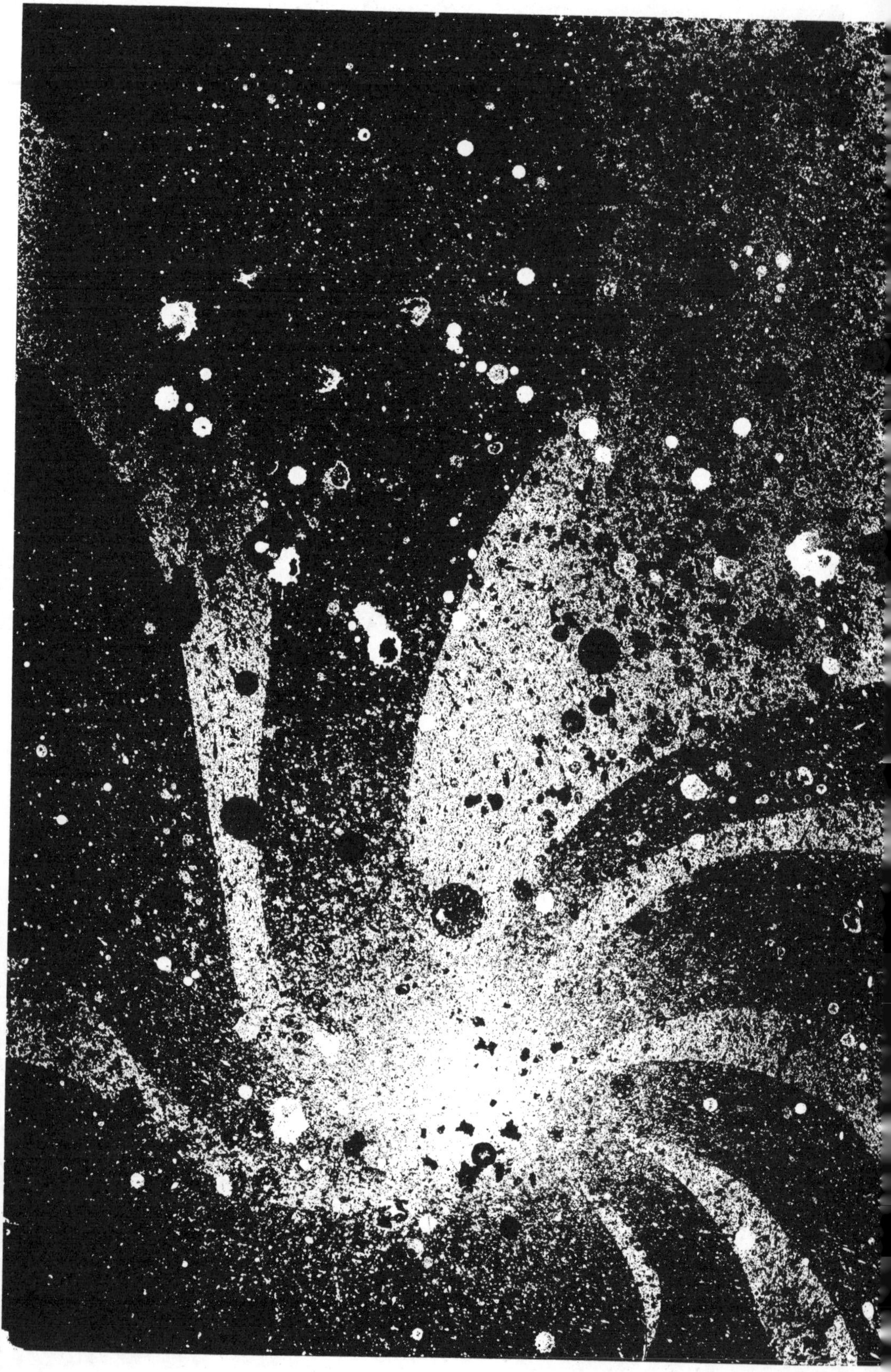

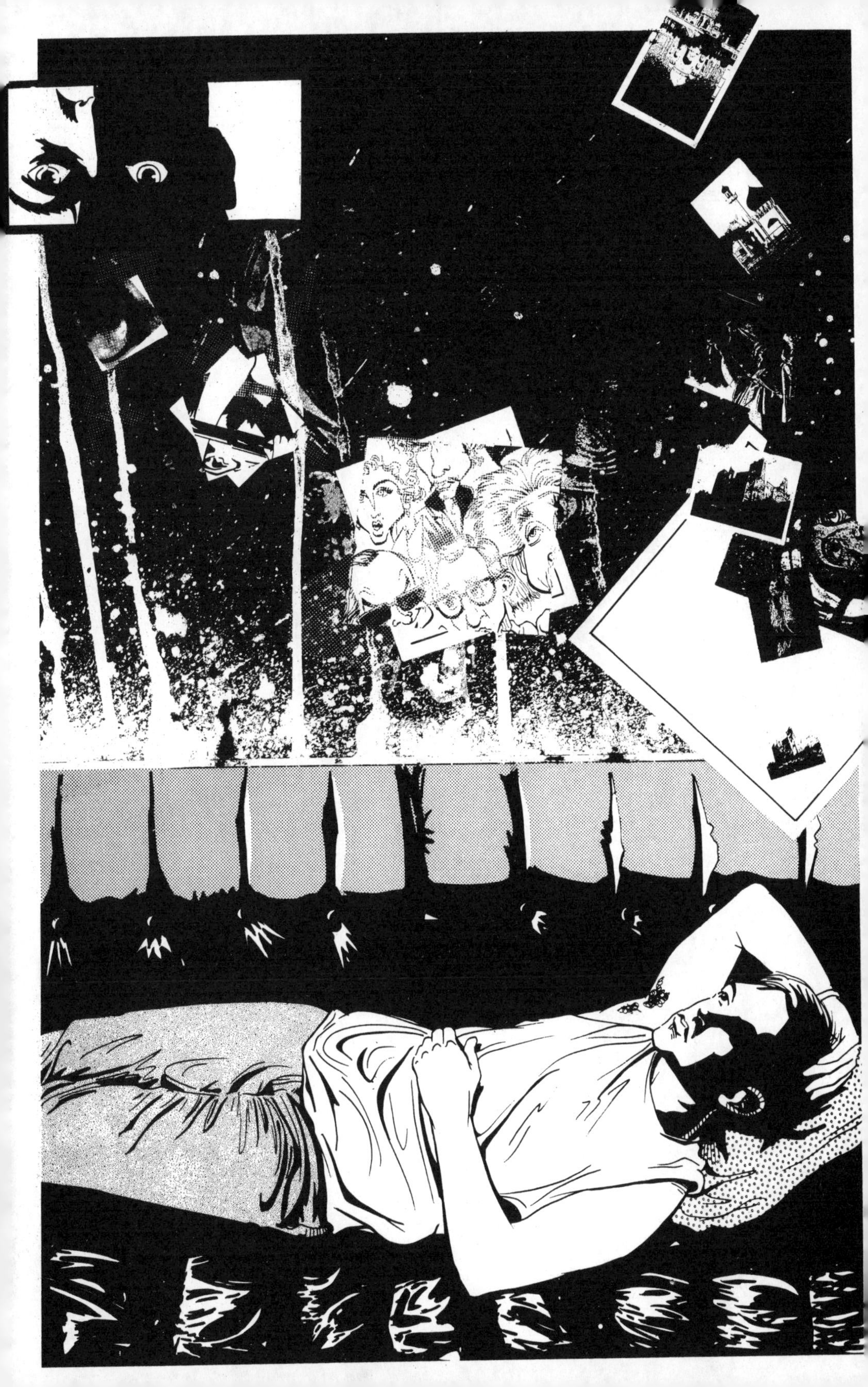

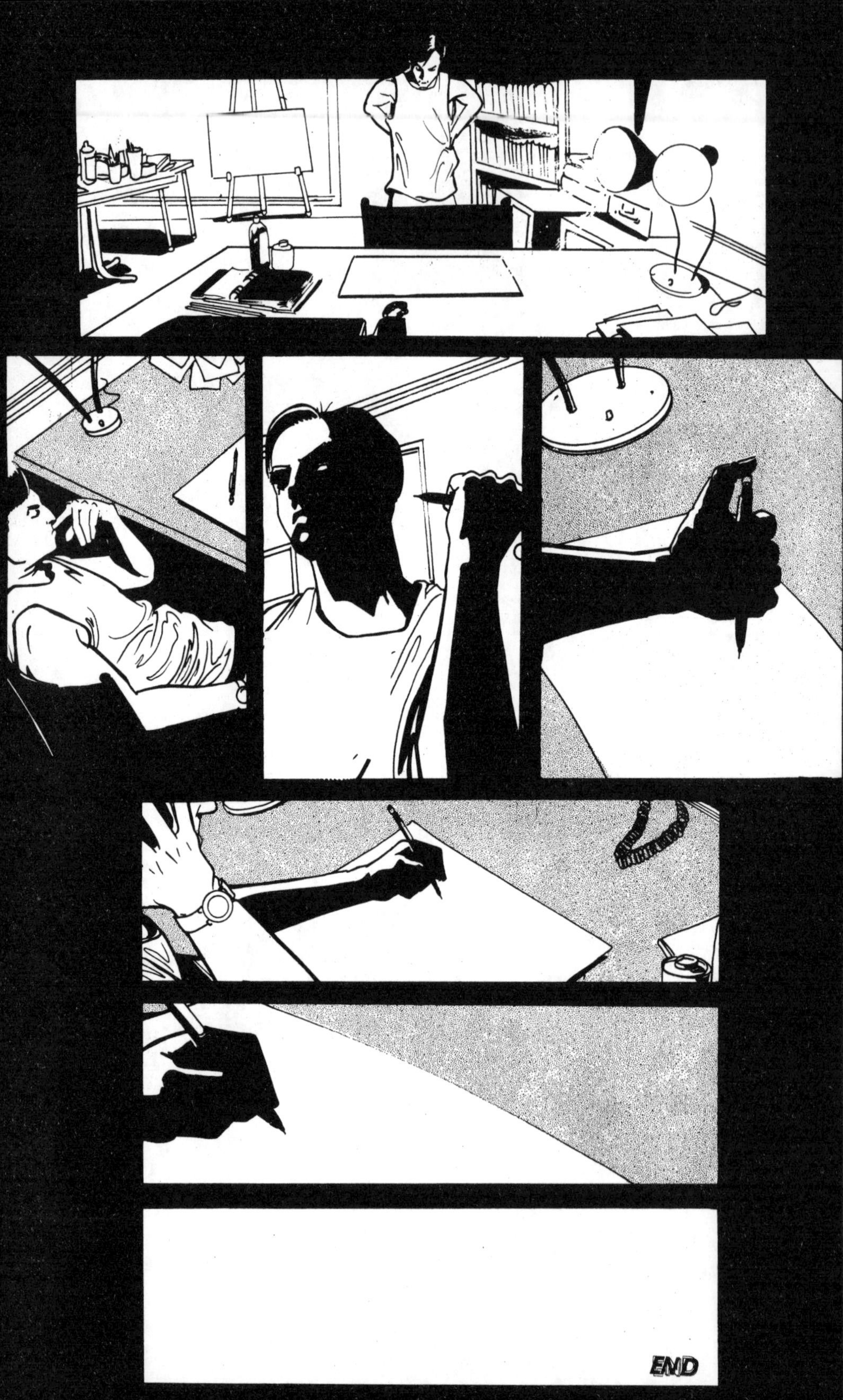
END

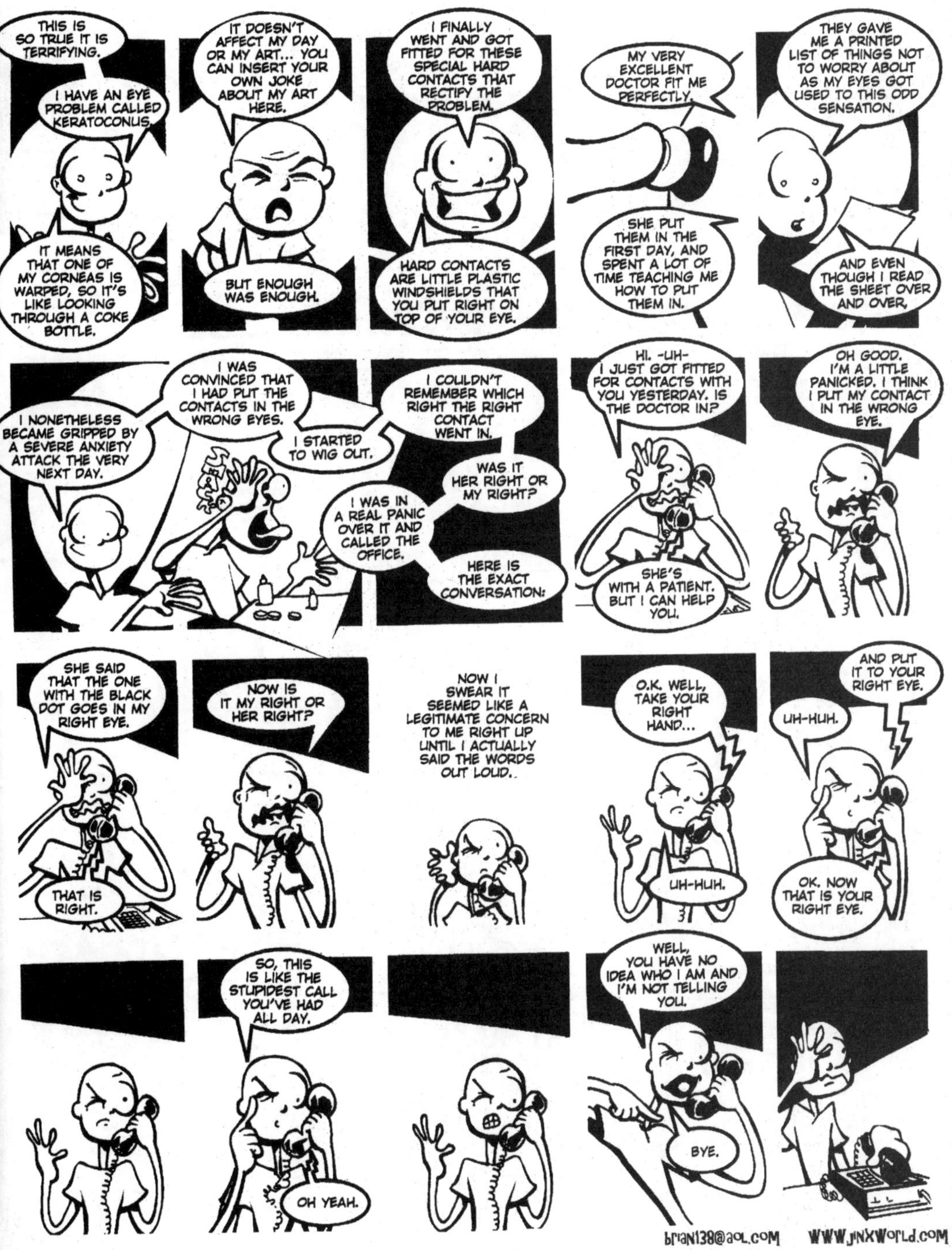
THIS IS SO TRUE IT IS TERRIFYING.
I HAVE AN EYE PROBLEM CALLED KERATOCONUS.
IT MEANS THAT ONE OF MY CORNEAS IS WARPED, SO IT'S LIKE LOOKING THROUGH A COKE BOTTLE.
IT DOESN'T AFFECT MY DAY OR MY ART... YOU CAN INSERT YOUR OWN JOKE ABOUT MY ART HERE.
BUT ENOUGH WAS ENOUGH.
I FINALLY WENT AND GOT FITTED FOR THESE SPECIAL HARD CONTACTS THAT RECTIFY THE PROBLEM.
HARD CONTACTS ARE LITTLE PLASTIC WINDSHIELDS THAT YOU PUT RIGHT ON TOP OF YOUR EYE.
MY VERY EXCELLENT DOCTOR FIT ME PERFECTLY.
SHE PUT THEM IN THE FIRST DAY, AND SPENT A LOT OF TIME TEACHING ME HOW TO PUT THEM IN.
THEY GAVE ME A PRINTED LIST OF THINGS NOT TO WORRY ABOUT AS MY EYES GOT USED TO THIS ODD SENSATION.
AND EVEN THOUGH I READ THE SHEET OVER AND OVER,
I NONETHELESS BECAME GRIPPED BY A SEVERE ANXIETY ATTACK THE VERY NEXT DAY.
I WAS CONVINCED THAT I HAD PUT THE CONTACTS IN THE WRONG EYES.
I STARTED TO WIG OUT.
I COULDN'T REMEMBER WHICH RIGHT THE RIGHT CONTACT WENT IN.
WAS IT HER RIGHT OR MY RIGHT?
I WAS IN A REAL PANIC OVER IT AND CALLED THE OFFICE.
HERE IS THE EXACT CONVERSATION:
HI. -UH- I JUST GOT FITTED FOR CONTACTS WITH YOU YESTERDAY. IS THE DOCTOR IN?
SHE'S WITH A PATIENT. BUT I CAN HELP YOU.
OH GOOD. I'M A LITTLE PANICKED. I THINK I PUT MY CONTACT IN THE WRONG EYE.
SHE SAID THAT THE ONE WITH THE BLACK DOT GOES IN MY RIGHT EYE.
THAT IS RIGHT.
NOW IS IT MY RIGHT OR HER RIGHT?
NOW I SWEAR IT SEEMED LIKE A LEGITIMATE CONCERN TO ME RIGHT UP UNTIL I ACTUALLY SAID THE WORDS OUT LOUD.
O.K. WELL, TAKE YOUR RIGHT HAND...
UH-HUH.
AND PUT IT TO YOUR RIGHT EYE.
UH-HUH.
OK. NOW THAT IS YOUR RIGHT EYE.
SO, THIS IS LIKE THE STUPIDEST CALL YOU'VE HAD ALL DAY.
OH YEAH.
WELL, YOU HAVE NO IDEA WHO I AM AND I'M NOT TELLING YOU.
BYE.
brian138@aol.com
WWW.JINXWORLD.COM

# THE MARKFRANK GIRLS

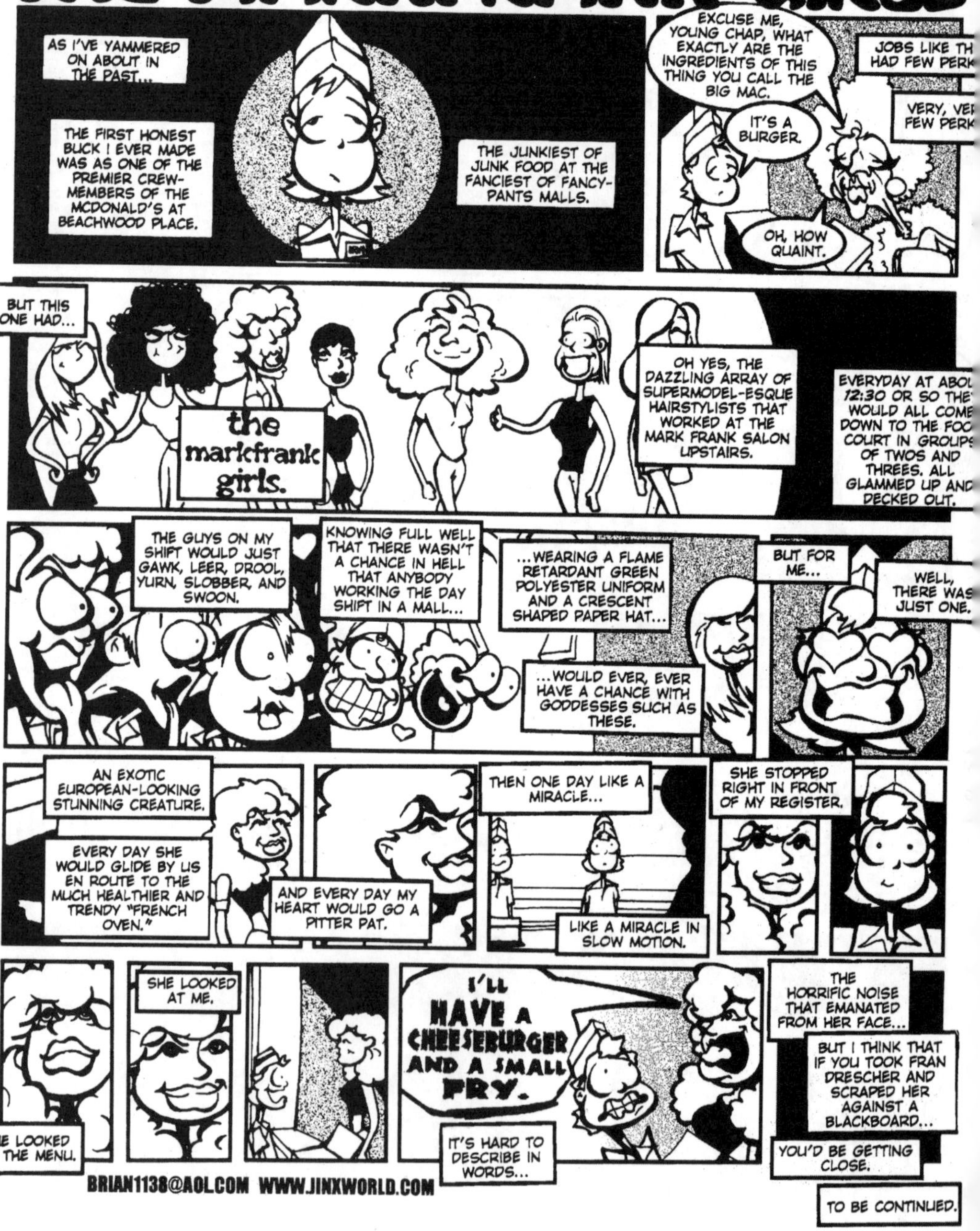
AS I'VE YAMMERED ON ABOUT IN THE PAST...
THE FIRST HONEST BUCK I EVER MADE WAS AS ONE OF THE PREMIER CREW-MEMBERS OF THE MCDONALD'S AT BEACHWOOD PLACE.
THE JUNKIEST OF JUNK FOOD AT THE FANCIEST OF FANCY-PANTS MALLS.
EXCUSE ME, YOUNG CHAP, WHAT EXACTLY ARE THE INGREDIENTS OF THIS THING YOU CALL THE BIG MAC.
IT'S A BURGER.
OH, HOW QUAINT.
JOBS LIKE TH
HAD FEW PERK
VERY, VE
FEW PERK
BUT THIS ONE HAD...
the markfrank girls.
OH YES, THE DAZZLING ARRAY OF SUPERMODEL-ESQUE HAIRSTYLISTS THAT WORKED AT THE MARK FRANK SALON UPSTAIRS.
EVERYDAY AT ABO
12:30 OR SO THE
WOULD ALL COME
DOWN TO THE FOO
COURT IN GROUP
OF TWOS AND
THREES. ALL
GLAMMED UP AND
DECKED OUT.
THE GUYS ON MY SHIFT WOULD JUST GAWK, LEER, DROOL, YURN, SLOBBER, AND SWOON.
KNOWING FULL WELL THAT THERE WASN'T A CHANCE IN HELL THAT ANYBODY WORKING THE DAY SHIFT IN A MALL...
...WEARING A FLAME RETARDANT GREEN POLYESTER UNIFORM AND A CRESCENT SHAPED PAPER HAT...
...WOULD EVER, EVER HAVE A CHANCE WITH GODDESSES SUCH AS THESE.
BUT FOR ME...
WELL, THERE WAS JUST ONE.
AN EXOTIC EUROPEAN-LOOKING STUNNING CREATURE.
EVERY DAY SHE WOULD GLIDE BY US EN ROUTE TO THE MUCH HEALTHIER AND TRENDY "FRENCH OVEN."
AND EVERY DAY MY HEART WOULD GO A PITTER PAT.
THEN ONE DAY LIKE A MIRACLE...
LIKE A MIRACLE IN SLOW MOTION.
SHE STOPPED RIGHT IN FRONT OF MY REGISTER.
SHE LOOKED AT THE MENU.
SHE LOOKED AT ME.
I'LL HAVE A CHEESEBURGER AND A SMALL FRY.
IT'S HARD TO DESCRIBE IN WORDS...
THE HORRIFIC NOISE THAT EMANATED FROM HER FACE...
BUT I THINK THAT IF YOU TOOK FRAN DRESCHER AND SCRAPED HER AGAINST A BLACKBOARD...
YOU'D BE GETTING CLOSE.
BRIAN1138@AOL.COM WWW.JINXWORLD.COM
TO BE CONTINUED.

# THE MARKFRANK GIRLS PART TWO

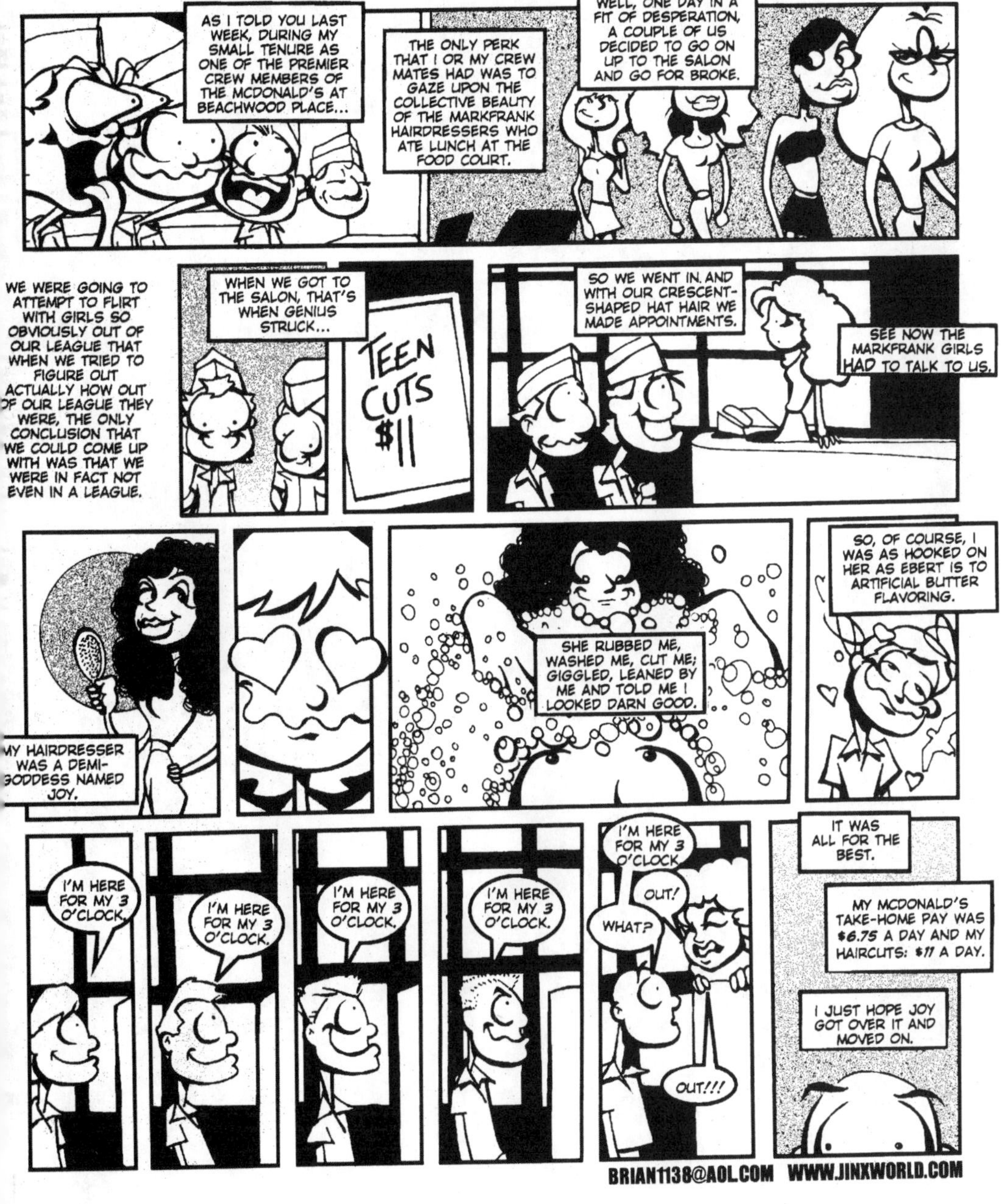
AS I TOLD YOU LAST WEEK, DURING MY SMALL TENURE AS ONE OF THE PREMIER CREW MEMBERS OF THE MCDONALD'S AT BEACHWOOD PLACE...
THE ONLY PERK THAT I OR MY CREW MATES HAD WAS TO GAZE UPON THE COLLECTIVE BEAUTY OF THE MARKFRANK HAIRDRESSERS WHO ATE LUNCH AT THE FOOD COURT.
WELL, ONE DAY IN A FIT OF DESPERATION, A COUPLE OF US DECIDED TO GO ON UP TO THE SALON AND GO FOR BROKE.
WE WERE GOING TO ATTEMPT TO FLIRT WITH GIRLS SO OBVIOUSLY OUT OF OUR LEAGUE THAT WHEN WE TRIED TO FIGURE OUT ACTUALLY HOW OUT OF OUR LEAGUE THEY WERE, THE ONLY CONCLUSION THAT WE COULD COME UP WITH WAS THAT WE WERE IN FACT NOT EVEN IN A LEAGUE.
WHEN WE GOT TO THE SALON, THAT'S WHEN GENIUS STRUCK...
TEEN CUTS $11
SO WE WENT IN. AND WITH OUR CRESCENT-SHAPED HAT HAIR WE MADE APPOINTMENTS.
SEE NOW THE MARKFRANK GIRLS HAD TO TALK TO US.
MY HAIRDRESSER WAS A DEMI-GODDESS NAMED JOY.
SHE RUBBED ME, WASHED ME, CUT ME; GIGGLED, LEANED BY ME AND TOLD ME I LOOKED DARN GOOD.
SO, OF COURSE, I WAS AS HOOKED ON HER AS EBERT IS TO ARTIFICIAL BUTTER FLAVORING.
I'M HERE FOR MY 3 O'CLOCK.
I'M HERE FOR MY 3 O'CLOCK.
I'M HERE FOR MY 3 O'CLOCK.
I'M HERE FOR MY 3 O'CLOCK.
I'M HERE FOR MY 3 O'CLOCK.
OUT!
WHAT?
OUT!!!
IT WAS ALL FOR THE BEST.
MY MCDONALD'S TAKE-HOME PAY WAS $6.75 A DAY AND MY HAIRCUTS: $11 A DAY.
I JUST HOPE JOY GOT OVER IT AND MOVED ON.

BRIAN1138@AOL.COM WWW.JINXWORLD.COM

# OTHER PEOPLE'S STORIES

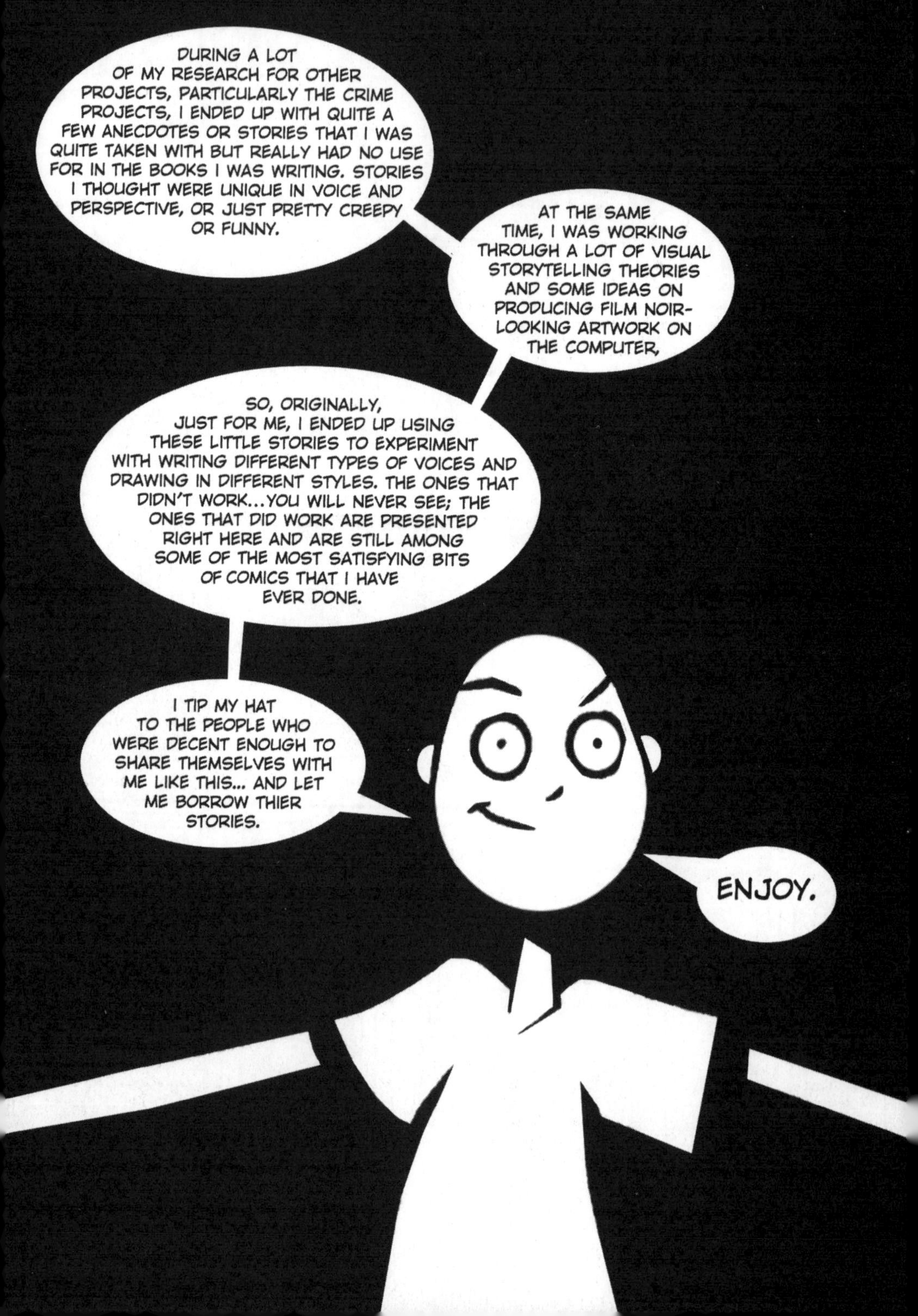
DURING A LOT OF MY RESEARCH FOR OTHER PROJECTS, PARTICULARLY THE CRIME PROJECTS, I ENDED UP WITH QUITE A FEW ANECDOTES OR STORIES THAT I WAS QUITE TAKEN WITH BUT REALLY HAD NO USE FOR IN THE BOOKS I WAS WRITING. STORIES I THOUGHT WERE UNIQUE IN VOICE AND PERSPECTIVE, OR JUST PRETTY CREEPY OR FUNNY.
AT THE SAME TIME, I WAS WORKING THROUGH A LOT OF VISUAL STORYTELLING THEORIES AND SOME IDEAS ON PRODUCING FILM NOIR-LOOKING ARTWORK ON THE COMPUTER,
SO, ORIGINALLY, JUST FOR ME, I ENDED UP USING THESE LITTLE STORIES TO EXPERIMENT WITH WRITING DIFFERENT TYPES OF VOICES AND DRAWING IN DIFFERENT STYLES. THE ONES THAT DIDN'T WORK...YOU WILL NEVER SEE; THE ONES THAT DID WORK ARE PRESENTED RIGHT HERE AND ARE STILL AMONG SOME OF THE MOST SATISFYING BITS OF COMICS THAT I HAVE EVER DONE.
I TIP MY HAT TO THE PEOPLE WHO WERE DECENT ENOUGH TO SHARE THEMSELVES WITH ME LIKE THIS... AND LET ME BORROW THIER STORIES.
ENJOY.

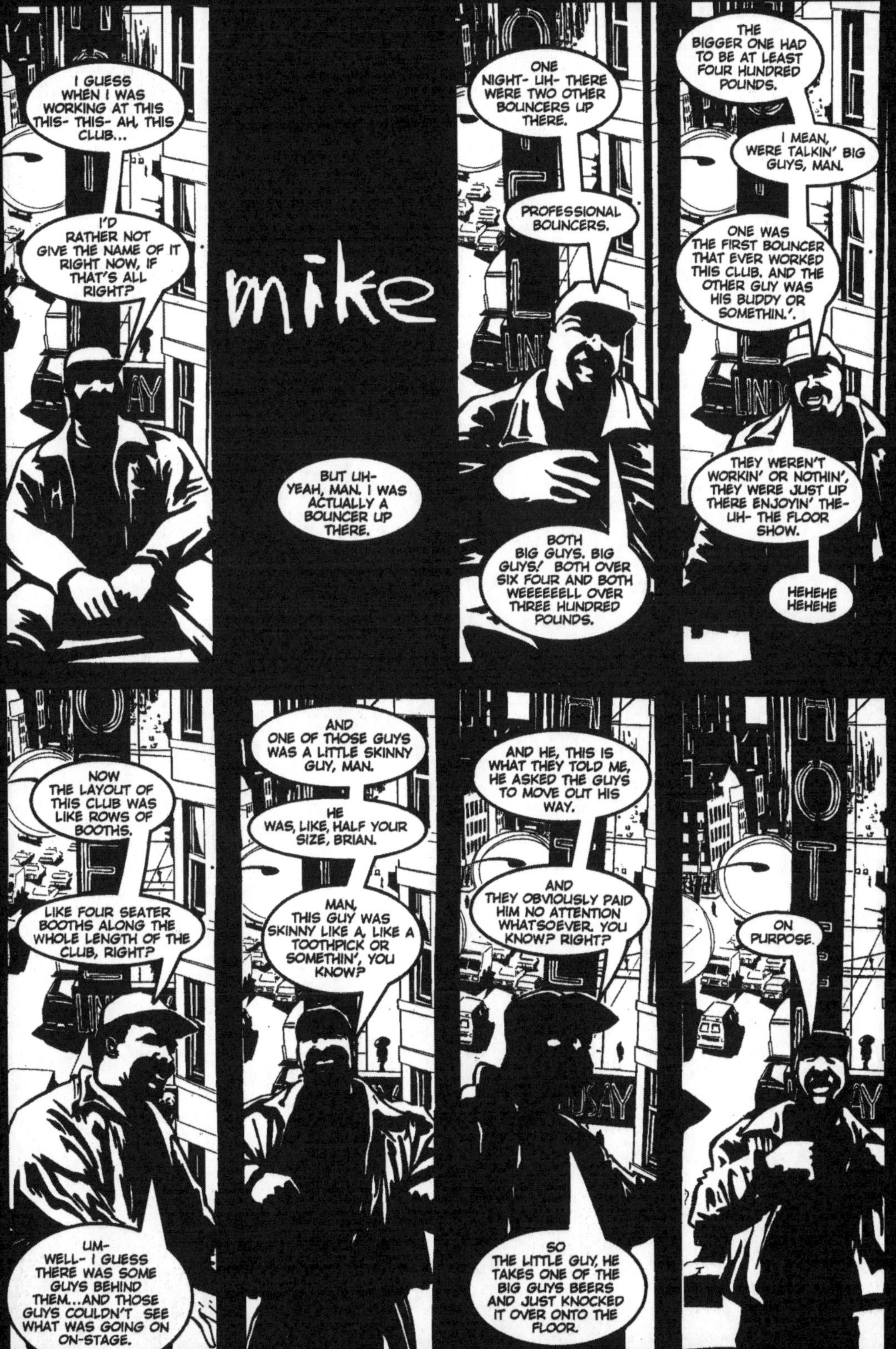
I GUESS WHEN I WAS WORKING AT THIS THIS- THIS- AH, THIS CLUB...
I'D RATHER NOT GIVE THE NAME OF IT RIGHT NOW, IF THAT'S ALL RIGHT?
mike
BUT UH- YEAH, MAN. I WAS ACTUALLY A BOUNCER UP THERE.
ONE NIGHT- UH- THERE WERE TWO OTHER BOUNCERS UP THERE.
PROFESSIONAL BOUNCERS.
BOTH BIG GUYS. BIG GUYS! BOTH OVER SIX FOUR AND BOTH WEEEEEELL OVER THREE HUNDRED POUNDS.
THE BIGGER ONE HAD TO BE AT LEAST FOUR HUNDRED POUNDS.
I MEAN, WERE TALKIN' BIG GUYS, MAN.
ONE WAS THE FIRST BOUNCER THAT EVER WORKED THIS CLUB. AND THE OTHER GUY WAS HIS BUDDY OR SOMETHIN.'.
THEY WEREN'T WORKIN' OR NOTHIN', THEY WERE JUST UP THERE ENJOYIN' THE- UH- THE FLOOR SHOW.
HEHEHE HEHEHE
NOW THE LAYOUT OF THIS CLUB WAS LIKE ROWS OF BOOTHS.
LIKE FOUR SEATER BOOTHS ALONG THE WHOLE LENGTH OF THE CLUB, RIGHT?
UM- WELL- I GUESS THERE WAS SOME GUYS BEHIND THEM...AND THOSE GUYS COULDN'T SEE WHAT WAS GOING ON ON-STAGE.
AND ONE OF THOSE GUYS WAS A LITTLE SKINNY GUY, MAN.
HE WAS, LIKE, HALF YOUR SIZE, BRIAN.
MAN, THIS GUY WAS SKINNY LIKE A, LIKE A TOOTHPICK OR SOMETHIN', YOU KNOW?
AND HE, THIS IS WHAT THEY TOLD ME, HE ASKED THE GUYS TO MOVE OUT HIS WAY.
AND THEY OBVIOUSLY PAID HIM NO ATTENTION WHATSOEVER. YOU KNOW? RIGHT?
SO THE LITTLE GUY, HE TAKES ONE OF THE BIG GUYS BEERS AND JUST KNOCKED IT OVER ONTO THE FLOOR.
ON PURPOSE.

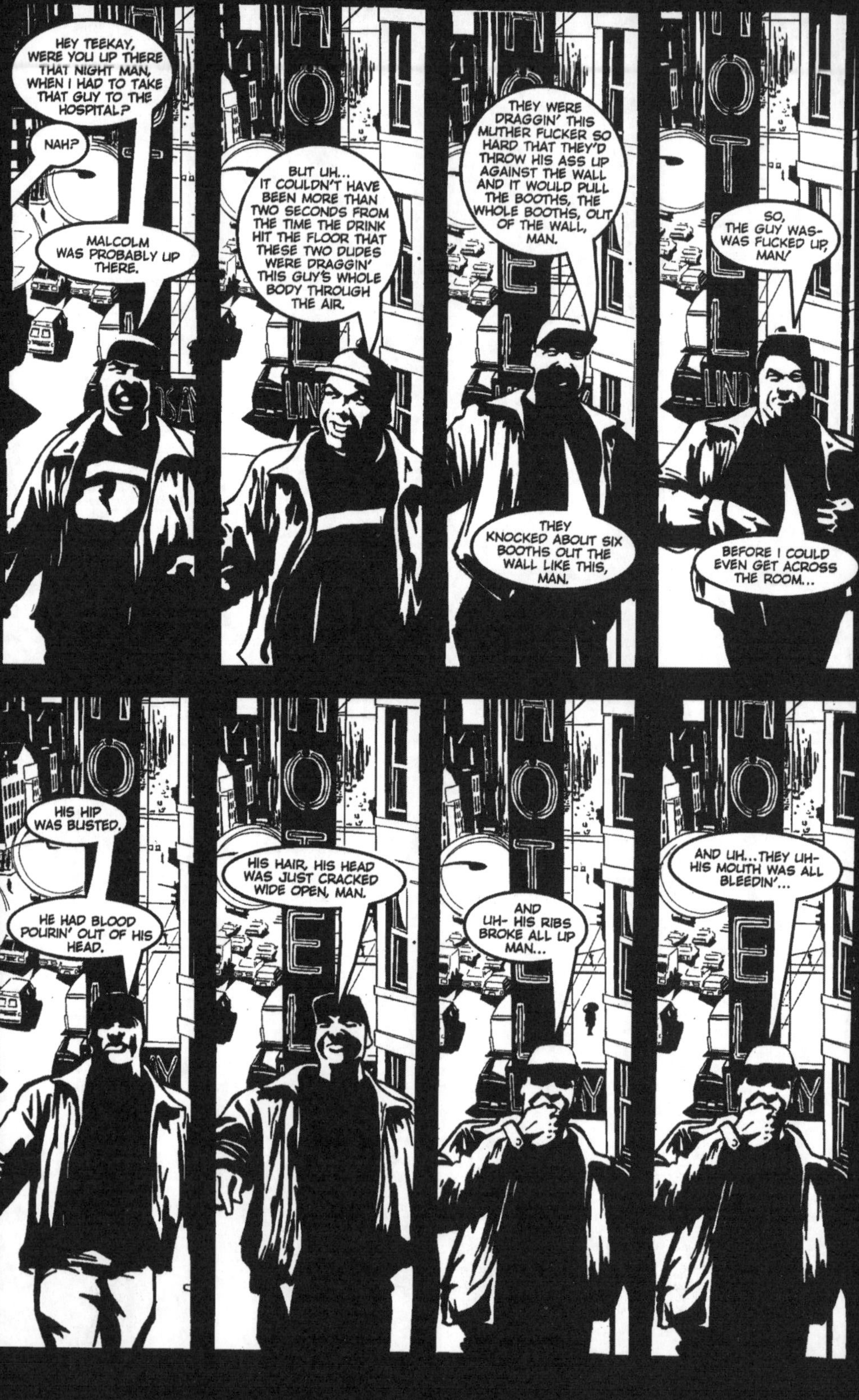
HEY TEEKAY, WERE YOU UP THERE THAT NIGHT MAN, WHEN I HAD TO TAKE THAT GUY TO THE HOSPITAL?
NAH?
MALCOLM WAS PROBABLY UP THERE.
BUT UH... IT COULDN'T HAVE BEEN MORE THAN TWO SECONDS FROM THE TIME THE DRINK HIT THE FLOOR THAT THESE TWO DUDES WERE DRAGGIN' THIS GUY'S WHOLE BODY THROUGH THE AIR.
THEY WERE DRAGGIN' THIS MUTHER FUCKER SO HARD THAT THEY'D THROW HIS ASS UP AGAINST THE WALL AND IT WOULD PULL THE BOOTHS, THE WHOLE BOOTHS, OUT OF THE WALL, MAN.
THEY KNOCKED ABOUT SIX BOOTHS OUT THE WALL LIKE THIS, MAN.
SO, THE GUY WAS- WAS FUCKED UP, MAN!
BEFORE I COULD EVEN GET ACROSS THE ROOM...
HIS HIP WAS BUSTED.
HE HAD BLOOD POURIN' OUT OF HIS HEAD.
HIS HAIR, HIS HEAD WAS JUST CRACKED WIDE OPEN, MAN.
AND UH- HIS RIBS BROKE ALL UP MAN...
AND UH...THEY UH- HIS MOUTH WAS ALL BLEEDIN'...

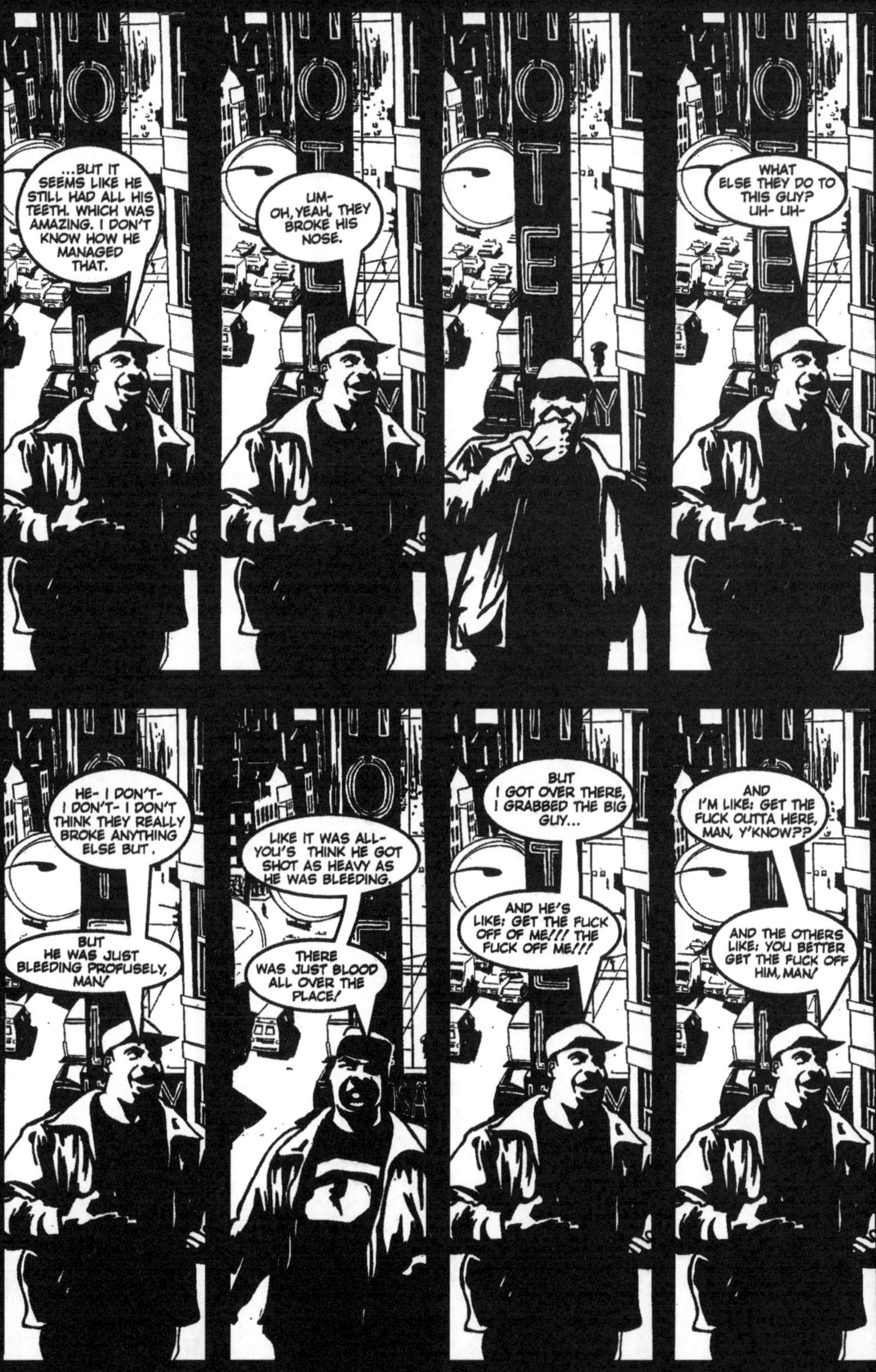
...BUT IT SEEMS LIKE HE STILL HAD ALL HIS TEETH. WHICH WAS AMAZING. I DON'T KNOW HOW HE MANAGED THAT.
UM- OH, YEAH, THEY BROKE HIS NOSE.
WHAT ELSE THEY DO TO THIS GUY? UH- UH-
HE- I DON'T- I DON'T- I DON'T THINK THEY REALLY BROKE ANYTHING ELSE BUT.
BUT HE WAS JUST BLEEDING PROFUSELY, MAN!
LIKE IT WAS ALL- YOU'S THINK HE GOT SHOT AS HEAVY AS HE WAS BLEEDING.
THERE WAS JUST BLOOD ALL OVER THE PLACE!
BUT I GOT OVER THERE, I GRABBED THE BIG GUY...
AND HE'S LIKE: GET THE FUCK OFF OF ME!!! THE FUCK OFF ME!!!
AND I'M LIKE: GET THE FUCK OUTTA HERE, MAN, Y'KNOW??
AND THE OTHERS LIKE: YOU BETTER GET THE FUCK OFF HIM, MAN!

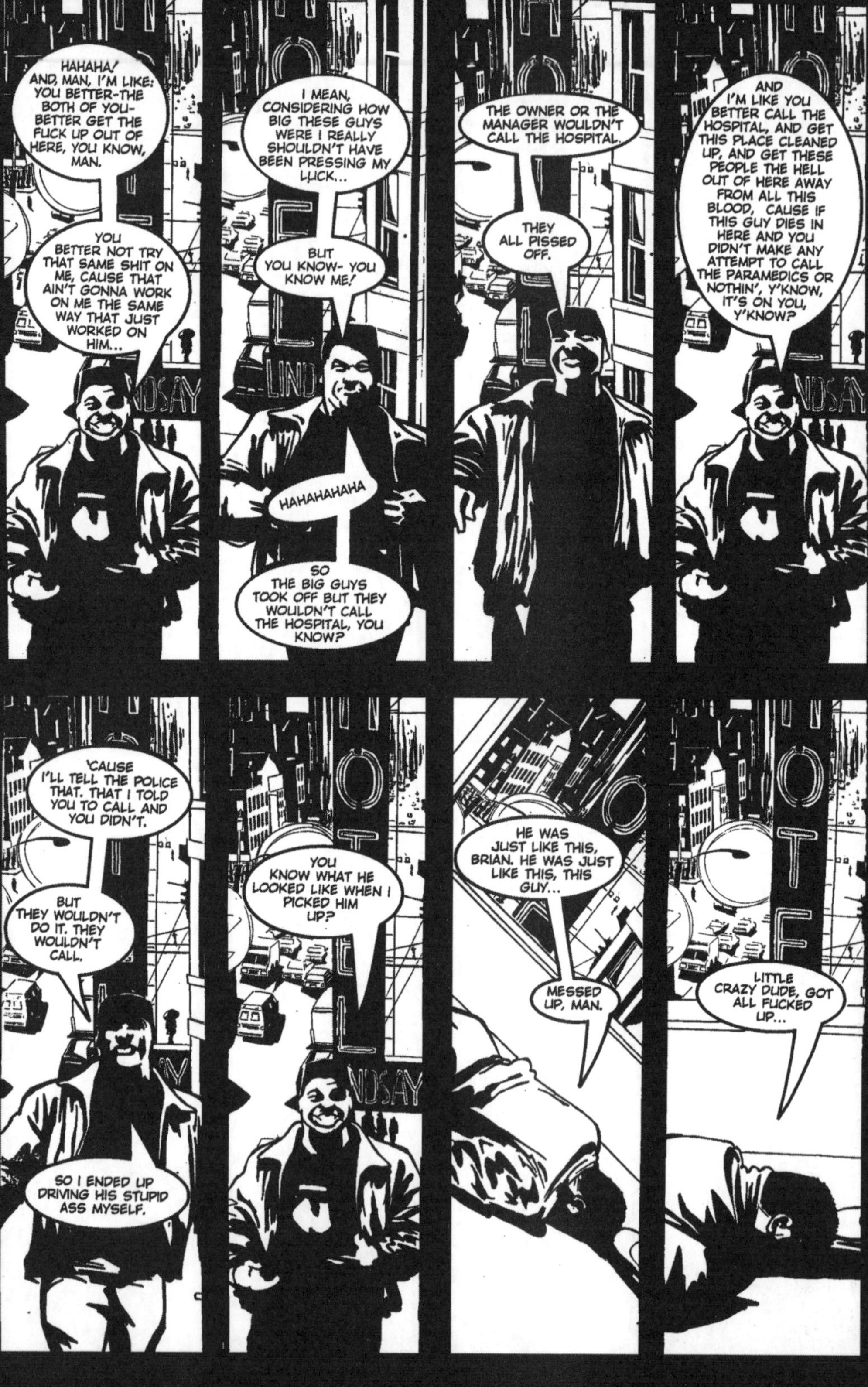
HAHAHA! AND, MAN, I'M LIKE: YOU BETTER-THE BOTH OF YOU-BETTER GET THE FUCK UP OUT OF HERE, YOU KNOW, MAN.
YOU BETTER NOT TRY THAT SAME SHIT ON ME, CAUSE THAT AIN'T GONNA WORK ON ME THE SAME WAY THAT JUST WORKED ON HIM...
I MEAN, CONSIDERING HOW BIG THESE GUYS WERE I REALLY SHOULDN'T HAVE BEEN PRESSING MY LUCK...
BUT YOU KNOW- YOU KNOW ME!
HAHAHAHAHA
SO THE BIG GUYS TOOK OFF BUT THEY WOULDN'T CALL THE HOSPITAL, YOU KNOW?
THE OWNER OR THE MANAGER WOULDN'T CALL THE HOSPITAL.
THEY ALL PISSED OFF.
AND I'M LIKE YOU BETTER CALL THE HOSPITAL, AND GET THIS PLACE CLEANED UP, AND GET THESE PEOPLE THE HELL OUT OF HERE AWAY FROM ALL THIS BLOOD, CAUSE IF THIS GUY DIES IN HERE AND YOU DIDN'T MAKE ANY ATTEMPT TO CALL THE PARAMEDICS OR NOTHIN', Y'KNOW, IT'S ON YOU, Y'KNOW?
'CAUSE I'LL TELL THE POLICE THAT. THAT I TOLD YOU TO CALL AND YOU DIDN'T.
BUT THEY WOULDN'T DO IT. THEY WOULDN'T CALL.
SO I ENDED UP DRIVING HIS STUPID ASS MYSELF.
YOU KNOW WHAT HE LOOKED LIKE WHEN I PICKED HIM UP?
HE WAS JUST LIKE THIS, BRIAN. HE WAS JUST LIKE THIS, THIS GUY...
MESSED UP, MAN.
LITTLE CRAZY DUDE, GOT ALL FUCKED UP...

THIS LITTLE YARN COMES FROM THE LT. WHO IS MY INTERN ADVISOR.

IT ALL COMES FROM A SURVEILLANCE TAPE THAT WAS REPORTEDLY USED IN TRIAL.

THE NAMES HAVE BEEN FORGOTTEN AND I DIDN'T ASK ANYWAY.

SO, THERE IS THIS SHOP, A LITTLE MA AND PA PLACE, BUT IT'S IN DETROIT SO ITS FORTIFIED.

IT'S GOT POWER DOORS THAT THE OWNER CAN TURN OFF WITH THE FLIP OF A SWITCH.

THE DOORS ARE MADE OUT OF THE SAME SHIT THE BOOTH HE SITS IN IS. REAL THICK PLEXIGLASS.

AS FOR THE BOOTH, IT'S ONLY GOT ONE METAL SLOT FOR PASSING CASH THROUGH, WHICH IS LEVER OPERATED AND OPENS OUTWARD.

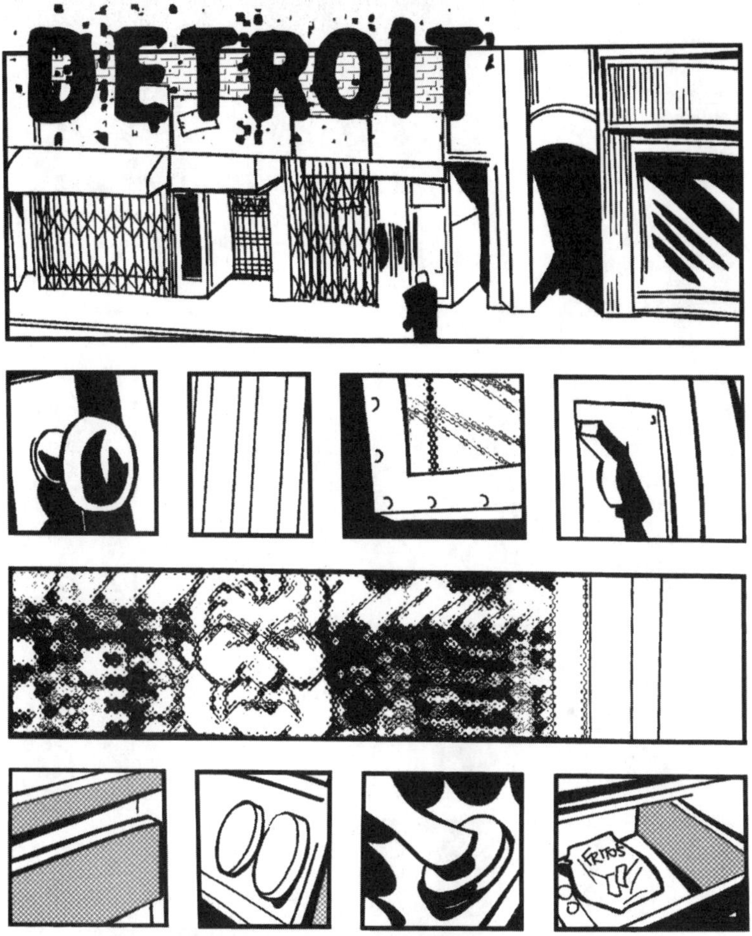
DETROIT
FRITOS

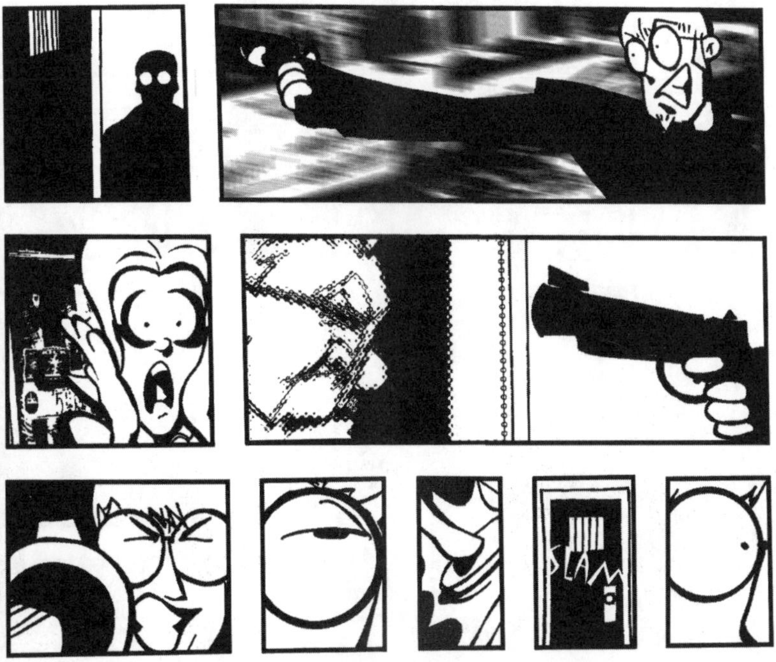
SLAM

SO THIS GUY, I NEVER GET A DESCRIPTION OF HIM, COMES IN THE STORE WITH A REVOLVER.

AT THE TIME, THERE IS ONLY ONE OTHER CUSTOMER...

A WOMAN,

AND THE OWNER, WHO IS IN HIS BOOTH.

SO THIS GUY POINTS THE REVOLVER AT THE BOOTH AND DEMANDS MONEY.

THE STORE OWNER JUST GLARES AT HIM AND PUSHES HIS BUTTON ...

THE DOORS SLAM CLOSE.

SO THE PERP **FREAKS.**

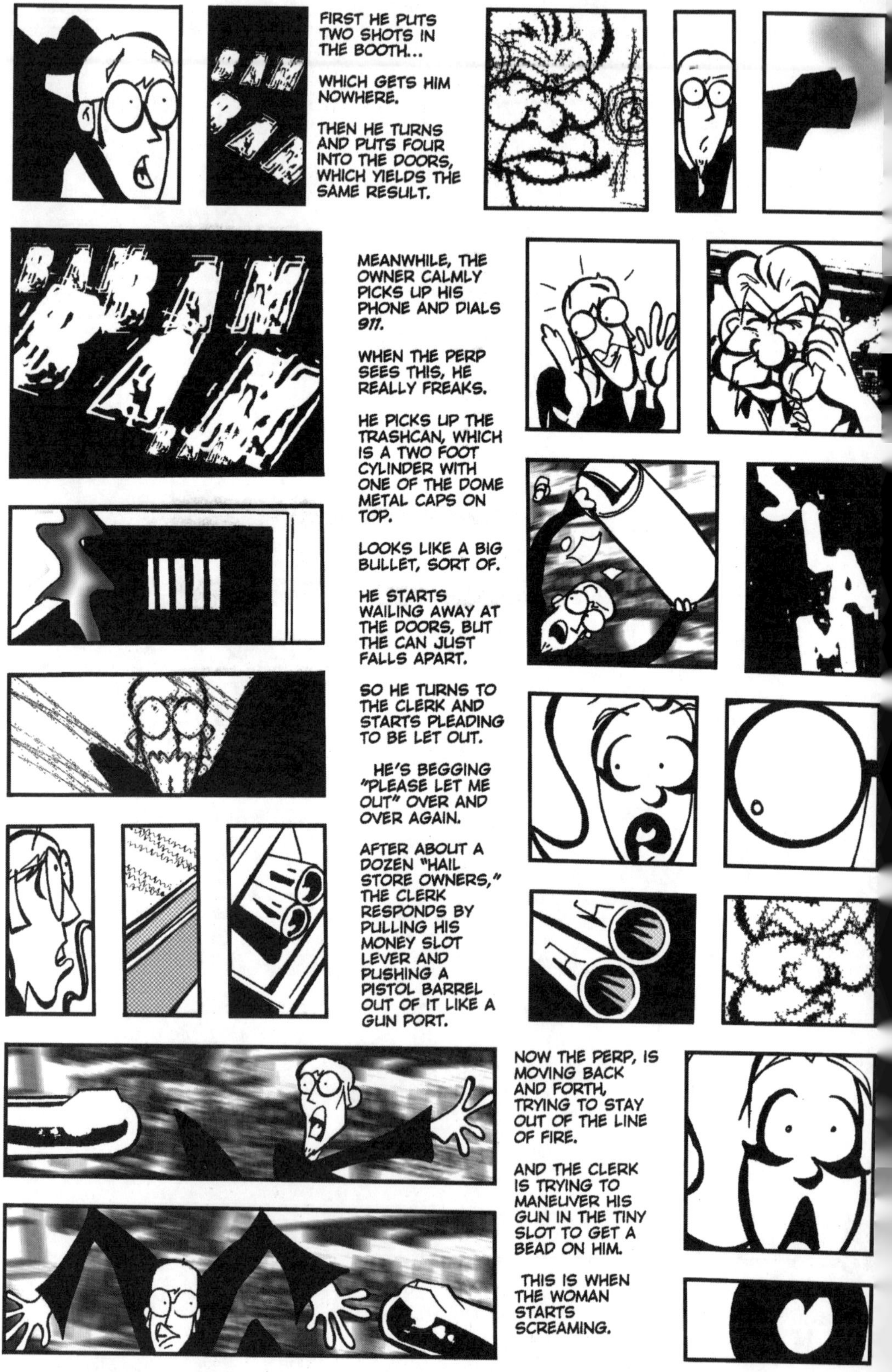

FIRST HE PUTS TWO SHOTS IN THE BOOTH...
WHICH GETS HIM NOWHERE.
THEN HE TURNS AND PUTS FOUR INTO THE DOORS, WHICH YIELDS THE SAME RESULT.
MEANWHILE, THE OWNER CALMLY PICKS UP HIS PHONE AND DIALS 911.
WHEN THE PERP SEES THIS, HE REALLY FREAKS.
HE PICKS UP THE TRASHCAN, WHICH IS A TWO FOOT CYLINDER WITH ONE OF THE DOME METAL CAPS ON TOP.
LOOKS LIKE A BIG BULLET, SORT OF.
HE STARTS WAILING AWAY AT THE DOORS, BUT THE CAN JUST FALLS APART.
SLAM
SO HE TURNS TO THE CLERK AND STARTS PLEADING TO BE LET OUT.
HE'S BEGGING "PLEASE LET ME OUT" OVER AND OVER AGAIN.
AFTER ABOUT A DOZEN "HAIL STORE OWNERS," THE CLERK RESPONDS BY PULLING HIS MONEY SLOT LEVER AND PUSHING A PISTOL BARREL OUT OF IT LIKE A GUN PORT.
NOW THE PERP, IS MOVING BACK AND FORTH, TRYING TO STAY OUT OF THE LINE OF FIRE.
AND THE CLERK IS TRYING TO MANEUVER HIS GUN IN THE TINY SLOT TO GET A BEAD ON HIM.
THIS IS WHEN THE WOMAN STARTS SCREAMING.

"DON'T SHOOT HIM!"

SHE REPEATS THIS OVER AND OVER AGAIN LIKE A MANTRA.

SO THIS GOES ON FOR A FEW MINUTES UNTIL THE POLICE SIRENS CAN BE CLEARLY HEARD.

WHEN THE PERP HEARS THE SIREN, HE **FLIPS** AND STARTS FRANTICALLY LOOKING FOR SOME WAY TO GET THROUGH THE DOORS.

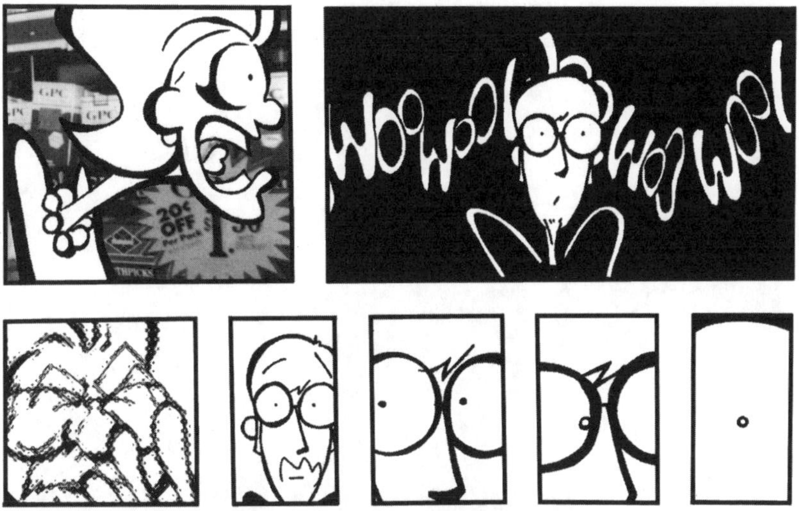
20¢ OFF
Per Pack

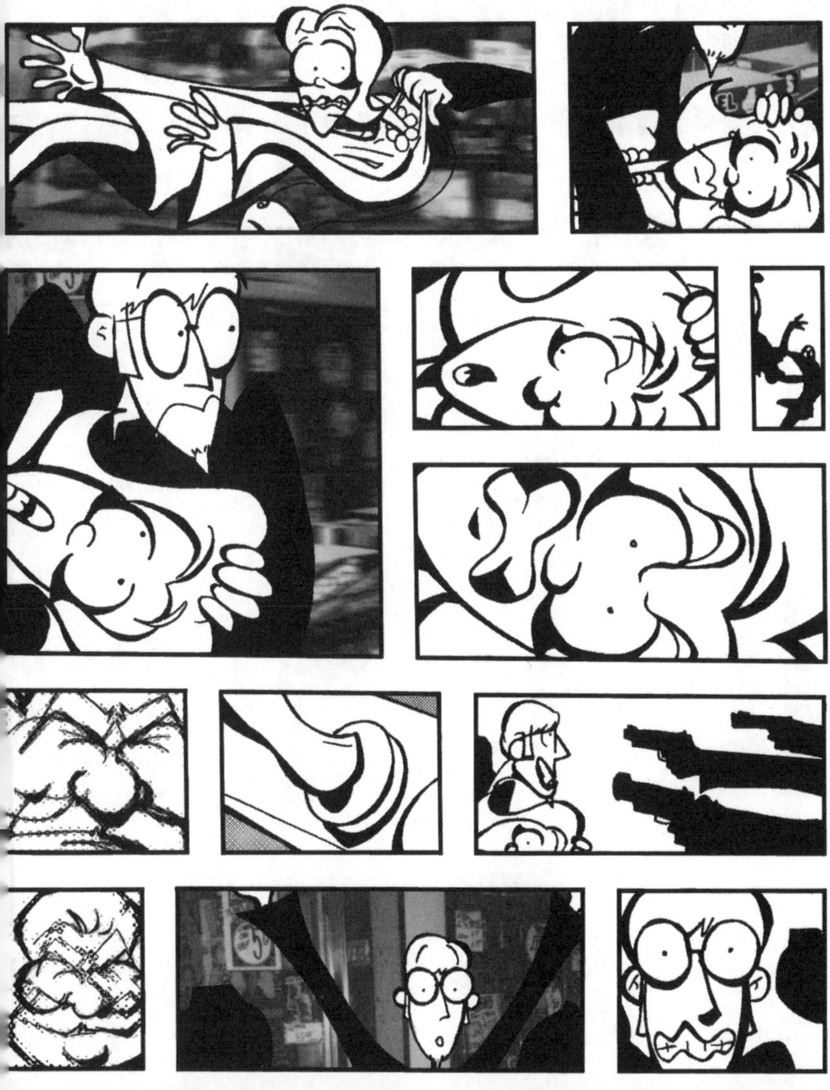

HE RUNS OVER TO THE WOMAN, WHO THE WHOLE TIME HAS BEEN YELLING "DON'T SHOOT HIM..."

HE GRABS HER, AND POSITIONS HER HORIZONTALLY UNDER HIS ARM LIKE A BATTERING RAM.

AT THIS POINT THE WOMAN STARTS SCREAMING AT THE TOP OF HER LUNGS:

**"SHOOT HIM!"**

BUT ALL THE STOREKEEPER DOES IS HIT THE DOOR BUTTON.

LETTING THE COPS IN.

THEY HAVE THEIR GLOCKS IN THEIR HANDS AND ONE SHOUTS **"HANDS IN THE AIR!"**

SO THE PERP DOES.

END OF STORY.

WHILE THIS MAY NOT BE TRUE, IT'S THE STORY I WAS TOLD.

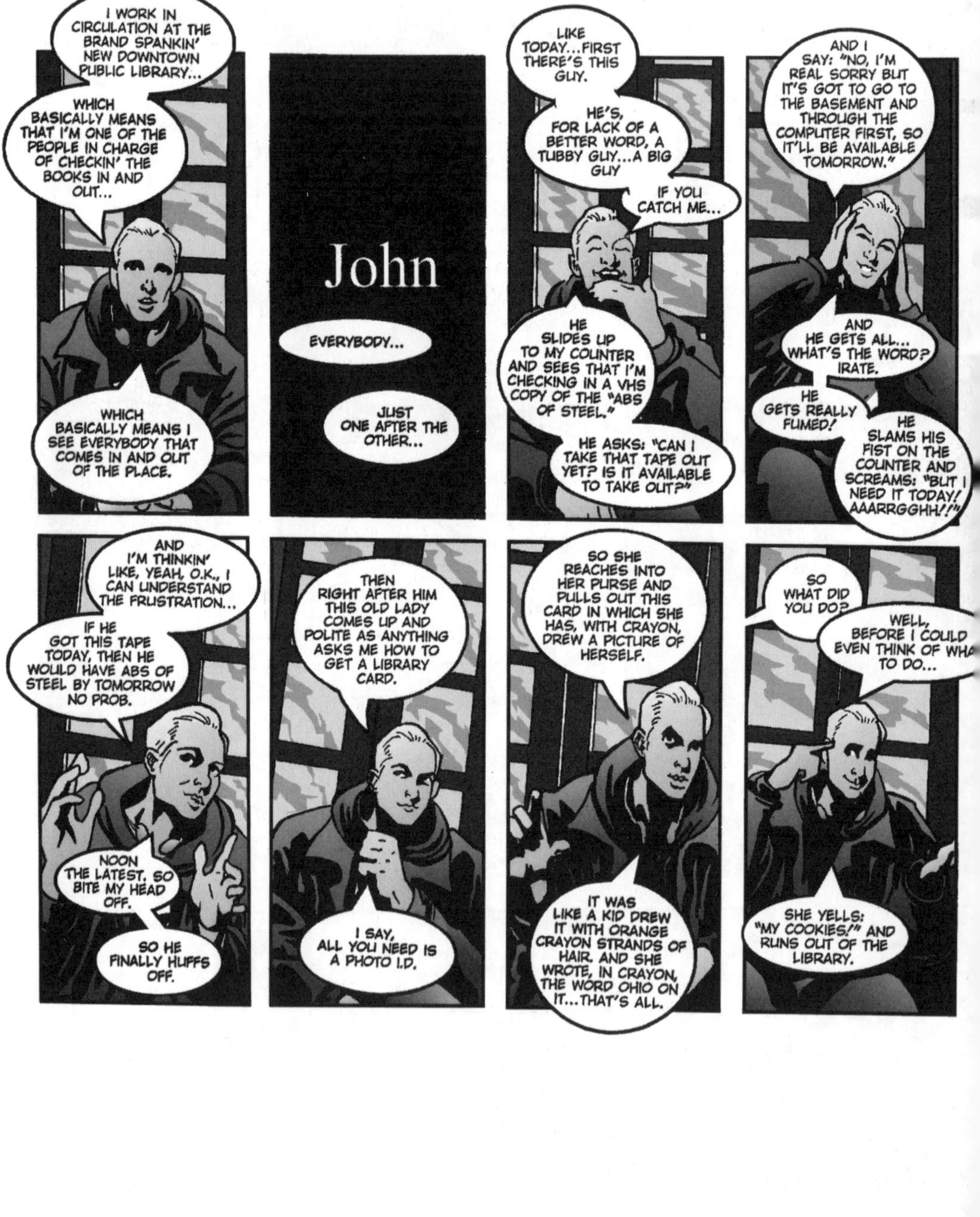
I WORK IN CIRCULATION AT THE BRAND SPANKIN' NEW DOWNTOWN PUBLIC LIBRARY...
WHICH BASICALLY MEANS THAT I'M ONE OF THE PEOPLE IN CHARGE OF CHECKIN' THE BOOKS IN AND OUT...
WHICH BASICALLY MEANS I SEE EVERYBODY THAT COMES IN AND OUT OF THE PLACE.
John
EVERYBODY...
JUST ONE AFTER THE OTHER...
LIKE TODAY...FIRST THERE'S THIS GUY.
HE'S, FOR LACK OF A BETTER WORD, A TUBBY GUY...A BIG GUY
IF YOU CATCH ME...
HE SLIDES UP TO MY COUNTER AND SEES THAT I'M CHECKING IN A VHS COPY OF THE "ABS OF STEEL."
HE ASKS: "CAN I TAKE THAT TAPE OUT YET? IS IT AVAILABLE TO TAKE OUT?"
AND I SAY: "NO, I'M REAL SORRY BUT IT'S GOT TO GO TO THE BASEMENT AND THROUGH THE COMPUTER FIRST, SO IT'LL BE AVAILABLE TOMORROW."
AND HE GETS ALL... WHAT'S THE WORD? IRATE.
HE GETS REALLY FUMED!
HE SLAMS HIS FIST ON THE COUNTER AND SCREAMS: "BUT I NEED IT TODAY! AAARRGGHH!!"
AND I'M THINKIN' LIKE, YEAH, O.K., I CAN UNDERSTAND THE FRUSTRATION...
IF HE GOT THIS TAPE TODAY, THEN HE WOULD HAVE ABS OF STEEL BY TOMORROW NO PROB.
NOON THE LATEST. SO BITE MY HEAD OFF.
SO HE FINALLY HUFFS OFF.
THEN RIGHT AFTER HIM THIS OLD LADY COMES UP AND POLITE AS ANYTHING ASKS ME HOW TO GET A LIBRARY CARD.
I SAY, ALL YOU NEED IS A PHOTO I.D.
SO SHE REACHES INTO HER PURSE AND PULLS OUT THIS CARD IN WHICH SHE HAS, WITH CRAYON, DREW A PICTURE OF HERSELF.
IT WAS LIKE A KID DREW IT WITH ORANGE CRAYON STRANDS OF HAIR. AND SHE WROTE, IN CRAYON, THE WORD OHIO ON IT...THAT'S ALL.
SO WHAT DID YOU DO?
WELL, BEFORE I COULD EVEN THINK OF WHA TO DO...
SHE YELLS: "MY COOKIES!" AND RUNS OUT OF THE LIBRARY.

# buffalo chips

WE WERE COVERING A GROUP...

THE WHITE BUFFALO SOCIETY.

AND BASICALLY THEY WERE LIKE A GROUP OF INDIAN WANNA BES.

THEY'RE NON-INDIAN PEOPLE WHO STUDY INDIAN CULTURE AND...AND...

...WHAT DO I WANNA SAY?

RELIGION.

THEY'RE HOLDING A- A- A- SUNDANCE.

WHICH IS A VERY RELIGIOUS *RITE* OF THE LAKOTA SOIUX INDIANS.

AND ITS A RITUAL THAT INVOLVES HANGING.

YOU- YOU INSERT FISHHOOKS...

NOT FISHHOOKS...

BONEHOOKS INTO YOUR CHEST.

YEAH.

AND THEN THEY ARE ATTACHED INTO A TREE OR A POLE.

AND YOU LEAN BACK AND YOU HANG.

YOU JUST HANG.

THEY WERE DOING ONE OF THESE AND THE REAL INDIANS...

WHEN THEY HEARD ABOUT IT...

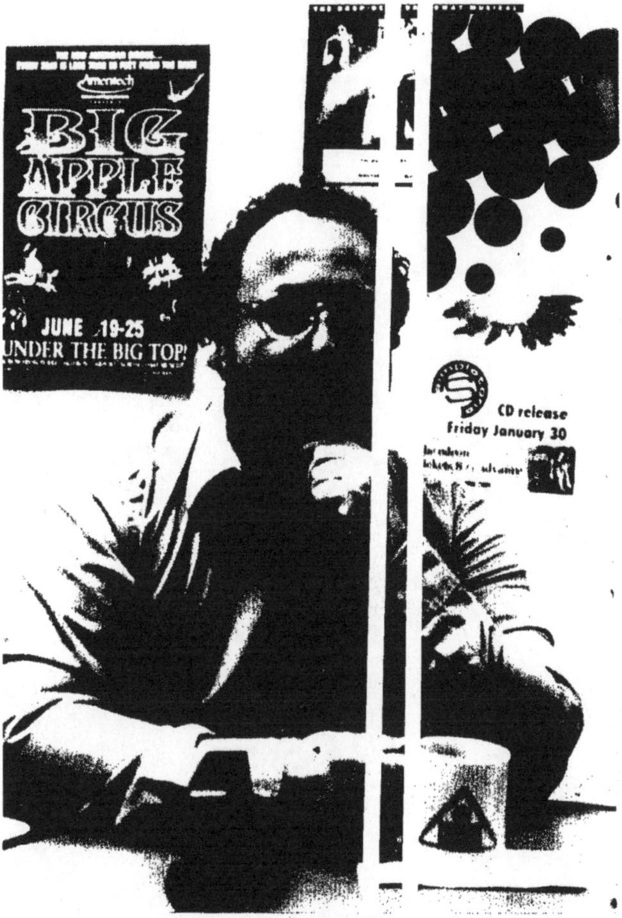
BIG APPLE CIRCUS
JUNE 19-25
UNDER THE BIG TOP!
CD release
Friday January 30

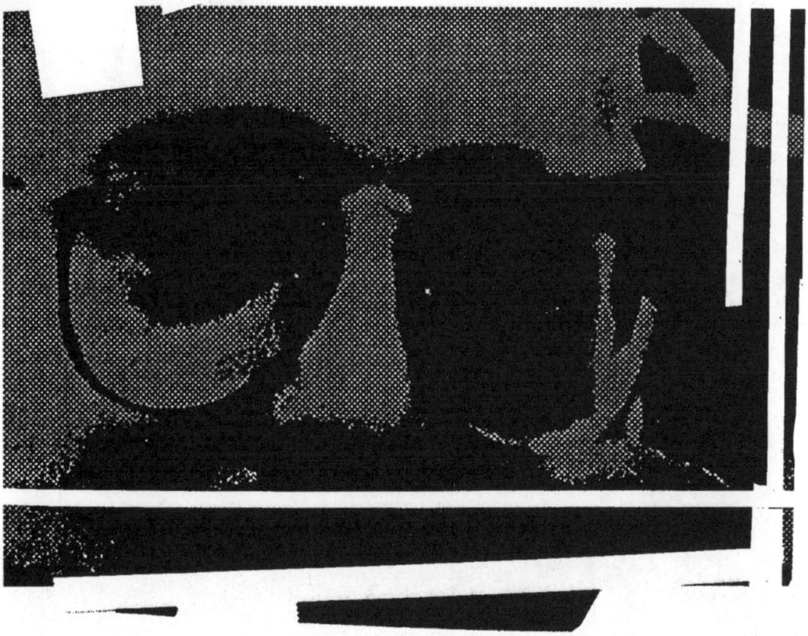

THEY WERE- THEY WERE VERY UPSET.

IT WOULD BE THE EQUIVALENT OF -OF - OF CATHOLICS TAKING COMMUNION.

IT'S- IT'S- IT'S A SACRAMENT.

A RITUAL.

SO THE REAL INDIANS ARE PRETTY UPSET

SO THEY TOLD US AT PAPER THEY WERE GOING TO PROTEST SO...

WE MET THEM THERE.

THE EVENT WAS BEING HELD IN THIS LITTLE TOWN CALLED SUMMERFIELD.

WHICH IS NEAR CAMBRIDGE, OHIO.

WAY, WAY DOWN SOUTH,

ANYWAY, I WENT DOWN THERE WITH A PHOTOGRAPHER.

WE GOT THERE EARLY.

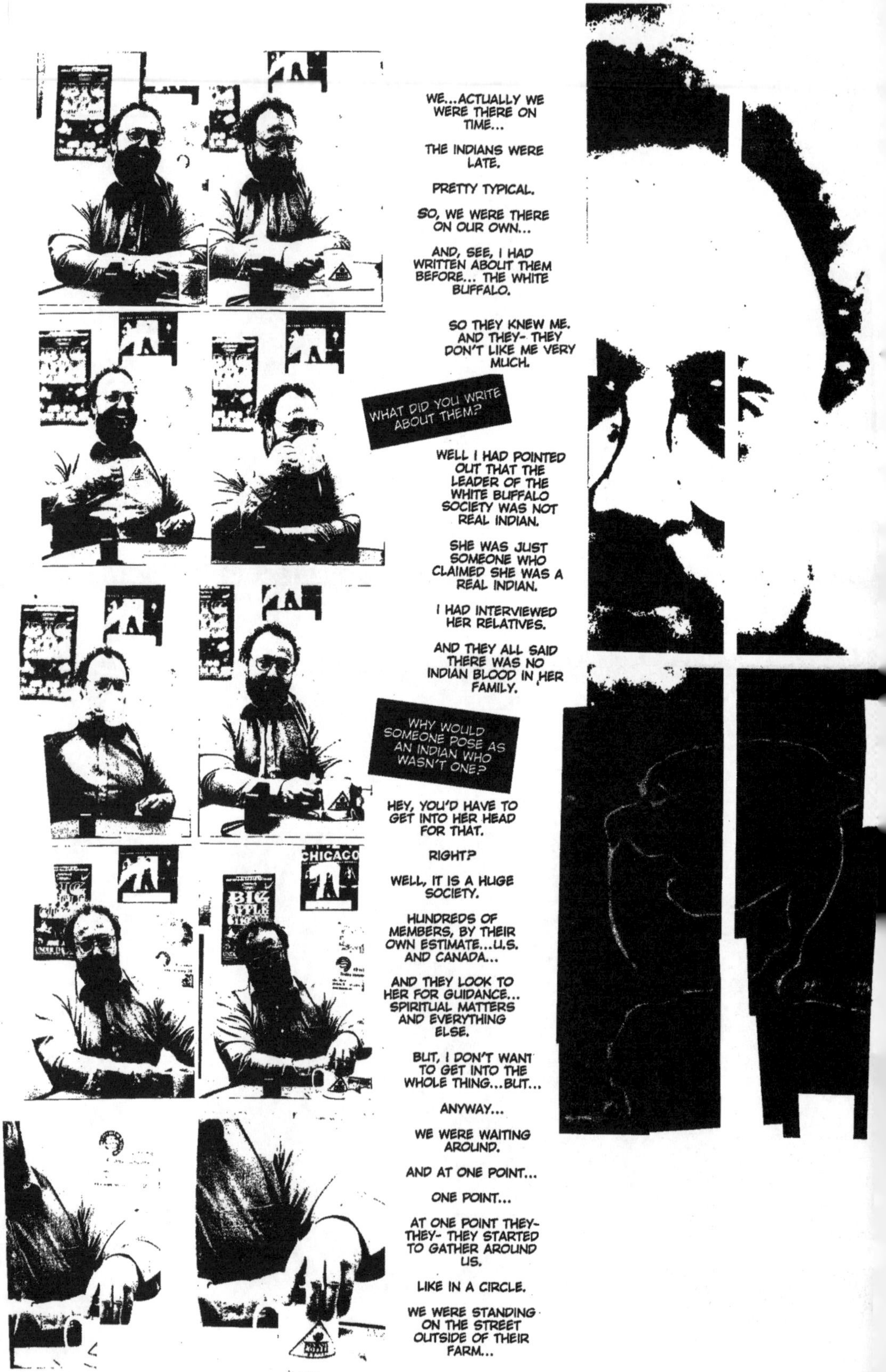

WE...ACTUALLY WE WERE THERE ON TIME...
THE INDIANS WERE LATE.
PRETTY TYPICAL.
SO, WE WERE THERE ON OUR OWN...
AND, SEE, I HAD WRITTEN ABOUT THEM BEFORE... THE WHITE BUFFALO.
SO THEY KNEW ME. AND THEY- THEY DON'T LIKE ME VERY MUCH.
WHAT DID YOU WRITE ABOUT THEM?
WELL I HAD POINTED OUT THAT THE LEADER OF THE WHITE BUFFALO SOCIETY WAS NOT REAL INDIAN.
SHE WAS JUST SOMEONE WHO CLAIMED SHE WAS A REAL INDIAN.
I HAD INTERVIEWED HER RELATIVES.
AND THEY ALL SAID THERE WAS NO INDIAN BLOOD IN HER FAMILY.
WHY WOULD SOMEONE POSE AS AN INDIAN WHO WASN'T ONE?
HEY, YOU'D HAVE TO GET INTO HER HEAD FOR THAT.
RIGHT?
WELL, IT IS A HUGE SOCIETY.
HUNDREDS OF MEMBERS, BY THEIR OWN ESTIMATE...U.S. AND CANADA...
AND THEY LOOK TO HER FOR GUIDANCE... SPIRITUAL MATTERS AND EVERYTHING ELSE.
BUT, I DON'T WANT TO GET INTO THE WHOLE THING...BUT...
ANYWAY...
WE WERE WAITING AROUND.
AND AT ONE POINT...
ONE POINT...
AT ONE POINT THEY- THEY- THEY STARTED TO GATHER AROUND US.
LIKE IN A CIRCLE.
WE WERE STANDING ON THE STREET OUTSIDE OF THEIR FARM...

IT WAS A VERY HOT DAY.

ABOUT A HUNDRED.

VERY RURAL...

FEELING VERY VULNERABLE...

HEH HEH

AND -UH- ALL THESE GUYS STARTED STANDING AROUND US AND THEN THEY STARTED SHOVING!

THEY STARTED SHOVING THE PHOTOGRAPHER RAMONE...

THEY ACTUALLY PUSHED HIM!

SO, A FIGHT ALMOST STARTED RIGHT THERE.

AND THEN ONE OF THE GROUP LEADERS BROKE IN AND SAID: "NO WE DON'T WANT ANY TROUBLE."

"JUST LEAVE THEM ALONE."

"AS LONG AS THEY STAY ON THE STREET IT'S FINE."

AND THIS IS THE FUNNY PART...

WHAT THEY ACTUALLY DID...

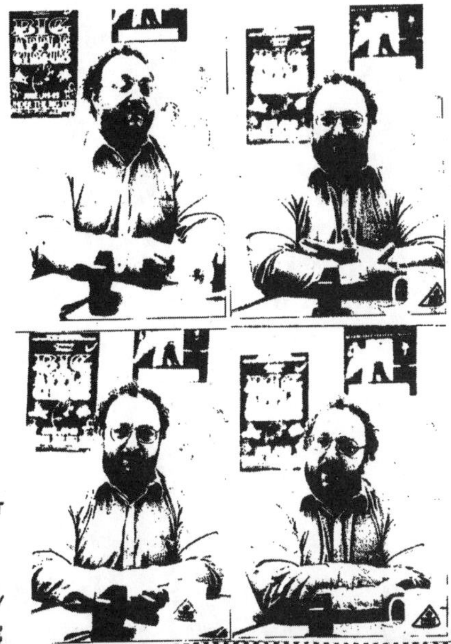

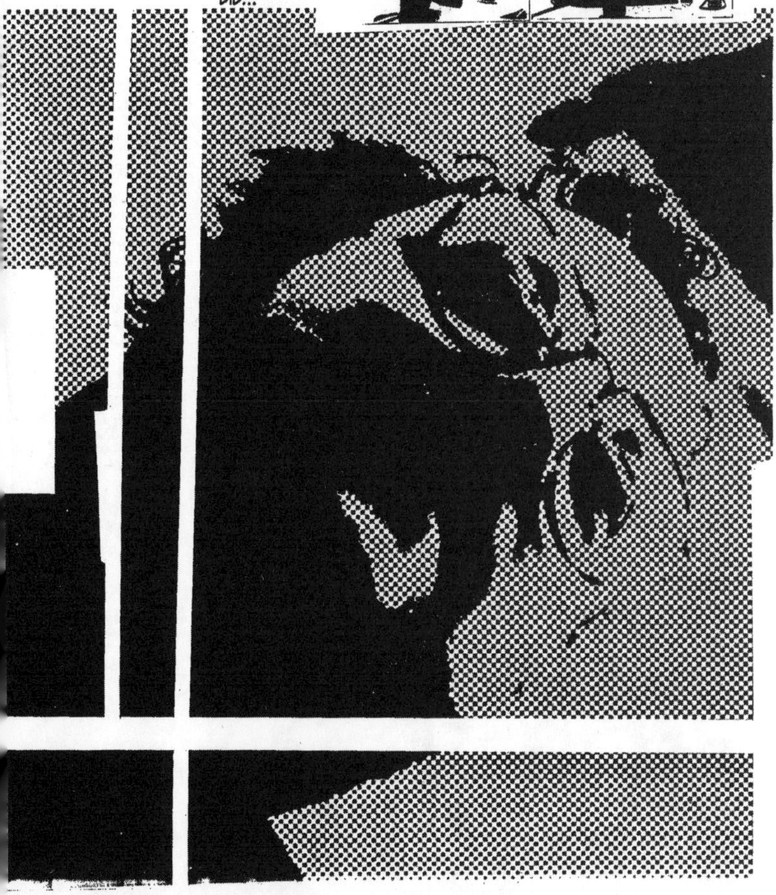

I GUESS THEY FELT SINCE THEY COULDN'T MANHANDLE US...

COULDN'T BULLY US TO GO AWAY...

THEY...

WELL, WE HAD SAT DOWN ON A LOG.

JUST TO WAIT FOR THE INDIANS...THE REAL INDIANS TO COME.

AND TWO WHITE BUFFALO GUYS CAME OVER...

AND GET THIS...

THEY WERE COVERED IN HUMAN SHIT!

HUMAN SHIT!

AND...

THEY WERE CHEWING CLOVES OF GARLIC.

RAW GARLIC!

AND THEY WERE CHOMPING AWAY...

THEY CAME AND SAT ON EITHER SIDE OF US....

...AND...

THEY WERE BREATHING IN OUR FACES LIKE THIS...

WHOOOOOOO

BREATHING THE GARLIC RIGHT IN OUR FACES.

AND...

Y'KNOW, THAT DIDN'T BOTHER ME...

'CAUSE I'M ITALIAN.

BUT THEY SMELLED LIKE SHIT!

'CAUSE THEY WERE COVERED IN SHIT!

THEN THEY STARTED TO GO LIKE THIS...

FLICKING THE SHIT OFF OF THEM ONTO US!

HAHAHAHAHA

I ACTUALLY THOUGHT IT WAS FUNNY.

WHAT DID YOU DO?

WELL, YOU KNOW, I KNOW THIS SOUNDS ODD...

BUT I JUST LAUGHED AT THEM.

I MEAN IT WAS SO OUTRAGEOUS.

I THOUGH IT WAS CLEVER IN A WEIRD WAY.

SO, WE JUST GOT UP AND WALKED AWAY FROM THEM...

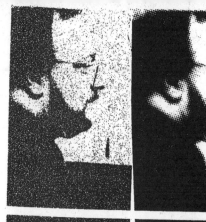

BUT A SECOND LATE
THE REAL INDIANS
ARRIVED.

WELL, IT WOULDN'T
EVEN EVER OCCUR TO
ME TO DO THAT IN A
MILLION YEARS...

WHAT? TO COVER
YOURSELF IN YOUR
OWN SHIT AND FLICK
IT AT SOMEONE??

NO.

THE FUNNY THING IS,
IS THAT THE
STORY...WHEN I
REPORTED IT TO THE
PAPER...

AND I SAID IT JUST
LIKE I TOLD YOU...

THE EDITOR'S FIRST
QUESTION WAS....

HAHA

HOW DO WE KNOW IT
WAS HUMAN SHIT??

HA HA

AND I TOLD HIM...I'VE
BEEN A REPORTER
LONG ENOUGH TO
KNOW WHAT KIND OF
SHIT I'M SMELLIN'.

SO, OUR PAPER RAN
THE STORY AND THEY
RAN IT AS THAT THEY
FLICKED "APPARENT
HUMAN WASTE."

HAHAHAHAHA

AND AN INDIAN PAPER
CALLED SHIT "SHIT..."

IT ACTUALLY HAD ME
QUOTED AS SAYING I
HAD SHIT FLICKED ON
ME...

SO THAT'S THAT
STORY.

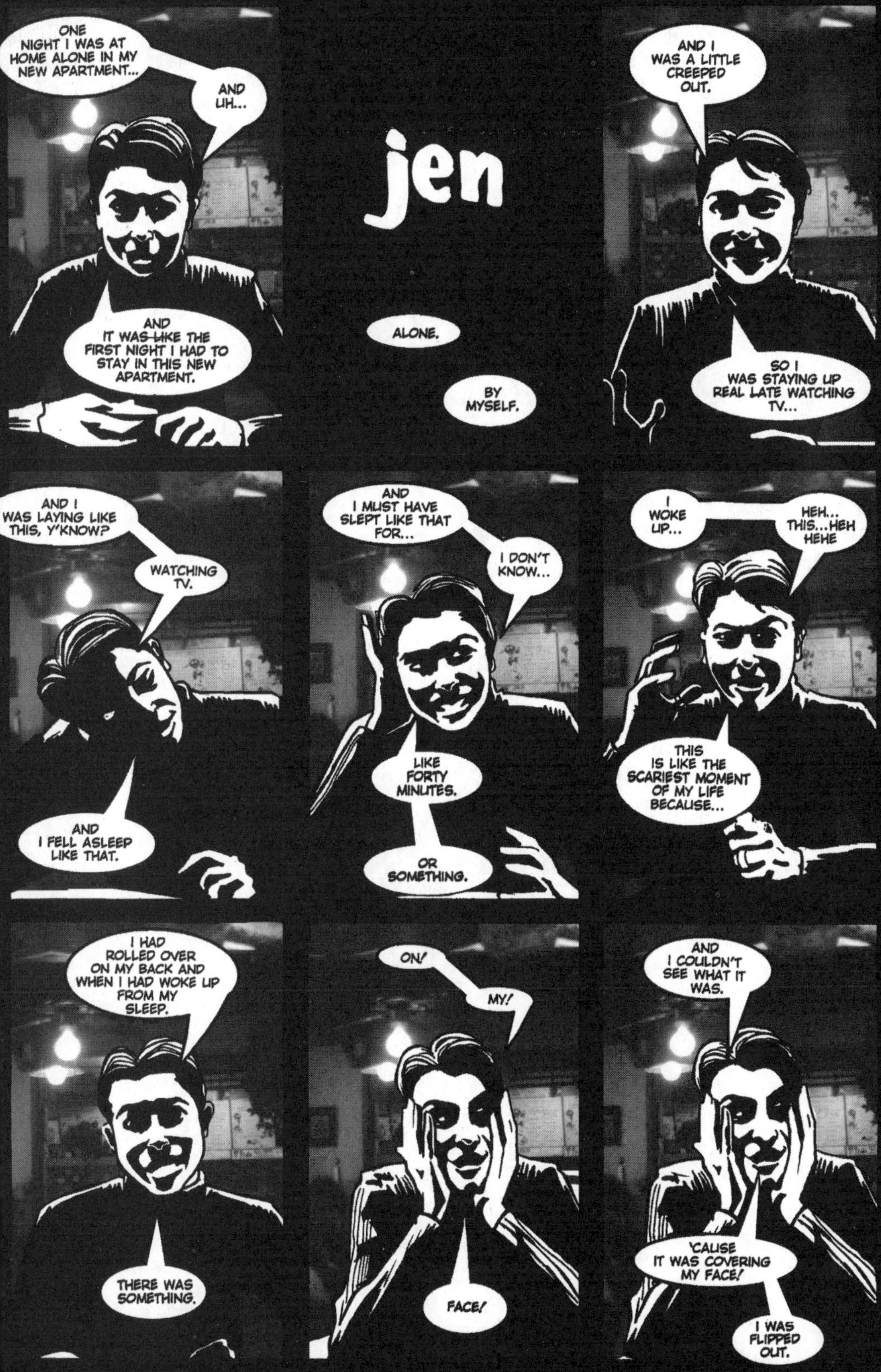
ONE NIGHT I WAS AT HOME ALONE IN MY NEW APARTMENT...
AND UH...
AND IT WAS LIKE THE FIRST NIGHT I HAD TO STAY IN THIS NEW APARTMENT.
jen
ALONE.
BY MYSELF.
AND I WAS A LITTLE CREEPED OUT.
SO I WAS STAYING UP REAL LATE WATCHING TV...
AND I WAS LAYING LIKE THIS, Y'KNOW?
WATCHING TV.
AND I FELL ASLEEP LIKE THAT.
AND I MUST HAVE SLEPT LIKE THAT FOR...
I DON'T KNOW...
LIKE FORTY MINUTES.
OR SOMETHING.
I WOKE UP...
HEH... THIS...HEH HEHE
THIS IS LIKE THE SCARIEST MOMENT OF MY LIFE BECAUSE...
I HAD ROLLED OVER ON MY BACK AND WHEN I HAD WOKE UP FROM MY SLEEP.
THERE WAS SOMETHING.
ON!
MY!
FACE!
AND I COULDN'T SEE WHAT IT WAS.
'CAUSE IT WAS COVERING MY FACE!
I WAS FLIPPED OUT.

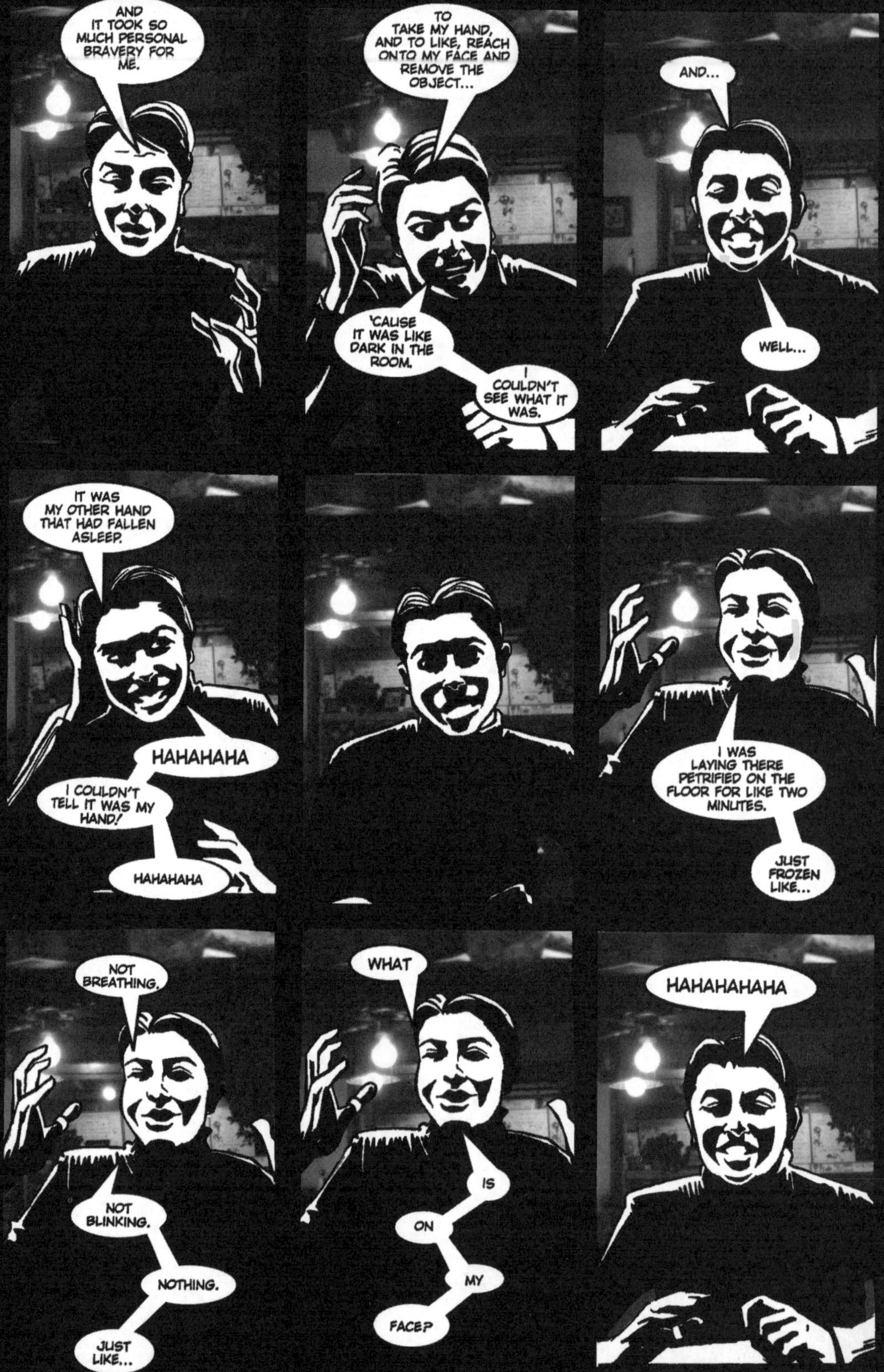
AND IT TOOK SO MUCH PERSONAL BRAVERY FOR ME.
TO TAKE MY HAND, AND TO LIKE, REACH ONTO MY FACE AND REMOVE THE OBJECT...
'CAUSE IT WAS LIKE DARK IN THE ROOM.
I COULDN'T SEE WHAT IT WAS.
AND...
WELL...
IT WAS MY OTHER HAND THAT HAD FALLEN ASLEEP.
HAHAHAHA
I COULDN'T TELL IT WAS MY HAND!
HAHAHAHA
I WAS LAYING THERE PETRIFIED ON THE FLOOR FOR LIKE TWO MINUTES.
JUST FROZEN LIKE...
NOT BREATHING.
NOT BLINKING.
NOTHING.
JUST LIKE...
WHAT
IS
ON
MY
FACE?
HAHAHAHAHA

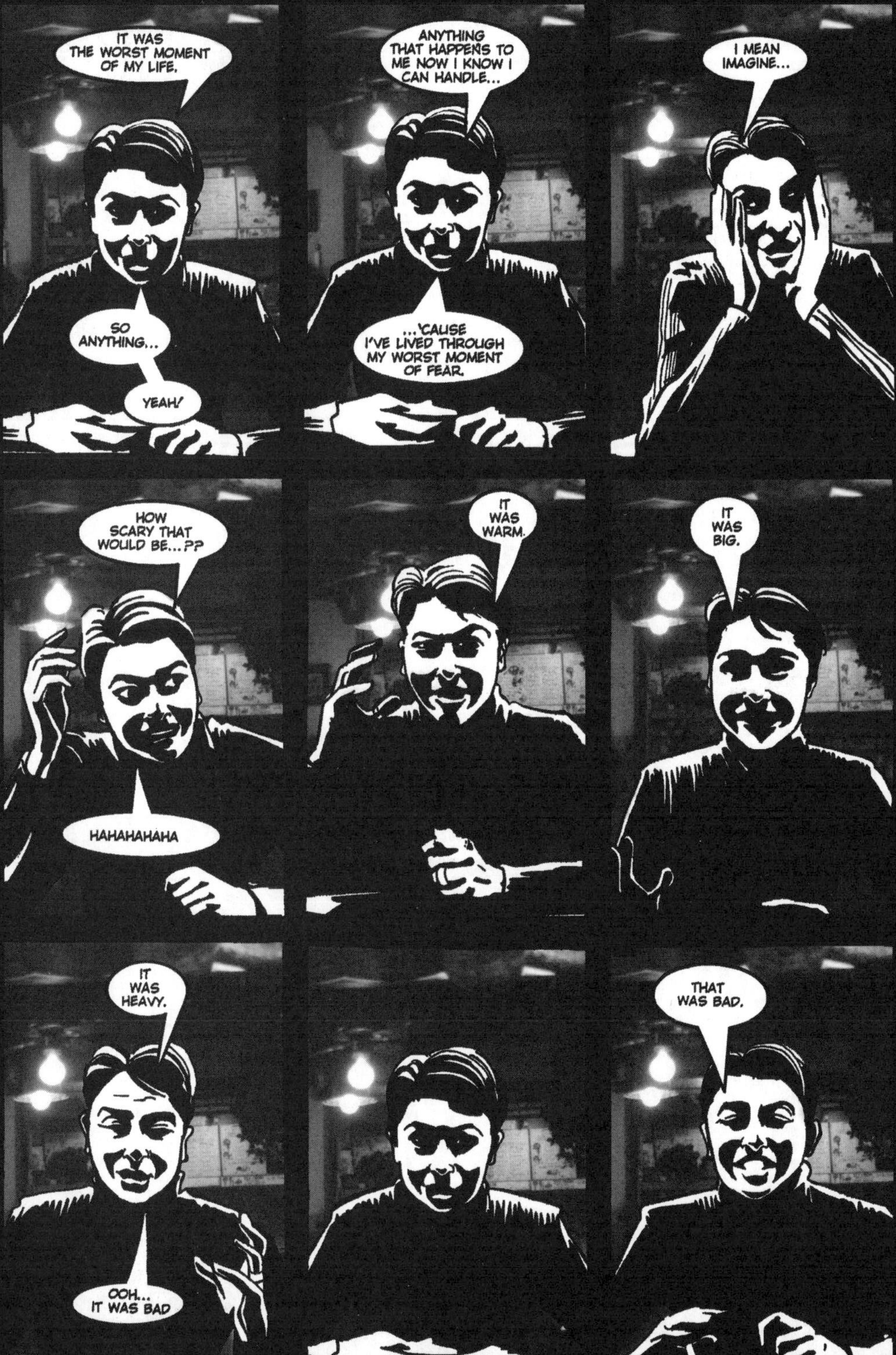
IT WAS THE WORST MOMENT OF MY LIFE.
SO ANYTHING...
YEAH!
ANYTHING THAT HAPPENS TO ME NOW I KNOW I CAN HANDLE...
...'CAUSE I'VE LIVED THROUGH MY WORST MOMENT OF FEAR.
I MEAN IMAGINE...
HOW SCARY THAT WOULD BE...??
HAHAHAHAHA
IT WAS WARM.
IT WAS BIG.
IT WAS HEAVY.
OOH... IT WAS BAD
THAT WAS BAD.

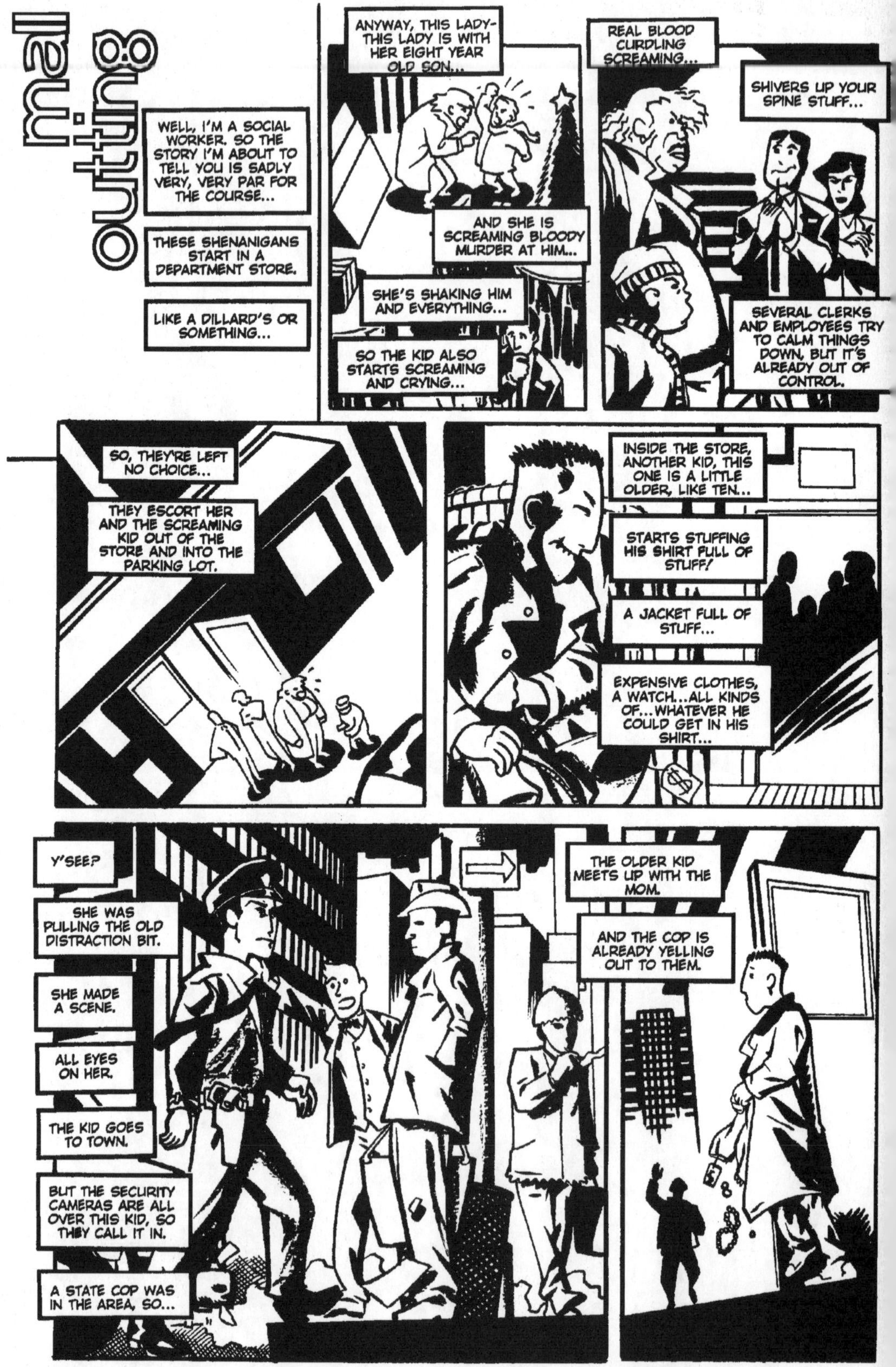
mall outing
WELL, I'M A SOCIAL WORKER. SO THE STORY I'M ABOUT TO TELL YOU IS SADLY VERY, VERY PAR FOR THE COURSE...
THESE SHENANIGANS START IN A DEPARTMENT STORE.
LIKE A DILLARD'S OR SOMETHING...
ANYWAY, THIS LADY- THIS LADY IS WITH HER EIGHT YEAR OLD SON...
AND SHE IS SCREAMING BLOODY MURDER AT HIM...
SHE'S SHAKING HIM AND EVERYTHING...
SO THE KID ALSO STARTS SCREAMING AND CRYING...
REAL BLOOD CURDLING SCREAMING...
SHIVERS UP YOUR SPINE STUFF...
SEVERAL CLERKS AND EMPLOYEES TRY TO CALM THINGS DOWN, BUT IT'S ALREADY OUT OF CONTROL.
SO, THEY'RE LEFT NO CHOICE...
THEY ESCORT HER AND THE SCREAMING KID OUT OF THE STORE AND INTO THE PARKING LOT.
INSIDE THE STORE, ANOTHER KID, THIS ONE IS A LITTLE OLDER, LIKE TEN...
STARTS STUFFING HIS SHIRT FULL OF STUFF!
A JACKET FULL OF STUFF...
EXPENSIVE CLOTHES, A WATCH...ALL KINDS OF...WHATEVER HE COULD GET IN HIS SHIRT...
Y'SEE?
SHE WAS PULLING THE OLD DISTRACTION BIT.
SHE MADE A SCENE.
ALL EYES ON HER.
THE KID GOES TO TOWN.
BUT THE SECURITY CAMERAS ARE ALL OVER THIS KID, SO THEY CALL IT IN.
A STATE COP WAS IN THE AREA, SO...
THE OLDER KID MEETS UP WITH THE MOM.
AND THE COP IS ALREADY YELLING OUT TO THEM.

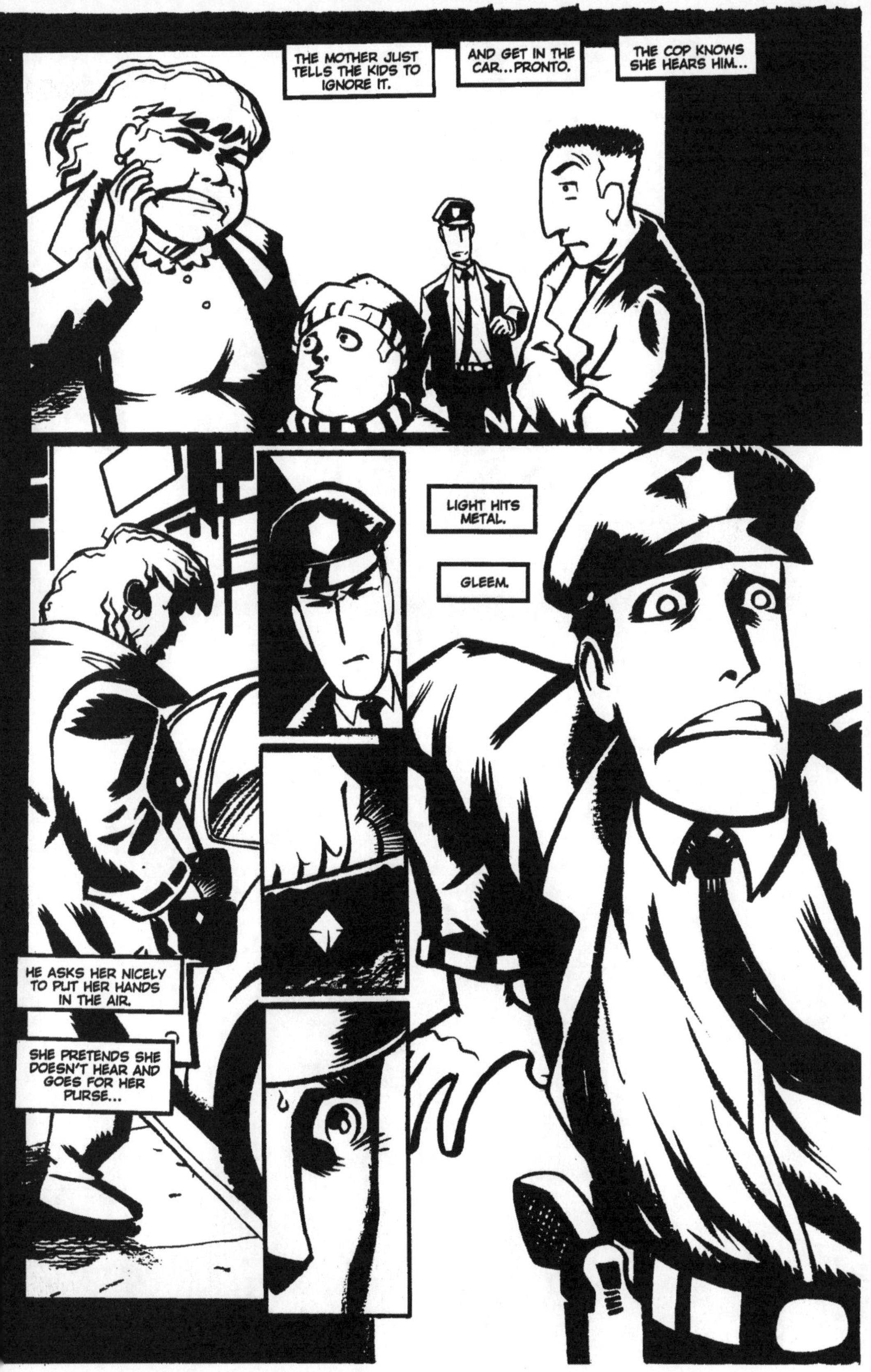
THE MOTHER JUST TELLS THE KIDS TO IGNORE IT.
AND GET IN THE CAR...PRONTO.
THE COP KNOWS SHE HEARS HIM...
HE ASKS HER NICELY TO PUT HER HANDS IN THE AIR.
SHE PRETENDS SHE DOESN'T HEAR AND GOES FOR HER PURSE...
LIGHT HITS METAL.
GLEEM.

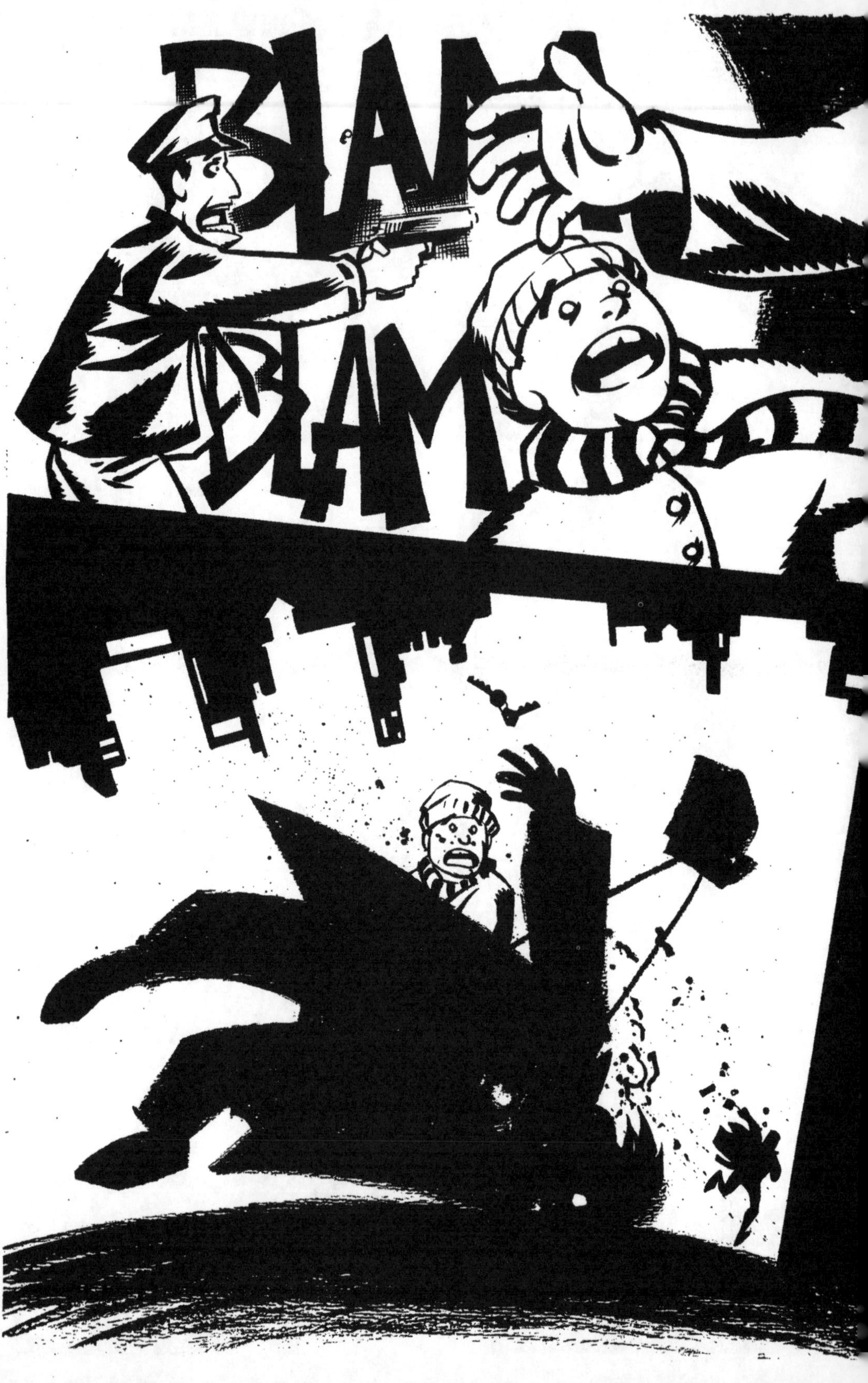
BLAM
BLAM

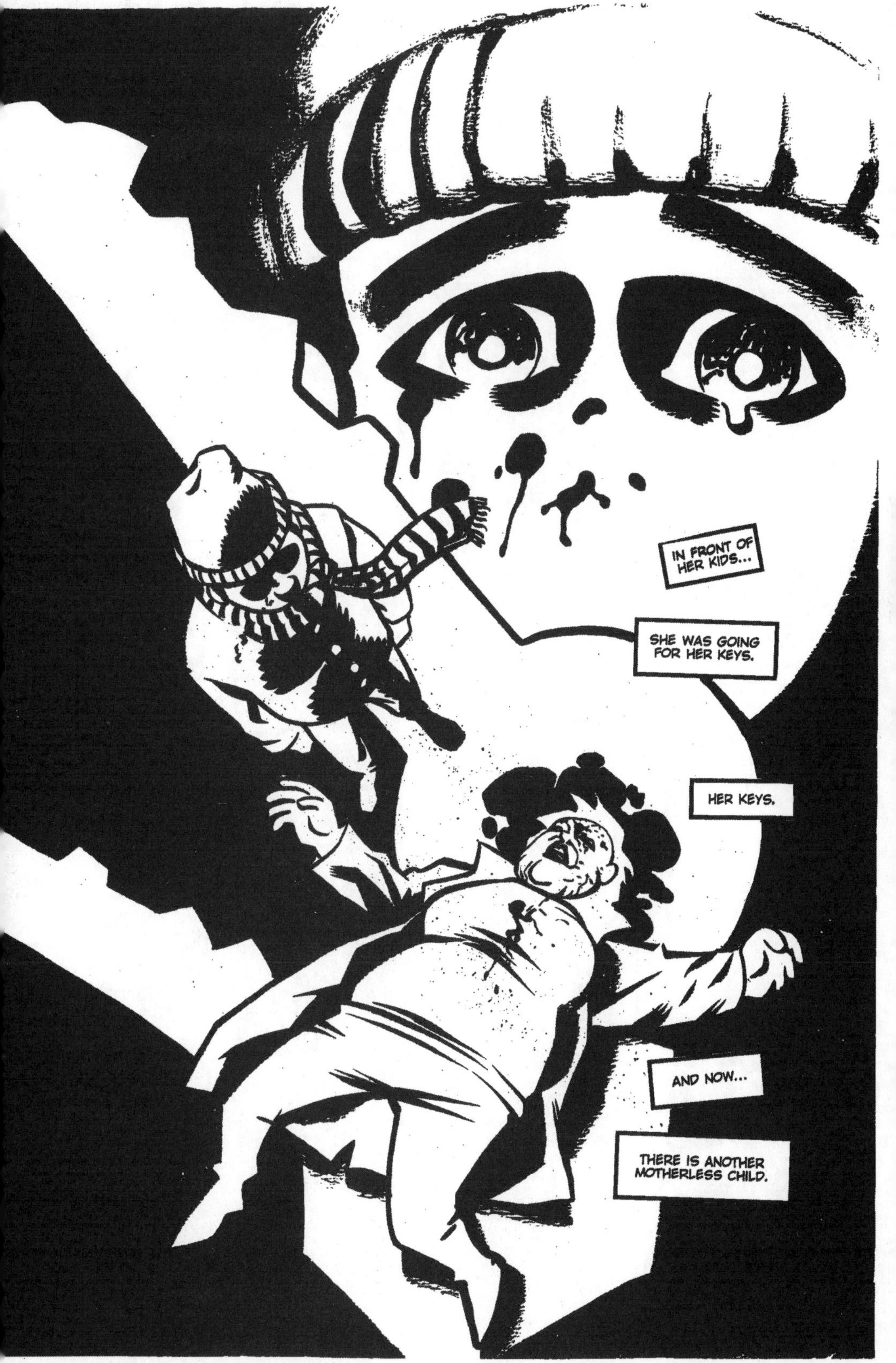
IN FRONT OF HER KIDS...
SHE WAS GOING FOR HER KEYS.
HER KEYS.
AND NOW...
THERE IS ANOTHER MOTHERLESS CHILD.

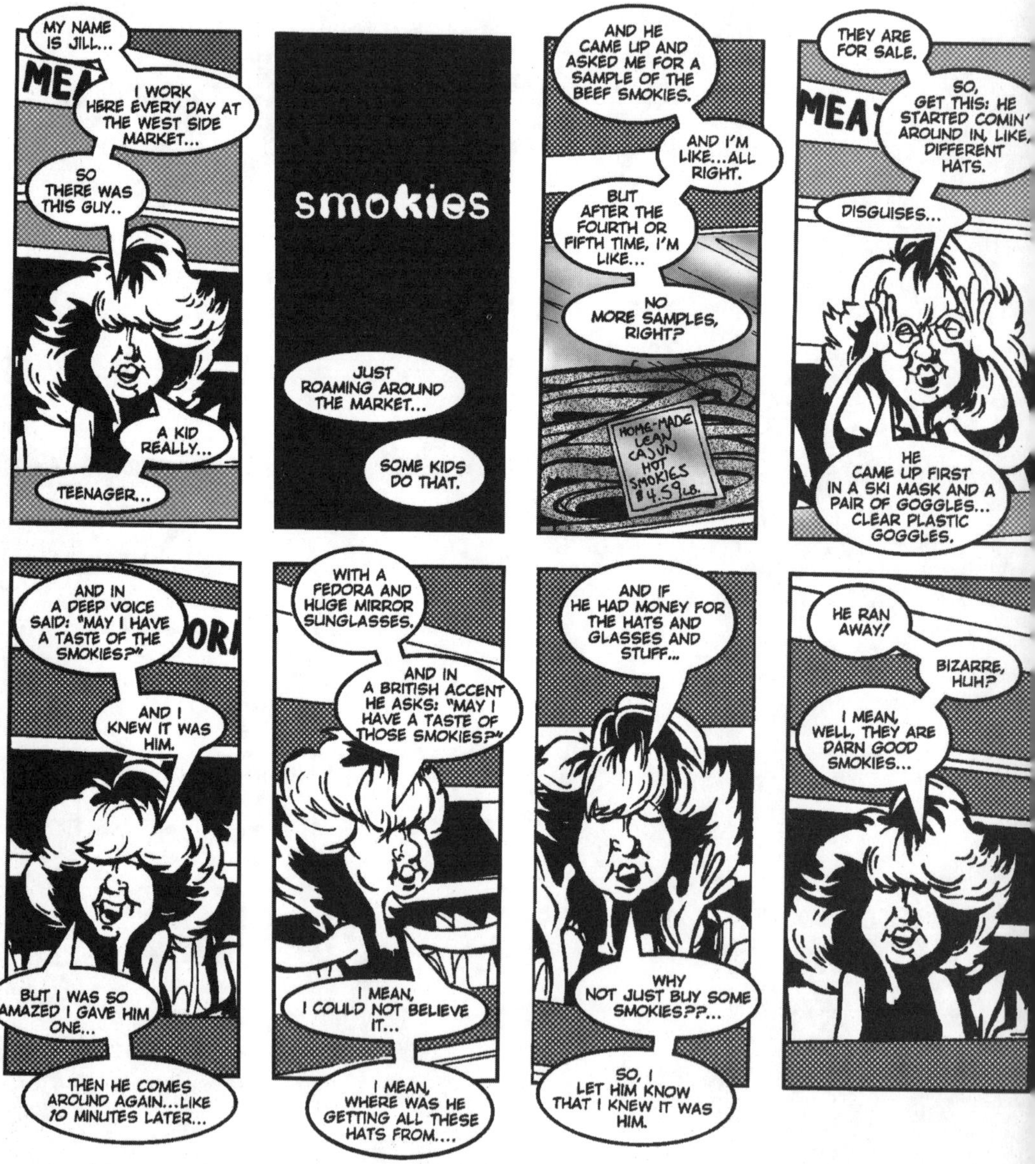
MY NAME IS JILL...
I WORK HERE EVERY DAY AT THE WEST SIDE MARKET...
SO THERE WAS THIS GUY..
A KID REALLY...
TEENAGER...
smokies
JUST ROAMING AROUND THE MARKET...
SOME KIDS DO THAT.
AND HE CAME UP AND ASKED ME FOR A SAMPLE OF THE BEEF SMOKIES.
AND I'M LIKE...ALL RIGHT.
BUT AFTER THE FOURTH OR FIFTH TIME, I'M LIKE...
NO MORE SAMPLES, RIGHT?
HOME-MADE LEAN CAJUN HOT SMOKIES $4.59 LB.
THEY ARE FOR SALE.
SO, GET THIS: HE STARTED COMIN' AROUND IN, LIKE, DIFFERENT HATS.
DISGUISES...
HE CAME UP FIRST IN A SKI MASK AND A PAIR OF GOGGLES... CLEAR PLASTIC GOGGLES.
AND IN A DEEP VOICE SAID: "MAY I HAVE A TASTE OF THE SMOKIES?"
AND I KNEW IT WAS HIM.
BUT I WAS SO AMAZED I GAVE HIM ONE...
THEN HE COMES AROUND AGAIN...LIKE 10 MINUTES LATER...
WITH A FEDORA AND HUGE MIRROR SUNGLASSES.
AND IN A BRITISH ACCENT HE ASKS: "MAY I HAVE A TASTE OF THOSE SMOKIES?"
I MEAN, I COULD NOT BELIEVE IT...
I MEAN, WHERE WAS HE GETTING ALL THESE HATS FROM....
AND IF HE HAD MONEY FOR THE HATS AND GLASSES AND STUFF...
WHY NOT JUST BUY SOME SMOKIES??...
SO, I LET HIM KNOW THAT I KNEW IT WAS HIM.
HE RAN AWAY!
BIZARRE, HUH?
I MEAN, WELL, THEY ARE DARN GOOD SMOKIES...

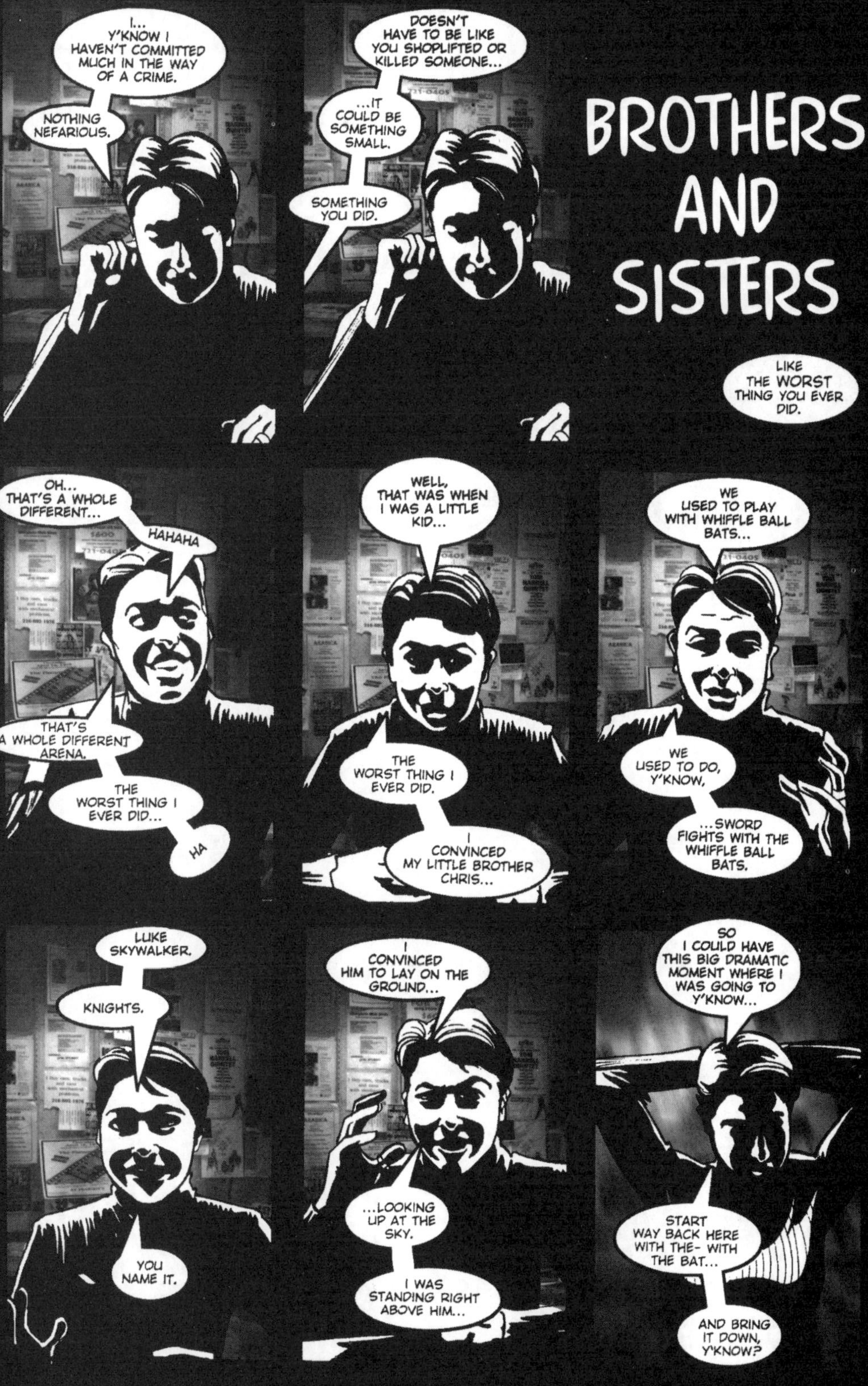
I... Y'KNOW I HAVEN'T COMMITTED MUCH IN THE WAY OF A CRIME.
NOTHING NEFARIOUS.
DOESN'T HAVE TO BE LIKE YOU SHOPLIFTED OR KILLED SOMEONE...
...IT COULD BE SOMETHING SMALL.
SOMETHING YOU DID.
BROTHERS AND SISTERS
LIKE THE WORST THING YOU EVER DID.
OH... THAT'S A WHOLE DIFFERENT...
HAHAHA
THAT'S A WHOLE DIFFERENT ARENA.
THE WORST THING I EVER DID...
HA
WELL, THAT WAS WHEN I WAS A LITTLE KID...
THE WORST THING I EVER DID.
I CONVINCED MY LITTLE BROTHER CHRIS...
WE USED TO PLAY WITH WHIFFLE BALL BATS...
WE USED TO DO, Y'KNOW,
...SWORD FIGHTS WITH THE WHIFFLE BALL BATS.
LUKE SKYWALKER.
KNIGHTS.
YOU NAME IT.
I CONVINCED HIM TO LAY ON THE GROUND...
...LOOKING UP AT THE SKY.
I WAS STANDING RIGHT ABOVE HIM...
SO I COULD HAVE THIS BIG DRAMATIC MOMENT WHERE I WAS GOING TO Y'KNOW...
START WAY BACK HERE WITH THE- WITH THE BAT...
AND BRING IT DOWN, Y'KNOW?

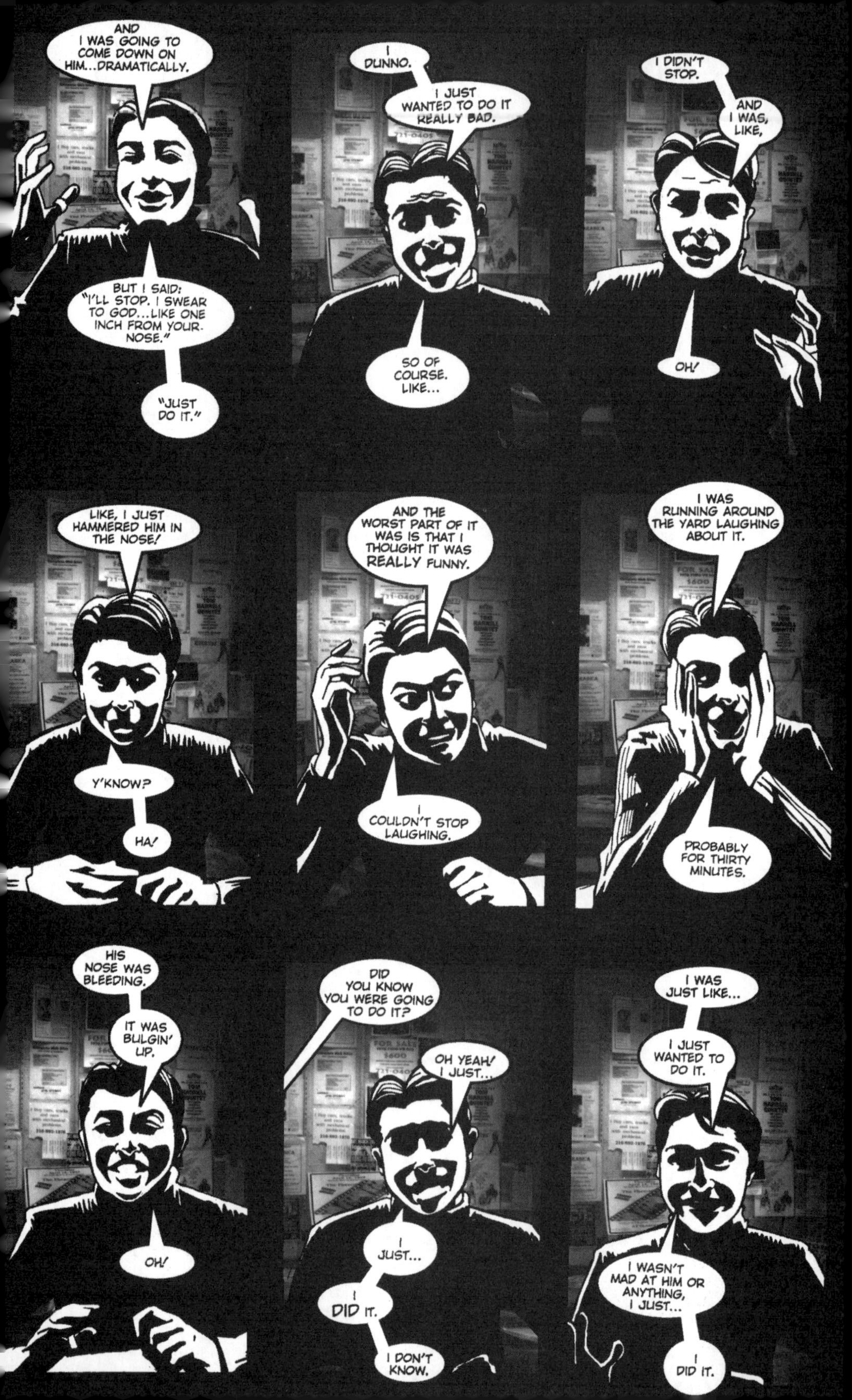
AND I WAS GOING TO COME DOWN ON HIM...DRAMATICALLY.
BUT I SAID: "I'LL STOP. I SWEAR TO GOD...LIKE ONE INCH FROM YOUR NOSE."
"JUST DO IT."
I DUNNO.
I JUST WANTED TO DO IT REALLY BAD.
SO OF COURSE. LIKE...
I DIDN'T STOP.
AND I WAS, LIKE,
OH!
LIKE, I JUST HAMMERED HIM IN THE NOSE!
Y'KNOW?
HA!
AND THE WORST PART OF IT WAS IS THAT I THOUGHT IT WAS REALLY FUNNY.
I COULDN'T STOP LAUGHING.
I WAS RUNNING AROUND THE YARD LAUGHING ABOUT IT.
PROBABLY FOR THIRTY MINUTES.
HIS NOSE WAS BLEEDING.
IT WAS BULGIN' UP.
OH!
DID YOU KNOW YOU WERE GOING TO DO IT?
OH YEAH! I JUST...
I JUST...
I DID IT.
I DON'T KNOW.
I WAS JUST LIKE...
I JUST WANTED TO DO IT.
I WASN'T MAD AT HIM OR ANYTHING, I JUST...
I DID IT.

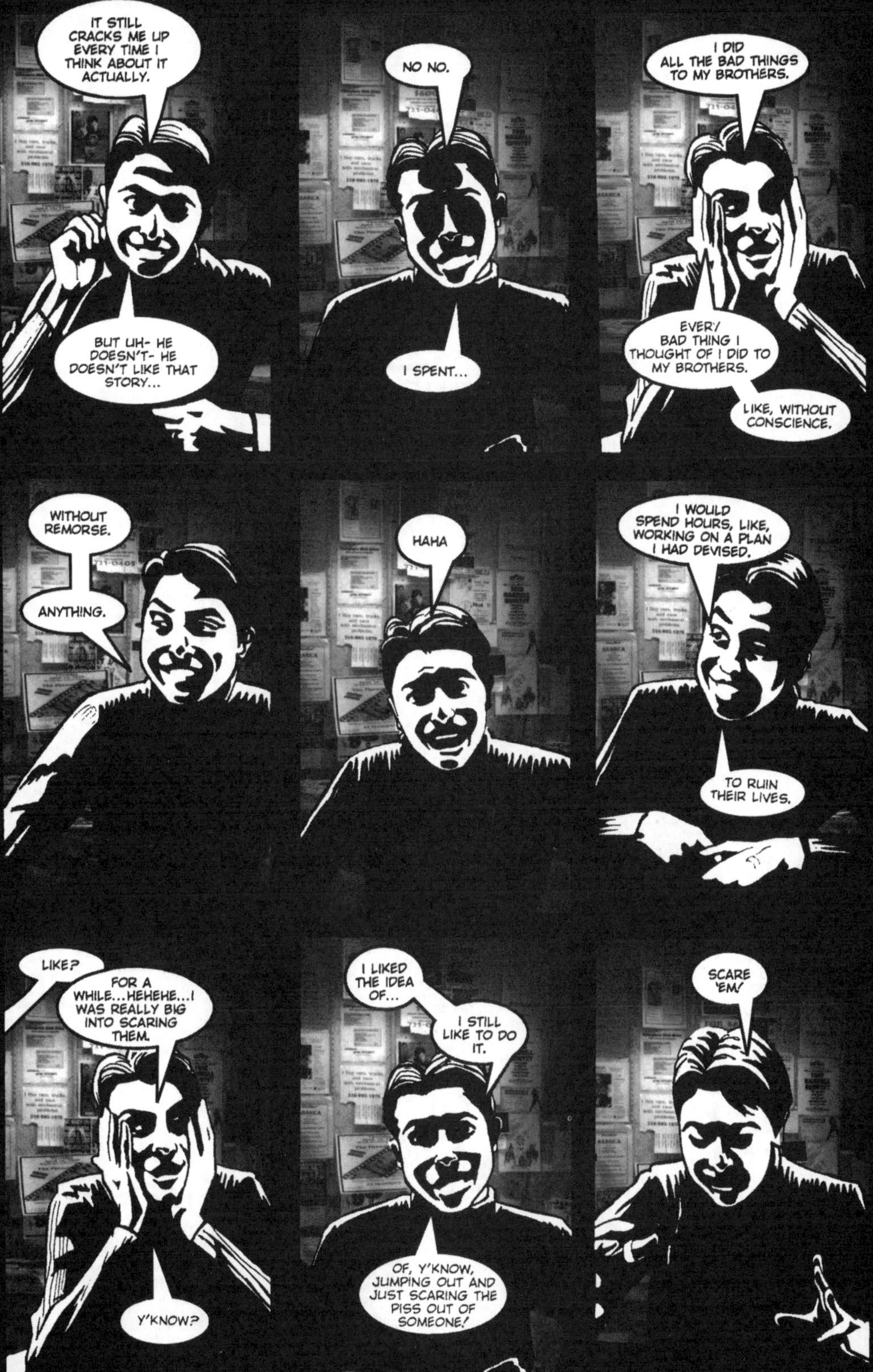
IT STILL CRACKS ME UP EVERY TIME I THINK ABOUT IT ACTUALLY.
BUT UH- HE DOESN'T- HE DOESN'T LIKE THAT STORY...
NO NO.
I SPENT...
I DID ALL THE BAD THINGS TO MY BROTHERS.
EVERY BAD THING I THOUGHT OF I DID TO MY BROTHERS.
LIKE, WITHOUT CONSCIENCE.
WITHOUT REMORSE.
ANYTHING.
HAHA
I WOULD SPEND HOURS, LIKE, WORKING ON A PLAN I HAD DEVISED.
TO RUIN THEIR LIVES.
LIKE?
FOR A WHILE...HEHEHE...I WAS REALLY BIG INTO SCARING THEM.
Y'KNOW?
I LIKED THE IDEA OF...
I STILL LIKE TO DO IT.
OF, Y'KNOW, JUMPING OUT AND JUST SCARING THE PISS OUT OF SOMEONE!
SCARE 'EM!

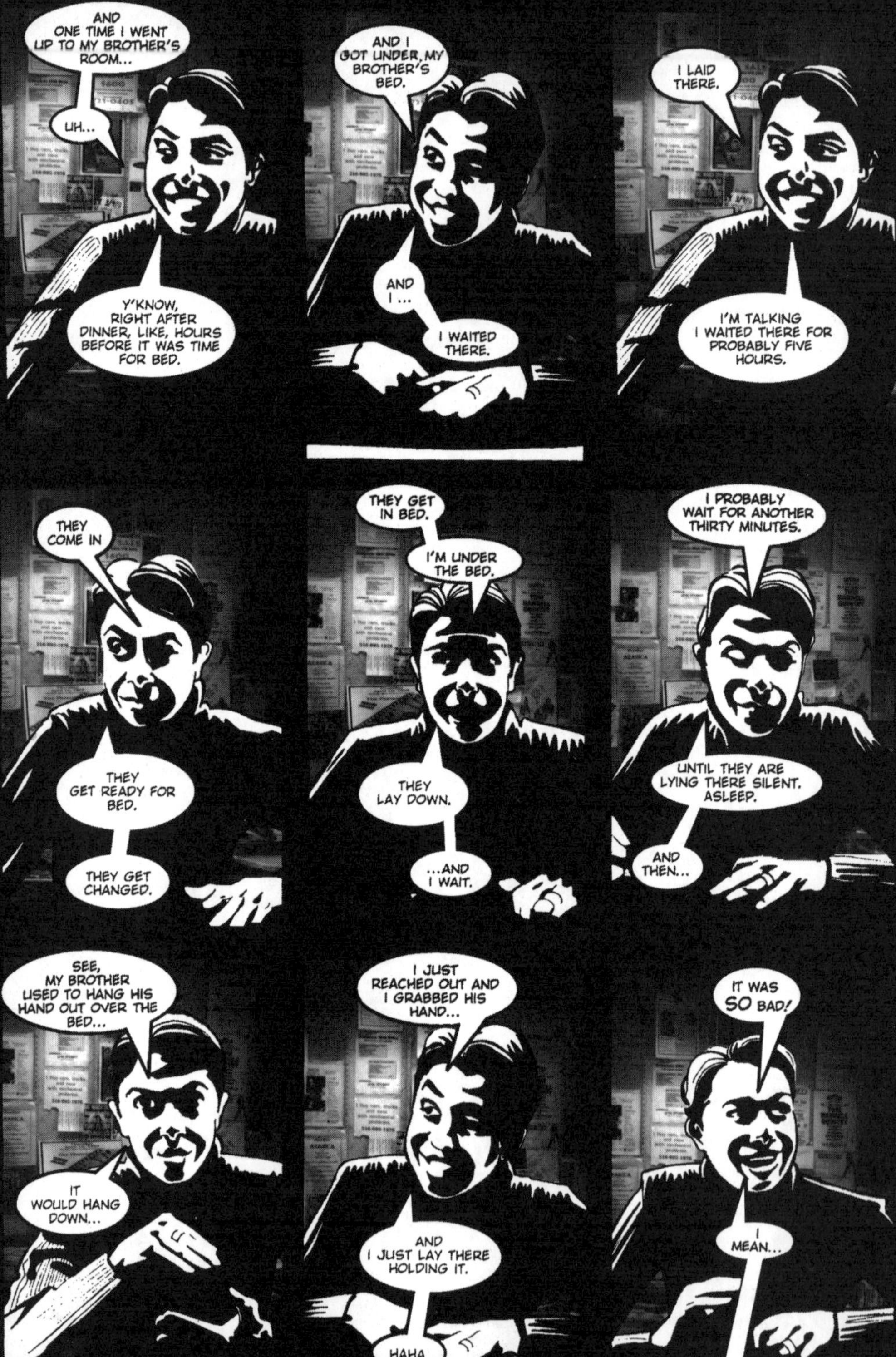
AND ONE TIME I WENT UP TO MY BROTHER'S ROOM...
UH...
Y'KNOW, RIGHT AFTER DINNER, LIKE, HOURS BEFORE IT WAS TIME FOR BED.
AND I GOT UNDER MY BROTHER'S BED.
AND I ...
I WAITED THERE.
I LAID THERE.
I'M TALKING I WAITED THERE FOR PROBABLY FIVE HOURS.
THEY COME IN
THEY GET READY FOR BED.
THEY GET CHANGED.
THEY GET IN BED.
I'M UNDER THE BED.
THEY LAY DOWN.
...AND I WAIT.
I PROBABLY WAIT FOR ANOTHER THIRTY MINUTES.
UNTIL THEY ARE LYING THERE SILENT. ASLEEP.
AND THEN...
SEE, MY BROTHER USED TO HANG HIS HAND OUT OVER THE BED...
IT WOULD HANG DOWN...
I JUST REACHED OUT AND I GRABBED HIS HAND...
AND I JUST LAY THERE HOLDING IT.
HAHA
IT WAS SO BAD!
I MEAN...
IT WAS REALLY INTERESTING THOUGH...

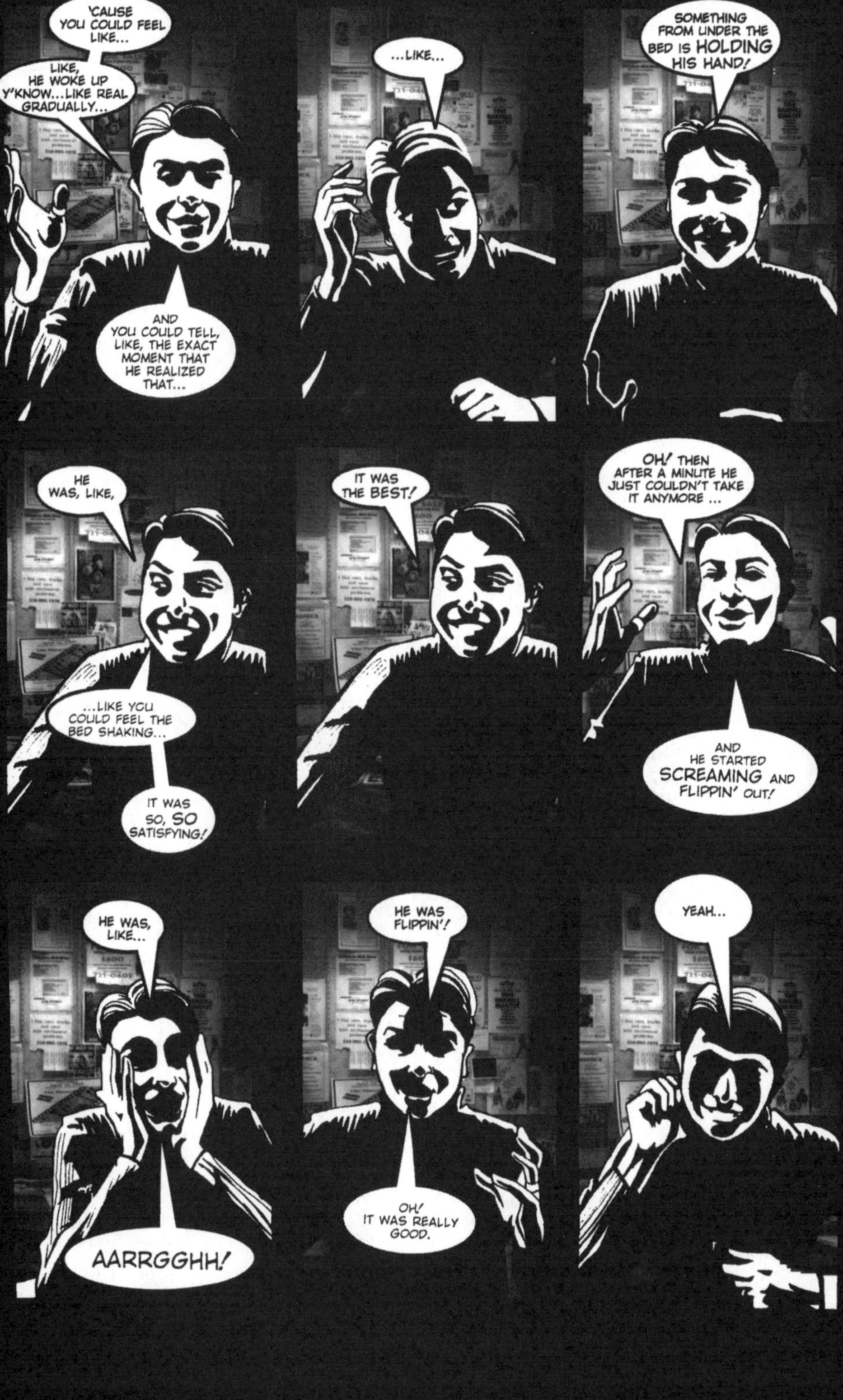
'CAUSE YOU COULD FEEL LIKE...
LIKE, HE WOKE UP Y'KNOW...LIKE REAL GRADUALLY...
AND YOU COULD TELL, LIKE, THE EXACT MOMENT THAT HE REALIZED THAT...
...LIKE...
SOMETHING FROM UNDER THE BED IS HOLDING HIS HAND!
HE WAS, LIKE,
...LIKE YOU COULD FEEL THE BED SHAKING...
IT WAS SO, SO SATISFYING!
IT WAS THE BEST!
OH! THEN AFTER A MINUTE HE JUST COULDN'T TAKE IT ANYMORE ...
AND HE STARTED SCREAMING AND FLIPPIN' OUT!
HE WAS, LIKE...
AARRGGHH!
HE WAS FLIPPIN'!
OH! IT WAS REALLY GOOD.
YEAH...

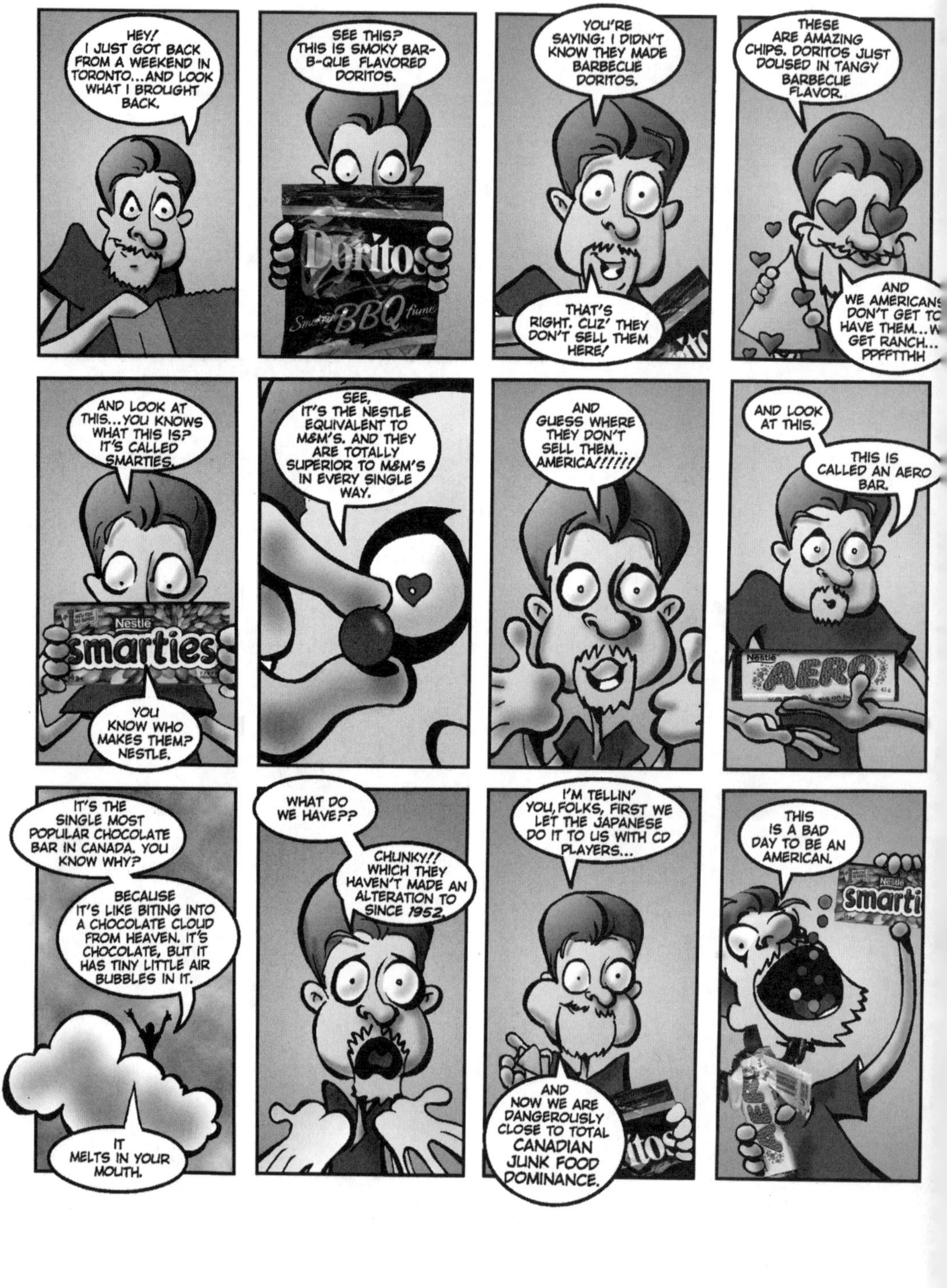
HEY! I JUST GOT BACK FROM A WEEKEND IN TORONTO...AND LOOK WHAT I BROUGHT BACK.
SEE THIS? THIS IS SMOKY BAR-B-QUE FLAVORED DORITOS.
Doritos
BBQ
YOU'RE SAYING: I DIDN'T KNOW THEY MADE BARBECUE DORITOS.
THAT'S RIGHT. CUZ' THEY DON'T SELL THEM HERE!
THESE ARE AMAZING CHIPS. DORITOS JUST DOUSED IN TANGY BARBECUE FLAVOR.
AND WE AMERICANS DON'T GET TO HAVE THEM...W GET RANCH... PPFFTTHH
AND LOOK AT THIS...YOU KNOWS WHAT THIS IS? IT'S CALLED SMARTIES.
Nestlé smarties
YOU KNOW WHO MAKES THEM? NESTLE.
SEE, IT'S THE NESTLE EQUIVALENT TO M&M'S. AND THEY ARE TOTALLY SUPERIOR TO M&M'S IN EVERY SINGLE WAY.
AND GUESS WHERE THEY DON'T SELL THEM... AMERICA!!!!!!
AND LOOK AT THIS.
THIS IS CALLED AN AERO BAR.
Nestlé AERO
IT'S THE SINGLE MOST POPULAR CHOCOLATE BAR IN CANADA. YOU KNOW WHY?
BECAUSE IT'S LIKE BITING INTO A CHOCOLATE CLOUD FROM HEAVEN. IT'S CHOCOLATE, BUT IT HAS TINY LITTLE AIR BUBBLES IN IT.
IT MELTS IN YOUR MOUTH.
WHAT DO WE HAVE??
CHUNKY!! WHICH THEY HAVEN'T MADE AN ALTERATION TO SINCE 1952.
I'M TELLIN' YOU, FOLKS, FIRST WE LET THE JAPANESE DO IT TO US WITH CD PLAYERS...
AND NOW WE ARE DANGEROUSLY CLOSE TO TOTAL CANADIAN JUNK FOOD DOMINANCE.
THIS IS A BAD DAY TO BE AN AMERICAN.

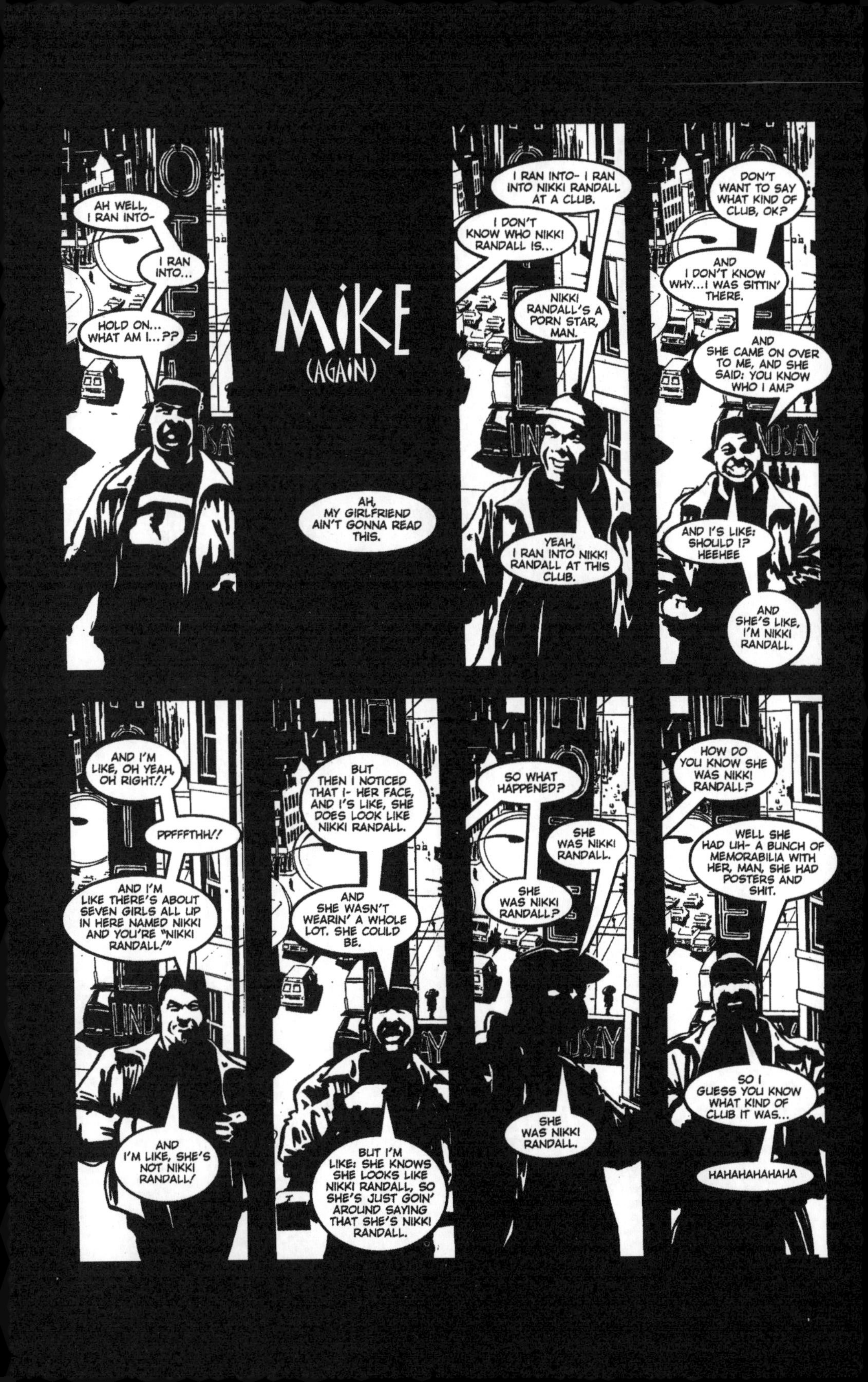
AH WELL, I RAN INTO-
I RAN INTO...
HOLD ON... WHAT AM I...??
MiKE (AGAiN)
AH, MY GIRLFRIEND AIN'T GONNA READ THIS.
I RAN INTO- I RAN INTO NIKKI RANDALL AT A CLUB.
I DON'T KNOW WHO NIKKI RANDALL IS...
NIKKI RANDALL'S A PORN STAR, MAN.
YEAH, I RAN INTO NIKKI RANDALL AT THIS CLUB.
DON'T WANT TO SAY WHAT KIND OF CLUB, OK?
AND I DON'T KNOW WHY...I WAS SITTIN' THERE.
AND SHE CAME ON OVER TO ME, AND SHE SAID: YOU KNOW WHO I AM?
AND I'S LIKE: SHOULD I? HEEHEE
AND SHE'S LIKE, I'M NIKKI RANDALL.
AND I'M LIKE, OH YEAH, OH RIGHT!!
PPFFFTHH!!
AND I'M LIKE THERE'S ABOUT SEVEN GIRLS ALL UP IN HERE NAMED NIKKI AND YOU'RE "NIKKI RANDALL!"
AND I'M LIKE, SHE'S NOT NIKKI RANDALL!
BUT THEN I NOTICED THAT I- HER FACE, AND I'S LIKE, SHE DOES LOOK LIKE NIKKI RANDALL.
AND SHE WASN'T WEARIN' A WHOLE LOT. SHE COULD BE.
BUT I'M LIKE: SHE KNOWS SHE LOOKS LIKE NIKKI RANDALL, SO SHE'S JUST GOIN' AROUND SAYING THAT SHE'S NIKKI RANDALL.
SO WHAT HAPPENED?
SHE WAS NIKKI RANDALL.
SHE WAS NIKKI RANDALL?
SHE WAS NIKKI RANDALL.
HOW DO YOU KNOW SHE WAS NIKKI RANDALL?
WELL SHE HAD UH- A BUNCH OF MEMORABILIA WITH HER, MAN, SHE HAD POSTERS AND SHIT.
SO I GUESS YOU KNOW WHAT KIND OF CLUB IT WAS...
HAHAHAHAHAHA

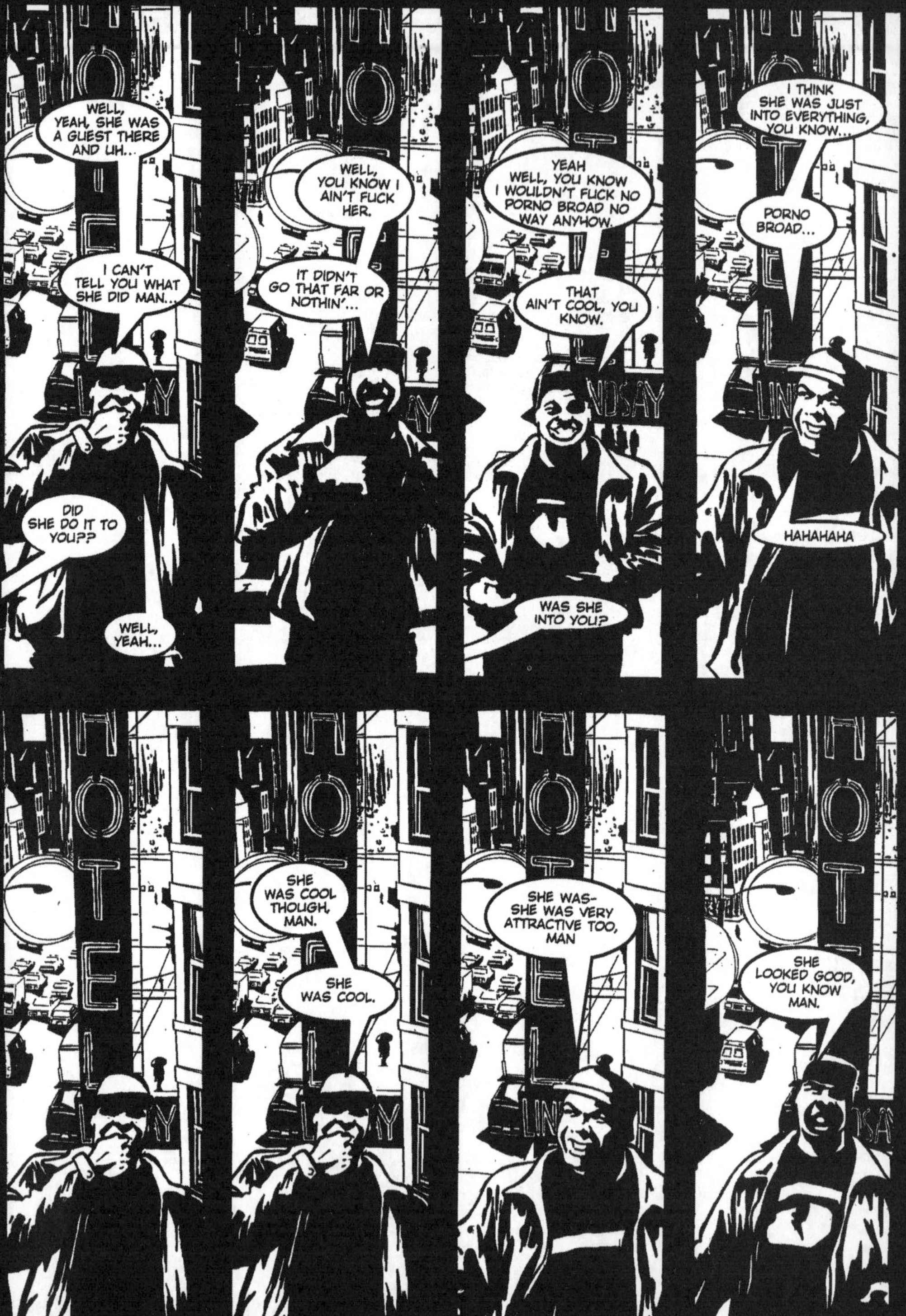
WELL, YEAH, SHE WAS A GUEST THERE AND UH...
I CAN'T TELL YOU WHAT SHE DID MAN...
DID SHE DO IT TO YOU??
WELL, YEAH...
WELL, YOU KNOW I AIN'T FUCK HER.
IT DIDN'T GO THAT FAR OR NOTHIN'...
YEAH WELL, YOU KNOW I WOULDN'T FUCK NO PORNO BROAD NO WAY ANYHOW.
THAT AIN'T COOL, YOU KNOW.
WAS SHE INTO YOU?
I THINK SHE WAS JUST INTO EVERYTHING, YOU KNOW...
PORNO BROAD...
HAHAHAHA
SHE WAS COOL THOUGH, MAN.
SHE WAS COOL.
SHE WAS- SHE WAS VERY ATTRACTIVE TOO, MAN
SHE LOOKED GOOD, YOU KNOW MAN.

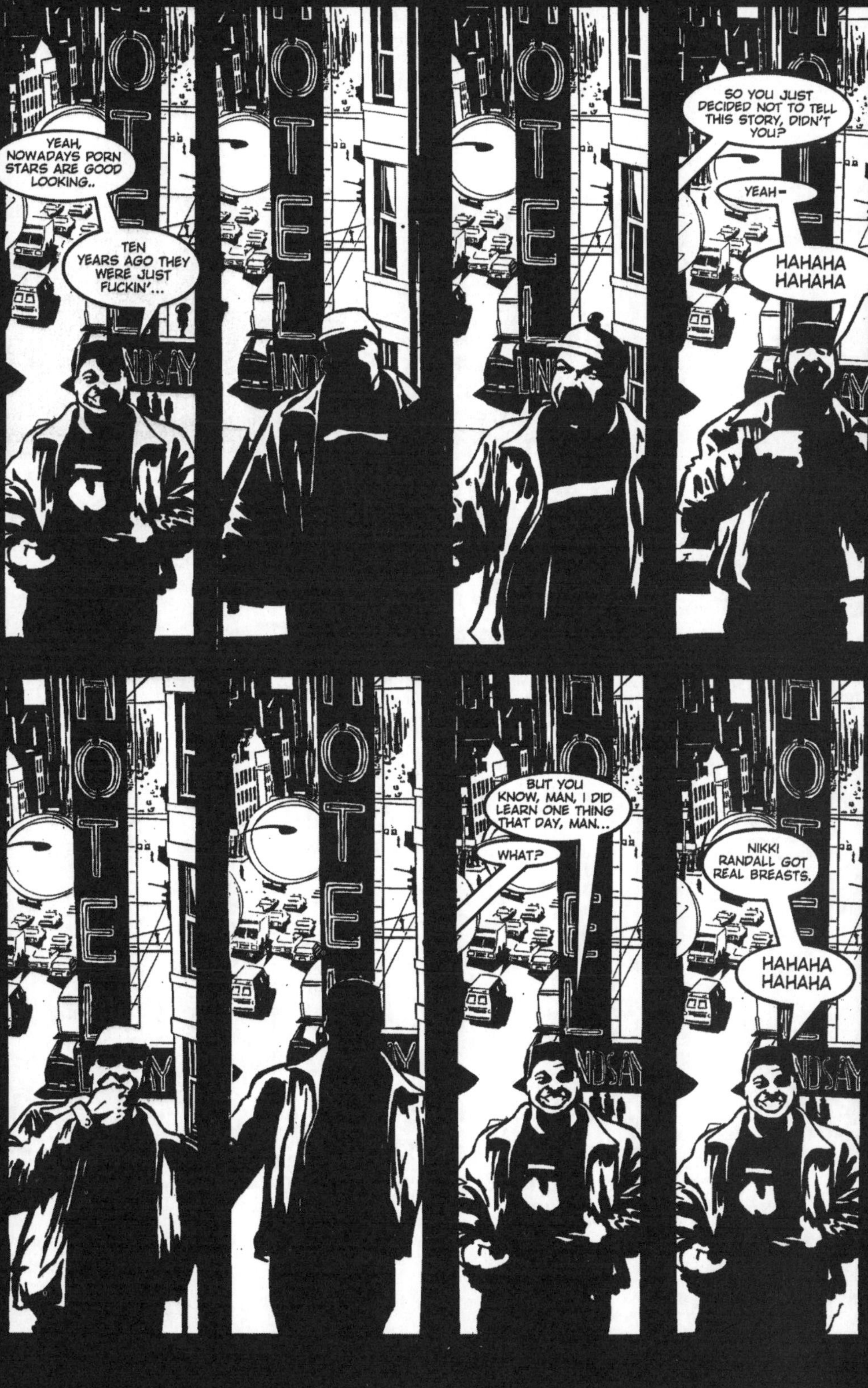
YEAH, NOWADAYS PORN STARS ARE GOOD LOOKING..
TEN YEARS AGO THEY WERE JUST FUCKIN'...
SO YOU JUST DECIDED NOT TO TELL THIS STORY, DIDN'T YOU?
YEAH-
HAHAHA HAHAHA
BUT YOU KNOW, MAN, I DID LEARN ONE THING THAT DAY, MAN...
WHAT?
NIKKI RANDALL GOT REAL BREASTS.
HAHAHA HAHAHA

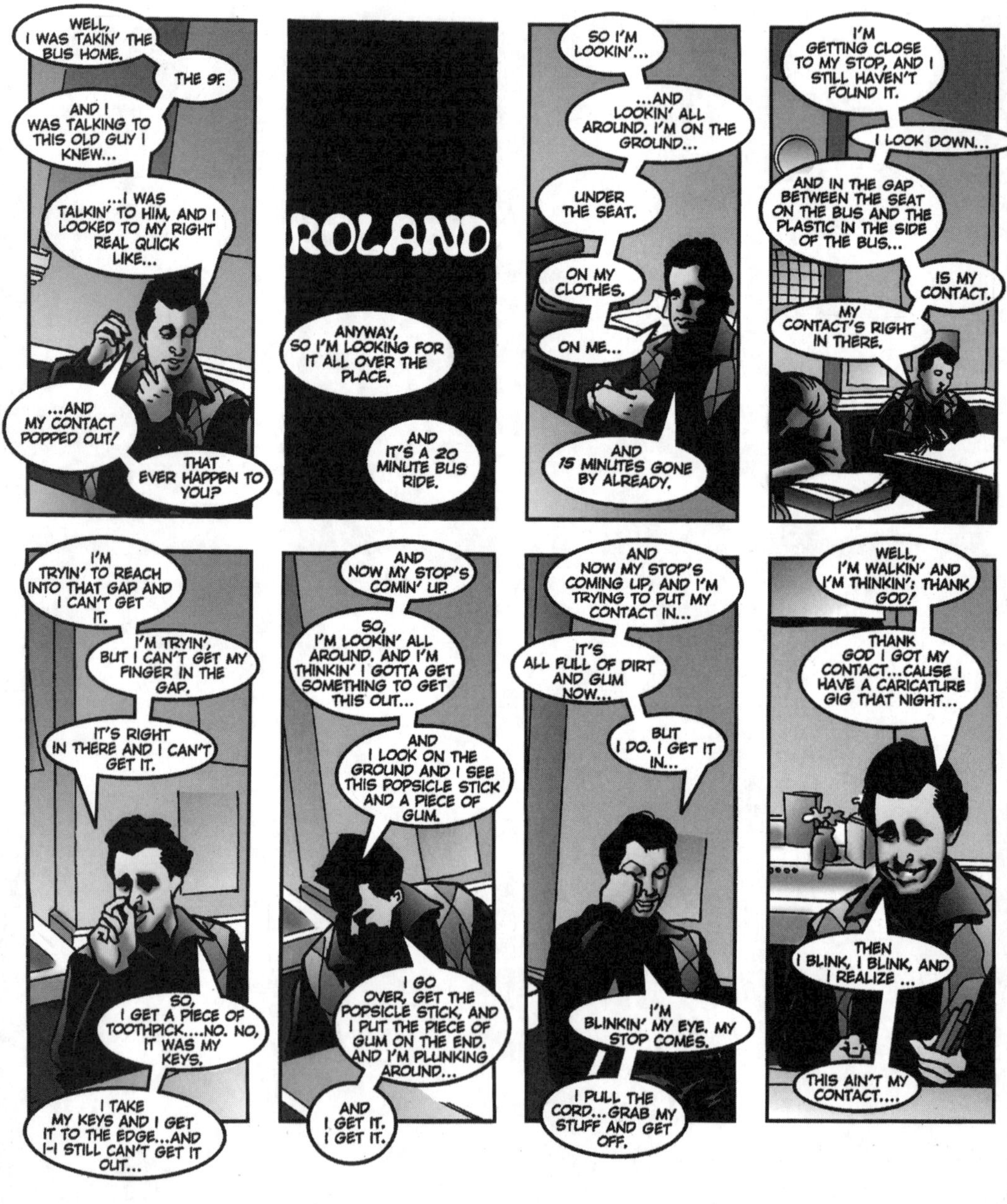
WELL, I WAS TAKIN' THE BUS HOME.
THE 9F.
AND I WAS TALKING TO THIS OLD GUY I KNEW...
...I WAS TALKIN' TO HIM, AND I LOOKED TO MY RIGHT REAL QUICK LIKE...
...AND MY CONTACT POPPED OUT!
THAT EVER HAPPEN TO YOU?
ROLAND
ANYWAY, SO I'M LOOKING FOR IT ALL OVER THE PLACE.
AND IT'S A 20 MINUTE BUS RIDE.
SO I'M LOOKIN'...
...AND LOOKIN' ALL AROUND. I'M ON THE GROUND...
UNDER THE SEAT.
ON MY CLOTHES.
ON ME...
AND 15 MINUTES GONE BY ALREADY.
I'M GETTING CLOSE TO MY STOP, AND I STILL HAVEN'T FOUND IT.
I LOOK DOWN...
AND IN THE GAP BETWEEN THE SEAT ON THE BUS AND THE PLASTIC IN THE SIDE OF THE BUS...
IS MY CONTACT.
MY CONTACT'S RIGHT IN THERE.
I'M TRYIN' TO REACH INTO THAT GAP AND I CAN'T GET IT.
I'M TRYIN', BUT I CAN'T GET MY FINGER IN THE GAP.
IT'S RIGHT IN THERE AND I CAN'T GET IT.
SO, I GET A PIECE OF TOOTHPICK....NO. NO, IT WAS MY KEYS.
I TAKE MY KEYS AND I GET IT TO THE EDGE...AND I-I STILL CAN'T GET IT OUT...
AND NOW MY STOP'S COMIN' UP.
SO, I'M LOOKIN' ALL AROUND. AND I'M THINKIN' I GOTTA GET SOMETHING TO GET THIS OUT...
AND I LOOK ON THE GROUND AND I SEE THIS POPSICLE STICK AND A PIECE OF GUM.
I GO OVER, GET THE POPSICLE STICK, AND I PUT THE PIECE OF GUM ON THE END. AND I'M PLUNKING AROUND...
AND I GET IT. I GET IT.
AND NOW MY STOP'S COMING UP, AND I'M TRYING TO PUT MY CONTACT IN...
IT'S ALL FULL OF DIRT AND GUM NOW...
BUT I DO. I GET IT IN...
I'M BLINKIN' MY EYE. MY STOP COMES.
I PULL THE CORD...GRAB MY STUFF AND GET OFF.
WELL, I'M WALKIN' AND I'M THINKIN': THANK GOD!
THANK GOD I GOT MY CONTACT...CAUSE I HAVE A CARICATURE GIG THAT NIGHT...
THEN I BLINK, I BLINK, AND I REALIZE ...
THIS AIN'T MY CONTACT....

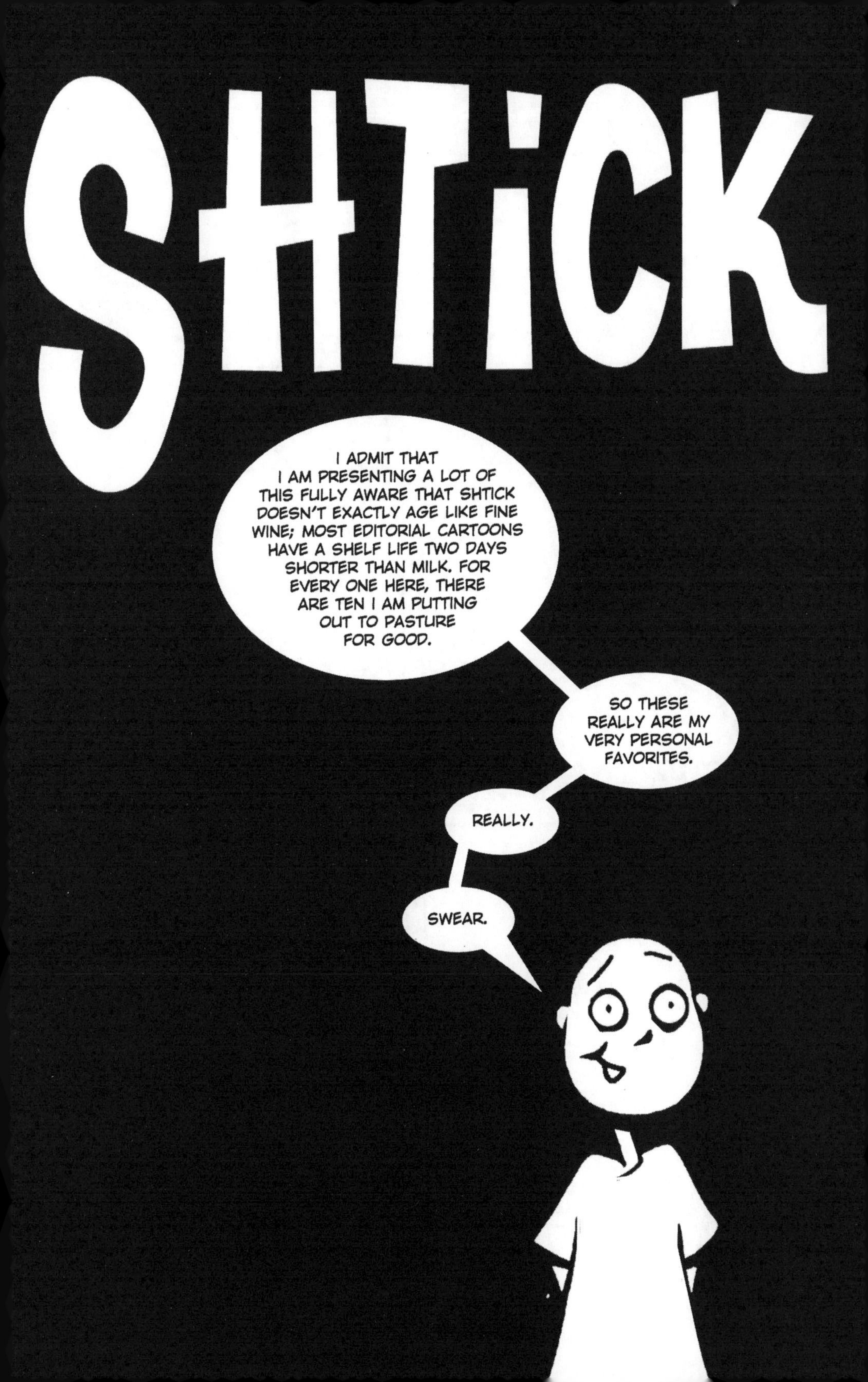
SHTICK
I ADMIT THAT I AM PRESENTING A LOT OF THIS FULLY AWARE THAT SHTICK DOESN'T EXACTLY AGE LIKE FINE WINE; MOST EDITORIAL CARTOONS HAVE A SHELF LIFE TWO DAYS SHORTER THAN MILK. FOR EVERY ONE HERE, THERE ARE TEN I AM PUTTING OUT TO PASTURE FOR GOOD.
SO THESE REALLY ARE MY VERY PERSONAL FAVORITES.
REALLY.
SWEAR.

# THINGS THAT ALWAYS FUCKING BOTHERED ME ABOUT THE

# SUNDAY FUNNIES

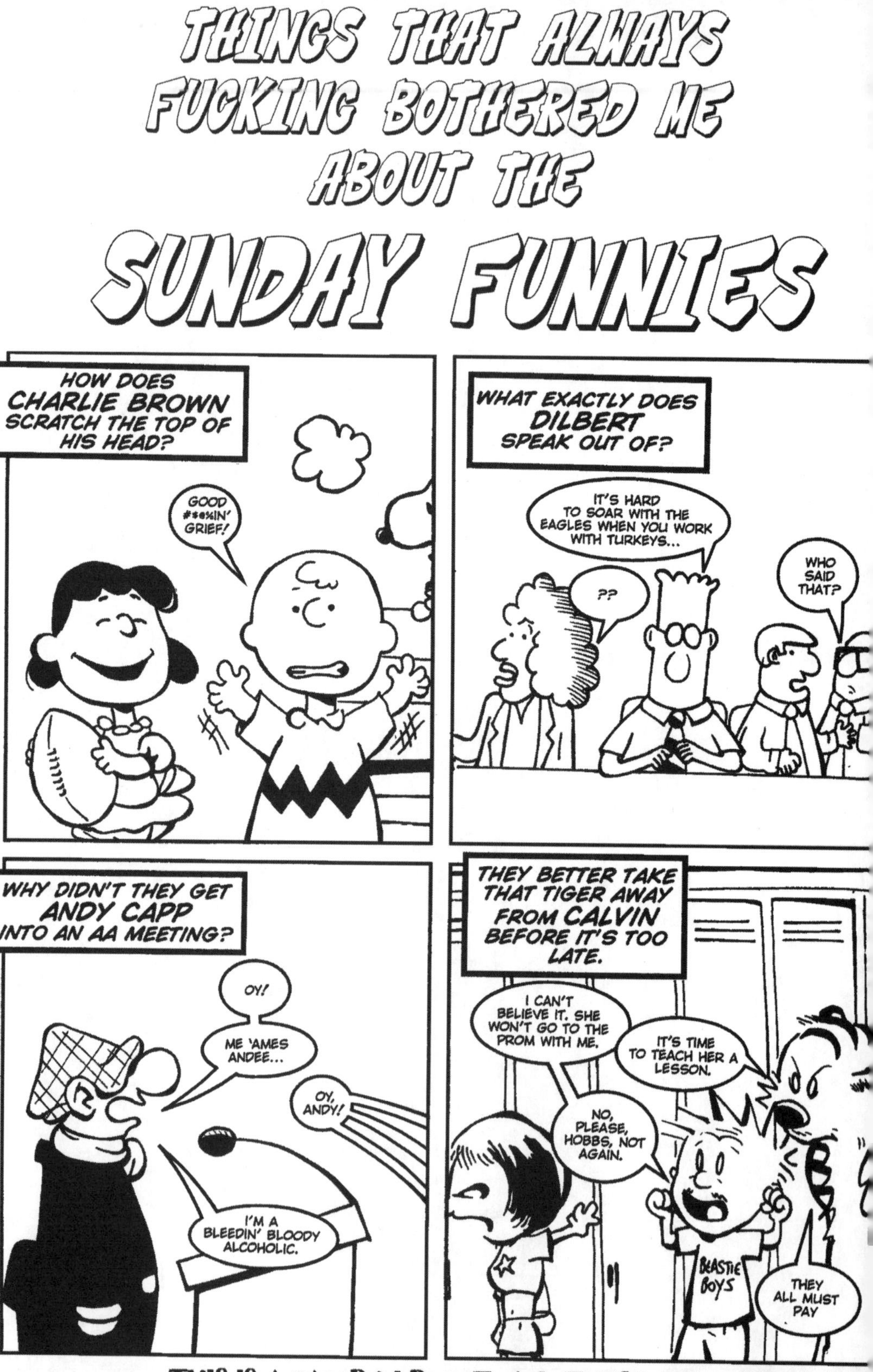
HOW DOES CHARLIE BROWN SCRATCH THE TOP OF HIS HEAD?
GOOD #$@%IN' GRIEF!
WHAT EXACTLY DOES DILBERT SPEAK OUT OF?
IT'S HARD TO SOAR WITH THE EAGLES WHEN YOU WORK WITH TURKEYS...
??
WHO SAID THAT?
WHY DIDN'T THEY GET ANDY CAPP INTO AN AA MEETING?
OY!
ME 'AMES ANDEE...
OY, ANDY!
I'M A BLEEDIN' BLOODY ALCOHOLIC.
THEY BETTER TAKE THAT TIGER AWAY FROM CALVIN BEFORE IT'S TOO LATE.
I CAN'T BELIEVE IT. SHE WON'T GO TO THE PROM WITH ME.
IT'S TIME TO TEACH HER A LESSON.
NO, PLEASE, HOBBS, NOT AGAIN.
BEASTIE BOYS
THEY ALL MUST PAY

THIS IS A PARODY. I DO NOT OWN THESE CHARACTERS..DUH

# ACTUAL CONVERSATIONS OVERHEARD AT THE LOCAL ARTHOUSE MOVIE THEATRE

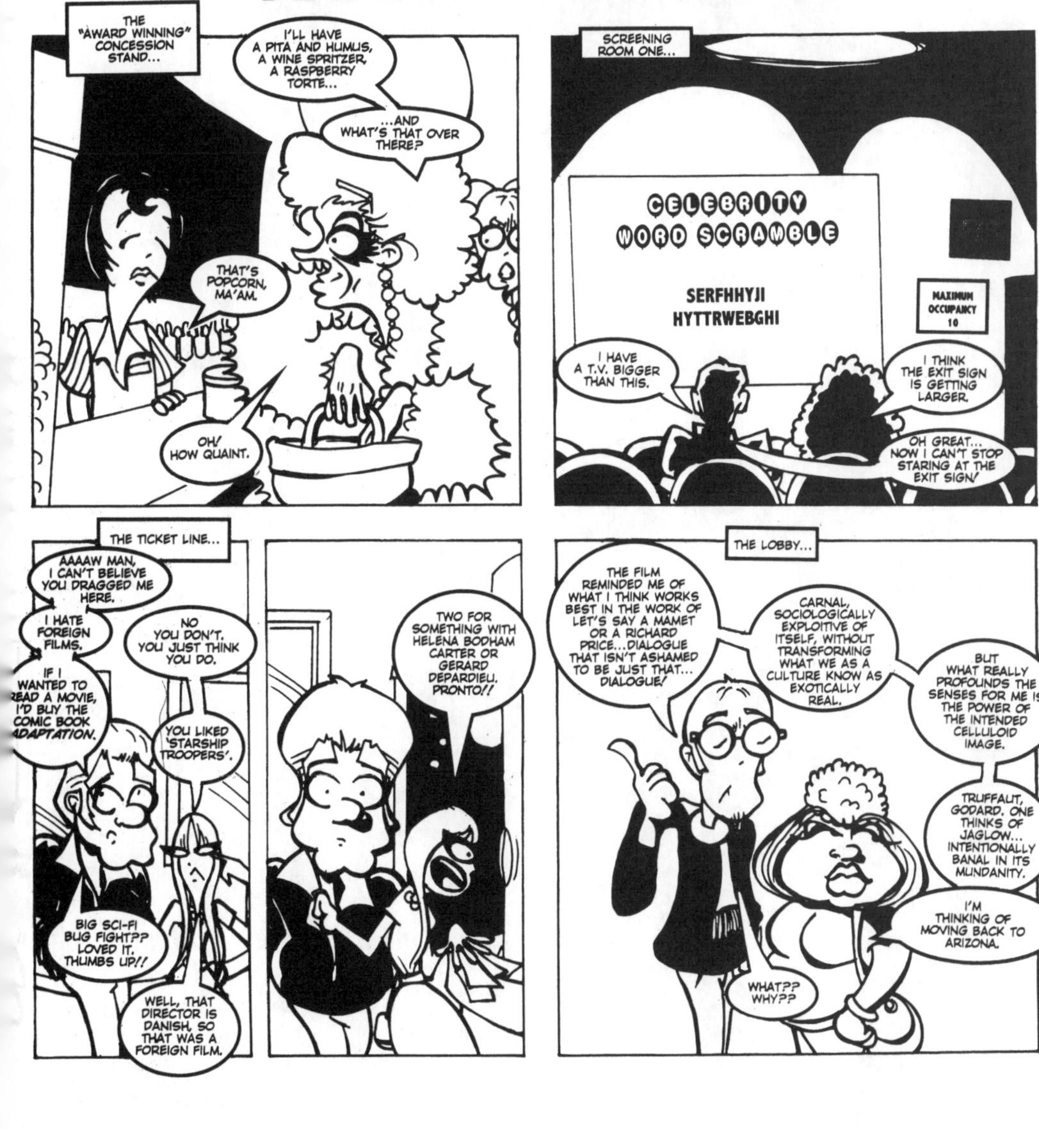
THE "AWARD WINNING" CONCESSION STAND...
I'LL HAVE A PITA AND HUMUS, A WINE SPRITZER, A RASPBERRY TORTE...
...AND WHAT'S THAT OVER THERE?
THAT'S POPCORN, MA'AM.
OH! HOW QUAINT.
SCREENING ROOM ONE...
CELEBRITY WORD SCRAMBLE
SERFHHYJI
HYTTRWEBGHI
MAXIMUM OCCUPANCY 10
I HAVE A T.V. BIGGER THAN THIS.
I THINK THE EXIT SIGN IS GETTING LARGER.
OH GREAT... NOW I CAN'T STOP STARING AT THE EXIT SIGN!
THE TICKET LINE...
AAAAW MAN, I CAN'T BELIEVE YOU DRAGGED ME HERE.
I HATE FOREIGN FILMS.
NO YOU DON'T. YOU JUST THINK YOU DO.
IF I WANTED TO READ A MOVIE, I'D BUY THE COMIC BOOK ADAPTATION.
YOU LIKED 'STARSHIP TROOPERS'.
BIG SCI-FI BUG FIGHT?? LOVED IT. THUMBS UP!!
WELL, THAT DIRECTOR IS DANISH, SO THAT WAS A FOREIGN FILM.
TWO FOR SOMETHING WITH HELENA BODHAM CARTER OR GERARD DEPARDIEU. PRONTO!!
THE LOBBY...
THE FILM REMINDED ME OF WHAT I THINK WORKS BEST IN THE WORK OF LET'S SAY A MAMET OR A RICHARD PRICE...DIALOGUE THAT ISN'T ASHAMED TO BE JUST THAT... DIALOGUE!
CARNAL, SOCIOLOGICALLY EXPLOITIVE OF ITSELF, WITHOUT TRANSFORMING WHAT WE AS A CULTURE KNOW AS EXOTICALLY REAL.
BUT WHAT REALLY PROFOUNDS THE SENSES FOR ME IS THE POWER OF THE INTENDED CELLULOID IMAGE.
TRUFFAUT, GODARD. ONE THINKS OF JAGLOW... INTENTIONALLY BANAL IN ITS MUNDANITY.
I'M THINKING OF MOVING BACK TO ARIZONA.
WHAT?? WHY??

## A DAY IN THE LIFE OF...
# A HOWARD STERN FAN

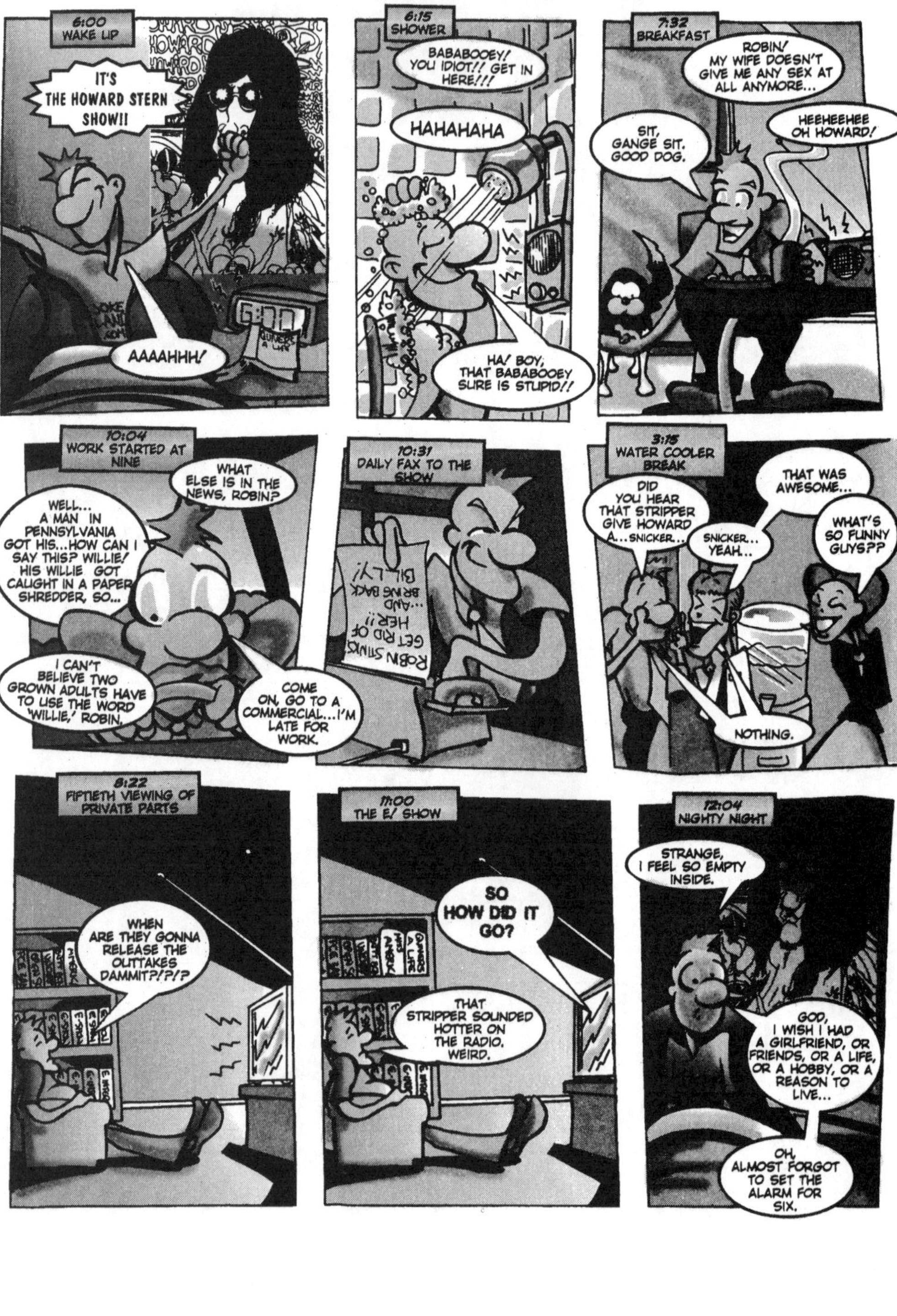

6:00 WAKE UP
IT'S THE HOWARD STERN SHOW!!
AAAAHHH!
6:15 SHOWER
BABABOOEY! YOU IDIOT!! GET IN HERE!!!
HAHAHAHA
HA! BOY, THAT BABABOOEY SURE IS STUPID!!
7:32 BREAKFAST
ROBIN! MY WIFE DOESN'T GIVE ME ANY SEX AT ALL ANYMORE...
HEEHEEHEE OH HOWARD!
SIT, GANGE SIT. GOOD DOG.
10:04 WORK STARTED AT NINE
WHAT ELSE IS IN THE NEWS, ROBIN?
WELL... A MAN IN PENNSYLVANIA GOT HIS...HOW CAN I SAY THIS? WILLIE! HIS WILLIE GOT CAUGHT IN A PAPER SHREDDER, SO...
I CAN'T BELIEVE TWO GROWN ADULTS HAVE TO USE THE WORD 'WILLIE,' ROBIN.
COME ON, GO TO A COMMERCIAL...I'M LATE FOR WORK.
10:31 DAILY FAX TO THE SHOW
ROBIN STINKS! GET RID OF HER!! ...AND BRING BACK BILLY!
3:15 WATER COOLER BREAK
DID YOU HEAR THAT STRIPPER GIVE HOWARD A...SNICKER...
SNICKER... YEAH...
THAT WAS AWESOME...
WHAT'S SO FUNNY GUYS??
NOTHING.
8:22 FIFTIETH VIEWING OF PRIVATE PARTS
WHEN ARE THEY GONNA RELEASE THE OUTTAKES DAMMIT?!?!?
11:00 THE E! SHOW
SO HOW DID IT GO?
THAT STRIPPER SOUNDED HOTTER ON THE RADIO. WEIRD.
12:04 NIGHTY NIGHT
STRANGE, I FEEL SO EMPTY INSIDE.
GOD, I WISH I HAD A GIRLFRIEND, OR FRIENDS, OR A LIFE, OR A HOBBY, OR A REASON TO LIVE...
OH, ALMOST FORGOT TO SET THE ALARM FOR SIX.

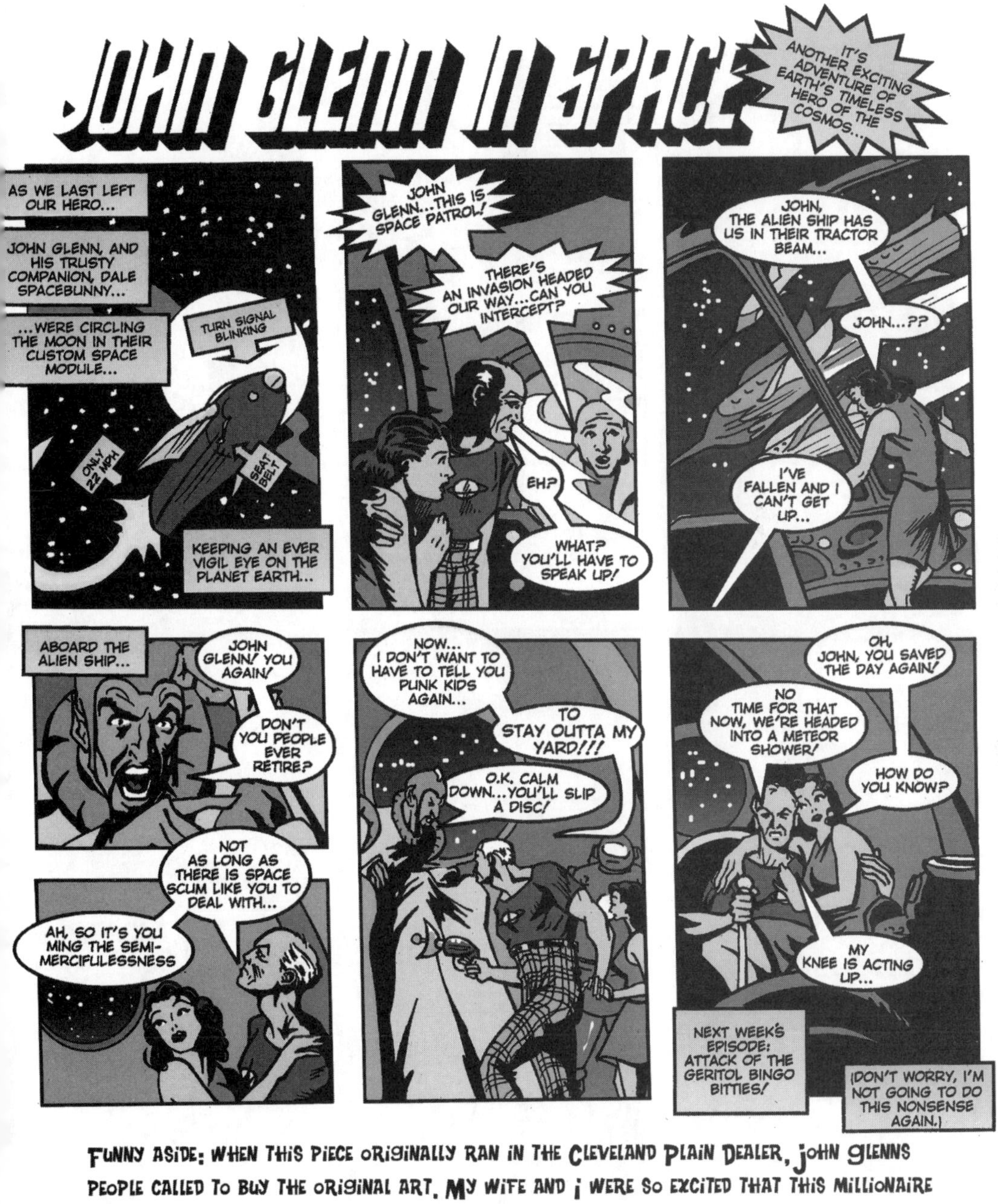
JOHN GLENN IN SPACE
IT'S ANOTHER EXCITING ADVENTURE OF EARTH'S TIMELESS HERO OF THE COSMOS...
AS WE LAST LEFT OUR HERO...
JOHN GLENN, AND HIS TRUSTY COMPANION, DALE SPACEBUNNY...
...WERE CIRCLING THE MOON IN THEIR CUSTOM SPACE MODULE...
TURN SIGNAL BLINKING
ONLY 22 MPH
SEAT BELT
KEEPING AN EVER VIGIL EYE ON THE PLANET EARTH...
JOHN GLENN...THIS IS SPACE PATROL!
THERE'S AN INVASION HEADED OUR WAY...CAN YOU INTERCEPT?
EH?
WHAT? YOU'LL HAVE TO SPEAK UP!
JOHN, THE ALIEN SHIP HAS US IN THEIR TRACTOR BEAM...
JOHN...??
I'VE FALLEN AND I CAN'T GET UP...
ABOARD THE ALIEN SHIP...
JOHN GLENN! YOU AGAIN!
DON'T YOU PEOPLE EVER RETIRE?
NOT AS LONG AS THERE IS SPACE SCUM LIKE YOU TO DEAL WITH...
AH, SO IT'S YOU MING THE SEMI-MERCIFULESSNESS
NOW... I DON'T WANT TO HAVE TO TELL YOU PUNK KIDS AGAIN...
TO STAY OUTTA MY YARD!!!
O.K. CALM DOWN...YOU'LL SLIP A DISC!
OH, JOHN, YOU SAVED THE DAY AGAIN!
NO TIME FOR THAT NOW, WE'RE HEADED INTO A METEOR SHOWER!
HOW DO YOU KNOW?
MY KNEE IS ACTING UP...
NEXT WEEK'S EPISODE: ATTACK OF THE GERITOL BINGO BITTIES!
(DON'T WORRY, I'M NOT GOING TO DO THIS NONSENSE AGAIN.)

FUNNY ASIDE: WHEN THIS PIECE ORIGINALLY RAN IN THE CLEVELAND PLAIN DEALER, JOHN GLENNS PEOPLE CALLED TO BUY THE ORIGINAL ART. MY WIFE AND I WERE SO EXCITED THAT THIS MILLIONAIRE ASTRONAUT WANTED TO BUY IT THAT WE ACTUALLY HAGGLED WITH EACH OTHER ON HOW MUCH WE THOUGHT WE COULD GET.

WE CAME BACK WITH WHAT WE THOUGHT WAS A PRICE THAT WAS HIGH BUT NOT TOO HIGH, THEY PRETTY MUCH HUNG UP ON US. OUR PRICE WAS TOO HIGH. I FELT BAD, CALLED BACK AND OFFERED JUST TO GIVE IT TO THEM, BUT THEY HUNG UP ON US AGAIN.

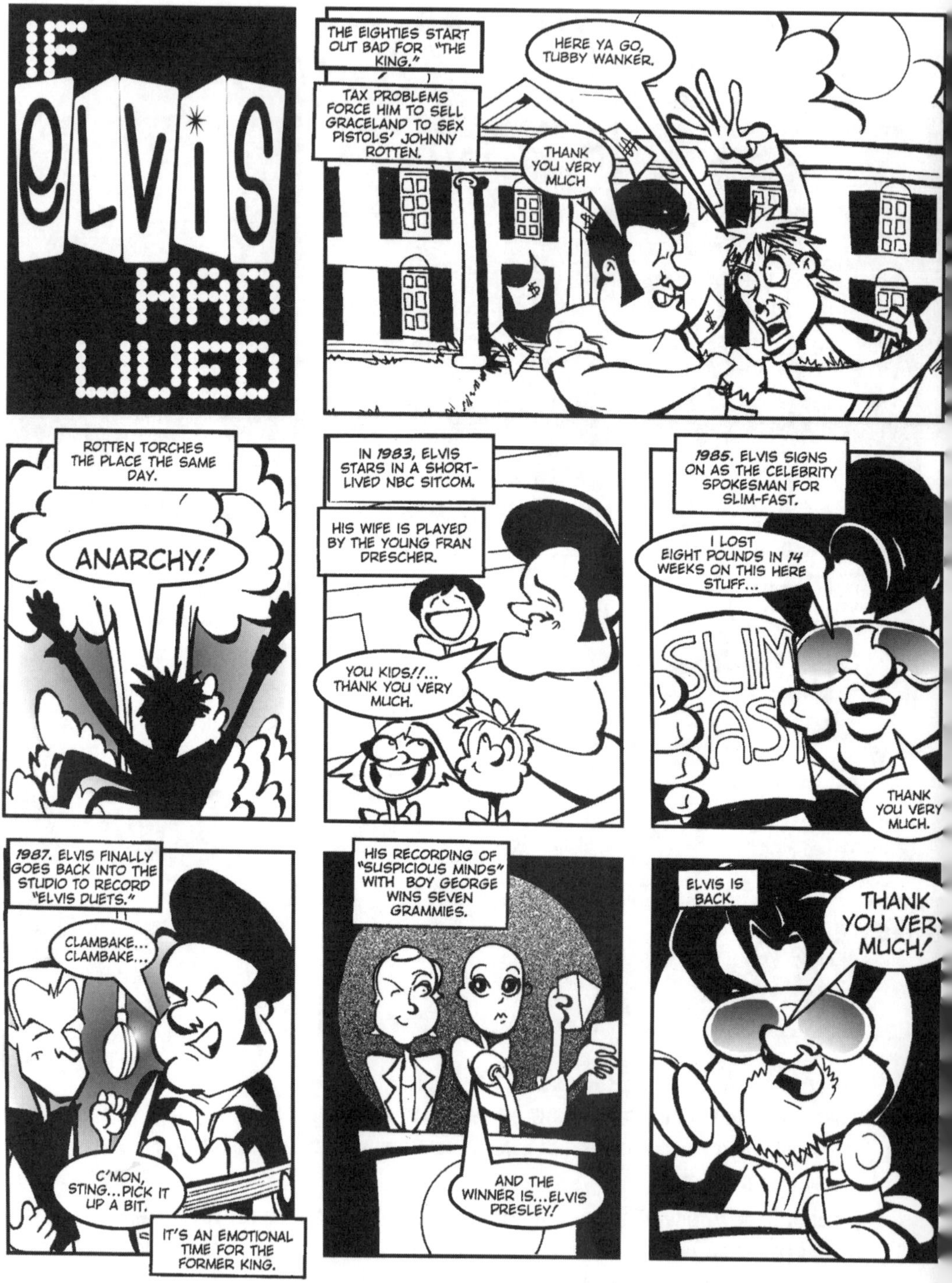
IF ELVIS HAD LIVED
THE EIGHTIES START OUT BAD FOR "THE KING."
TAX PROBLEMS FORCE HIM TO SELL GRACELAND TO SEX PISTOLS' JOHNNY ROTTEN.
HERE YA GO, TUBBY WANKER.
THANK YOU VERY MUCH
ROTTEN TORCHES THE PLACE THE SAME DAY.
ANARCHY!
IN 1983, ELVIS STARS IN A SHORT-LIVED NBC SITCOM.
HIS WIFE IS PLAYED BY THE YOUNG FRAN DRESCHER.
YOU KIDS!!... THANK YOU VERY MUCH.
1985. ELVIS SIGNS ON AS THE CELEBRITY SPOKESMAN FOR SLIM-FAST.
I LOST EIGHT POUNDS IN 14 WEEKS ON THIS HERE STUFF...
SLIM FAST
THANK YOU VERY MUCH.
1987. ELVIS FINALLY GOES BACK INTO THE STUDIO TO RECORD "ELVIS DUETS."
CLAMBAKE... CLAMBAKE...
C'MON, STING...PICK IT UP A BIT.
IT'S AN EMOTIONAL TIME FOR THE FORMER KING.
HIS RECORDING OF "SUSPICIOUS MINDS" WITH BOY GEORGE WINS SEVEN GRAMMIES.
AND THE WINNER IS...ELVIS PRESLEY!
ELVIS IS BACK.
THANK YOU VERY MUCH!

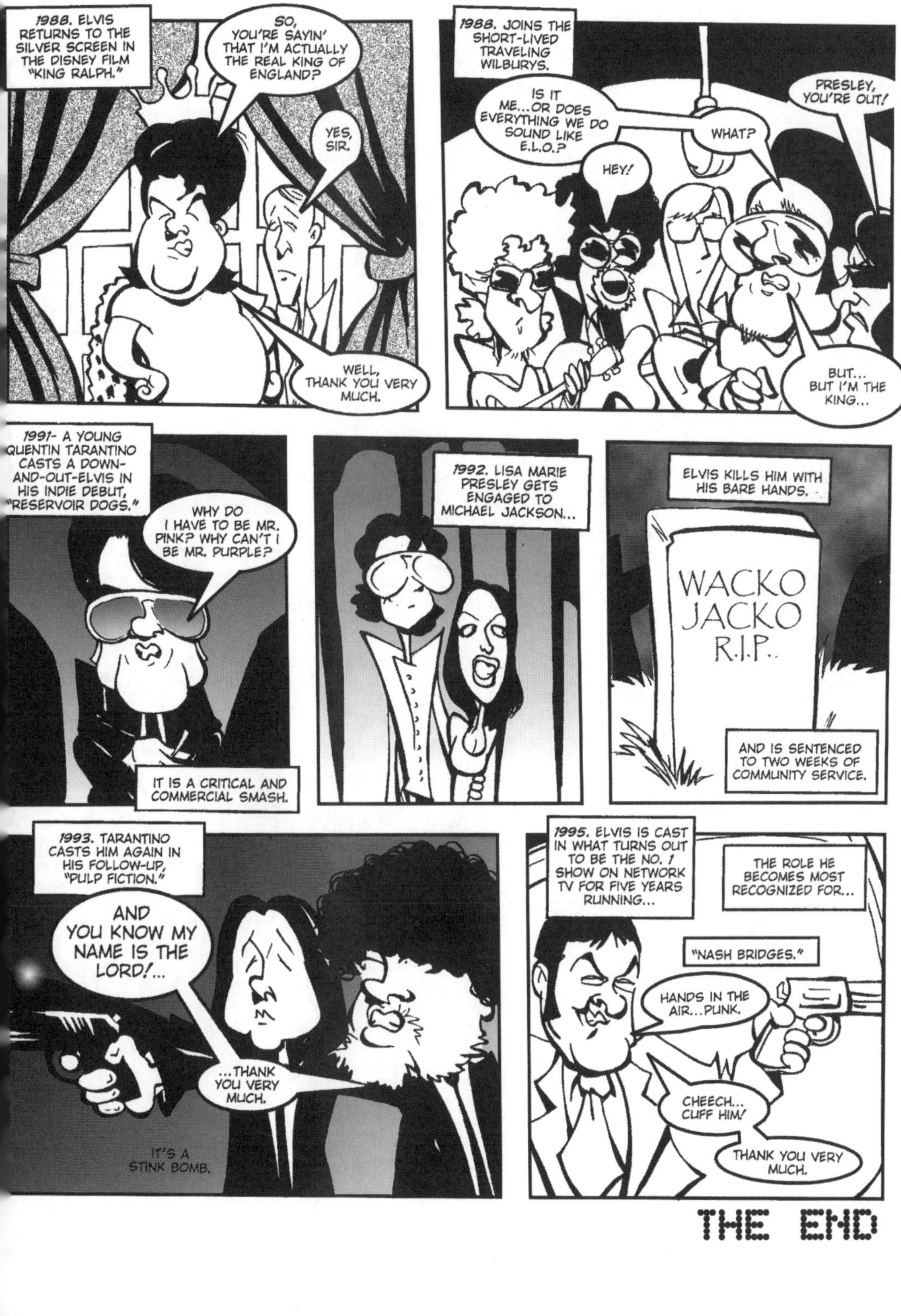
1988. ELVIS RETURNS TO THE SILVER SCREEN IN THE DISNEY FILM "KING RALPH."
SO, YOU'RE SAYIN' THAT I'M ACTUALLY THE REAL KING OF ENGLAND?
YES, SIR.
WELL, THANK YOU VERY MUCH.
1988. JOINS THE SHORT-LIVED TRAVELING WILBURYS.
IS IT ME...OR DOES EVERYTHING WE DO SOUND LIKE E.L.O.?
HEY!
WHAT?
PRESLEY, YOU'RE OUT!
BUT... BUT I'M THE KING...
1991- A YOUNG QUENTIN TARANTINO CASTS A DOWN-AND-OUT-ELVIS IN HIS INDIE DEBUT, "RESERVOIR DOGS."
WHY DO I HAVE TO BE MR. PINK? WHY CAN'T I BE MR. PURPLE?
IT IS A CRITICAL AND COMMERCIAL SMASH.
1992. LISA MARIE PRESLEY GETS ENGAGED TO MICHAEL JACKSON...
ELVIS KILLS HIM WITH HIS BARE HANDS.
WACKO JACKO R.I.P..
AND IS SENTENCED TO TWO WEEKS OF COMMUNITY SERVICE.
1993. TARANTINO CASTS HIM AGAIN IN HIS FOLLOW-UP, "PULP FICTION."
AND YOU KNOW MY NAME IS THE LORD!...
...THANK YOU VERY MUCH.
IT'S A STINK BOMB.
1995. ELVIS IS CAST IN WHAT TURNS OUT TO BE THE NO. 1 SHOW ON NETWORK TV FOR FIVE YEARS RUNNING...
THE ROLE HE BECOMES MOST RECOGNIZED FOR...
"NASH BRIDGES."
HANDS IN THE AIR...PUNK.
CHEECH... CUFF HIM!
THANK YOU VERY MUCH.

THE END

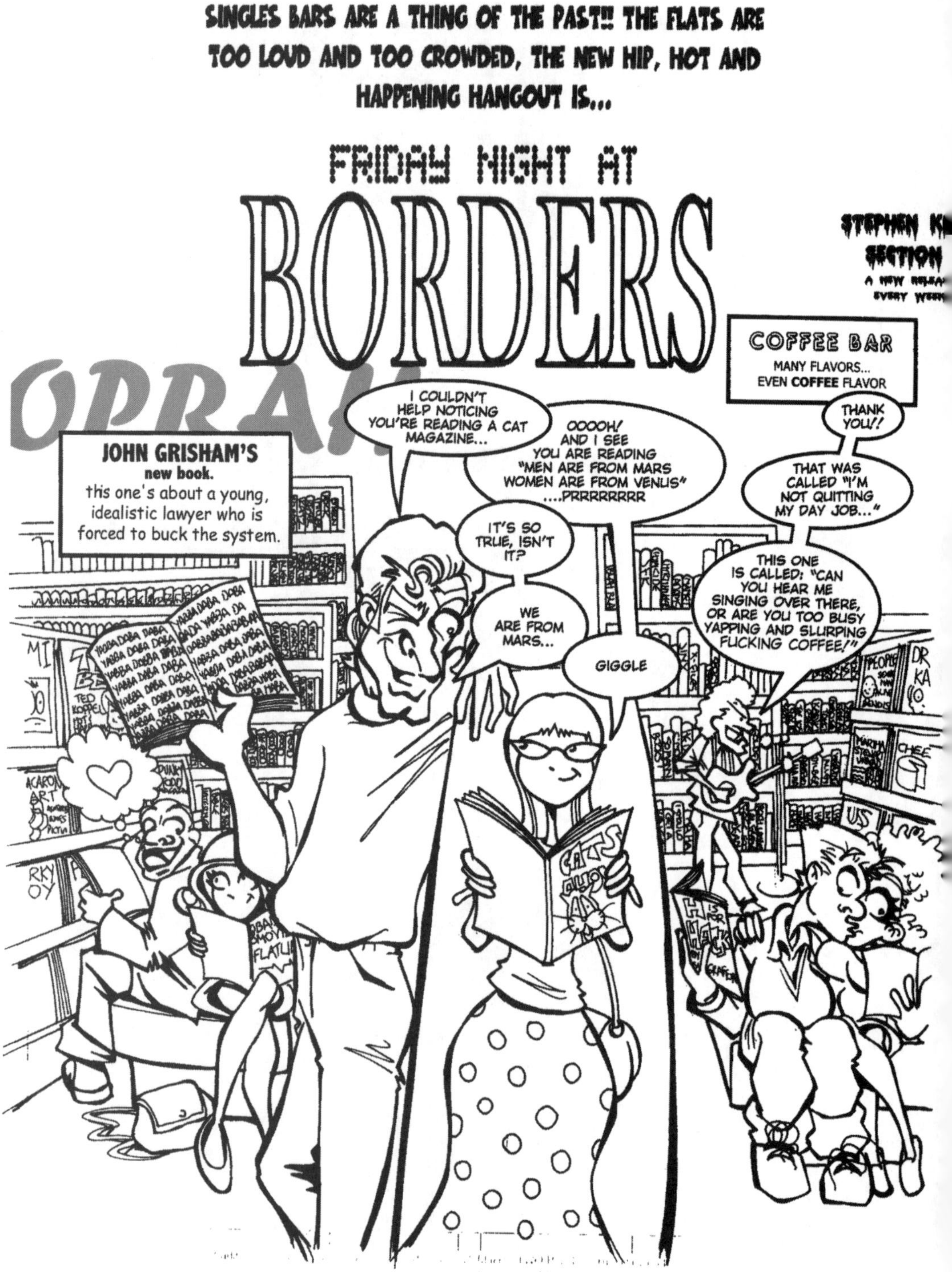
SINGLES BARS ARE A THING OF THE PAST!! THE FLATS ARE TOO LOUD AND TOO CROWDED, THE NEW HIP, HOT AND HAPPENING HANGOUT IS...
FRIDAY NIGHT AT
BORDERS
SECTION
COFFEE BAR
MANY FLAVORS... EVEN COFFEE FLAVOR
JOHN GRISHAM'S new book. this one's about a young, idealistic lawyer who is forced to buck the system.
I COULDN'T HELP NOTICING YOU'RE READING A CAT MAGAZINE...
OOOOH! AND I SEE YOU ARE READING "MEN ARE FROM MARS WOMEN ARE FROM VENUS" ....PRRRRRRRRR
IT'S SO TRUE, ISN'T IT?
WE ARE FROM MARS...
GIGGLE
THIS ONE IS CALLED: "CAN YOU HEAR ME SINGING OVER THERE, OR ARE YOU TOO BUSY YAPPING AND SLURPING FUCKING COFFEE!"
THAT WAS CALLED "I'M NOT QUITTING MY DAY JOB..."
THANK YOU!!

**Ever wonder what those local on-air news personalities are yammering on about???**

**Well, as a public service, we offer you....**

# NEWS BANTER SUBTITLES

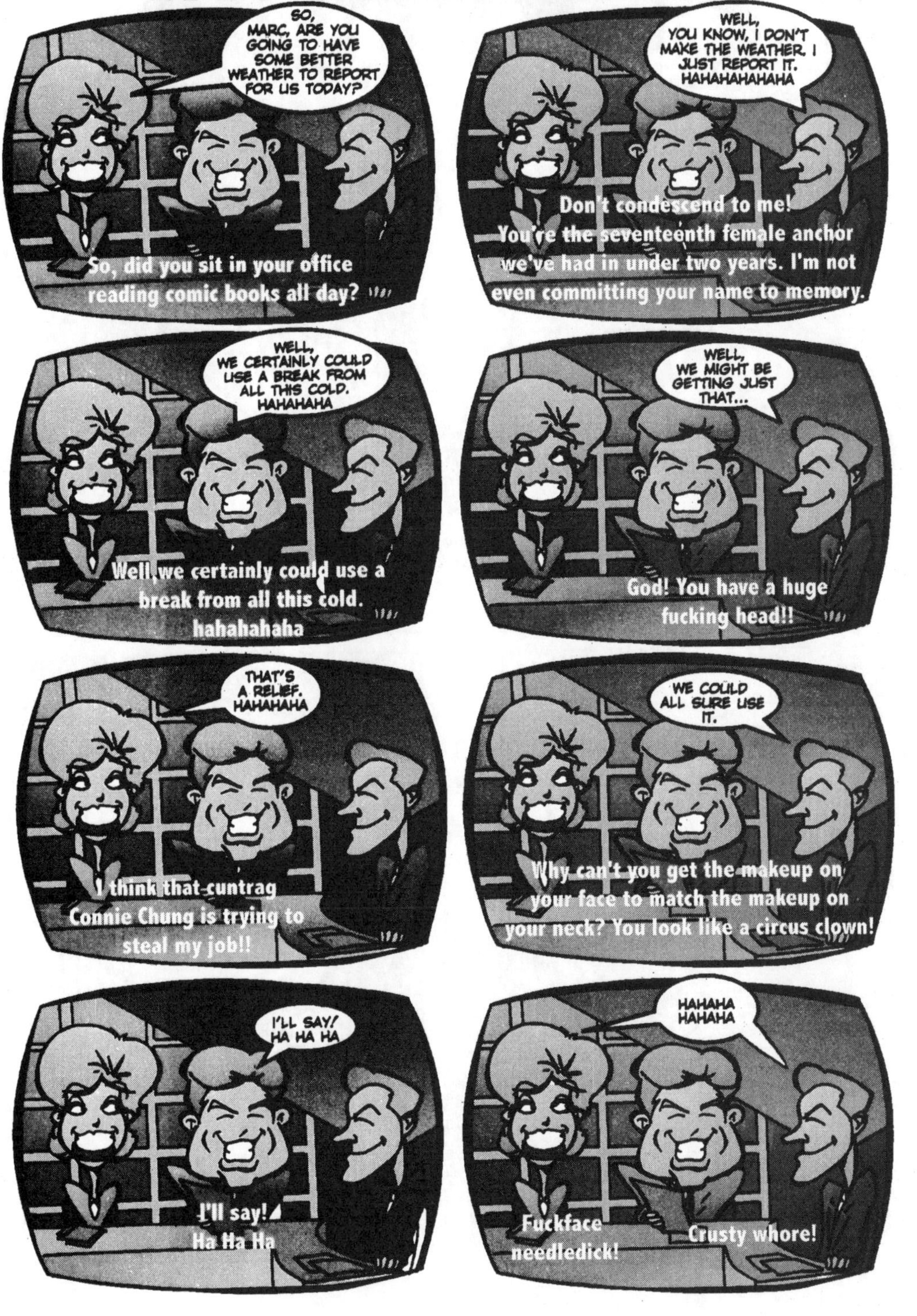

SO, MARC, ARE YOU GOING TO HAVE SOME BETTER WEATHER TO REPORT FOR US TODAY?
So, did you sit in your office reading comic books all day?
WELL, YOU KNOW, I DON'T MAKE THE WEATHER. I JUST REPORT IT. HAHAHAHAHAHAHA
Don't condescend to me! You're the seventeenth female anchor we've had in under two years. I'm not even committing your name to memory.
WELL, WE CERTAINLY COULD USE A BREAK FROM ALL THIS COLD. HAHAHAHA
Well, we certainly could use a break from all this cold. hahahahaha
WELL, WE MIGHT BE GETTING JUST THAT...
God! You have a huge fucking head!!
THAT'S A RELIEF. HAHAHAHA
I think that cuntrag Connie Chung is trying to steal my job!!
WE COULD ALL SURE USE IT.
Why can't you get the makeup on your face to match the makeup on your neck? You look like a circus clown!
I'LL SAY! HA HA HA
I'll say! Ha Ha Ha
HAHAHA HAHAHA
Fuckface needledick!
Crusty whore!

# HOW TO SPEND A TOTALLY FULFILLING DAY AT THE

# ART MUSEUM

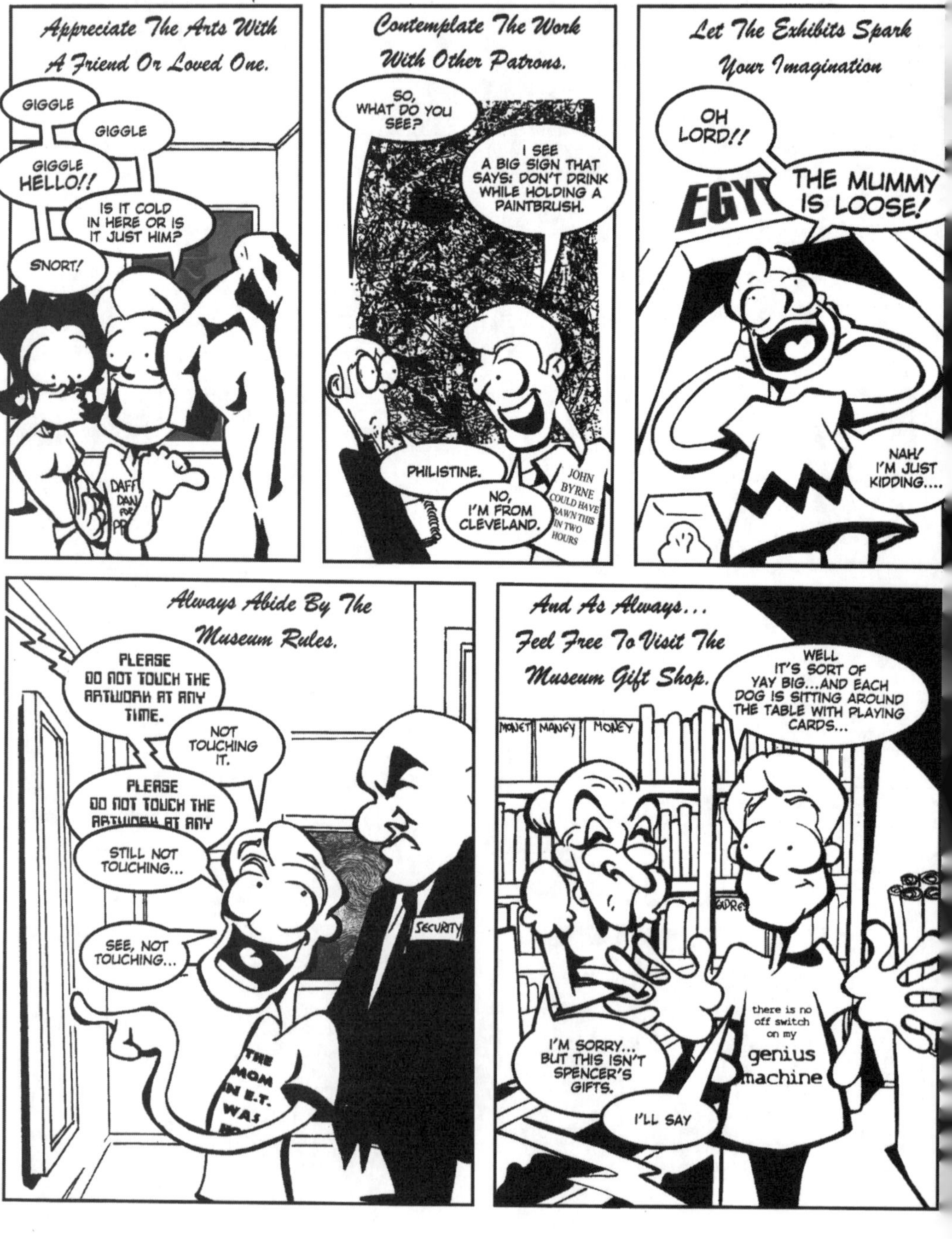

Appreciate The Arts With A Friend Or Loved One.
GIGGLE
GIGGLE
GIGGLE HELLO!!
IS IT COLD IN HERE OR IS IT JUST HIM?
SNORT!
Contemplate The Work With Other Patrons.
SO, WHAT DO YOU SEE?
I SEE A BIG SIGN THAT SAYS: DON'T DRINK WHILE HOLDING A PAINTBRUSH.
PHILISTINE.
NO, I'M FROM CLEVELAND.
JOHN BYRNE COULD HAVE DRAWN THIS IN TWO HOURS
Let The Exhibits Spark Your Imagination
OH LORD!!
THE MUMMY IS LOOSE!
NAH! I'M JUST KIDDING....
Always Abide By The Museum Rules.
PLEASE DO NOT TOUCH THE ARTWORK AT ANY TIME.
NOT TOUCHING IT.
PLEASE DO NOT TOUCH THE
STILL NOT TOUCHING...
SEE, NOT TOUCHING...
SECURITY
And As Always... Feel Free To Visit The Museum Gift Shop.
WELL IT'S SORT OF YAY BIG...AND EACH DOG IS SITTING AROUND THE TABLE WITH PLAYING CARDS...
MONET
MANEY
MONEY
I'M SORRY... BUT THIS ISN'T SPENCER'S GIFTS.
I'LL SAY
there is no off switch on my genius machine

# A DAY IN THE LIFE OF A FILM GEEK

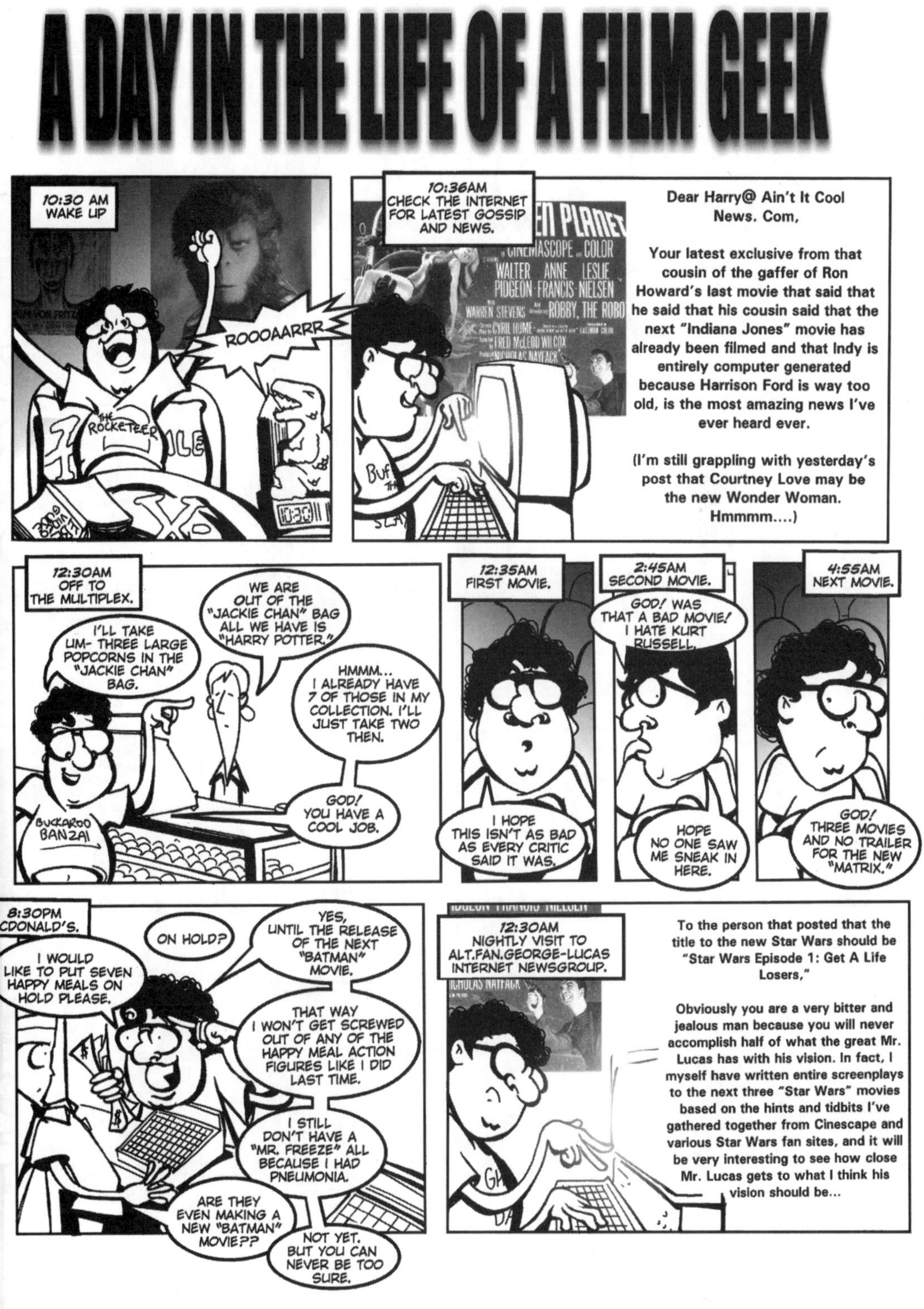

10:30 AM WAKE UP
ROOOAARRR
THE ROCKETEER
10:36AM CHECK THE INTERNET FOR LATEST GOSSIP AND NEWS.
Dear Harry@ Ain't It Cool News. Com,
Your latest exclusive from that cousin of the gaffer of Ron Howard's last movie that said that he said that his cousin said that the next "Indiana Jones" movie has already been filmed and that Indy is entirely computer generated because Harrison Ford is way too old, is the most amazing news I've ever heard ever.
(I'm still grappling with yesterday's post that Courtney Love may be the new Wonder Woman. Hmmmm....)
12:30AM OFF TO THE MULTIPLEX.
I'LL TAKE UM- THREE LARGE POPCORNS IN THE "JACKIE CHAN" BAG.
WE ARE OUT OF THE "JACKIE CHAN" BAG ALL WE HAVE IS "HARRY POTTER."
HMMM... I ALREADY HAVE 7 OF THOSE IN MY COLLECTION. I'LL JUST TAKE TWO THEN.
GOD! YOU HAVE A COOL JOB.
BUCKAROO BANZAI
12:35AM FIRST MOVIE.
I HOPE THIS ISN'T AS BAD AS EVERY CRITIC SAID IT WAS.
2:45AM SECOND MOVIE.
GOD! WAS THAT A BAD MOVIE! I HATE KURT RUSSELL.
HOPE NO ONE SAW ME SNEAK IN HERE.
4:55AM NEXT MOVIE.
GOD! THREE MOVIES AND NO TRAILER FOR THE NEW "MATRIX."
8:30PM CDONALD'S.
I WOULD LIKE TO PUT SEVEN HAPPY MEALS ON HOLD PLEASE.
ON HOLD?
YES, UNTIL THE RELEASE OF THE NEXT "BATMAN" MOVIE.
THAT WAY I WON'T GET SCREWED OUT OF ANY OF THE HAPPY MEAL ACTION FIGURES LIKE I DID LAST TIME.
I STILL DON'T HAVE A "MR. FREEZE" ALL BECAUSE I HAD PNEUMONIA.
ARE THEY EVEN MAKING A NEW "BATMAN" MOVIE??
NOT YET. BUT YOU CAN NEVER BE TOO SURE.
12:30AM NIGHTLY VISIT TO ALT.FAN.GEORGE-LUCAS INTERNET NEWSGROUP.
To the person that posted that the title to the new Star Wars should be "Star Wars Episode 1: Get A Life Losers,"
Obviously you are a very bitter and jealous man because you will never accomplish half of what the great Mr. Lucas has with his vision. In fact, I myself have written entire screenplays to the next three "Star Wars" movies based on the hints and tidbits I've gathered together from Cinescape and various Star Wars fan sites, and it will be very interesting to see how close Mr. Lucas gets to what I think his vision should be...

# ANOTHER DEFINING MOMENT IN BENDIS HISTORY

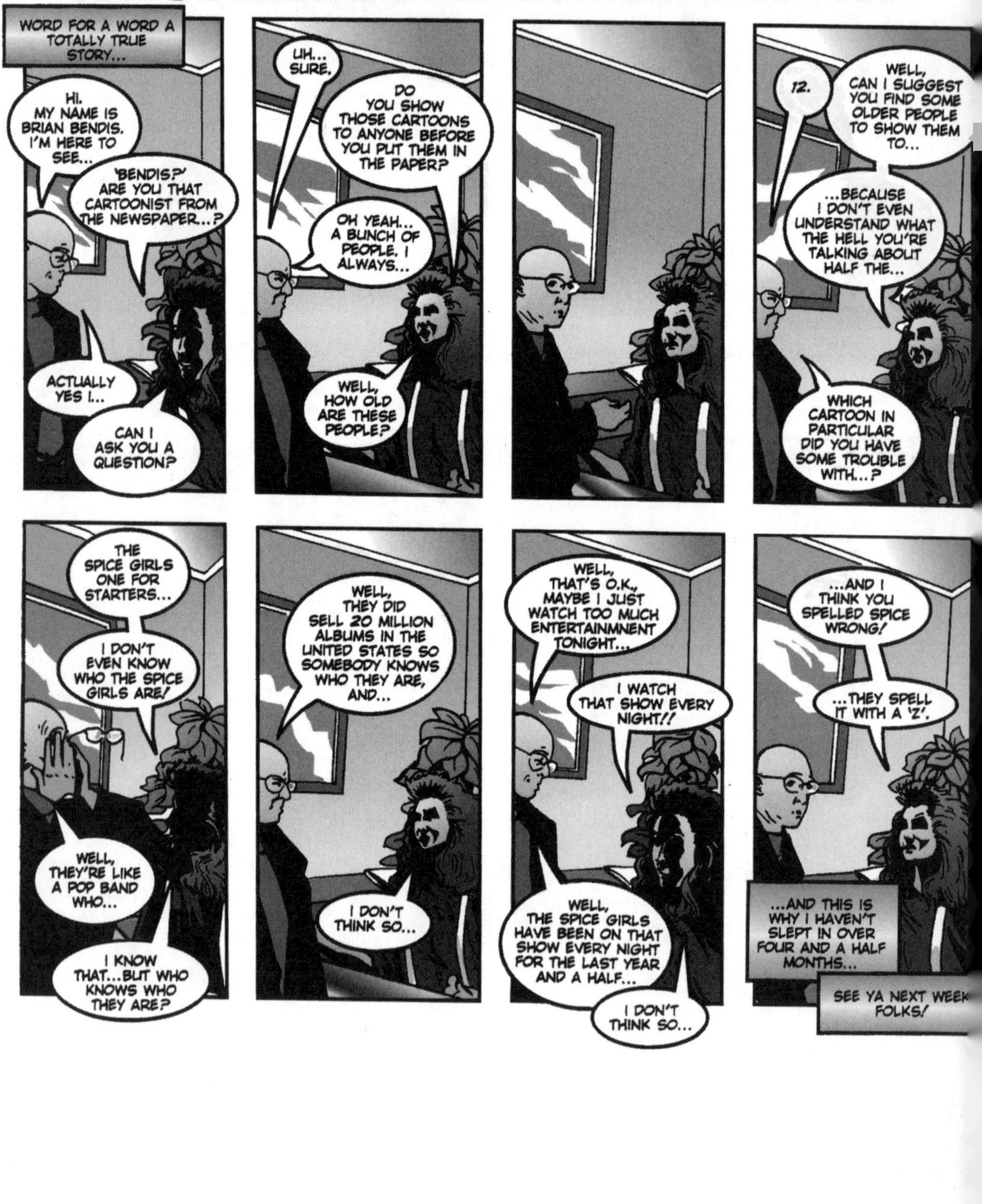
WORD FOR A WORD A TOTALLY TRUE STORY...
HI. MY NAME IS BRIAN BENDIS. I'M HERE TO SEE...
'BENDIS?' ARE YOU THAT CARTOONIST FROM THE NEWSPAPER...?
ACTUALLY YES I...
CAN I ASK YOU A QUESTION?
UH... SURE.
DO YOU SHOW THOSE CARTOONS TO ANYONE BEFORE YOU PUT THEM IN THE PAPER?
OH YEAH... A BUNCH OF PEOPLE. I ALWAYS...
WELL, HOW OLD ARE THESE PEOPLE?
12.
WELL, CAN I SUGGEST YOU FIND SOME OLDER PEOPLE TO SHOW THEM TO...
...BECAUSE I DON'T EVEN UNDERSTAND WHAT THE HELL YOU'RE TALKING ABOUT HALF THE...
WHICH CARTOON IN PARTICULAR DID YOU HAVE SOME TROUBLE WITH...?
THE SPICE GIRLS ONE FOR STARTERS...
I DON'T EVEN KNOW WHO THE SPICE GIRLS ARE!
WELL, THEY'RE LIKE A POP BAND WHO...
I KNOW THAT...BUT WHO KNOWS WHO THEY ARE?
WELL, THEY DID SELL 20 MILLION ALBUMS IN THE UNITED STATES SO SOMEBODY KNOWS WHO THEY ARE, AND...
I DON'T THINK SO...
WELL, THAT'S O.K., MAYBE I JUST WATCH TOO MUCH ENTERTAINMNENT TONIGHT...
I WATCH THAT SHOW EVERY NIGHT!!
WELL, THE SPICE GIRLS HAVE BEEN ON THAT SHOW EVERY NIGHT FOR THE LAST YEAR AND A HALF...
I DON'T THINK SO...
...AND I THINK YOU SPELLED SPICE WRONG!
...THEY SPELL IT WITH A 'Z'.
...AND THIS IS WHY I HAVEN'T SLEPT IN OVER FOUR AND A HALF MONTHS...
SEE YA NEXT WEEK FOLKS!

# THE COLLABORATIONS

## AND OTHER STUFF

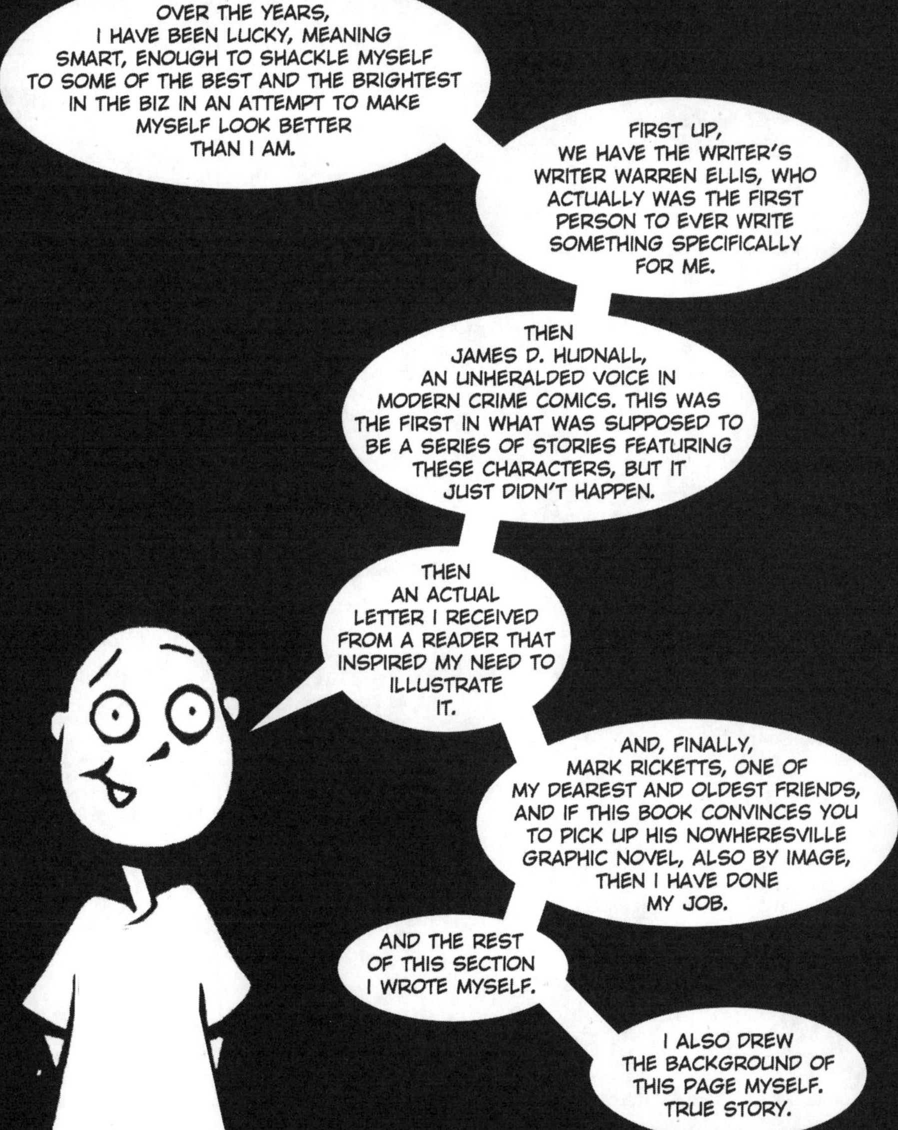
OVER THE YEARS, I HAVE BEEN LUCKY, MEANING SMART, ENOUGH TO SHACKLE MYSELF TO SOME OF THE BEST AND THE BRIGHTEST IN THE BIZ IN AN ATTEMPT TO MAKE MYSELF LOOK BETTER THAN I AM.
FIRST UP, WE HAVE THE WRITER'S WRITER WARREN ELLIS, WHO ACTUALLY WAS THE FIRST PERSON TO EVER WRITE SOMETHING SPECIFICALLY FOR ME.
THEN JAMES D. HUDNALL, AN UNHERALDED VOICE IN MODERN CRIME COMICS. THIS WAS THE FIRST IN WHAT WAS SUPPOSED TO BE A SERIES OF STORIES FEATURING THESE CHARACTERS, BUT IT JUST DIDN'T HAPPEN.
THEN AN ACTUAL LETTER I RECEIVED FROM A READER THAT INSPIRED MY NEED TO ILLUSTRATE IT.
AND, FINALLY, MARK RICKETTS, ONE OF MY DEAREST AND OLDEST FRIENDS, AND IF THIS BOOK CONVINCES YOU TO PICK UP HIS NOWHERESVILLE GRAPHIC NOVEL, ALSO BY IMAGE, THEN I HAVE DONE MY JOB.
AND THE REST OF THIS SECTION I WROTE MYSELF.
I ALSO DREW THE BACKGROUND OF THIS PAGE MYSELF. TRUE STORY.

# Better Living Through Chemistry

WARREN ELLIS - WRITER
BRIAN MICHAEL BENDIS - ARTIST
ROXANNE STARR - LETTERER

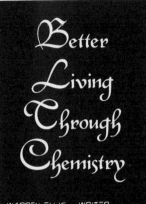

CALL ME LEARY.

I LIVE AND WORK HERE IN THE BIG CITY, AND I HAVE A GOOD JOB. HECK, YES.

I GOT MARRIED ONCE, BUT I SOBERED UP.

WHO NEEDS IT? I GOT MY PLEASURES AND I GOT MY JOB. RIGHT?

I DON'T TOUCH DRUGS.

DRUGS MESS WITH MY LIFE AND MY JOB.

U.S. Army Narcotic Environment Project

I'M HIGH ON LIFE.

SO YOU'RE WONDERING WHAT MY PLEASURES ARE NOW, RIGHT?

WELL, I'M NOT ASHAMED TO ADMIT IT.

I LIKE SITCOMS.

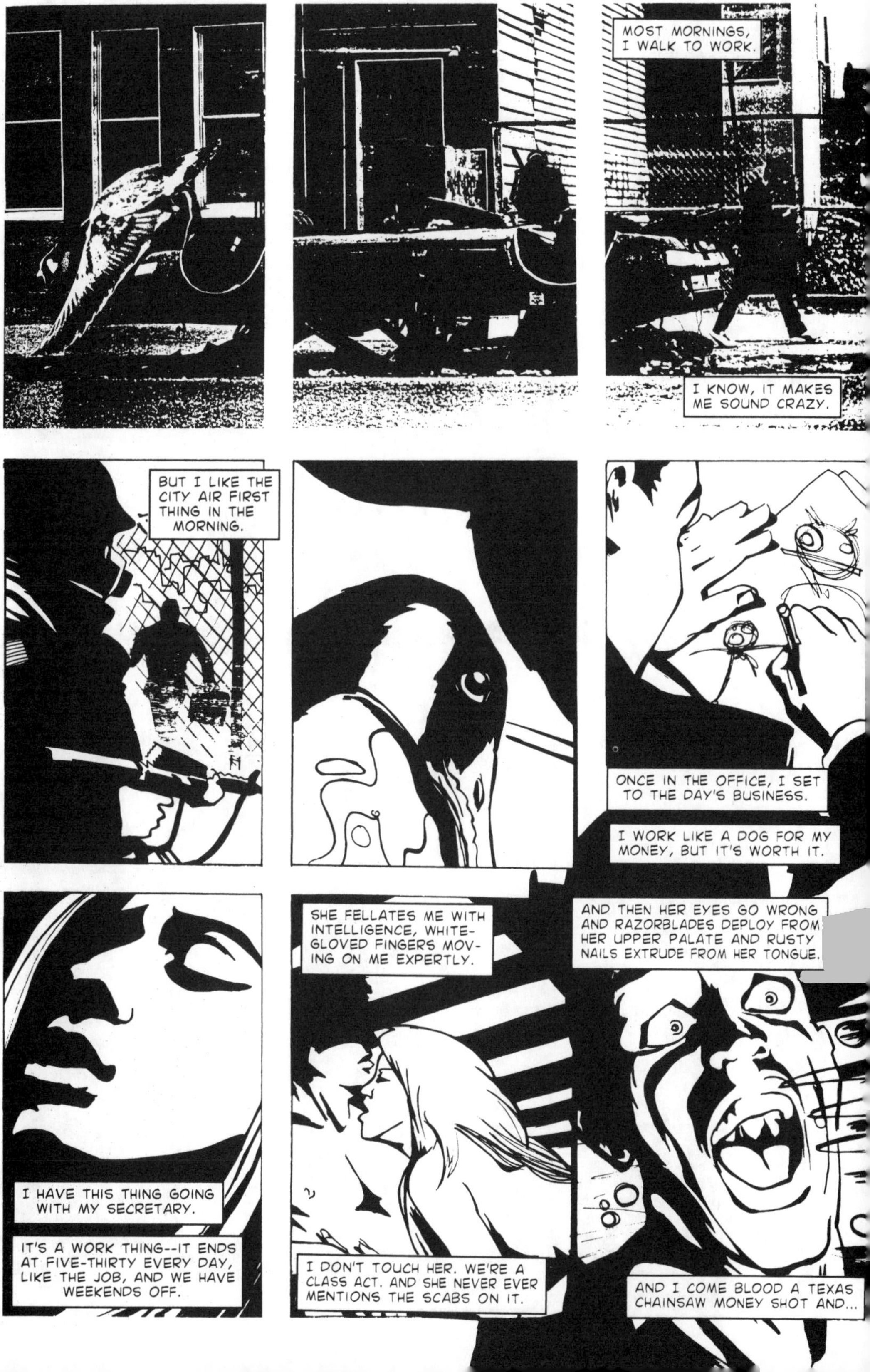
MOST MORNINGS, I WALK TO WORK.
I KNOW, IT MAKES ME SOUND CRAZY.
BUT I LIKE THE CITY AIR FIRST THING IN THE MORNING.
ONCE IN THE OFFICE, I SET TO THE DAY'S BUSINESS.
I WORK LIKE A DOG FOR MY MONEY, BUT IT'S WORTH IT.
I HAVE THIS THING GOING WITH MY SECRETARY.
IT'S A WORK THING--IT ENDS AT FIVE-THIRTY EVERY DAY, LIKE THE JOB, AND WE HAVE WEEKENDS OFF.
SHE FELLATES ME WITH INTELLIGENCE, WHITE-GLOVED FINGERS MOVING ON ME EXPERTLY.
I DON'T TOUCH HER. WE'RE A CLASS ACT. AND SHE NEVER EVER MENTIONS THE SCABS ON IT.
AND THEN HER EYES GO WRONG AND RAZORBLADES DEPLOY FROM HER UPPER PALATE AND RUSTY NAILS EXTRUDE FROM HER TONGUE.
AND I COME BLOOD A TEXAS CHAINSAW MONEY SHOT AND...

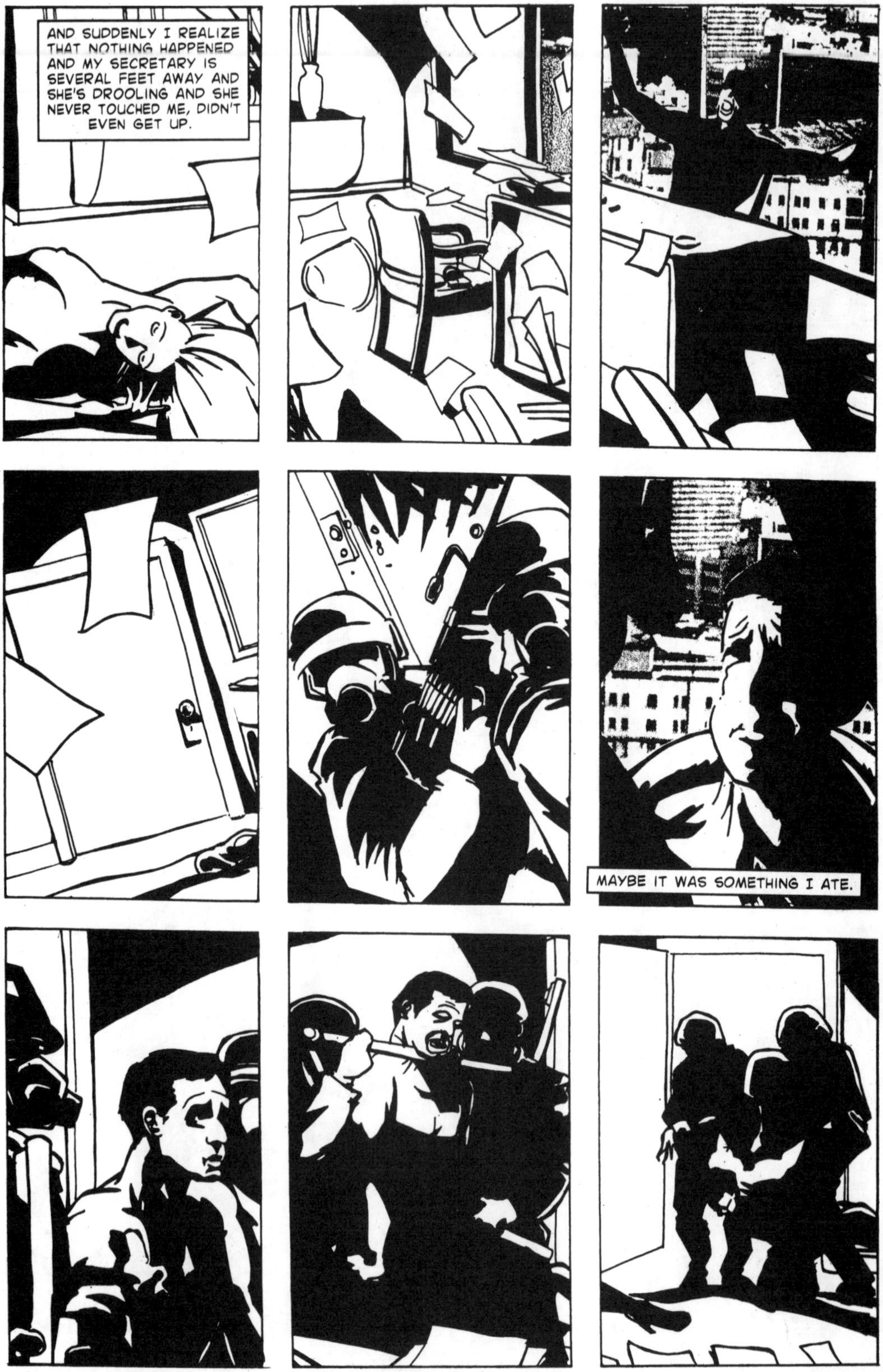
AND SUDDENLY I REALIZE THAT NOTHING HAPPENED AND MY SECRETARY IS SEVERAL FEET AWAY AND SHE'S DROOLING AND SHE NEVER TOUCHED ME, DIDN'T EVEN GET UP.
MAYBE IT WAS SOMETHING I ATE.

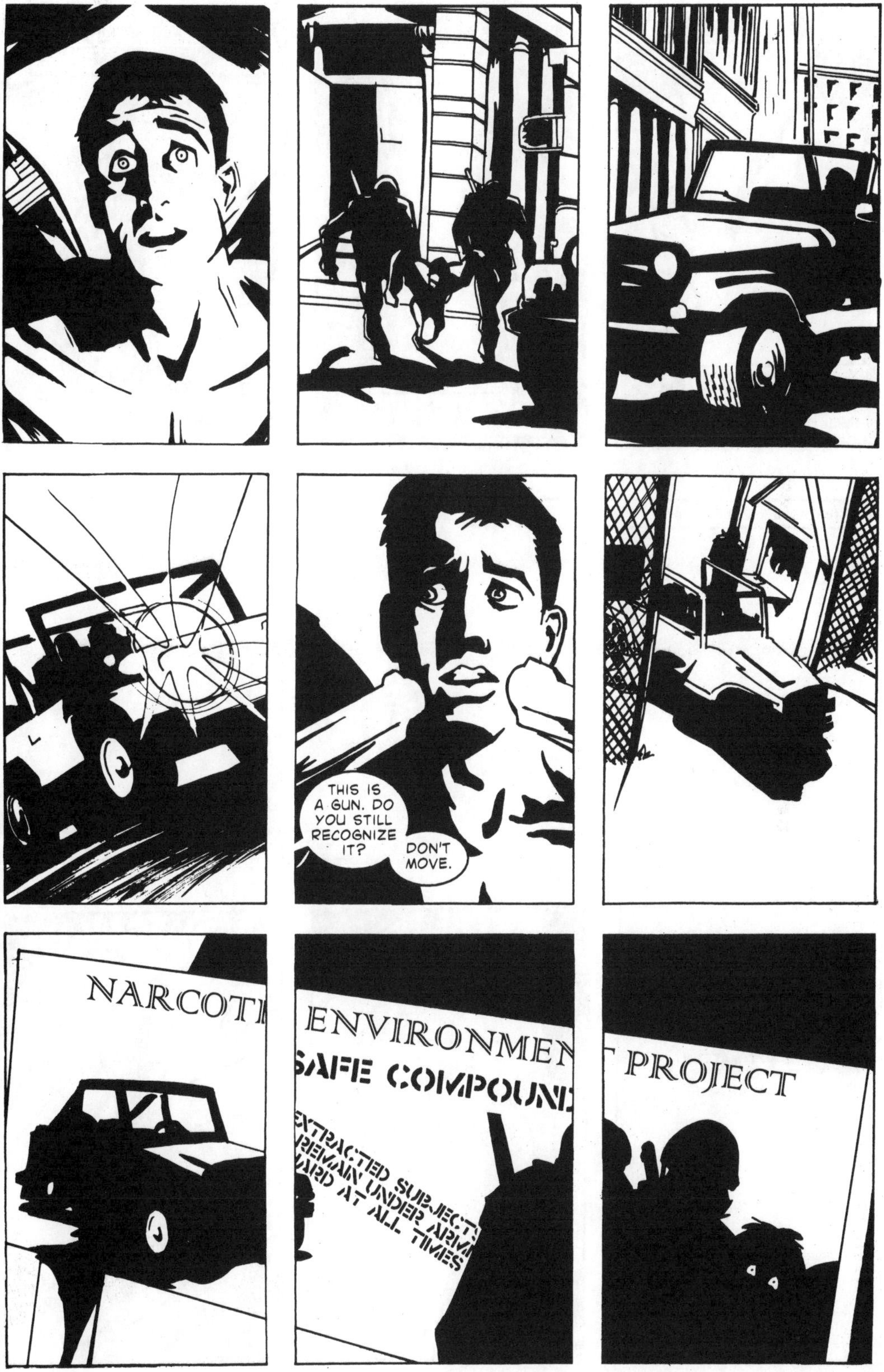
THIS IS A GUN. DO YOU STILL RECOGNIZE IT?
DON'T MOVE.
NARCOTI ENVIRONMEN PROJECT
SAFE COMPOUN
EXTRACTED SUBJECTS REMAIN UNDER ARM ARD AT ALL TIMES

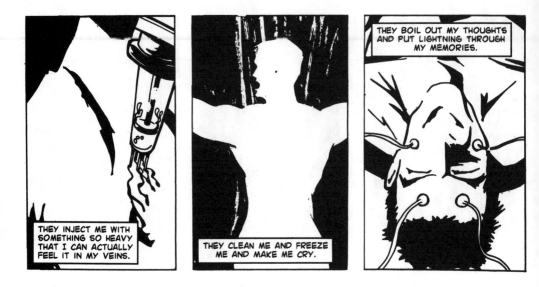

THEY INJECT ME WITH SOMETHING SO HEAVY THAT I CAN ACTUALLY FEEL IT IN MY VEINS.

THEY CLEAN ME AND FREEZE ME AND MAKE ME CRY.

THEY BOIL OUT MY THOUGHTS AND PUT LIGHTNING THROUGH MY MEMORIES.

AFTER A FEW DAYS, THEY DECIDE TO TALK TO ME.

THEY TELL ME I'M AN AMERICAN CITIZEN.

BUT THAT DOESN'T MATTER. DO YOU SEE?

WHEN WE NEEDED YOU, THAT DIDN'T MEAN ANYTHING. THIS PROJECT'S NEED IS GREATER THAN YOUR RIGHTS.

NATIONAL SECURITY. YOU UNDERSTAND *THAT*, DON'T YOU, SON?

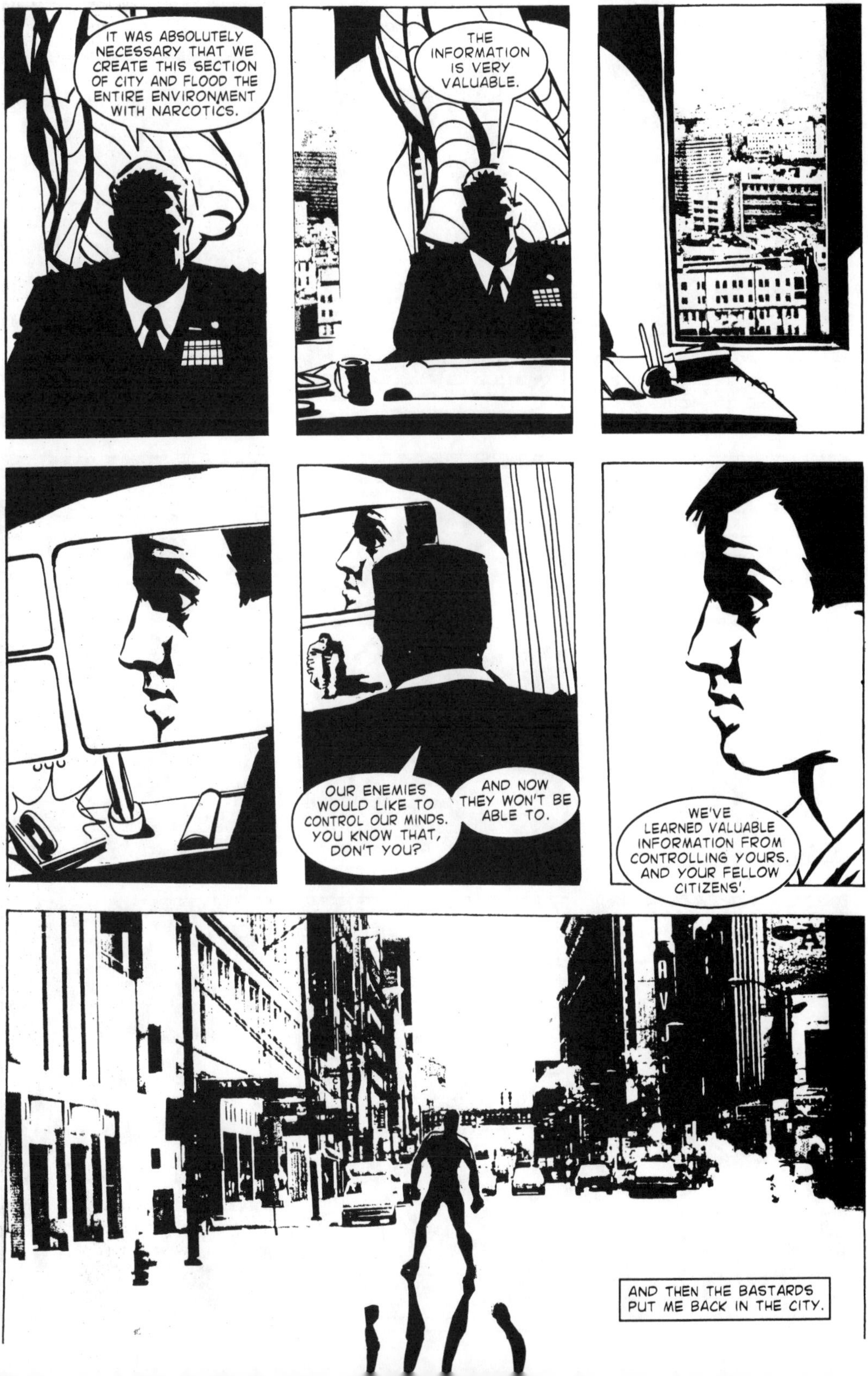

IT WAS ABSOLUTELY NECESSARY THAT WE CREATE THIS SECTION OF CITY AND FLOOD THE ENTIRE ENVIRONMENT WITH NARCOTICS.
THE INFORMATION IS VERY VALUABLE.
OUR ENEMIES WOULD LIKE TO CONTROL OUR MINDS. YOU KNOW THAT, DON'T YOU?
AND NOW THEY WON'T BE ABLE TO.
WE'VE LEARNED VALUABLE INFORMATION FROM CONTROLLING YOURS. AND YOUR FELLOW CITIZENS'.
AND THEN THE BASTARDS PUT ME BACK IN THE CITY.

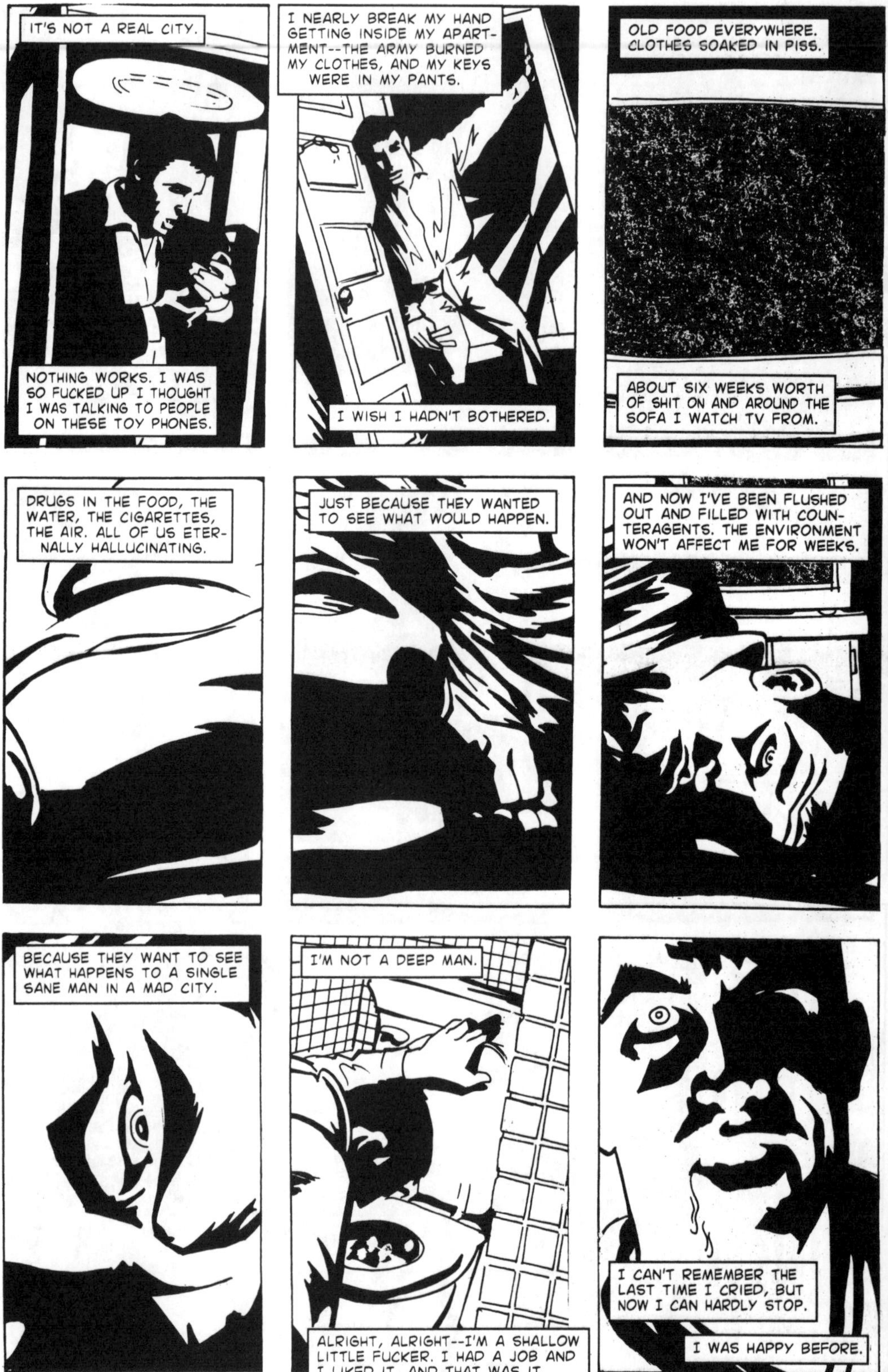
IT'S NOT A REAL CITY.
NOTHING WORKS. I WAS SO FUCKED UP I THOUGHT I WAS TALKING TO PEOPLE ON THESE TOY PHONES.
I NEARLY BREAK MY HAND GETTING INSIDE MY APARTMENT--THE ARMY BURNED MY CLOTHES, AND MY KEYS WERE IN MY PANTS.
I WISH I HADN'T BOTHERED.
OLD FOOD EVERYWHERE. CLOTHES SOAKED IN PISS.
ABOUT SIX WEEKS WORTH OF SHIT ON AND AROUND THE SOFA I WATCH TV FROM.
DRUGS IN THE FOOD, THE WATER, THE CIGARETTES, THE AIR. ALL OF US ETERNALLY HALLUCINATING.
JUST BECAUSE THEY WANTED TO SEE WHAT WOULD HAPPEN.
AND NOW I'VE BEEN FLUSHED OUT AND FILLED WITH COUNTERAGENTS. THE ENVIRONMENT WON'T AFFECT ME FOR WEEKS.
BECAUSE THEY WANT TO SEE WHAT HAPPENS TO A SINGLE SANE MAN IN A MAD CITY.
I'M NOT A DEEP MAN.
ALRIGHT, ALRIGHT--I'M A SHALLOW LITTLE FUCKER. I HAD A JOB AND I LIKED IT, AND THAT WAS IT.
I CAN'T REMEMBER THE LAST TIME I CRIED, BUT NOW I CAN HARDLY STOP.
I WAS HAPPY BEFORE.

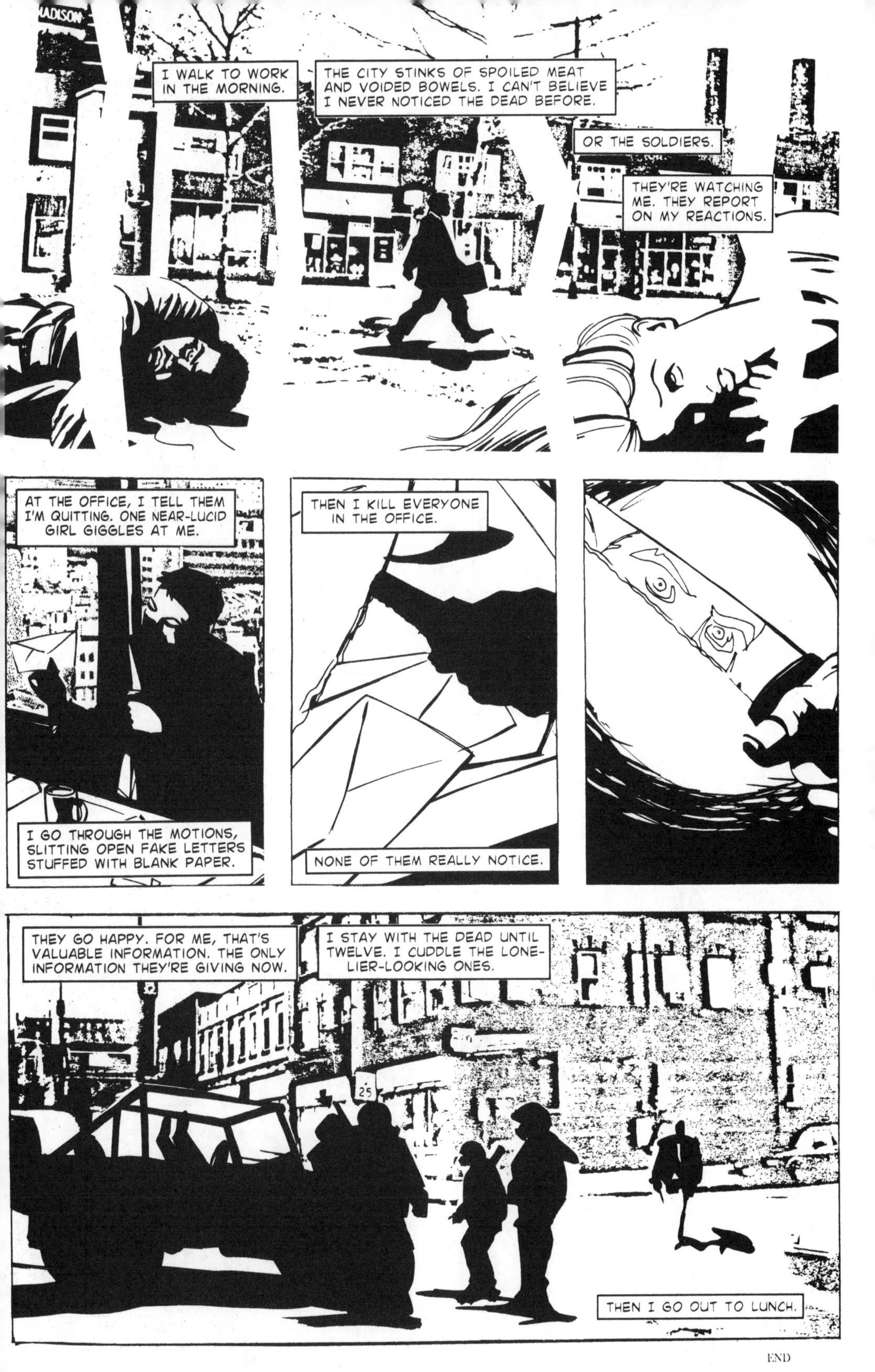
MADISON
I WALK TO WORK IN THE MORNING.
THE CITY STINKS OF SPOILED MEAT AND VOIDED BOWELS. I CAN'T BELIEVE I NEVER NOTICED THE DEAD BEFORE.
OR THE SOLDIERS.
THEY'RE WATCHING ME. THEY REPORT ON MY REACTIONS.
AT THE OFFICE, I TELL THEM I'M QUITTING. ONE NEAR-LUCID GIRL GIGGLES AT ME.
I GO THROUGH THE MOTIONS, SLITTING OPEN FAKE LETTERS STUFFED WITH BLANK PAPER.
THEN I KILL EVERYONE IN THE OFFICE.
NONE OF THEM REALLY NOTICE.
THEY GO HAPPY. FOR ME, THAT'S VALUABLE INFORMATION. THE ONLY INFORMATION THEY'RE GIVING NOW.
I STAY WITH THE DEAD UNTIL TWELVE. I CUDDLE THE LONE-LIER-LOOKING ONES.
25
THEN I GO OUT TO LUNCH.

END

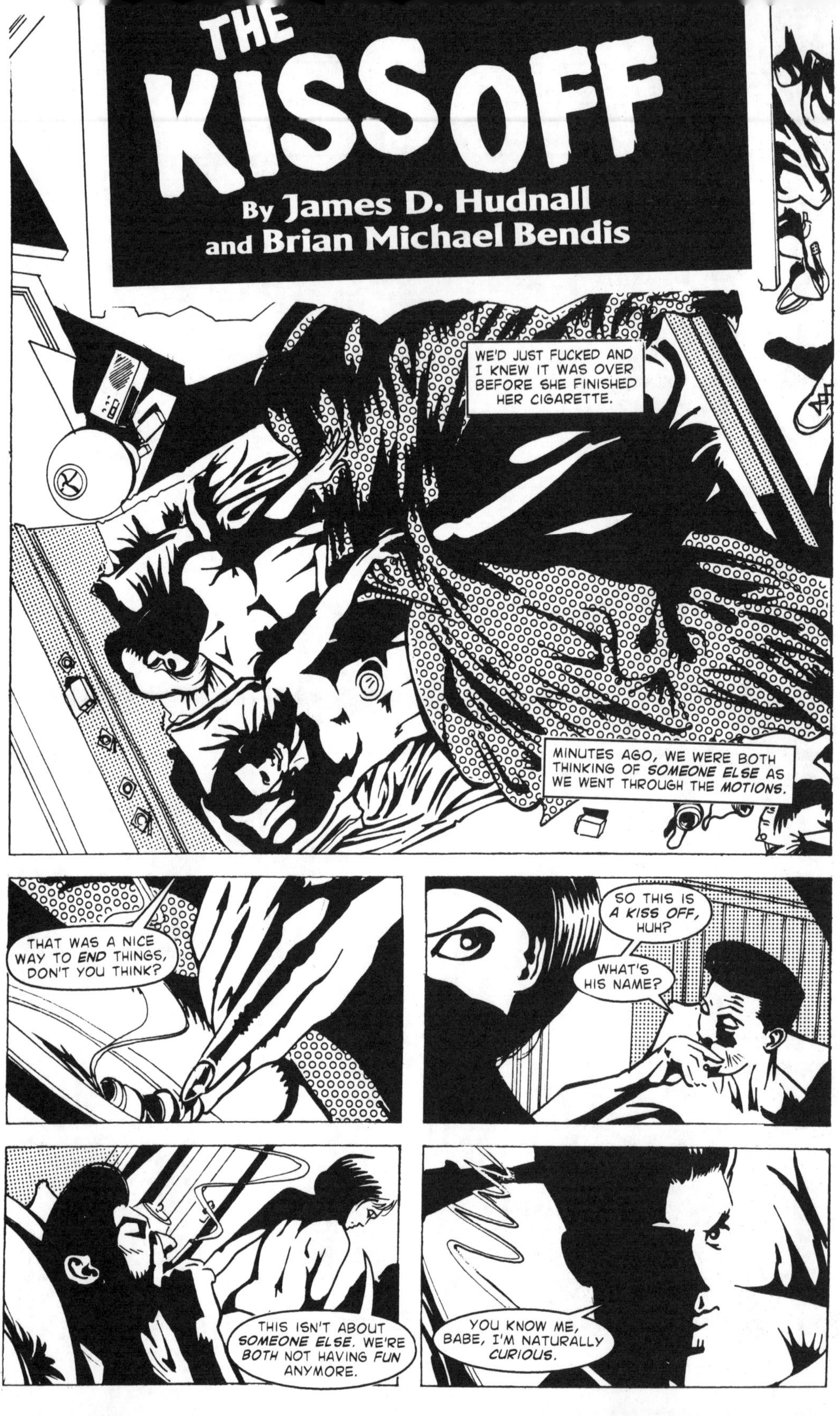
THE KISSOFF
By James D. Hudnall
and Brian Michael Bendis
WE'D JUST FUCKED AND I KNEW IT WAS OVER BEFORE SHE FINISHED HER CIGARETTE.
MINUTES AGO, WE WERE BOTH THINKING OF SOMEONE ELSE AS WE WENT THROUGH THE MOTIONS.
THAT WAS A NICE WAY TO END THINGS, DON'T YOU THINK?
SO THIS IS A KISS OFF, HUH?
WHAT'S HIS NAME?
THIS ISN'T ABOUT SOMEONE ELSE. WE'RE BOTH NOT HAVING FUN ANYMORE.
YOU KNOW ME, BABE, I'M NATURALLY CURIOUS.

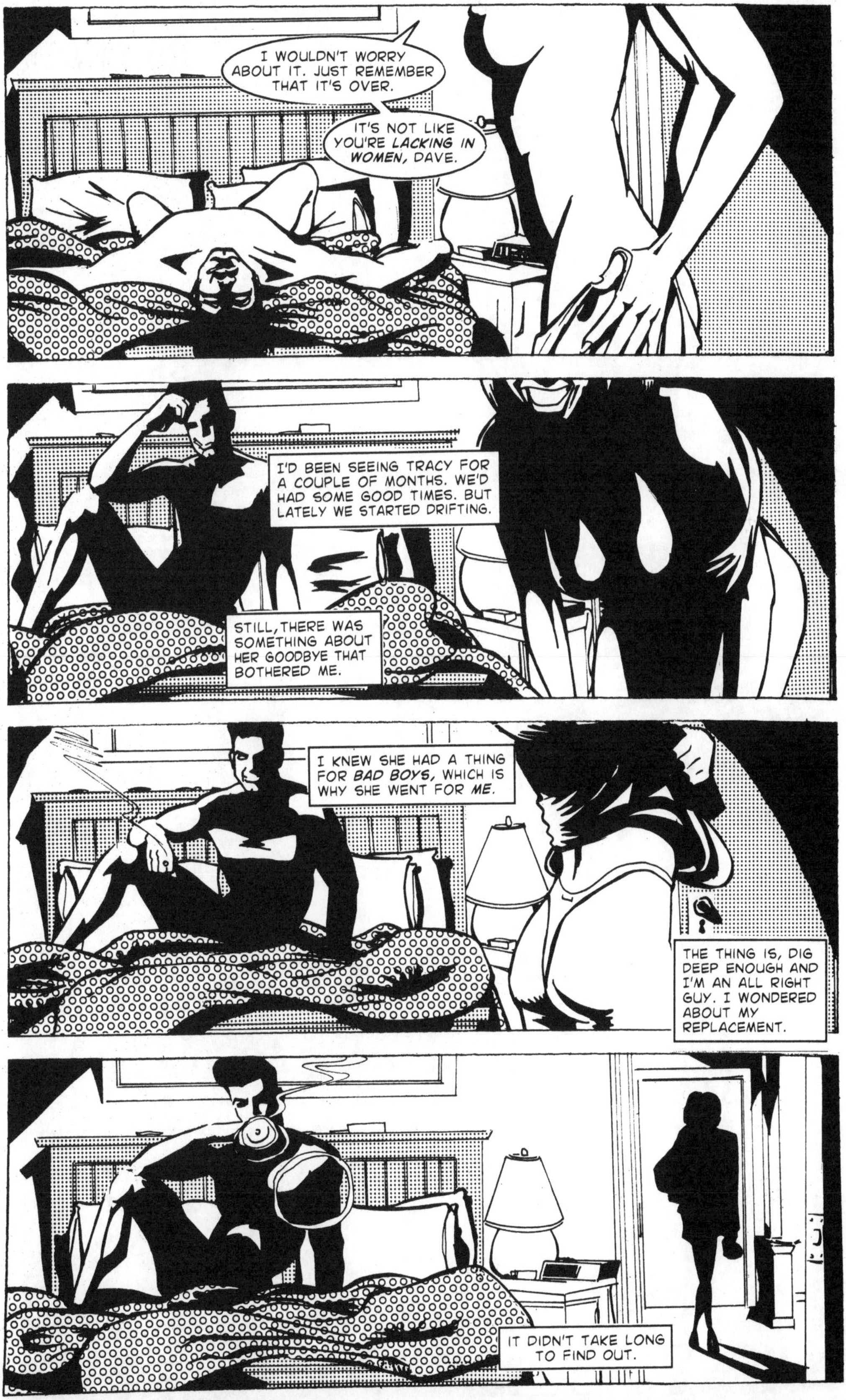
I WOULDN'T WORRY ABOUT IT. JUST REMEMBER THAT IT'S OVER.
IT'S NOT LIKE YOU'RE *LACKING IN WOMEN,* DAVE.
I'D BEEN SEEING TRACY FOR A COUPLE OF MONTHS. WE'D HAD SOME GOOD TIMES. BUT LATELY WE STARTED DRIFTING.
STILL, THERE WAS SOMETHING ABOUT HER GOODBYE THAT BOTHERED ME.
I KNEW SHE HAD A THING FOR *BAD BOYS,* WHICH IS WHY SHE WENT FOR *ME.*
THE THING IS, DIG DEEP ENOUGH AND I'M AN ALL RIGHT GUY. I WONDERED ABOUT MY REPLACEMENT.
IT DIDN'T TAKE LONG TO FIND OUT.

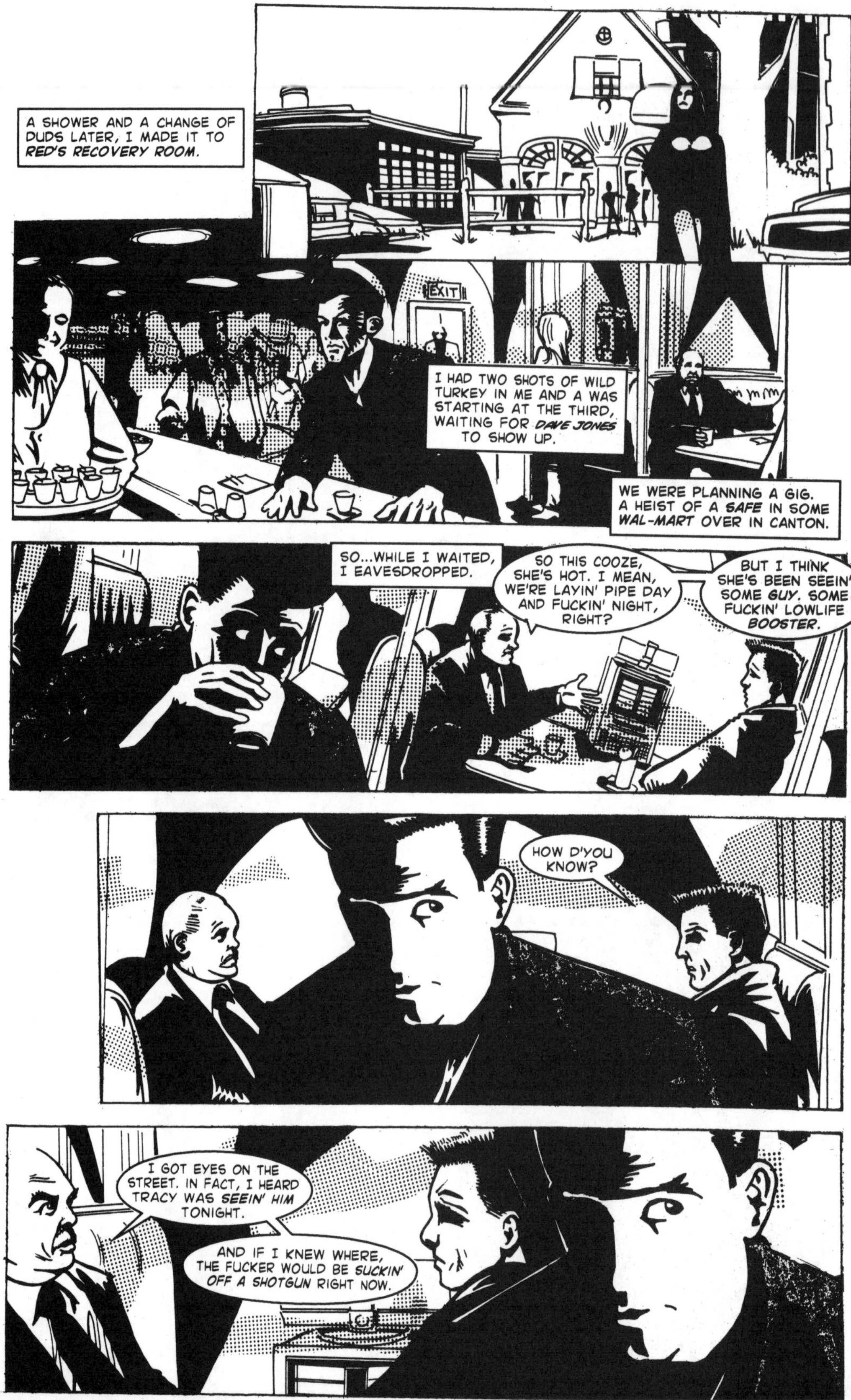
A SHOWER AND A CHANGE OF DUDS LATER, I MADE IT TO RED'S RECOVERY ROOM.
EXIT
I HAD TWO SHOTS OF WILD TURKEY IN ME AND A WAS STARTING AT THE THIRD, WAITING FOR DAVE JONES TO SHOW UP.
WE WERE PLANNING A GIG. A HEIST OF A SAFE IN SOME WAL-MART OVER IN CANTON.
SO...WHILE I WAITED, I EAVESDROPPED.
SO THIS COOZE, SHE'S HOT. I MEAN, WE'RE LAYIN' PIPE DAY AND FUCKIN' NIGHT, RIGHT?
BUT I THINK SHE'S BEEN SEEIN' SOME GUY. SOME FUCKIN' LOWLIFE BOOSTER.
HOW D'YOU KNOW?
I GOT EYES ON THE STREET. IN FACT, I HEARD TRACY WAS SEEIN' HIM TONIGHT.
AND IF I KNEW WHERE, THE FUCKER WOULD BE SUCKIN' OFF A SHOTGUN RIGHT NOW.

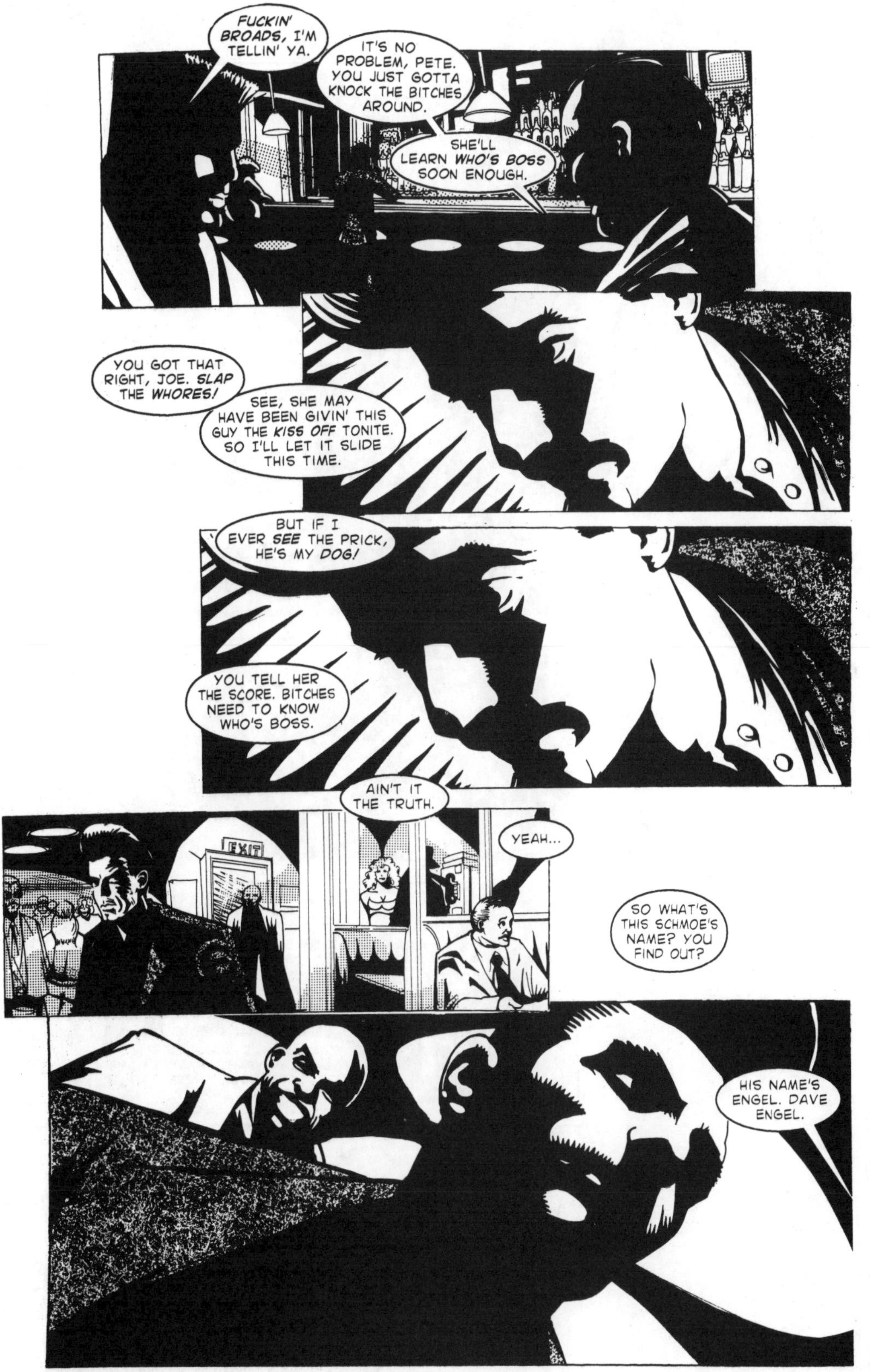
FUCKIN' BROADS, I'M TELLIN' YA.
IT'S NO PROBLEM, PETE. YOU JUST GOTTA KNOCK THE BITCHES AROUND.
SHE'LL LEARN WHO'S BOSS SOON ENOUGH.
YOU GOT THAT RIGHT, JOE. SLAP THE WHORES!
SEE, SHE MAY HAVE BEEN GIVIN' THIS GUY THE KISS OFF TONITE. SO I'LL LET IT SLIDE THIS TIME.
BUT IF I EVER SEE THE PRICK, HE'S MY DOG!
YOU TELL HER THE SCORE. BITCHES NEED TO KNOW WHO'S BOSS.
AIN'T IT THE TRUTH.
EXIT
YEAH...
SO WHAT'S THIS SCHMOE'S NAME? YOU FIND OUT?
HIS NAME'S ENGEL. DAVE ENGEL.

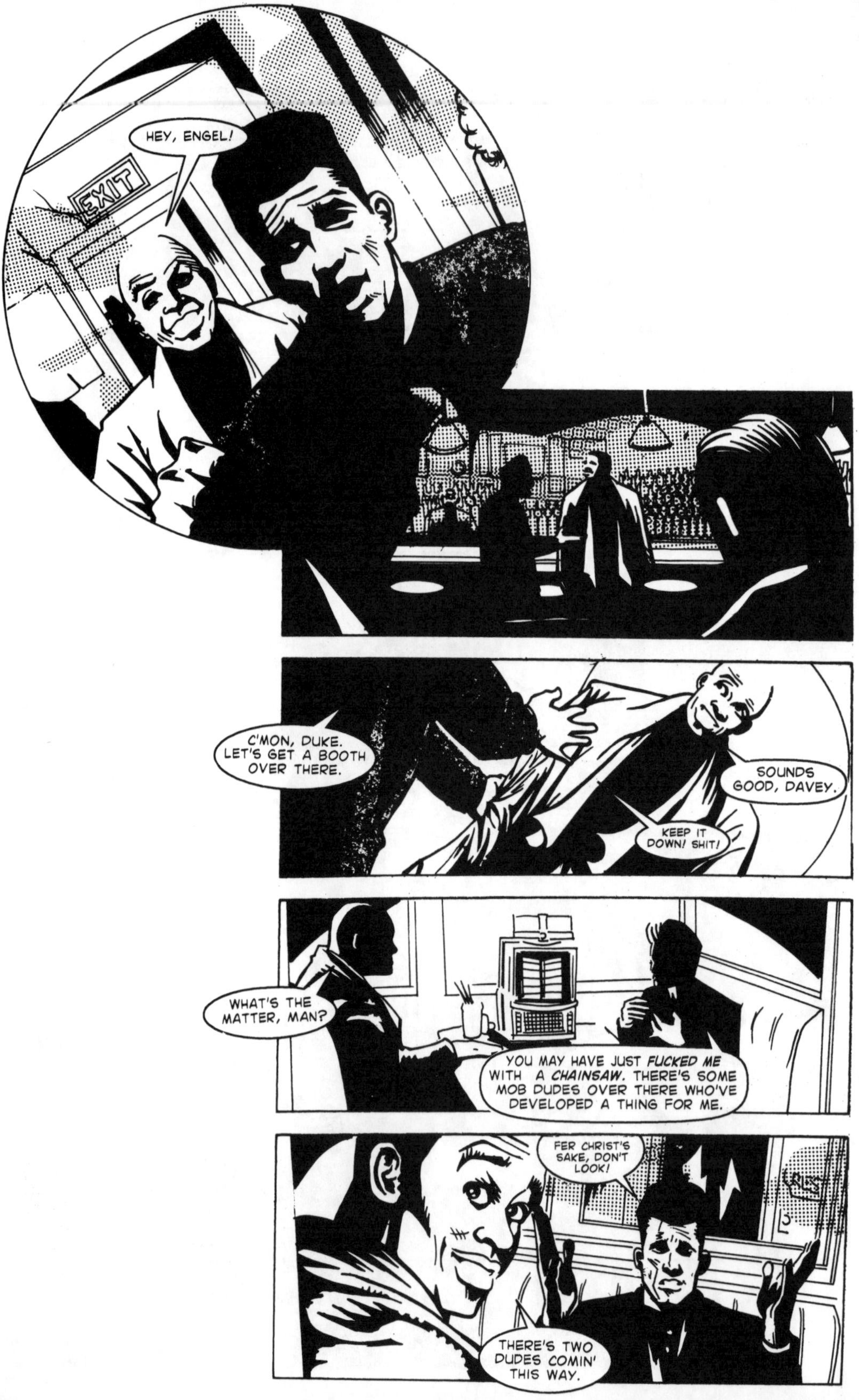
HEY, ENGEL!
EXIT
C'MON, DUKE. LET'S GET A BOOTH OVER THERE.
SOUNDS GOOD, DAVEY.
KEEP IT DOWN! SHIT!
WHAT'S THE MATTER, MAN?
YOU MAY HAVE JUST FUCKED ME WITH A CHAINSAW. THERE'S SOME MOB DUDES OVER THERE WHO'VE DEVELOPED A THING FOR ME.
FER CHRIST'S SAKE, DON'T LOOK!
THERE'S TWO DUDES COMIN' THIS WAY.

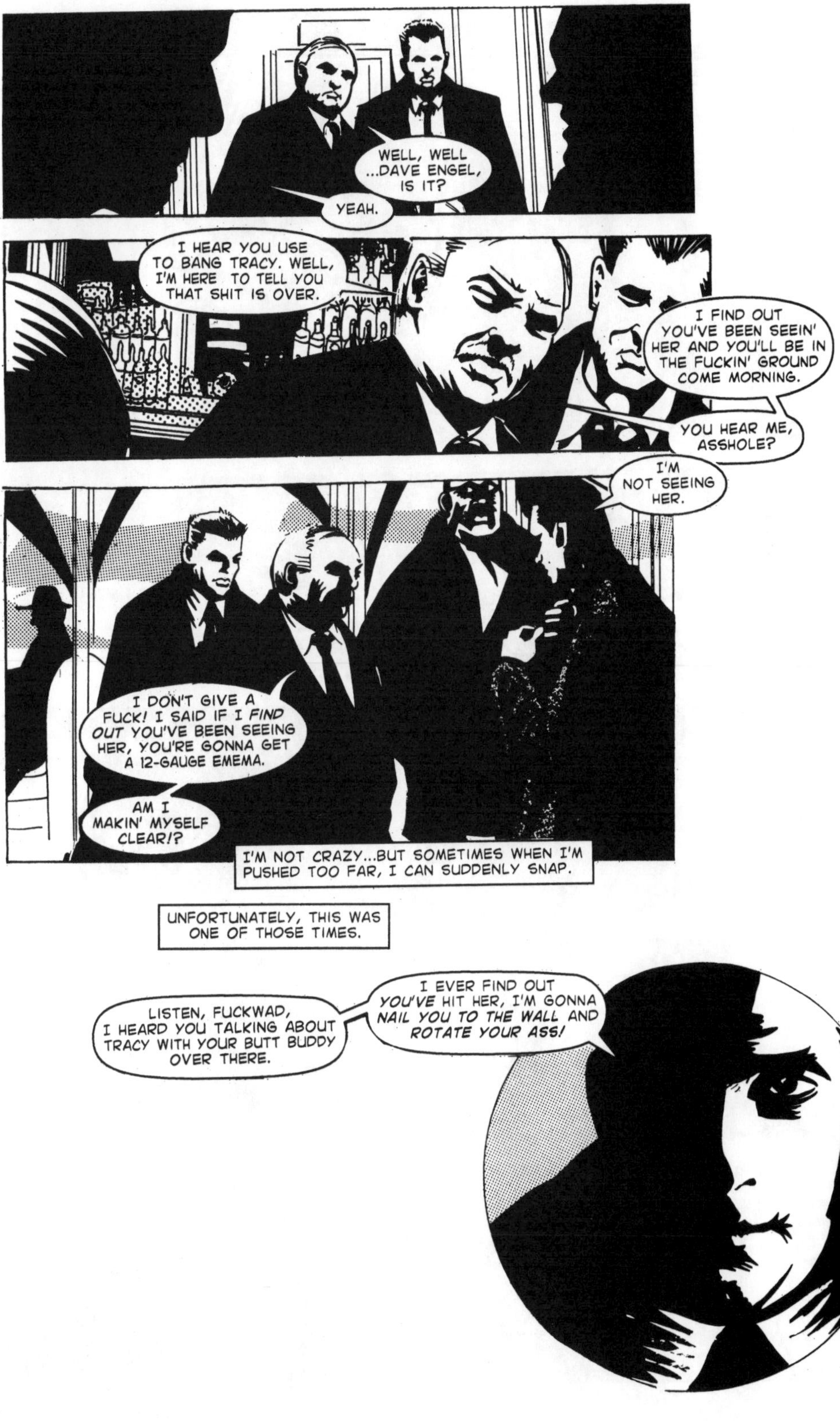
WELL, WELL ...DAVE ENGEL, IS IT?
YEAH.
I HEAR YOU USE TO BANG TRACY. WELL, I'M HERE TO TELL YOU THAT SHIT IS OVER.
I FIND OUT YOU'VE BEEN SEEIN' HER AND YOU'LL BE IN THE FUCKIN' GROUND COME MORNING.
YOU HEAR ME, ASSHOLE?
I'M NOT SEEING HER.
I DON'T GIVE A FUCK! I SAID IF I *FIND OUT* YOU'VE BEEN SEEING HER, YOU'RE GONNA GET A 12-GAUGE EMEMA.
AM I MAKIN' MYSELF CLEAR!?
I'M NOT CRAZY...BUT SOMETIMES WHEN I'M PUSHED TOO FAR, I CAN SUDDENLY SNAP.
UNFORTUNATELY, THIS WAS ONE OF THOSE TIMES.
LISTEN, FUCKWAD, I HEARD YOU TALKING ABOUT TRACY WITH YOUR BUTT BUDDY OVER THERE.
I EVER FIND OUT *YOU'VE* HIT HER, I'M GONNA *NAIL YOU TO THE WALL* AND *ROTATE YOUR ASS!*

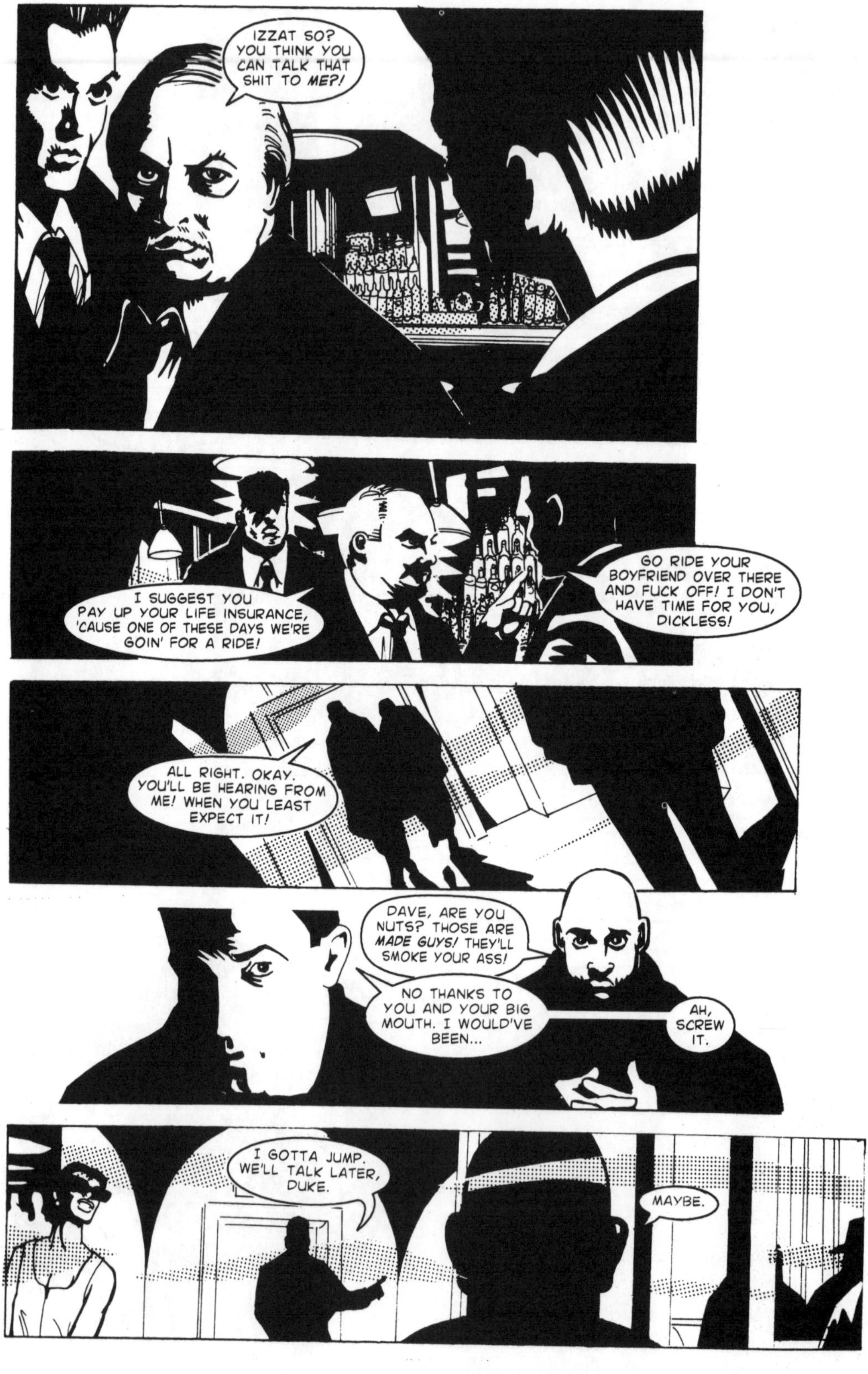
IZZAT SO? YOU THINK YOU CAN TALK THAT SHIT TO ME?!
I SUGGEST YOU PAY UP YOUR LIFE INSURANCE, 'CAUSE ONE OF THESE DAYS WE'RE GOIN' FOR A RIDE!
GO RIDE YOUR BOYFRIEND OVER THERE AND FUCK OFF! I DON'T HAVE TIME FOR YOU, DICKLESS!
ALL RIGHT. OKAY. YOU'LL BE HEARING FROM ME! WHEN YOU LEAST EXPECT IT!
DAVE, ARE YOU NUTS? THOSE ARE MADE GUYS! THEY'LL SMOKE YOUR ASS!
NO THANKS TO YOU AND YOUR BIG MOUTH. I WOULD'VE BEEN...
AH, SCREW IT.
I GOTTA JUMP. WE'LL TALK LATER, DUKE.
MAYBE.

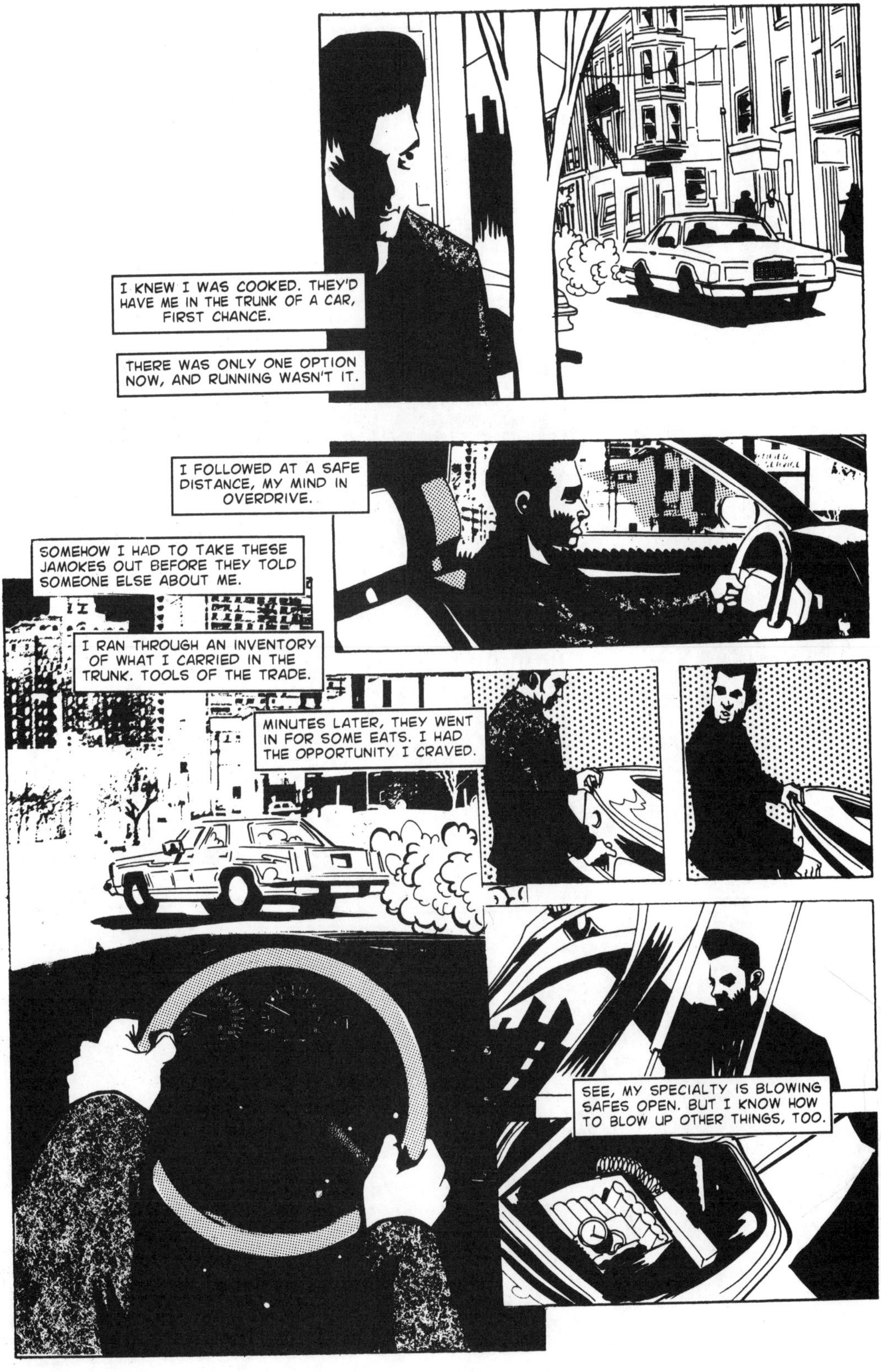
I KNEW I WAS COOKED. THEY'D HAVE ME IN THE TRUNK OF A CAR, FIRST CHANCE.
THERE WAS ONLY ONE OPTION NOW, AND RUNNING WASN'T IT.
I FOLLOWED AT A SAFE DISTANCE, MY MIND IN OVERDRIVE.
SOMEHOW I HAD TO TAKE THESE JAMOKES OUT BEFORE THEY TOLD SOMEONE ELSE ABOUT ME.
I RAN THROUGH AN INVENTORY OF WHAT I CARRIED IN THE TRUNK. TOOLS OF THE TRADE.
MINUTES LATER, THEY WENT IN FOR SOME EATS. I HAD THE OPPORTUNITY I CRAVED.
SEE, MY SPECIALTY IS BLOWING SAFES OPEN. BUT I KNOW HOW TO BLOW UP OTHER THINGS, TOO.

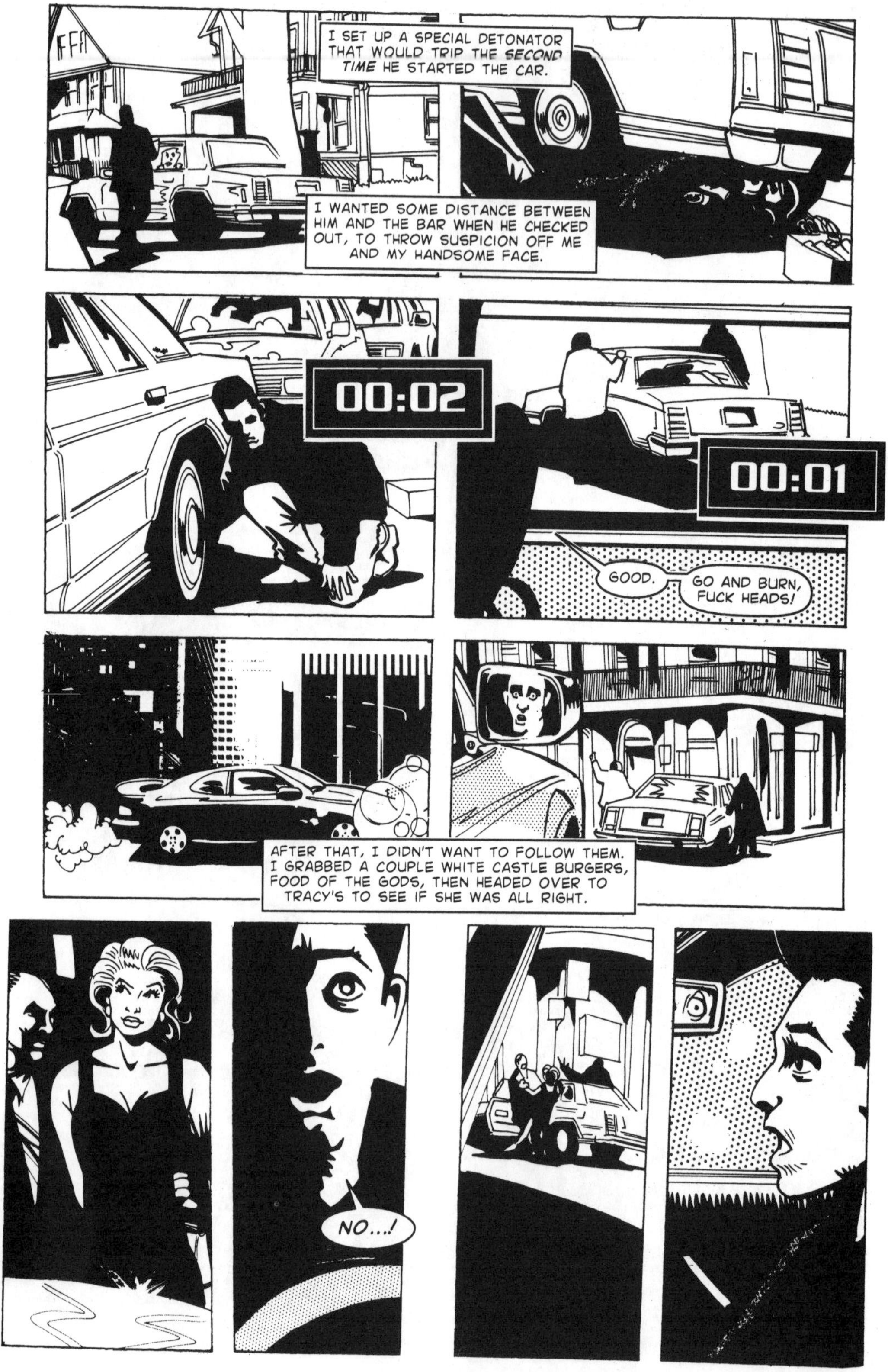
I SET UP A SPECIAL DETONATOR THAT WOULD TRIP THE *SECOND TIME* HE STARTED THE CAR.
I WANTED SOME DISTANCE BETWEEN HIM AND THE BAR WHEN HE CHECKED OUT, TO THROW SUSPICION OFF ME AND MY HANDSOME FACE.
00:02
00:01
GOOD.
GO AND BURN, FUCK HEADS!
AFTER THAT, I DIDN'T WANT TO FOLLOW THEM. I GRABBED A COUPLE WHITE CASTLE BURGERS, FOOD OF THE GODS, THEN HEADED OVER TO TRACY'S TO SEE IF SHE WAS ALL RIGHT.
NO...!

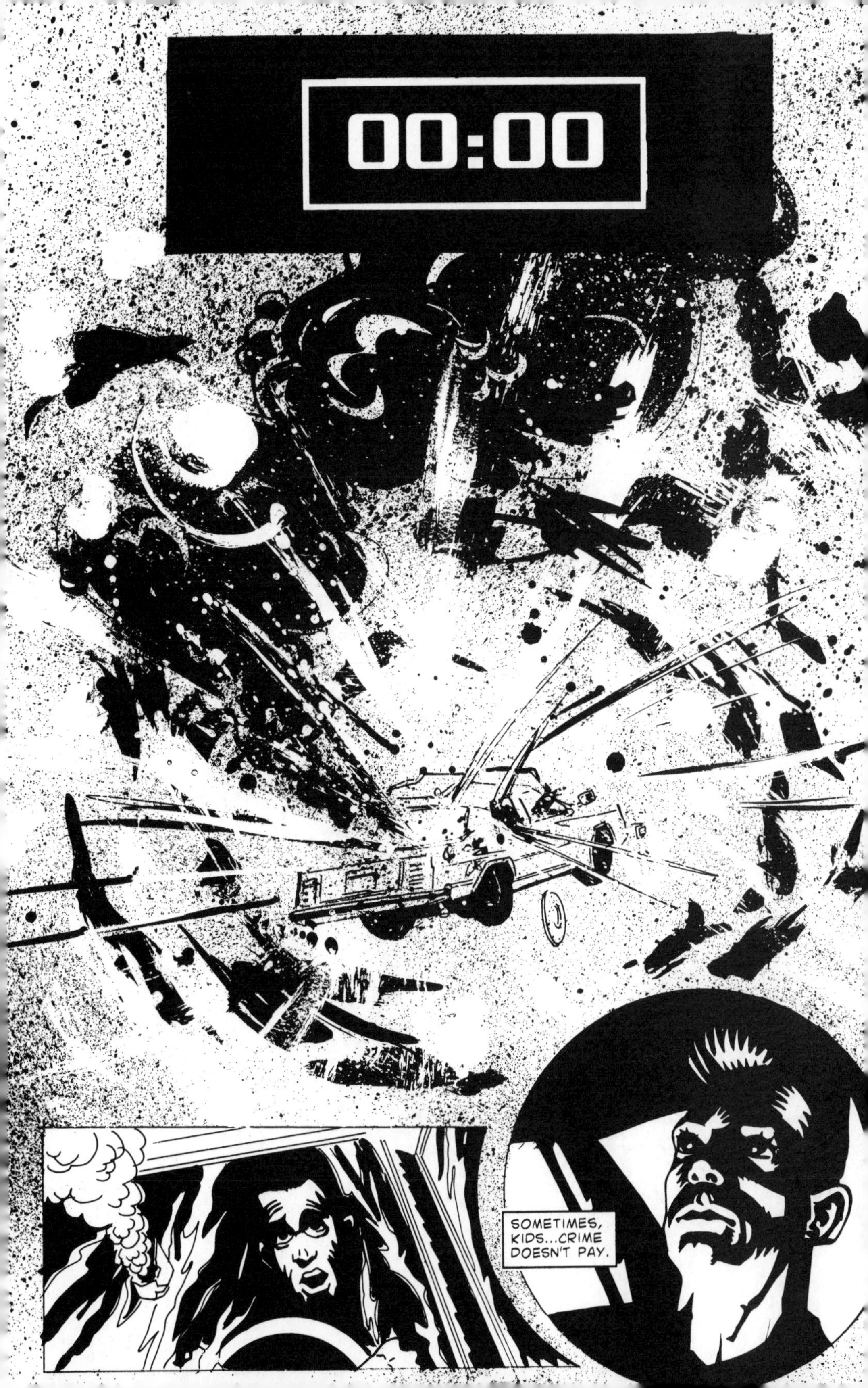
00:00
SOMETIMES, KIDS...CRIME DOESN'T PAY.

Dear Mr. Bendis,

I swear to you that the following is true.

This is a few years back. It was Christmas Eve, I was 13 years old.

My mom sent me out to the store to get something for dinner. We lived just a few blocks from Cedar Center so I could walk myself.

I don't think she realized how bad it had gotten outside, or she wouldn't have sent me.

I probably should have used common sense and told her how bad it was, but if I'm not in the house, I'm not cleaning for company, so out in the snow I went.

The snow and wind were blinding. I couldn't see two feet in front of me. I just pushed myself forward into the snow.

All of a sudden, the wind got very strong and deafening...

And I swear this is true.

I was pushed off my feet, like something pushed me by my tush up in the air and threw me forward five or six feet, where I landed in a snowbank.

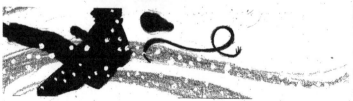

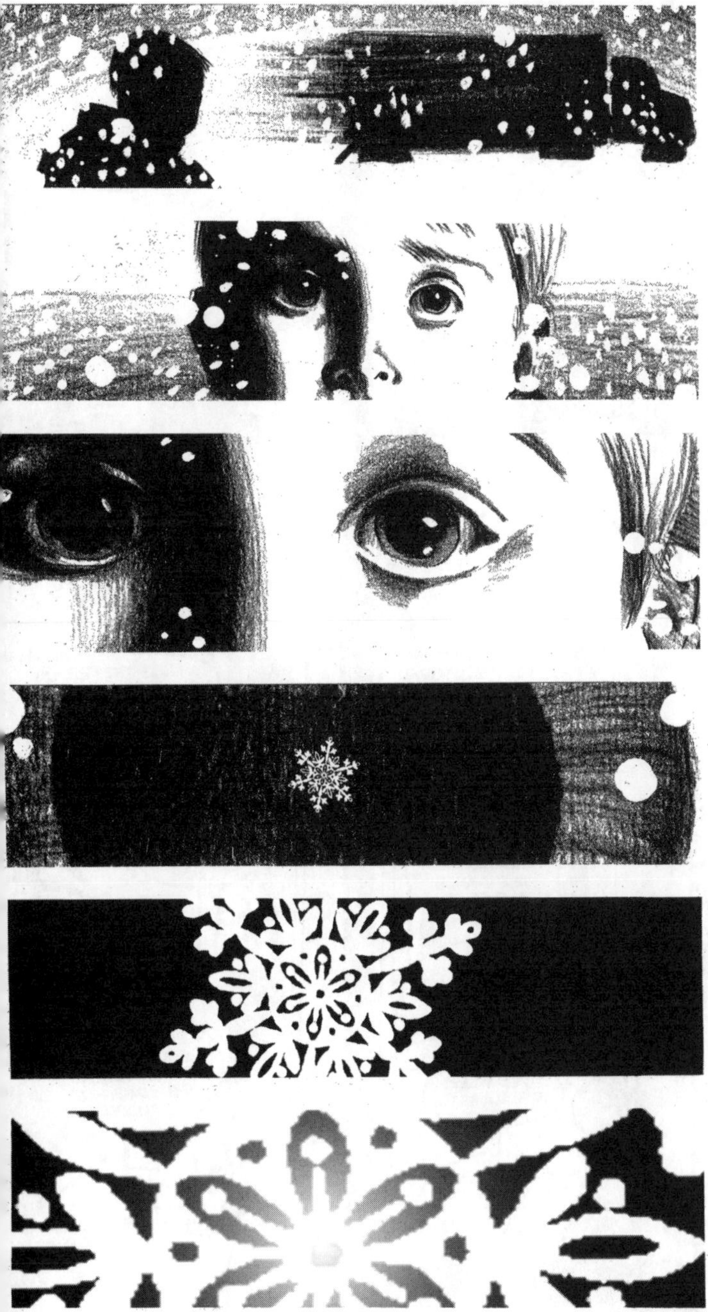

It was only at that moment that I realized that a truck had been barreling toward where I just stood. It had missed me by no more than an inch.

Now I'm not by any means what you'd call a religious person or a spiritual person, but I know what happened to me that day was an honest-to-god miracle.

I've thought about what it meant for a long time and why it happened, and I have no answers. I do think that it is important to tell people when things like this happen.

I think we live in complicated and jaded times. And even though it's not a parting of the sea or a burning bush, a miracle is a miracle.

And I think if you could take the time to let people know it happened, that things like this still happen, maybe people will feel a little better about the world,

maybe they could have as great a Christmas as I had that year, when I got to go home to my mom.

Thank you for making me laugh every week.

# JOHN CLEESE

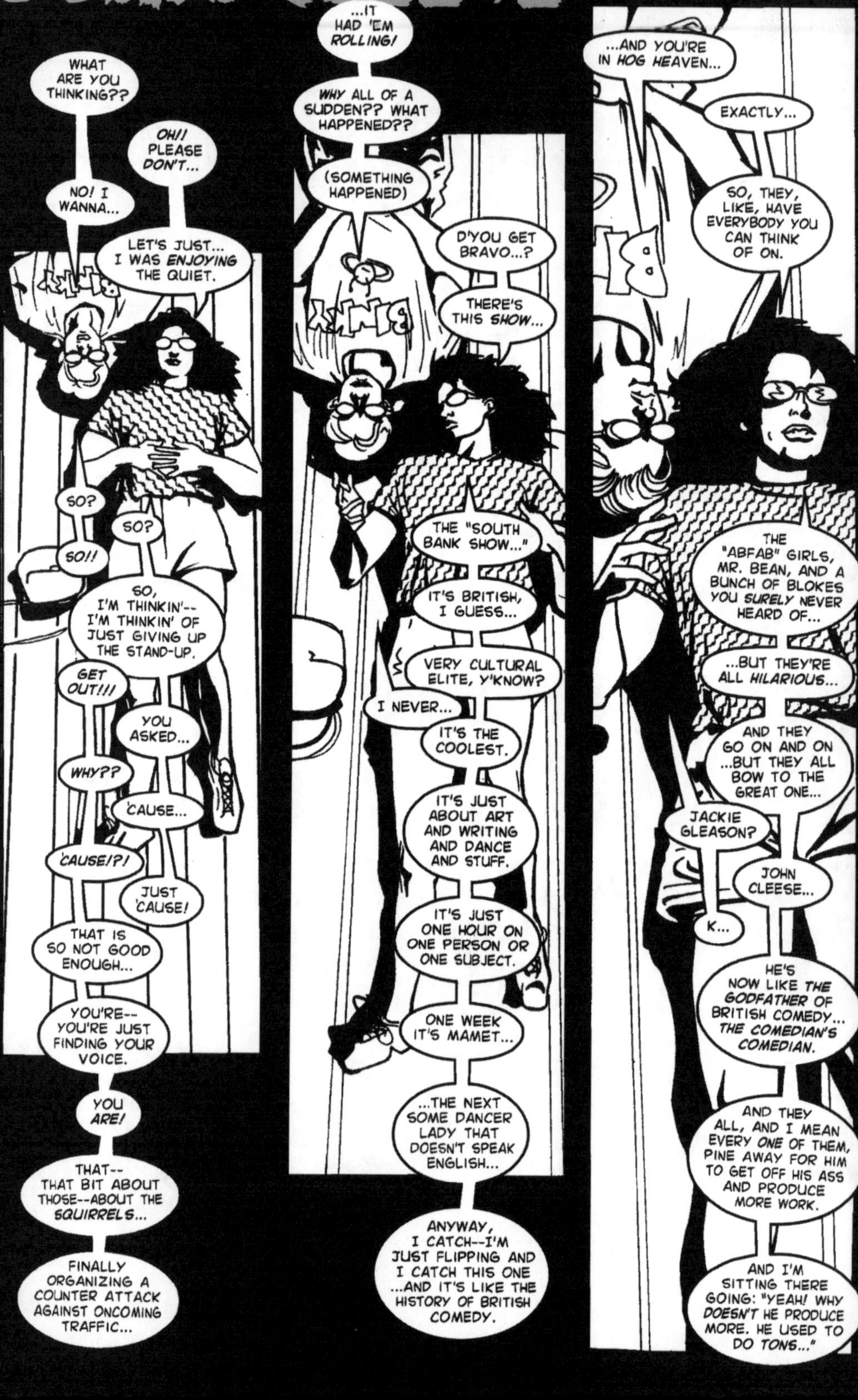
WHAT ARE YOU THINKING??
OH!! PLEASE DON'T...
NO! I WANNA...
LET'S JUST... I WAS ENJOYING THE QUIET.
SO?
SO?
SO!!
SO, I'M THINKIN'-- I'M THINKIN' OF JUST GIVING UP THE STAND-UP.
GET OUT!!!
YOU ASKED...
WHY??
'CAUSE...
'CAUSE!?!
JUST 'CAUSE!
THAT IS SO NOT GOOD ENOUGH...
YOU'RE-- YOU'RE JUST FINDING YOUR VOICE.
YOU ARE!
THAT-- THAT BIT ABOUT THOSE--ABOUT THE SQUIRRELS...
FINALLY ORGANIZING A COUNTER ATTACK AGAINST ONCOMING TRAFFIC...
...IT HAD 'EM ROLLING!
WHY ALL OF A SUDDEN?? WHAT HAPPENED??
(SOMETHING HAPPENED)
D'YOU GET BRAVO...?
THERE'S THIS SHOW...
THE "SOUTH BANK SHOW..."
IT'S BRITISH, I GUESS...
VERY CULTURAL ELITE, Y'KNOW?
I NEVER...
IT'S THE COOLEST.
IT'S JUST ABOUT ART AND WRITING AND DANCE AND STUFF.
IT'S JUST ONE HOUR ON ONE PERSON OR ONE SUBJECT.
ONE WEEK IT'S MAMET...
...THE NEXT SOME DANCER LADY THAT DOESN'T SPEAK ENGLISH...
ANYWAY, I CATCH--I'M JUST FLIPPING AND I CATCH THIS ONE ...AND IT'S LIKE THE HISTORY OF BRITISH COMEDY.
...AND YOU'RE IN HOG HEAVEN...
EXACTLY...
SO, THEY, LIKE, HAVE EVERYBODY YOU CAN THINK OF ON.
THE "ABFAB" GIRLS, MR. BEAN, AND A BUNCH OF BLOKES YOU SURELY NEVER HEARD OF...
...BUT THEY'RE ALL HILARIOUS...
AND THEY GO ON AND ON ...BUT THEY ALL BOW TO THE GREAT ONE...
JACKIE GLEASON?
JOHN CLEESE...
K...
HE'S NOW LIKE THE GODFATHER OF BRITISH COMEDY... THE COMEDIAN'S COMEDIAN.
AND THEY ALL, AND I MEAN EVERY ONE OF THEM, PINE AWAY FOR HIM TO GET OFF HIS ASS AND PRODUCE MORE WORK.
AND I'M SITTING THERE GOING: "YEAH! WHY DOESN'T HE PRODUCE MORE. HE USED TO DO TONS..."

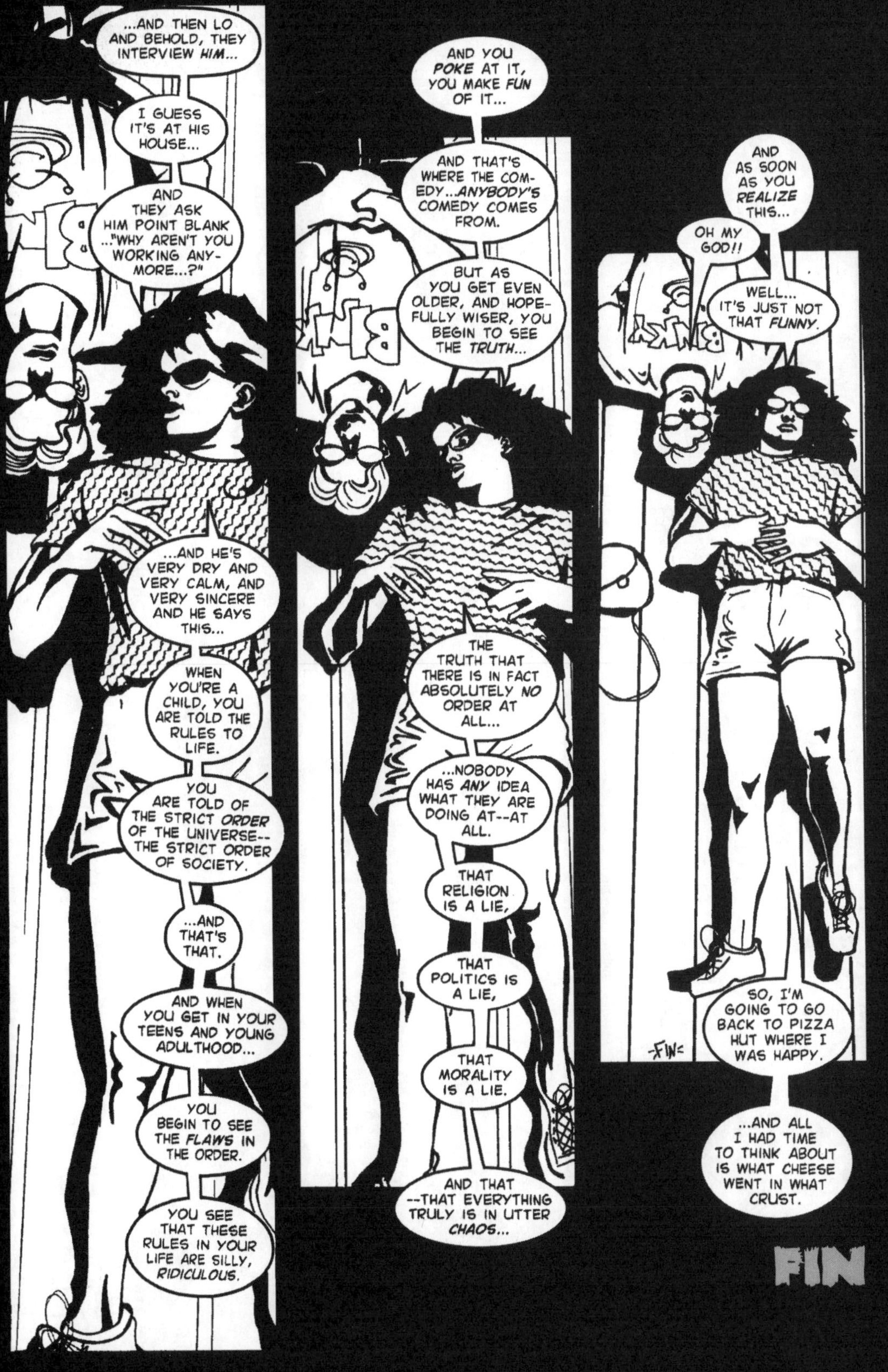
...AND THEN LO AND BEHOLD, THEY INTERVIEW HIM...
I GUESS IT'S AT HIS HOUSE...
AND THEY ASK HIM POINT BLANK ..."WHY AREN'T YOU WORKING ANY-MORE...?"
...AND HE'S VERY DRY AND VERY CALM, AND VERY SINCERE AND HE SAYS THIS...
WHEN YOU'RE A CHILD, YOU ARE TOLD THE RULES TO LIFE.
YOU ARE TOLD OF THE STRICT ORDER OF THE UNIVERSE-- THE STRICT ORDER OF SOCIETY.
...AND THAT'S THAT.
AND WHEN YOU GET IN YOUR TEENS AND YOUNG ADULTHOOD...
YOU BEGIN TO SEE THE FLAWS IN THE ORDER.
YOU SEE THAT THESE RULES IN YOUR LIFE ARE SILLY, RIDICULOUS.
AND YOU POKE AT IT, YOU MAKE FUN OF IT...
AND THAT'S WHERE THE COM-EDY...ANYBODY'S COMEDY COMES FROM.
BUT AS YOU GET EVEN OLDER, AND HOPE-FULLY WISER, YOU BEGIN TO SEE THE TRUTH...
THE TRUTH THAT THERE IS IN FACT ABSOLUTELY NO ORDER AT ALL...
...NOBODY HAS ANY IDEA WHAT THEY ARE DOING AT--AT ALL.
THAT RELIGION IS A LIE,
THAT POLITICS IS A LIE,
THAT MORALITY IS A LIE.
AND THAT --THAT EVERYTHING TRULY IS IN UTTER CHAOS...
AND AS SOON AS YOU REALIZE THIS...
OH MY GOD!!
WELL... IT'S JUST NOT THAT FUNNY.
SO, I'M GOING TO GO BACK TO PIZZA HUT WHERE I WAS HAPPY.
...AND ALL I HAD TIME TO THINK ABOUT IS WHAT CHEESE WENT IN WHAT CRUST.
-FIN-
FIN

# MYSTERY DATE

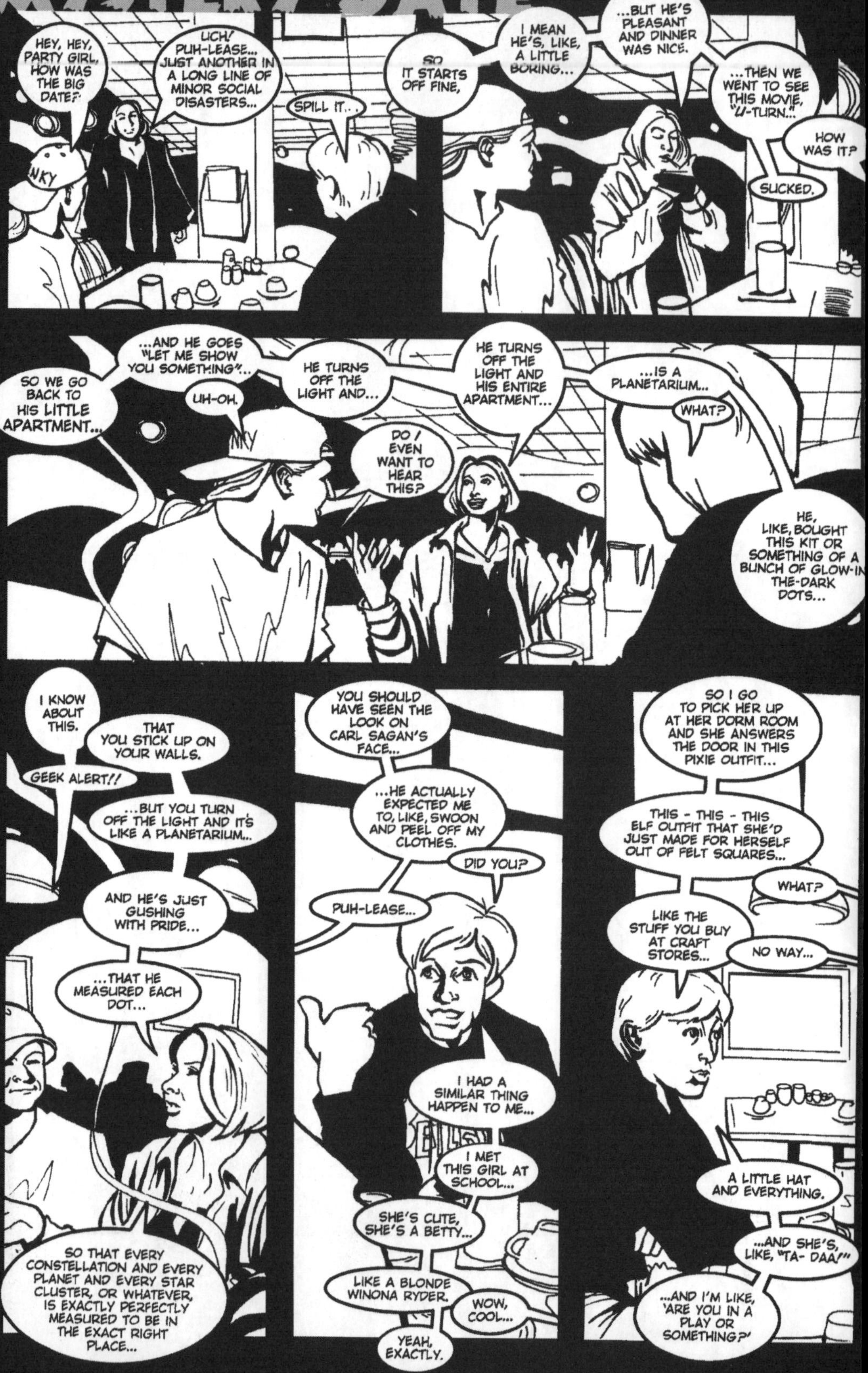
HEY, HEY, PARTY GIRL, HOW WAS THE BIG DATE?
UGH! PUH-LEASE... JUST ANOTHER IN A LONG LINE OF MINOR SOCIAL DISASTERS...
SPILL IT...
SO IT STARTS OFF FINE,
I MEAN HE'S, LIKE, A LITTLE BORING...
...BUT HE'S PLEASANT AND DINNER WAS NICE.
...THEN WE WENT TO SEE THIS MOVIE, "U-TURN."
HOW WAS IT?
SUCKED.
SO WE GO BACK TO HIS LITTLE APARTMENT...
...AND HE GOES "LET ME SHOW YOU SOMETHING"...
UH-OH.
HE TURNS OFF THE LIGHT AND...
DO I EVEN WANT TO HEAR THIS?
HE TURNS OFF THE LIGHT AND HIS ENTIRE APARTMENT...
...IS A PLANETARIUM...
WHAT?
HE, LIKE, BOUGHT THIS KIT OR SOMETHING OF A BUNCH OF GLOW-IN-THE-DARK DOTS...
I KNOW ABOUT THIS.
THAT YOU STICK UP ON YOUR WALLS.
GEEK ALERT!!
...BUT YOU TURN OFF THE LIGHT AND IT'S LIKE A PLANETARIUM...
AND HE'S JUST GUSHING WITH PRIDE...
...THAT HE MEASURED EACH DOT...
SO THAT EVERY CONSTELLATION AND EVERY PLANET AND EVERY STAR CLUSTER, OR WHATEVER, IS EXACTLY PERFECTLY MEASURED TO BE IN THE EXACT RIGHT PLACE...
YOU SHOULD HAVE SEEN THE LOOK ON CARL SAGAN'S FACE...
...HE ACTUALLY EXPECTED ME TO, LIKE, SWOON AND PEEL OFF MY CLOTHES.
DID YOU?
PUH-LEASE...
I HAD A SIMILAR THING HAPPEN TO ME...
I MET THIS GIRL AT SCHOOL...
SHE'S CUTE, SHE'S A BETTY...
LIKE A BLONDE WINONA RYDER.
WOW, COOL...
YEAH, EXACTLY.
SO I GO TO PICK HER UP AT HER DORM ROOM AND SHE ANSWERS THE DOOR IN THIS PIXIE OUTFIT...
THIS - THIS - THIS ELF OUTFIT THAT SHE'D JUST MADE FOR HERSELF OUT OF FELT SQUARES...
WHAT?
LIKE THE STUFF YOU BUY AT CRAFT STORES...
NO WAY...
A LITTLE HAT AND EVERYTHING.
...AND SHE'S, LIKE, "TA- DAA!"
...AND I'M LIKE, 'ARE YOU IN A PLAY OR SOMETHING?'

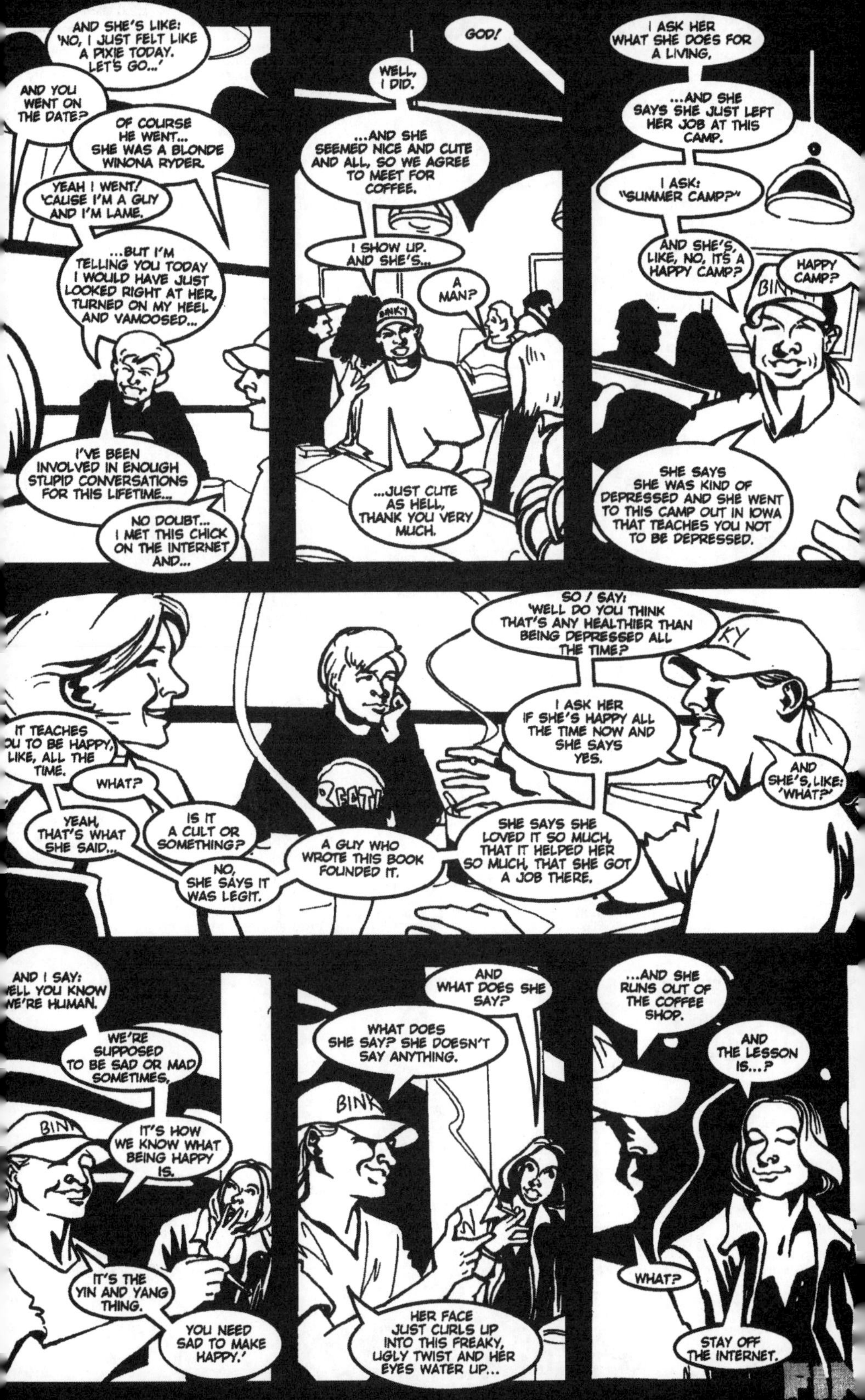
AND SHE'S LIKE: 'NO, I JUST FELT LIKE A PIXIE TODAY. LET'S GO...'
AND YOU WENT ON THE DATE?
OF COURSE HE WENT... SHE WAS A BLONDE WINONA RYDER.
YEAH I WENT! 'CAUSE I'M A GUY AND I'M LAME.
...BUT I'M TELLING YOU TODAY I WOULD HAVE JUST LOOKED RIGHT AT HER, TURNED ON MY HEEL AND VAMOOSED...
I'VE BEEN INVOLVED IN ENOUGH STUPID CONVERSATIONS FOR THIS LIFETIME...
NO DOUBT... I MET THIS CHICK ON THE INTERNET AND...
GOD!
WELL, I DID.
...AND SHE SEEMED NICE AND CUTE AND ALL, SO WE AGREE TO MEET FOR COFFEE.
I SHOW UP. AND SHE'S...
A MAN?
...JUST CUTE AS HELL, THANK YOU VERY MUCH.
I ASK HER WHAT SHE DOES FOR A LIVING,
...AND SHE SAYS SHE JUST LEFT HER JOB AT THIS CAMP.
I ASK: "SUMMER CAMP?"
AND SHE'S, LIKE, NO, IT'S A HAPPY CAMP?
HAPPY CAMP?
SHE SAYS SHE WAS KIND OF DEPRESSED AND SHE WENT TO THIS CAMP OUT IN IOWA THAT TEACHES YOU NOT TO BE DEPRESSED.
IT TEACHES OU TO BE HAPPY, LIKE, ALL THE TIME.
WHAT?
YEAH, THAT'S WHAT SHE SAID...
IS IT A CULT OR SOMETHING?
NO, SHE SAYS IT WAS LEGIT.
A GUY WHO WROTE THIS BOOK FOUNDED IT.
SHE SAYS SHE LOVED IT SO MUCH, THAT IT HELPED HER SO MUCH, THAT SHE GOT A JOB THERE.
I ASK HER IF SHE'S HAPPY ALL THE TIME NOW AND SHE SAYS YES.
SO I SAY: 'WELL DO YOU THINK THAT'S ANY HEALTHIER THAN BEING DEPRESSED ALL THE TIME?
AND SHE'S, LIKE: 'WHAT?'
AND I SAY: VELL YOU KNOW VE'RE HUMAN.
WE'RE SUPPOSED TO BE SAD OR MAD SOMETIMES,
IT'S HOW WE KNOW WHAT BEING HAPPY IS.
IT'S THE YIN AND YANG THING.
YOU NEED SAD TO MAKE HAPPY.'
AND WHAT DOES SHE SAY?
WHAT DOES SHE SAY? SHE DOESN'T SAY ANYTHING.
HER FACE JUST CURLS UP INTO THIS FREAKY, UGLY TWIST AND HER EYES WATER UP...
...AND SHE RUNS OUT OF THE COFFEE SHOP.
AND THE LESSON IS...?
WHAT?
STAY OFF THE INTERNET.
FIN

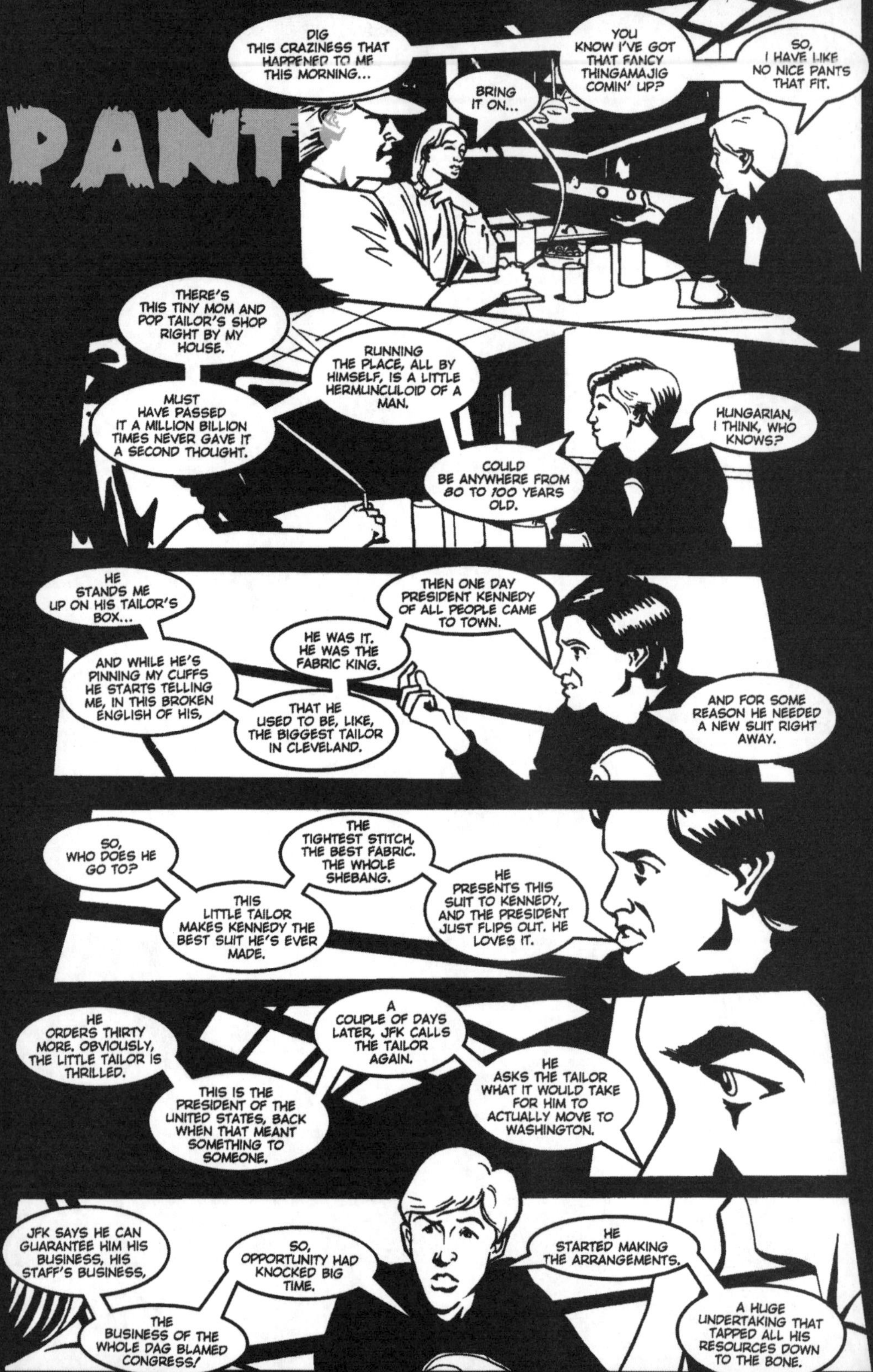
PANT
DIG THIS CRAZINESS THAT HAPPENED TO ME THIS MORNING...
BRING IT ON...
YOU KNOW I'VE GOT THAT FANCY THINGAMAJIG COMIN' UP?
SO, I HAVE LIKE NO NICE PANTS THAT FIT.
THERE'S THIS TINY MOM AND POP TAILOR'S SHOP RIGHT BY MY HOUSE.
MUST HAVE PASSED IT A MILLION BILLION TIMES NEVER GAVE IT A SECOND THOUGHT.
RUNNING THE PLACE, ALL BY HIMSELF, IS A LITTLE HERMUNCULOID OF A MAN.
COULD BE ANYWHERE FROM 80 TO 100 YEARS OLD.
HUNGARIAN, I THINK, WHO KNOWS?
HE STANDS ME UP ON HIS TAILOR'S BOX...
AND WHILE HE'S PINNING MY CUFFS HE STARTS TELLING ME, IN THIS BROKEN ENGLISH OF HIS,
THAT HE USED TO BE, LIKE, THE BIGGEST TAILOR IN CLEVELAND.
HE WAS IT. HE WAS THE FABRIC KING.
THEN ONE DAY PRESIDENT KENNEDY OF ALL PEOPLE CAME TO TOWN.
AND FOR SOME REASON HE NEEDED A NEW SUIT RIGHT AWAY.
SO, WHO DOES HE GO TO?
THIS LITTLE TAILOR MAKES KENNEDY THE BEST SUIT HE'S EVER MADE.
THE TIGHTEST STITCH, THE BEST FABRIC. THE WHOLE SHEBANG.
HE PRESENTS THIS SUIT TO KENNEDY, AND THE PRESIDENT JUST FLIPS OUT. HE LOVES IT.
HE ORDERS THIRTY MORE. OBVIOUSLY, THE LITTLE TAILOR IS THRILLED.
THIS IS THE PRESIDENT OF THE UNITED STATES, BACK WHEN THAT MEANT SOMETHING TO SOMEONE.
A COUPLE OF DAYS LATER, JFK CALLS THE TAILOR AGAIN.
HE ASKS THE TAILOR WHAT IT WOULD TAKE FOR HIM TO ACTUALLY MOVE TO WASHINGTON.
JFK SAYS HE CAN GUARANTEE HIM HIS BUSINESS, HIS STAFF'S BUSINESS,
THE BUSINESS OF THE WHOLE DAG BLAMED CONGRESS!
SO, OPPORTUNITY HAD KNOCKED BIG TIME.
HE STARTED MAKING THE ARRANGEMENTS.
A HUGE UNDERTAKING THAT TAPPED ALL HIS RESOURCES DOWN TO THE BONE.

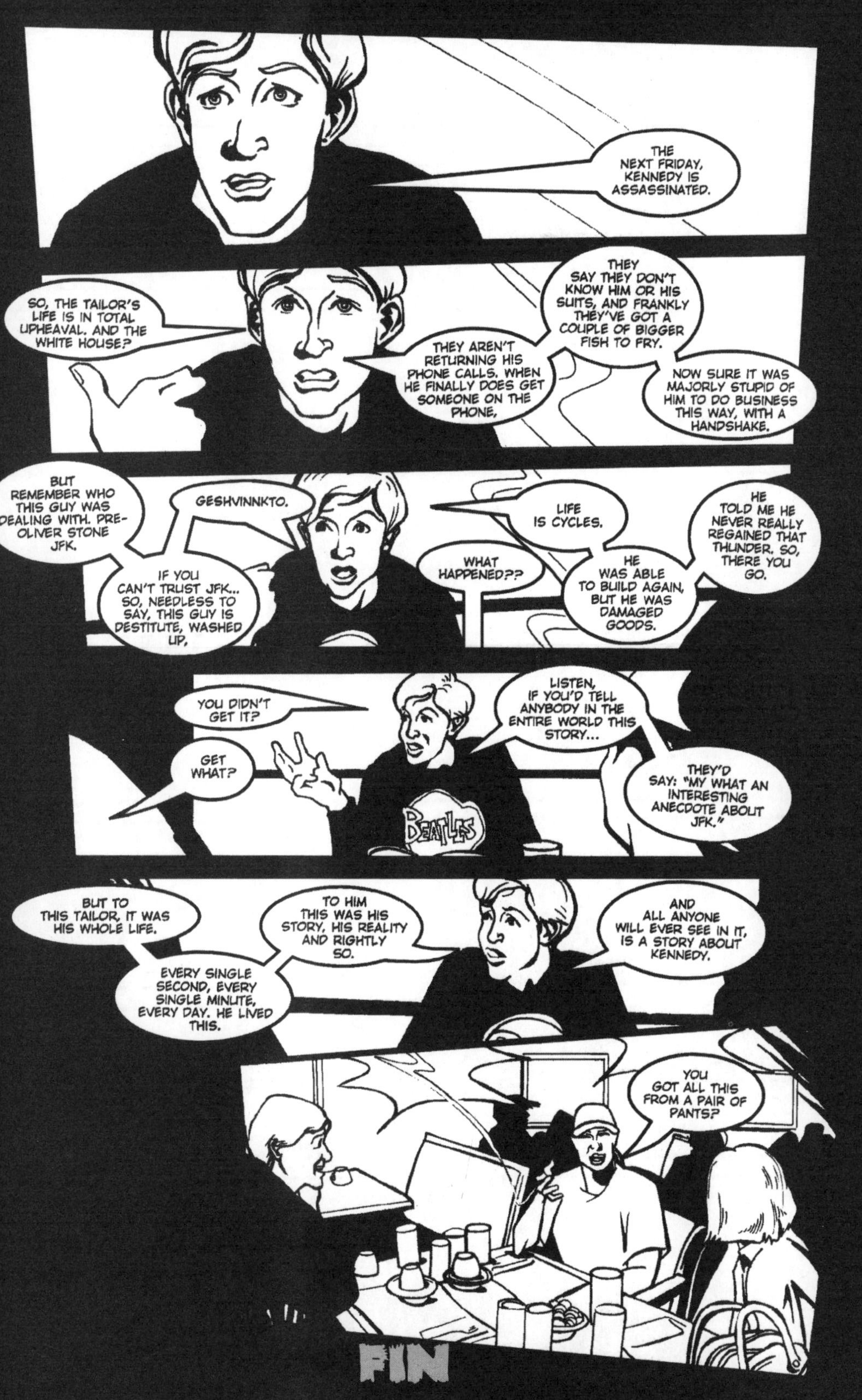
THE NEXT FRIDAY, KENNEDY IS ASSASSINATED.
SO, THE TAILOR'S LIFE IS IN TOTAL UPHEAVAL. AND THE WHITE HOUSE?
THEY AREN'T RETURNING HIS PHONE CALLS. WHEN HE FINALLY DOES GET SOMEONE ON THE PHONE,
THEY SAY THEY DON'T KNOW HIM OR HIS SUITS, AND FRANKLY THEY'VE GOT A COUPLE OF BIGGER FISH TO FRY.
NOW SURE IT WAS MAJORLY STUPID OF HIM TO DO BUSINESS THIS WAY, WITH A HANDSHAKE.
BUT REMEMBER WHO THIS GUY WAS DEALING WITH. PRE-OLIVER STONE JFK.
GESHVINNKTO.
IF YOU CAN'T TRUST JFK... SO, NEEDLESS TO SAY, THIS GUY IS DESTITUTE, WASHED UP,
WHAT HAPPENED??
LIFE IS CYCLES.
HE WAS ABLE TO BUILD AGAIN, BUT HE WAS DAMAGED GOODS.
HE TOLD ME HE NEVER REALLY REGAINED THAT THUNDER. SO, THERE YOU GO.
YOU DIDN'T GET IT?
GET WHAT?
LISTEN, IF YOU'D TELL ANYBODY IN THE ENTIRE WORLD THIS STORY...
THEY'D SAY: "MY WHAT AN INTERESTING ANECDOTE ABOUT JFK."
BEATLES
BUT TO THIS TAILOR, IT WAS HIS WHOLE LIFE.
EVERY SINGLE SECOND, EVERY SINGLE MINUTE, EVERY DAY. HE LIVED THIS.
TO HIM THIS WAS HIS STORY, HIS REALITY AND RIGHTLY SO.
AND ALL ANYONE WILL EVER SEE IN IT, IS A STORY ABOUT KENNEDY.
YOU GOT ALL THIS FROM A PAIR OF PANTS?
FIN

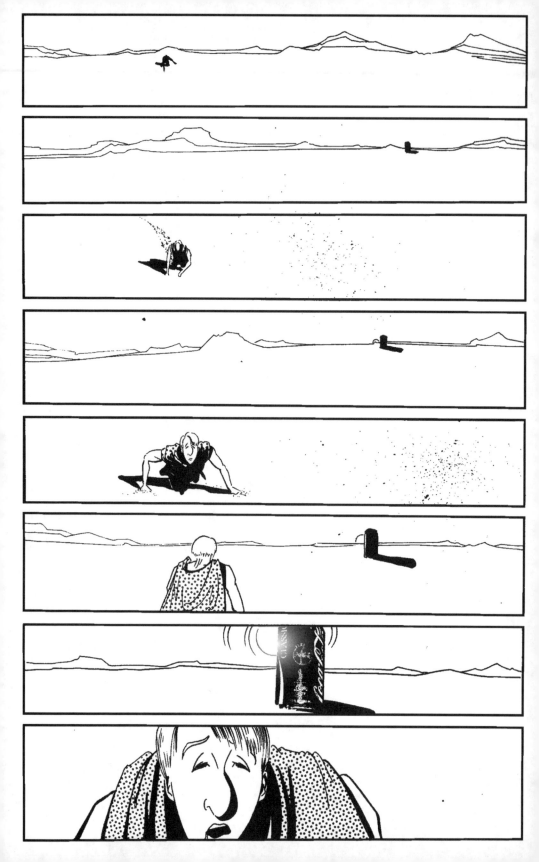

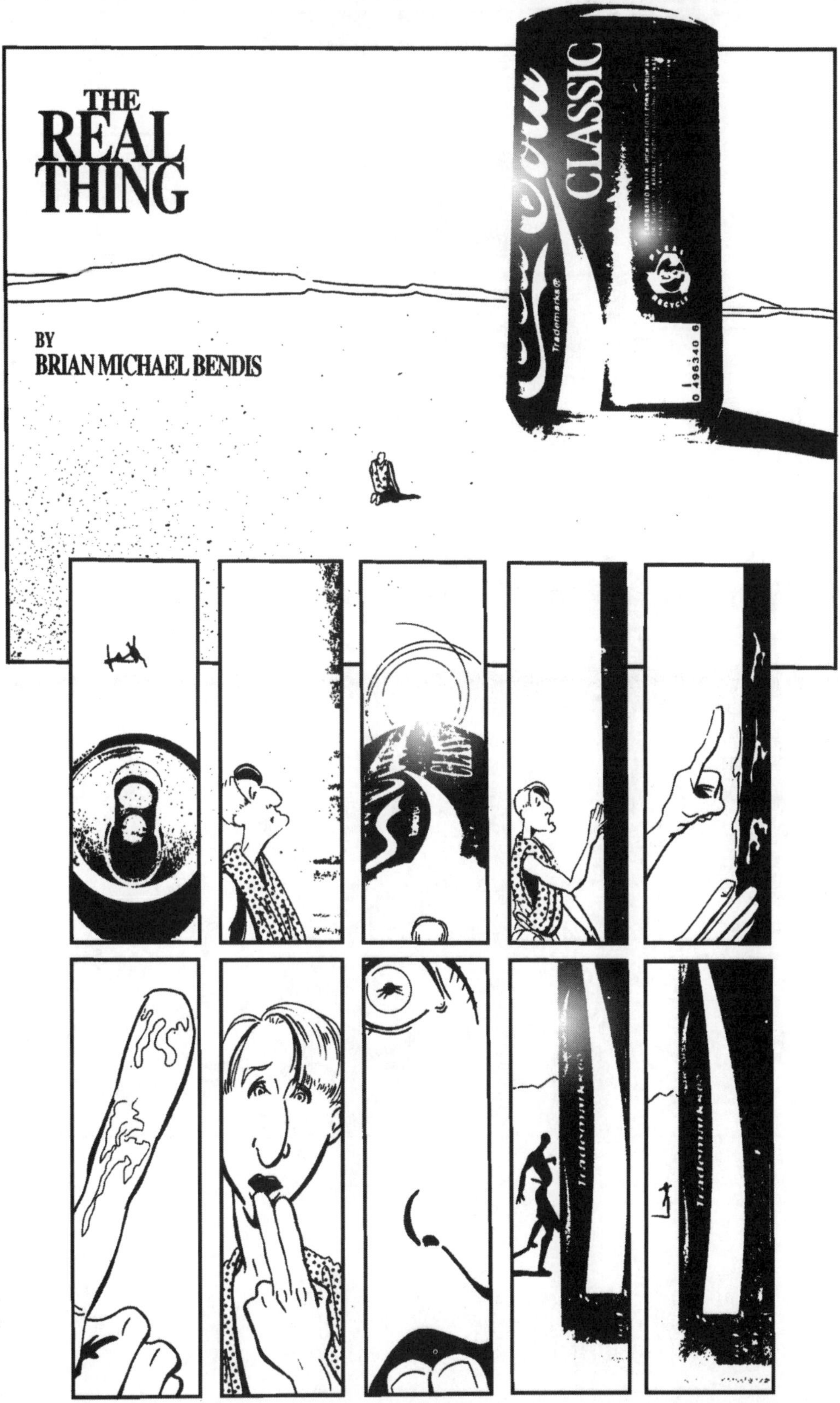
THE REAL THING
BY
BRIAN MICHAEL BENDIS
CLASSIC
Trademarks®
RECYCLE

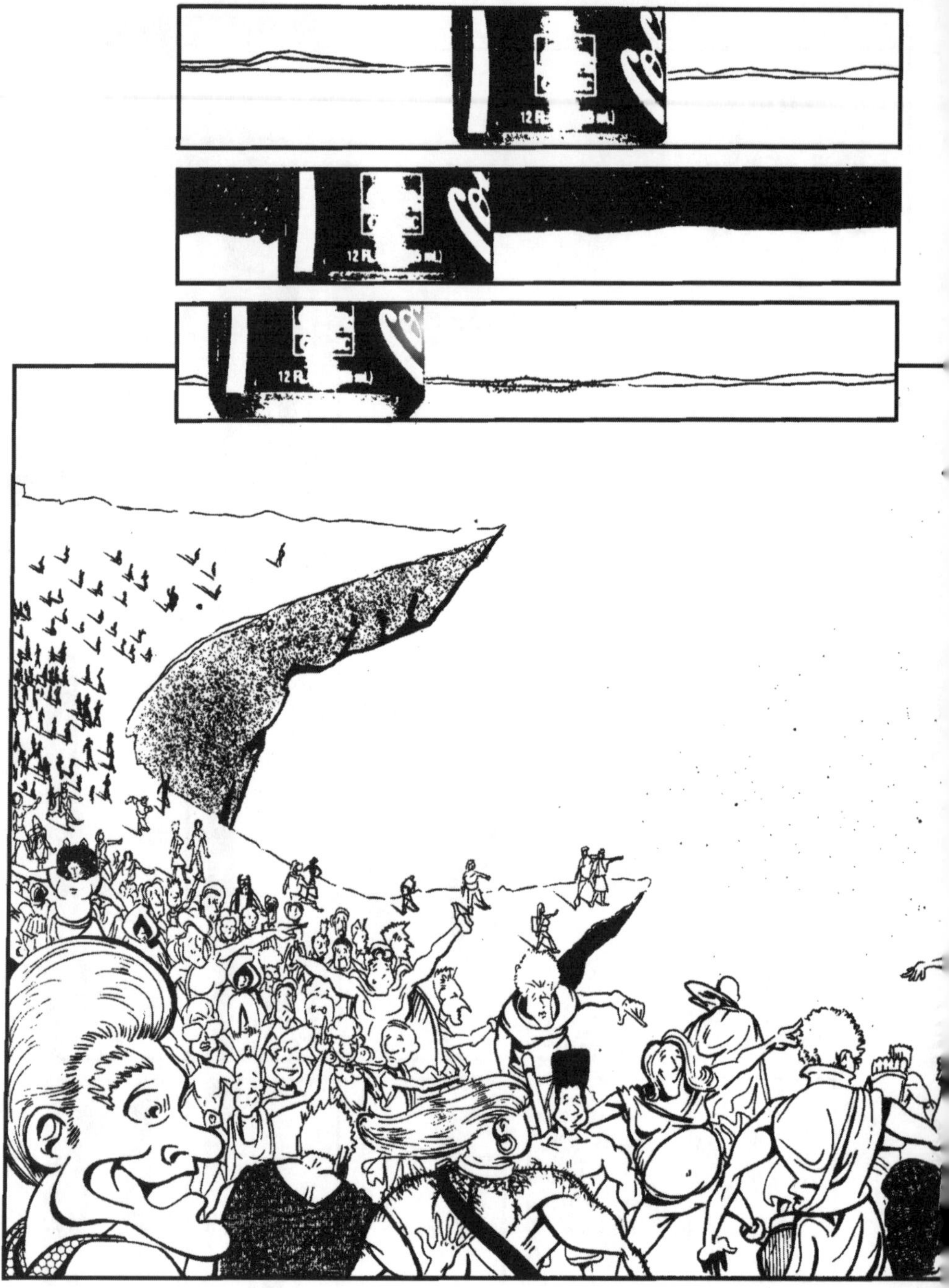

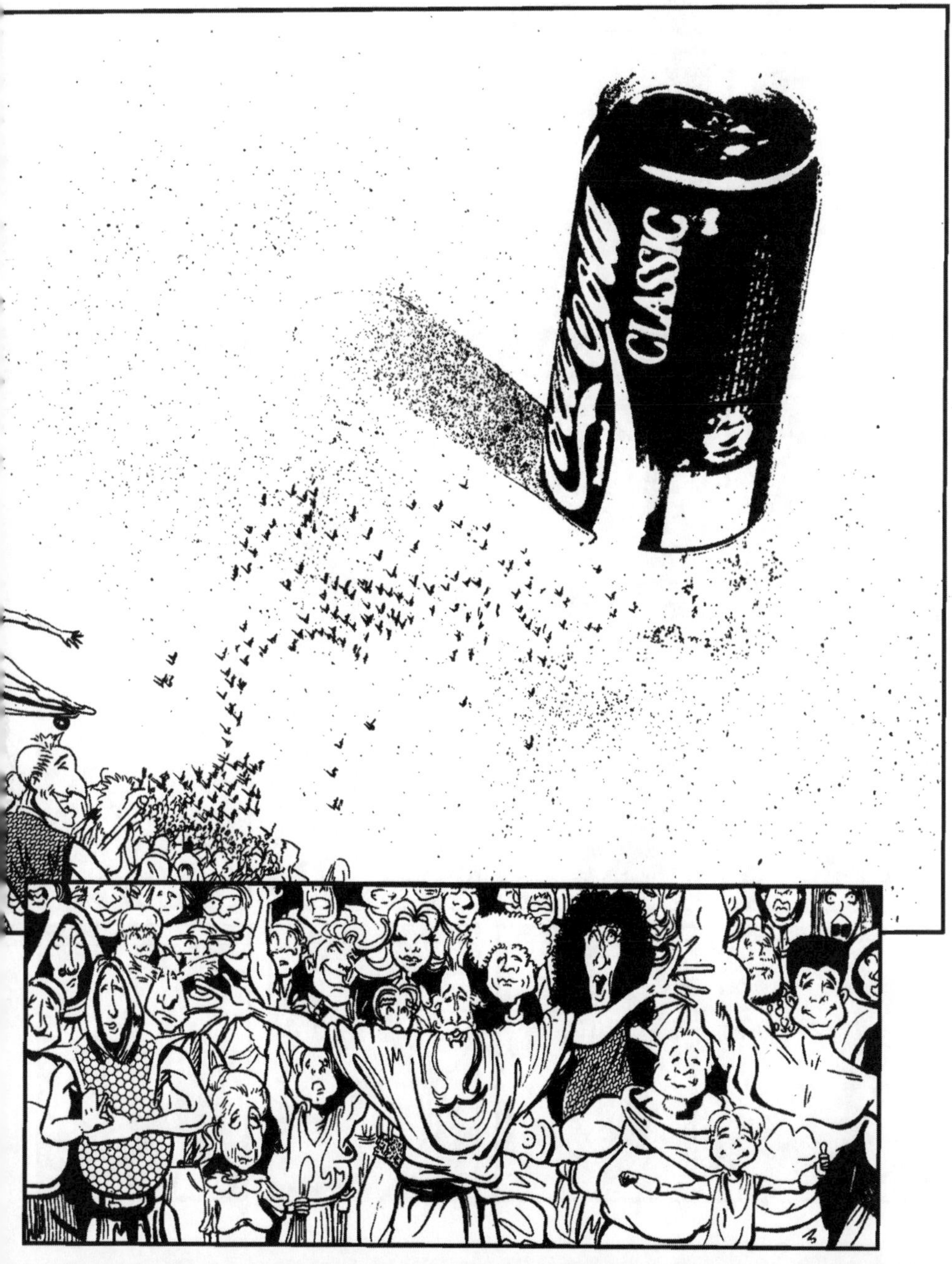
Coca-Cola
CLASSIC

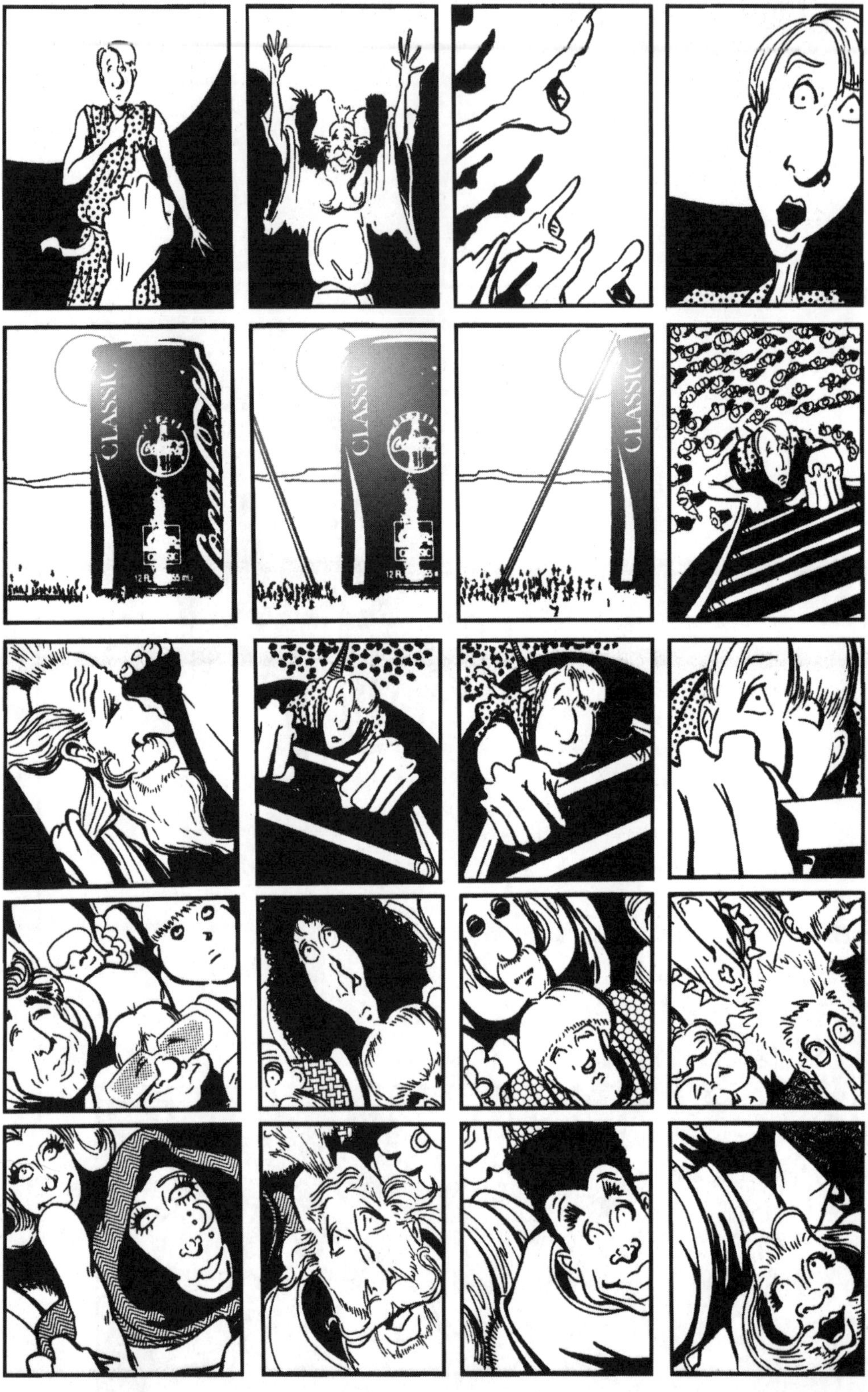
CLASSIC
Coca-Cola
CLASSIC
Coca-Cola
CLASSIC

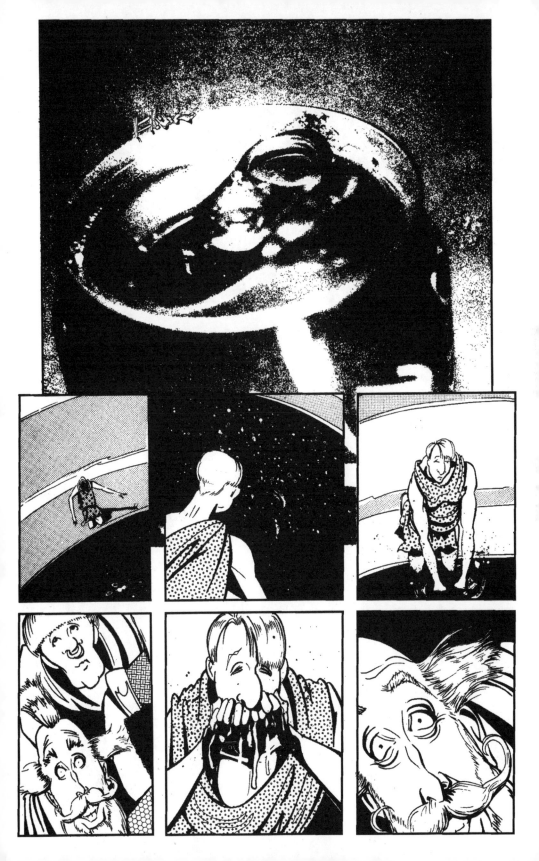

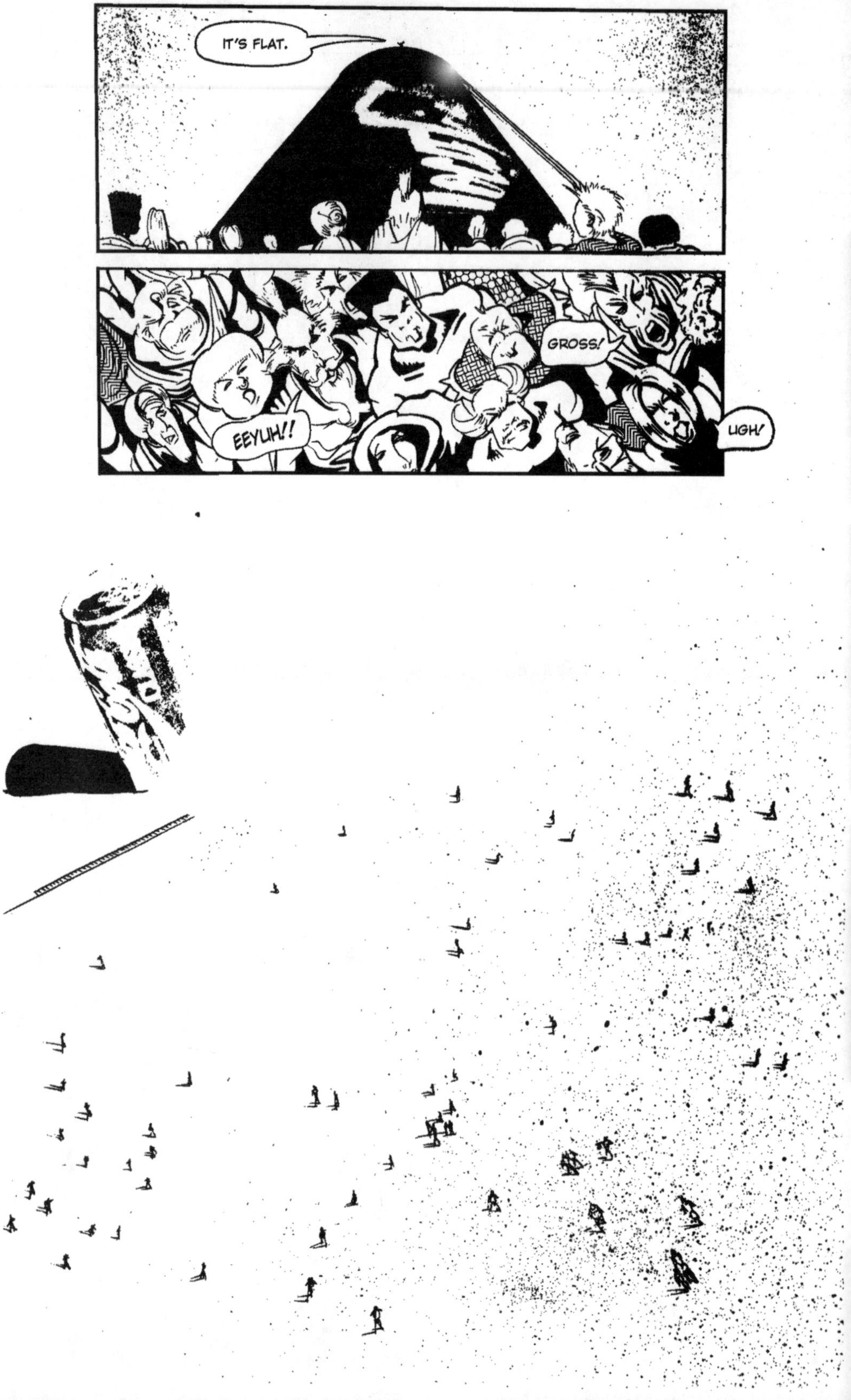
IT'S FLAT.
EEYUH!!
GROSS!
UGH!

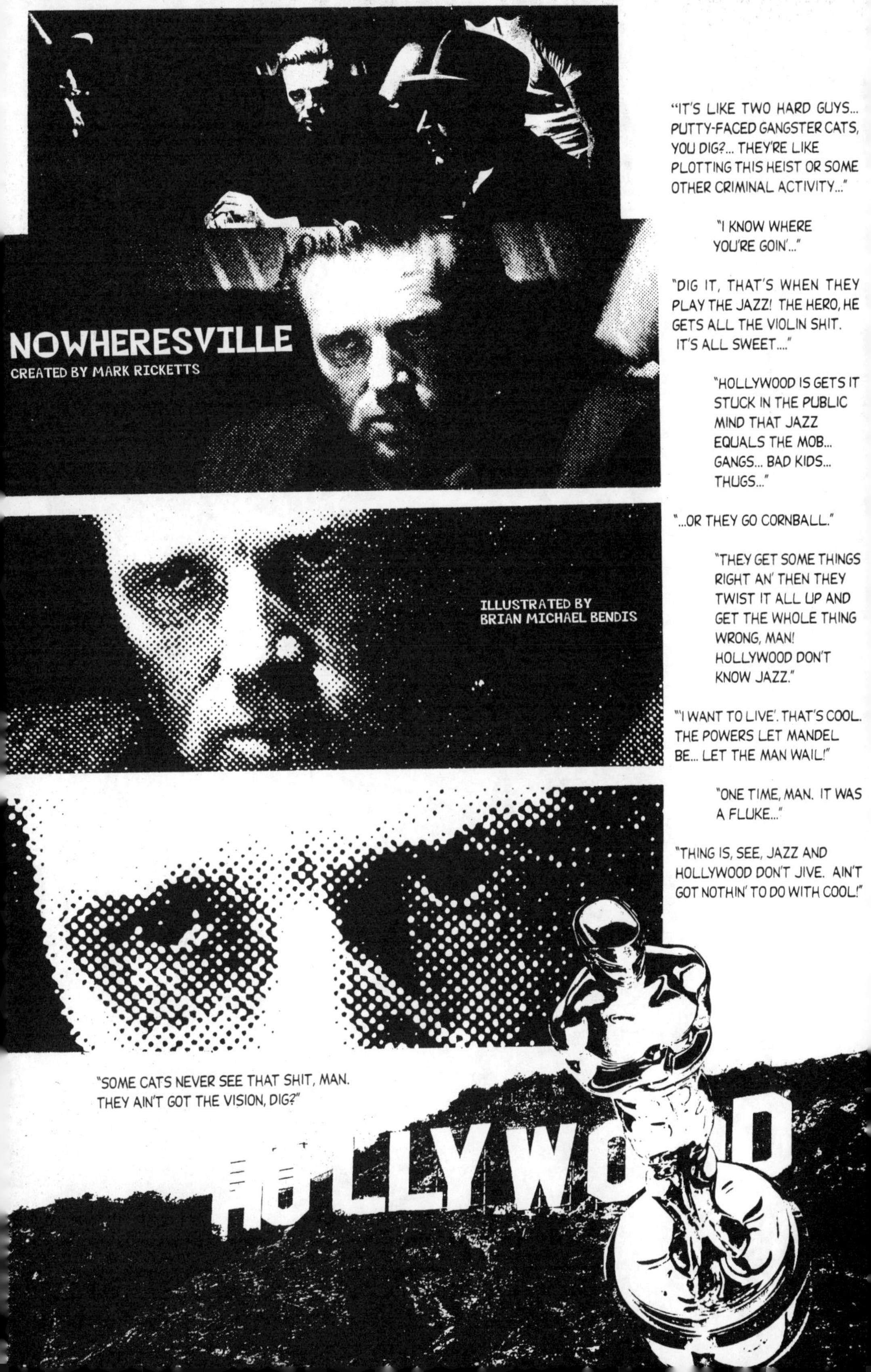

# NOWHERESVILLE

**CREATED BY MARK RICKETTS**

ILLUSTRATED BY
BRIAN MICHAEL BENDIS

"SOME CATS NEVER SEE THAT SHIT, MAN.
THEY AIN'T GOT THE VISION, DIG?"

HOLLYWOOD

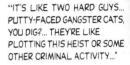

"IT'S LIKE TWO HARD GUYS...
PUTTY-FACED GANGSTER CATS,
YOU DIG?... THEY'RE LIKE
PLOTTING THIS HEIST OR SOME
OTHER CRIMINAL ACTIVITY..."

"I KNOW WHERE
YOU'RE GOIN'..."

"DIG IT, THAT'S WHEN THEY
PLAY THE JAZZ! THE HERO, HE
GETS ALL THE VIOLIN SHIT.
IT'S ALL SWEET...."

"HOLLYWOOD IS GETS IT
STUCK IN THE PUBLIC
MIND THAT JAZZ
EQUALS THE MOB...
GANGS... BAD KIDS...
THUGS..."

"...OR THEY GO CORNBALL."

"THEY GET SOME THINGS
RIGHT AN' THEN THEY
TWIST IT ALL UP AND
GET THE WHOLE THING
WRONG, MAN!
HOLLYWOOD DON'T
KNOW JAZZ."

"'I WANT TO LIVE'. THAT'S COOL.
THE POWERS LET MANDEL
BE... LET THE MAN WAIL!"

"ONE TIME, MAN. IT WAS
A FLUKE..."

"THING IS, SEE, JAZZ AND
HOLLYWOOD DON'T JIVE. AIN'T
GOT NOTHIN' TO DO WITH COOL!"

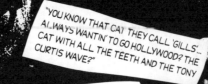

"YOU KNOW THAT CAT THEY CALL 'GILLS'... ALWAYS WANTIN' TO GO HOLLYWOOD? THE CAT WITH ALL THE TEETH AND THE TONY CURTIS WAVE?"

"THAT CAT HAD TALENT. HE WAS NO 'BIRD', BUT HE HAD SOME CHOPS."

"LOTTA FOLKS THINK HE GOT THAT NAME 'GILLS' 'CAUSE HE HAD THAT 'CIRCULAR BREATHING' THING DOWN, RIGHT? I MEAN HE COULD BE WAILIN' ALONG ON SOME KINDA BEBOP SOLO AND THEN HE'D CATCH THIS HIGH NOTE AND JUST HOLD IT THERE...LIKE FOREVER. LIKE HE WAS BREATHIN' THROUGH THE SIDE OF HIS NECK OR SOMETHIN'. 'GILLS', YOU DIG?"

"LIKE A FISH, MAN. YEAH, I'M WITH YOU."

" THAT AIN'T HOW HE GOT THE NAME. HE GOT THE NAME 'COS THE DAY JOB HE WAS WORKIN' AT THE PIER. HE WAS ONE THOSE CATS WHAT THROWS FISH...WRAPS 'EM... YOU KNOW, IN A OPEN MARKET. YOU SEEN THAT SHIT WHERE THEY PITCH BIG, FAT OL' FISH FROM ONE CAT TO THE NEXT, RIGHT?"

"YEAH, I SEEN THAT. FISH FLYIN' THROUGH THE AIR. S'COOL."

"THING IS, SEE... HE'D GET OFF WORK AN' GO TO HIS NIGHT GIG. BE WAITING OUTSIDE SOME CLUB SIDEDOOR ... A DOZEN ALLEYCATS WHAT CAUGHT THE SCENT CRAWLIN' UP HIS LEG.... CRYIN'! MAN, THE OTHER FELLAHS GET TO THE GIG AND THEY GOT INTO RIBBIN' HIM, YA KNOW. NOW, THAT'S HOW HE GOT THE NAME 'GILLS'... RIGHT THERE. THAT'S WHAT I THINK."

"YEAH, I KNOW ALL 'BOUT THAT CAT. I KNOW HIS WIFE AND I KNEW HIM FROM WHEN HE MET THAT LITTLE KITTY, TOO. NICE , BIG BLUE EYED SOUTHERN CHICK. KINDA FRAIL...AN' INNOCENT LITTLE APPLE. CALLED HER 'SWEET PEA'. "

"HIS 'DO WAS ALWAYS PERFECT."

"DON'T KNOW NO 'SWEET PEA'. MET A CAT NAMED 'BUTTER BEAN' ONE TIME."

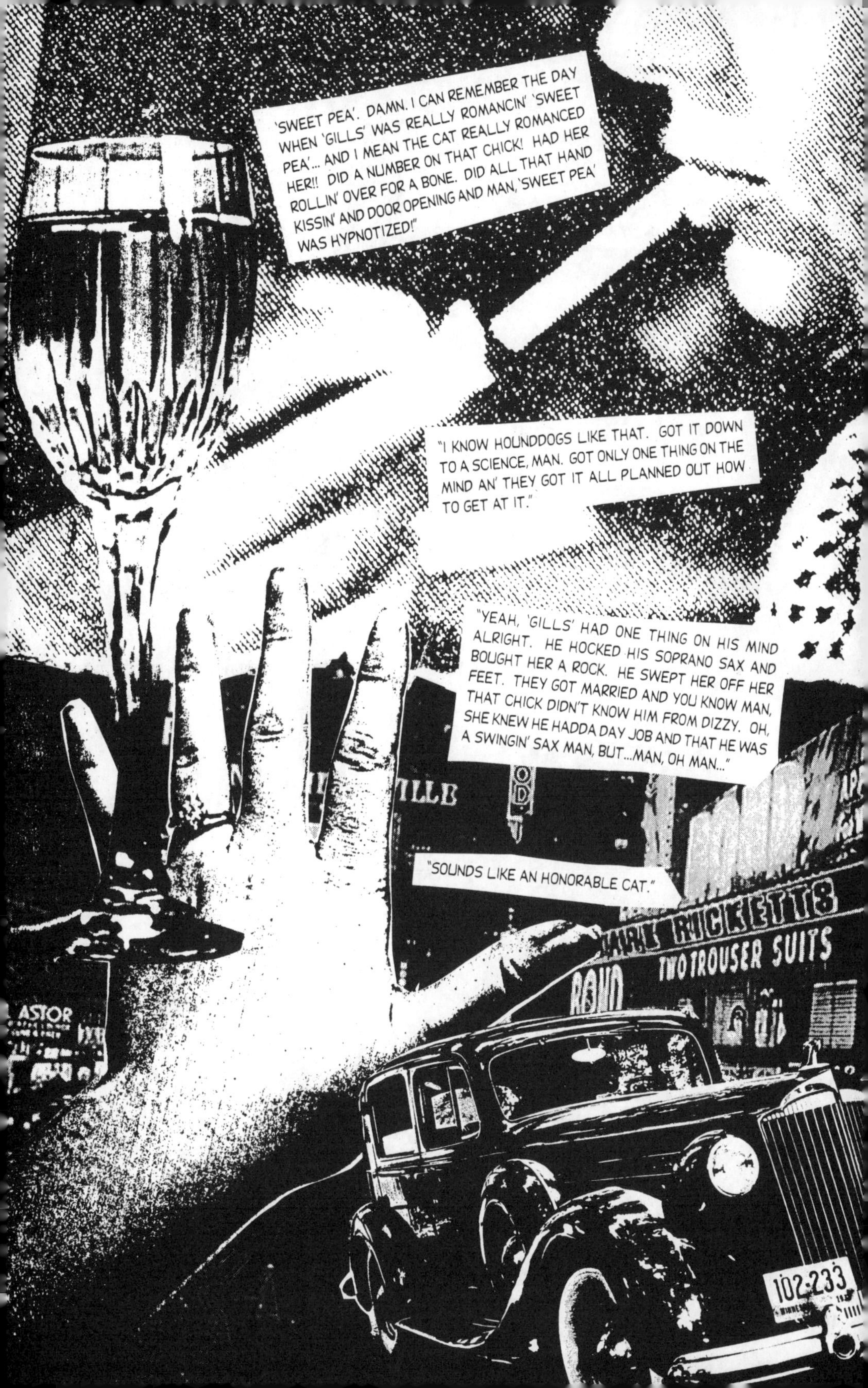
'SWEET PEA'. DAMN. I CAN REMEMBER THE DAY WHEN 'GILLS' WAS REALLY ROMANCIN' 'SWEET PEA'... AND I MEAN THE CAT REALLY ROMANCED HER!! DID A NUMBER ON THAT CHICK! HAD HER ROLLIN' OVER FOR A BONE. DID ALL THAT HAND KISSIN' AND DOOR OPENING AND MAN, 'SWEET PEA' WAS HYPNOTIZED!"
"I KNOW HOUNDDOGS LIKE THAT. GOT IT DOWN TO A SCIENCE, MAN. GOT ONLY ONE THING ON THE MIND AN' THEY GOT IT ALL PLANNED OUT HOW TO GET AT IT."
"YEAH, 'GILLS' HAD ONE THING ON HIS MIND ALRIGHT. HE HOCKED HIS SOPRANO SAX AND BOUGHT HER A ROCK. HE SWEPT HER OFF HER FEET. THEY GOT MARRIED AND YOU KNOW MAN, THAT CHICK DIDN'T KNOW HIM FROM DIZZY. OH, SHE KNEW HE HADDA DAY JOB AND THAT HE WAS A SWINGIN' SAX MAN, BUT...MAN, OH MAN..."
"SOUNDS LIKE AN HONORABLE CAT."
RICKETTS
TWO TROUSER SUITS
ASTOR
102-233

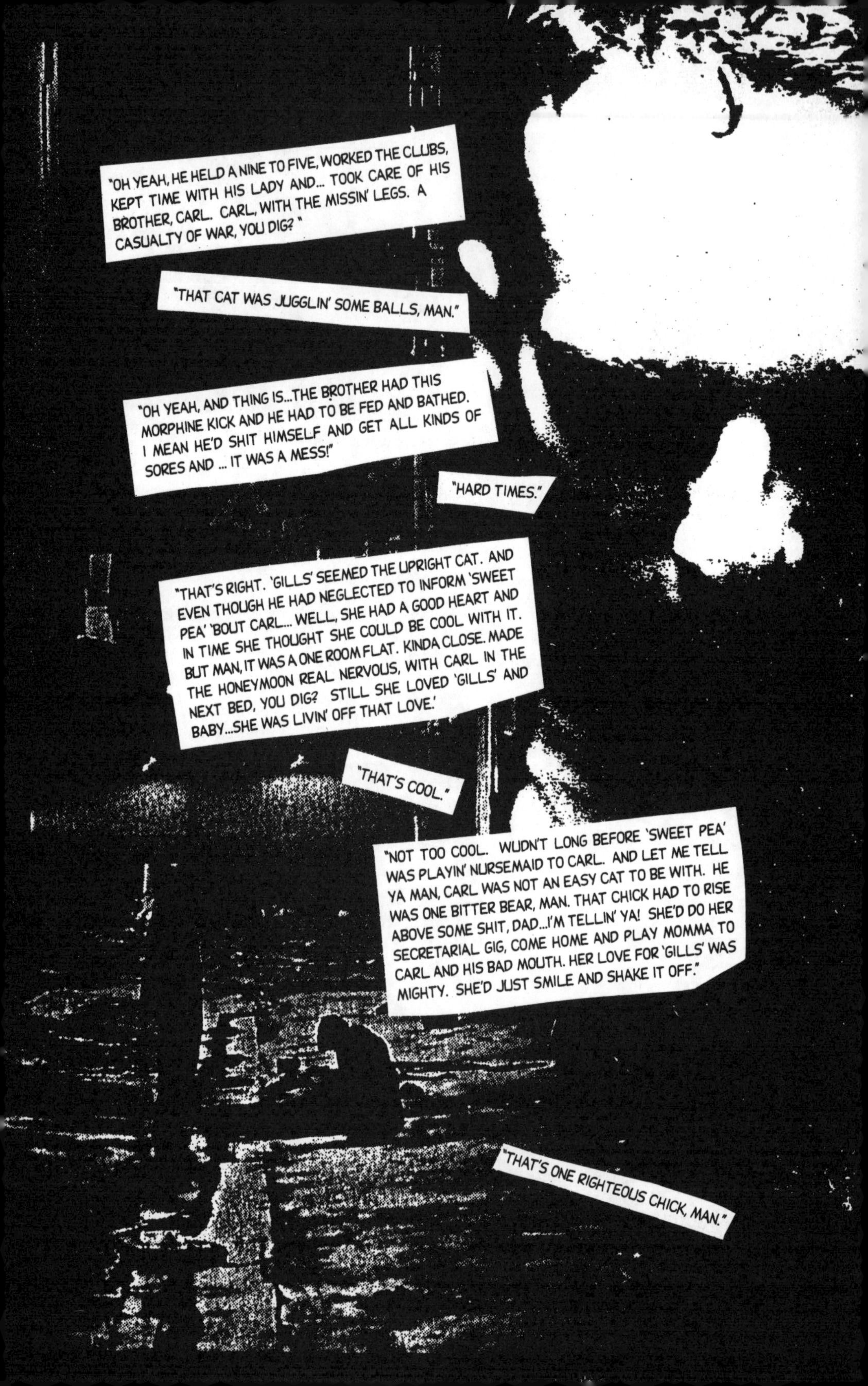
"OH YEAH, HE HELD A NINE TO FIVE, WORKED THE CLUBS, KEPT TIME WITH HIS LADY AND... TOOK CARE OF HIS BROTHER, CARL. CARL, WITH THE MISSIN' LEGS. A CASUALTY OF WAR, YOU DIG?"
"THAT CAT WAS JUGGLIN' SOME BALLS, MAN."
"OH YEAH, AND THING IS...THE BROTHER HAD THIS MORPHINE KICK AND HE HAD TO BE FED AND BATHED. I MEAN HE'D SHIT HIMSELF AND GET ALL KINDS OF SORES AND ... IT WAS A MESS!"
"HARD TIMES."
"THAT'S RIGHT. 'GILLS' SEEMED THE UPRIGHT CAT. AND EVEN THOUGH HE HAD NEGLECTED TO INFORM 'SWEET PEA' 'BOUT CARL... WELL, SHE HAD A GOOD HEART AND IN TIME SHE THOUGHT SHE COULD BE COOL WITH IT. BUT MAN, IT WAS A ONE ROOM FLAT. KINDA CLOSE. MADE THE HONEYMOON REAL NERVOUS, WITH CARL IN THE NEXT BED, YOU DIG? STILL SHE LOVED 'GILLS' AND BABY...SHE WAS LIVIN' OFF THAT LOVE.'
"THAT'S COOL."
"NOT TOO COOL. WUDN'T LONG BEFORE 'SWEET PEA' WAS PLAYIN' NURSEMAID TO CARL. AND LET ME TELL YA MAN, CARL WAS NOT AN EASY CAT TO BE WITH. HE WAS ONE BITTER BEAR, MAN. THAT CHICK HAD TO RISE ABOVE SOME SHIT, DAD...I'M TELLIN' YA! SHE'D DO HER SECRETARIAL GIG, COME HOME AND PLAY MOMMA TO CARL AND HIS BAD MOUTH. HER LOVE FOR 'GILLS' WAS MIGHTY. SHE'D JUST SMILE AND SHAKE IT OFF."
"THAT'S ONE RIGHTEOUS CHICK, MAN."

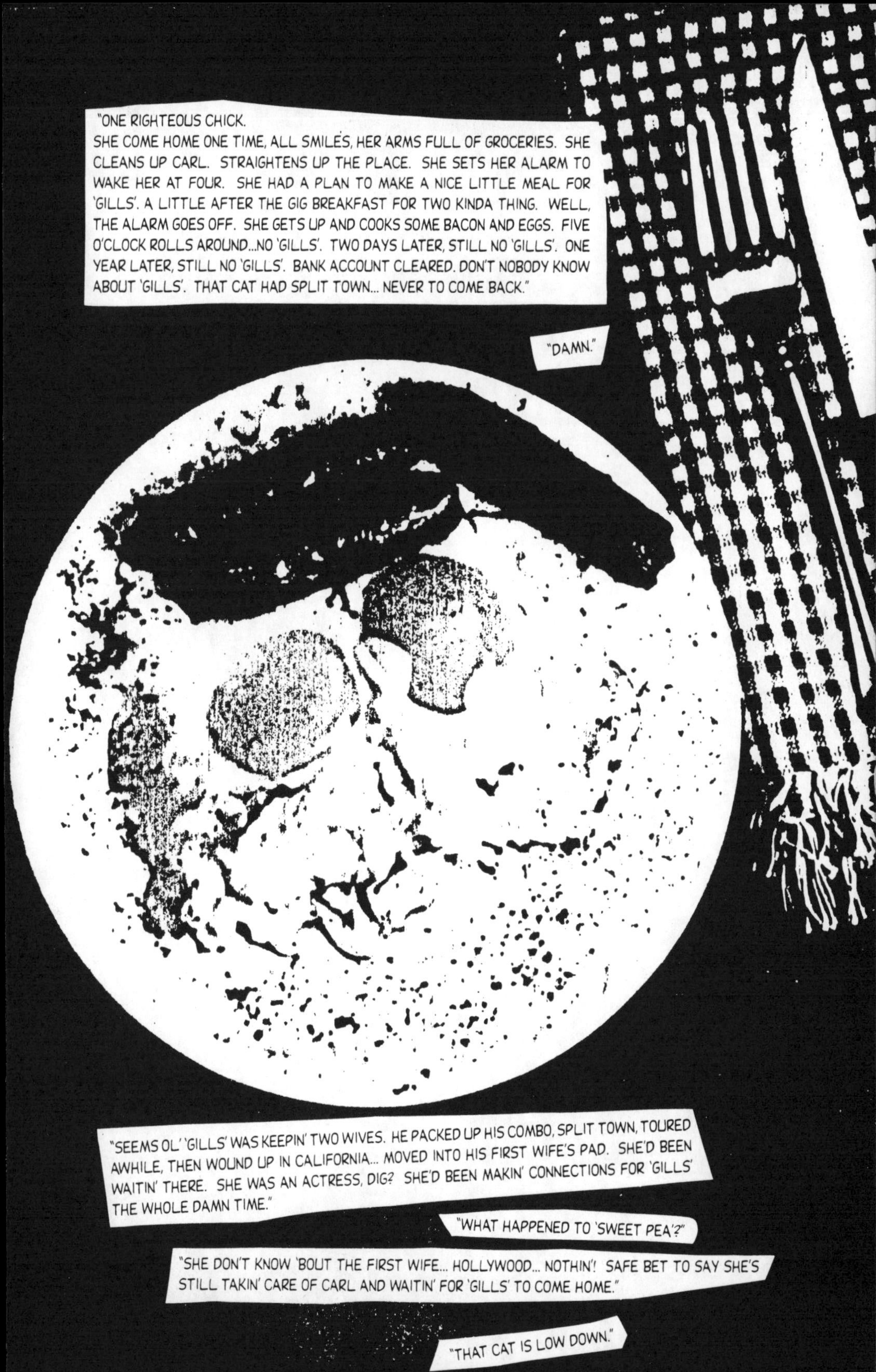
"ONE RIGHTEOUS CHICK.
SHE COME HOME ONE TIME, ALL SMILES, HER ARMS FULL OF GROCERIES. SHE CLEANS UP CARL. STRAIGHTENS UP THE PLACE. SHE SETS HER ALARM TO WAKE HER AT FOUR. SHE HAD A PLAN TO MAKE A NICE LITTLE MEAL FOR 'GILLS'. A LITTLE AFTER THE GIG BREAKFAST FOR TWO KINDA THING. WELL, THE ALARM GOES OFF. SHE GETS UP AND COOKS SOME BACON AND EGGS. FIVE O'CLOCK ROLLS AROUND...NO 'GILLS'. TWO DAYS LATER, STILL NO 'GILLS'. ONE YEAR LATER, STILL NO 'GILLS'. BANK ACCOUNT CLEARED. DON'T NOBODY KNOW ABOUT 'GILLS'. THAT CAT HAD SPLIT TOWN... NEVER TO COME BACK."
"DAMN."
"SEEMS OL' 'GILLS' WAS KEEPIN' TWO WIVES. HE PACKED UP HIS COMBO, SPLIT TOWN, TOURED AWHILE, THEN WOUND UP IN CALIFORNIA... MOVED INTO HIS FIRST WIFE'S PAD. SHE'D BEEN WAITIN' THERE. SHE WAS AN ACTRESS, DIG? SHE'D BEEN MAKIN' CONNECTIONS FOR 'GILLS' THE WHOLE DAMN TIME."
"WHAT HAPPENED TO 'SWEET PEA'?"
"SHE DON'T KNOW 'BOUT THE FIRST WIFE... HOLLYWOOD... NOTHIN'! SAFE BET TO SAY SHE'S STILL TAKIN' CARE OF CARL AND WAITIN' FOR 'GILLS' TO COME HOME."
"THAT CAT IS LOW DOWN."

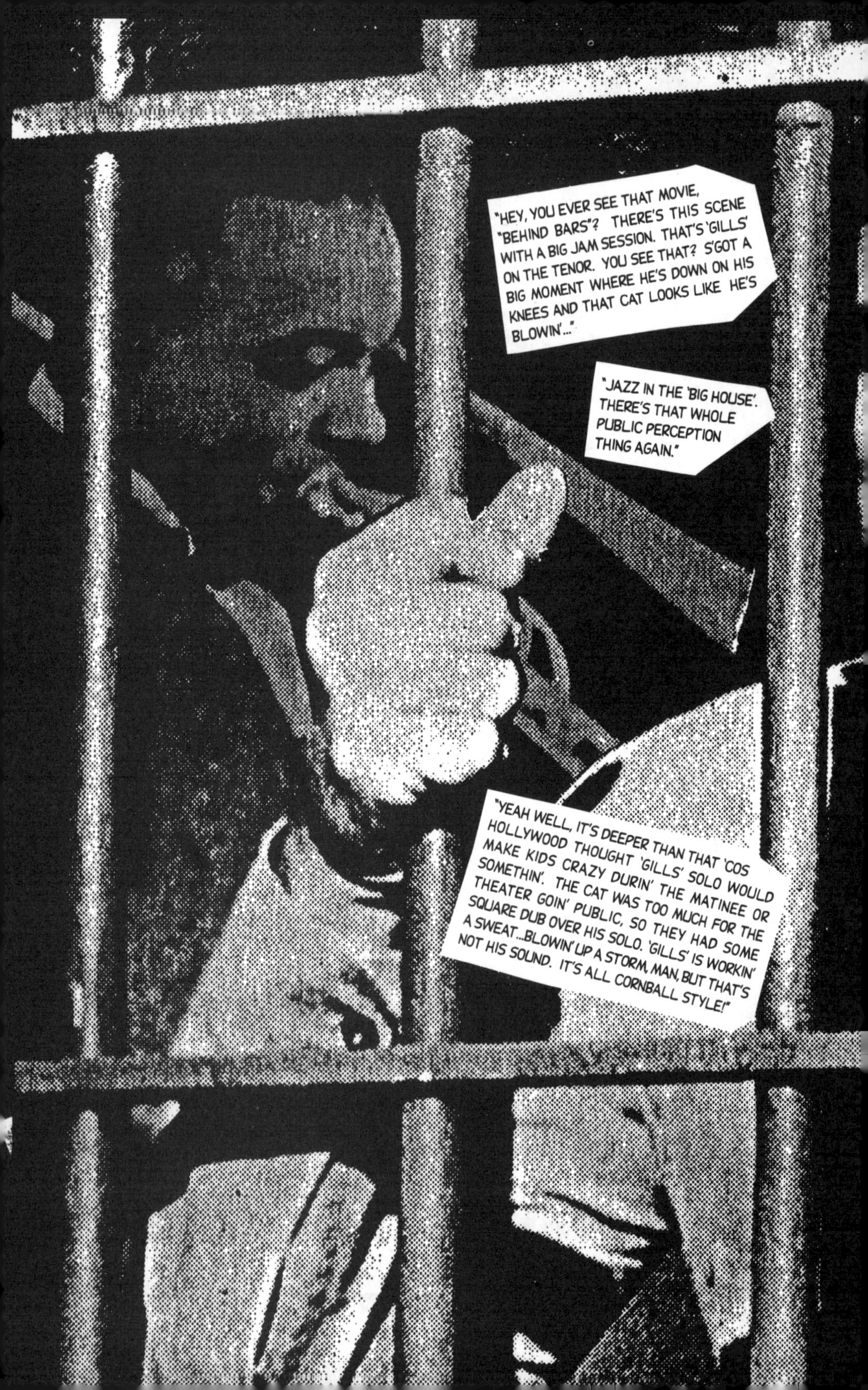
"HEY, YOU EVER SEE THAT MOVIE, "BEHIND BARS"? THERE'S THIS SCENE WITH A BIG JAM SESSION. THAT'S 'GILLS' ON THE TENOR. YOU SEE THAT? S'GOT A BIG MOMENT WHERE HE'S DOWN ON HIS KNEES AND THAT CAT LOOKS LIKE HE'S BLOWIN'..."
"JAZZ IN THE 'BIG HOUSE'. THERE'S THAT WHOLE PUBLIC PERCEPTION THING AGAIN."
"YEAH WELL, IT'S DEEPER THAN THAT 'COS HOLLYWOOD THOUGHT 'GILLS' SOLO WOULD MAKE KIDS CRAZY DURIN' THE MATINEE OR SOMETHIN'. THE CAT WAS TOO MUCH FOR THE THEATER GOIN' PUBLIC, SO THEY HAD SOME SQUARE DUB OVER HIS SOLO. 'GILLS' IS WORKIN' A SWEAT...BLOWIN' UP A STORM, MAN, BUT THAT'S NOT HIS SOUND. IT'S ALL CORNBALL STYLE!"

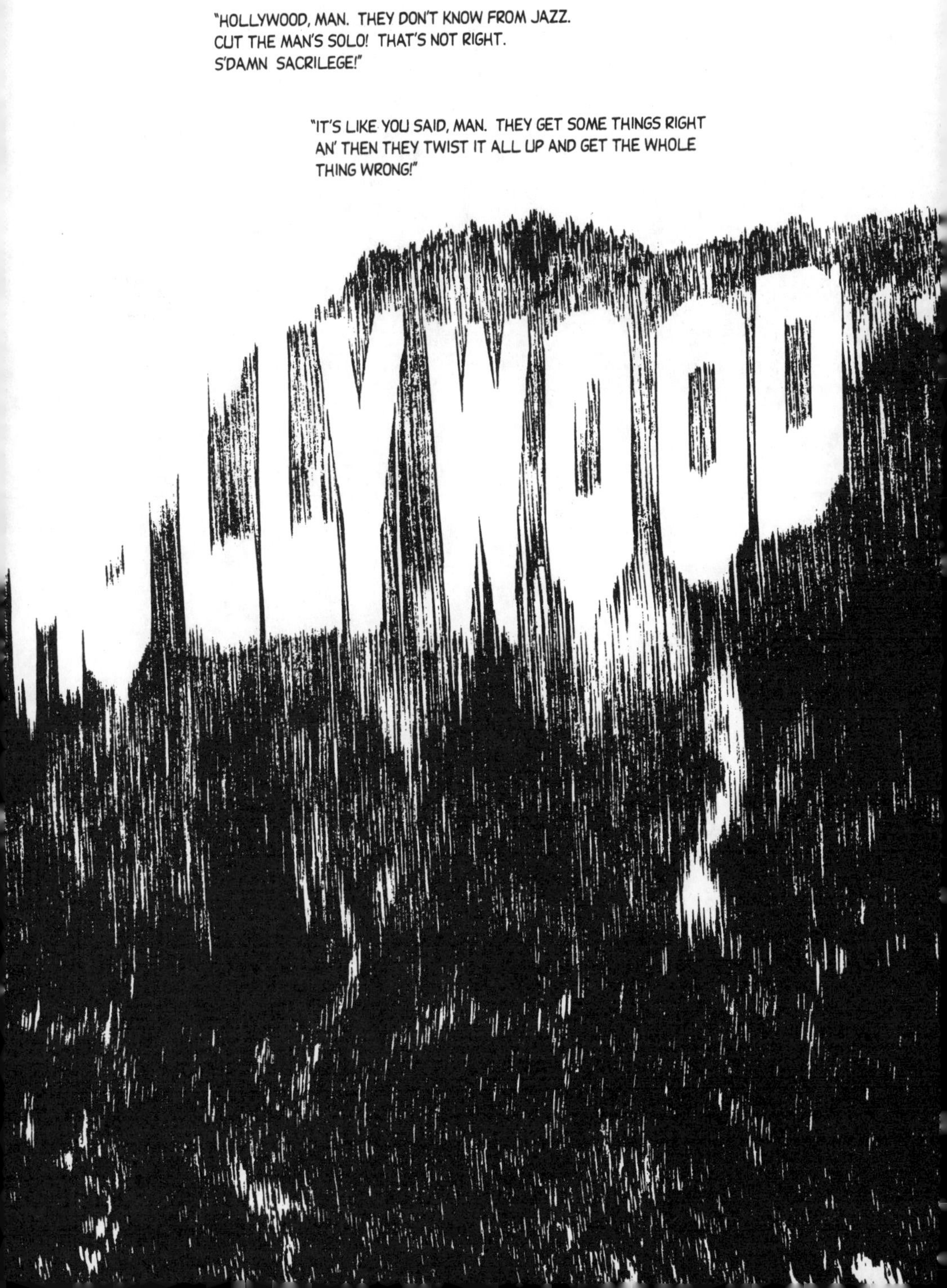
"HOLLYWOOD, MAN. THEY DON'T KNOW FROM JAZZ. CUT THE MAN'S SOLO! THAT'S NOT RIGHT. S'DAMN SACRILEGE!"
"IT'S LIKE YOU SAID, MAN. THEY GET SOME THINGS RIGHT AN' THEN THEY TWIST IT ALL UP AND GET THE WHOLE THING WRONG!"

# PORTFOLIO

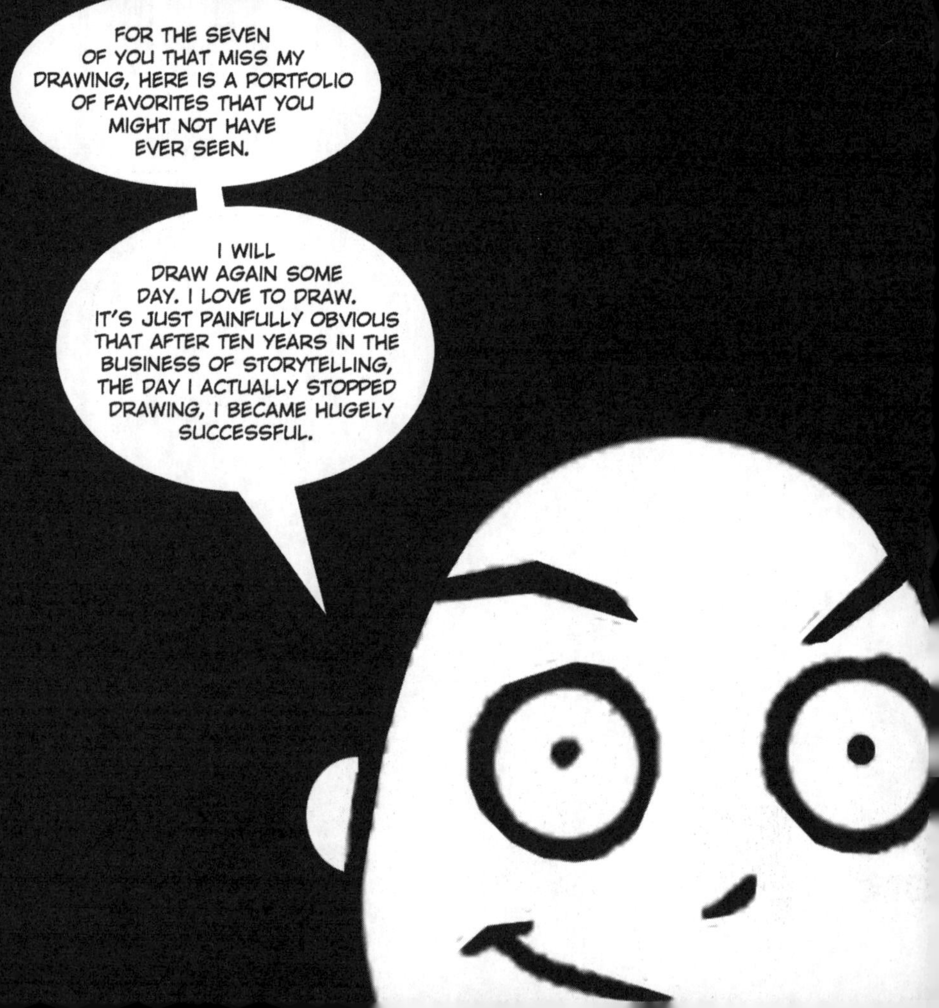
FOR THE SEVEN OF YOU THAT MISS MY DRAWING, HERE IS A PORTFOLIO OF FAVORITES THAT YOU MIGHT NOT HAVE EVER SEEN.
I WILL DRAW AGAIN SOME DAY. I LOVE TO DRAW. IT'S JUST PAINFULLY OBVIOUS THAT AFTER TEN YEARS IN THE BUSINESS OF STORYTELLING, THE DAY I ACTUALLY STOPPED DRAWING, I BECAME HUGELY SUCCESSFUL.

COVER TO LOCAL MAGAZINE. A STORY ON LOCAL FEDERAL CORRUPTION.

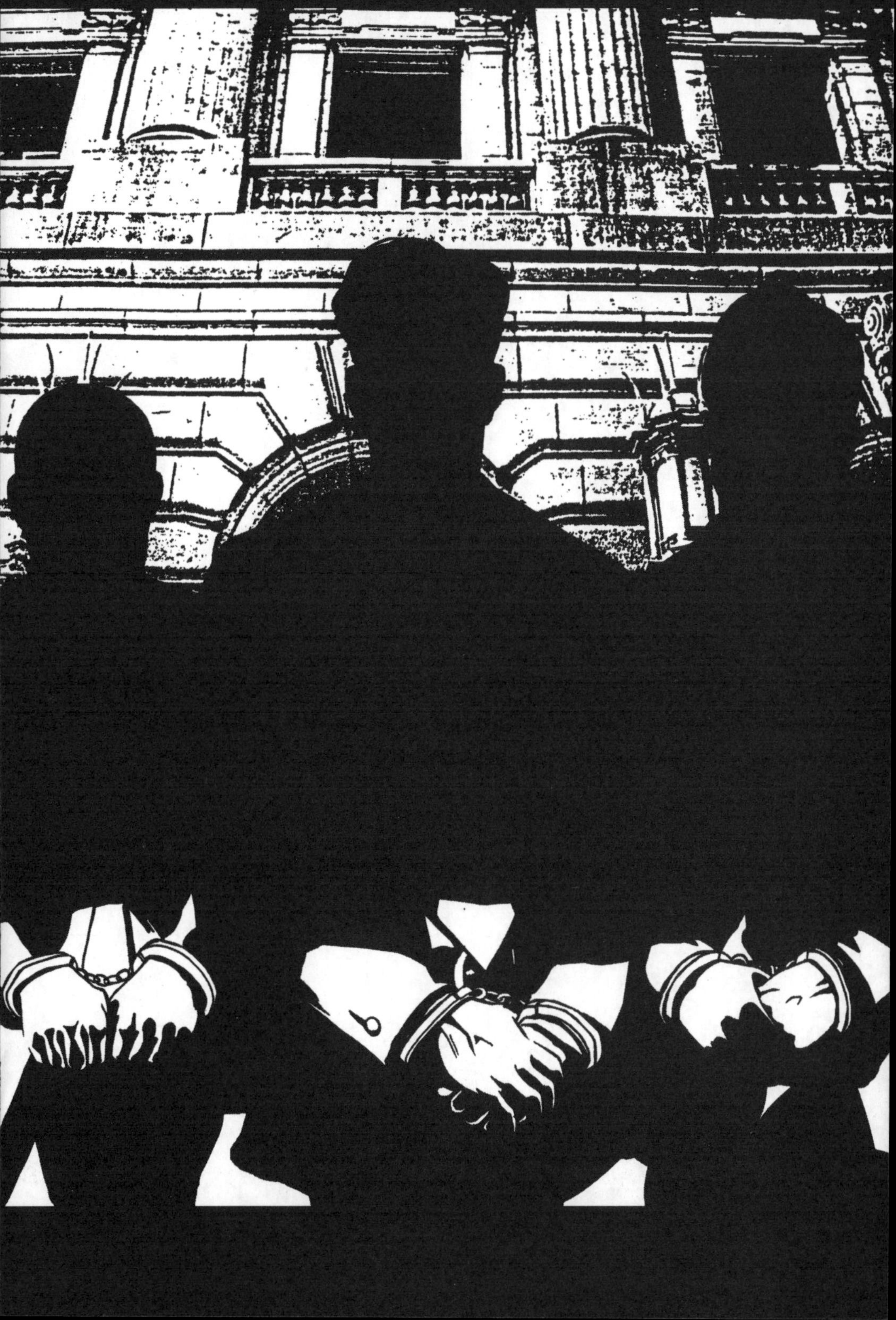

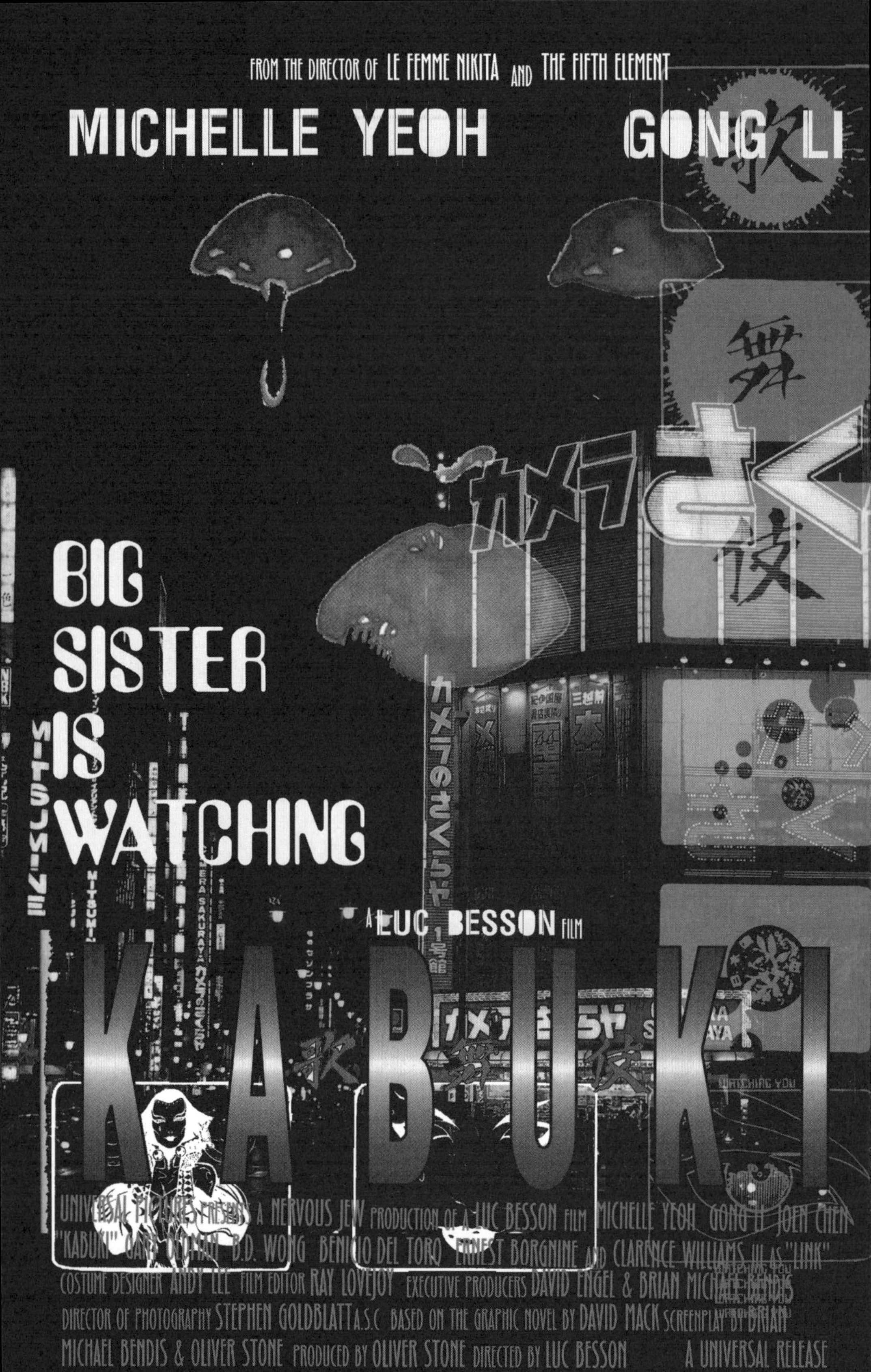
FROM THE DIRECTOR OF LE FEMME NIKITA AND THE FIFTH ELEMENT
MICHELLE YEOH
GONG LI
BIG SISTER IS WATCHING
A LUC BESSON FILM
KABUKI
UNIVERSAL PICTURES PRESENTS A NERVOUS JEW PRODUCTION OF A LUC BESSON FILM MICHELLE YEOH GONG LI JOEN CHEN "KABUKI" GARY OLDMAN B.D. WONG BENICIO DEL TORO ERNEST BORGNINE AND CLARENCE WILLIAMS III AS "LINK"
COSTUME DESIGNER ANDY LEE FILM EDITOR RAY LOVEJOY EXECUTIVE PRODUCERS DAVID ENGEL & BRIAN MICHAEL BENDIS
DIRECTOR OF PHOTOGRAPHY STEPHEN GOLDBLATT A.S.C BASED ON THE GRAPHIC NOVEL BY DAVID MACK SCREENPLAY BY BRIAN MICHAEL BENDIS & OLIVER STONE PRODUCED BY OLIVER STONE DIRECTED BY LUC BESSON
A UNIVERSAL RELEASE

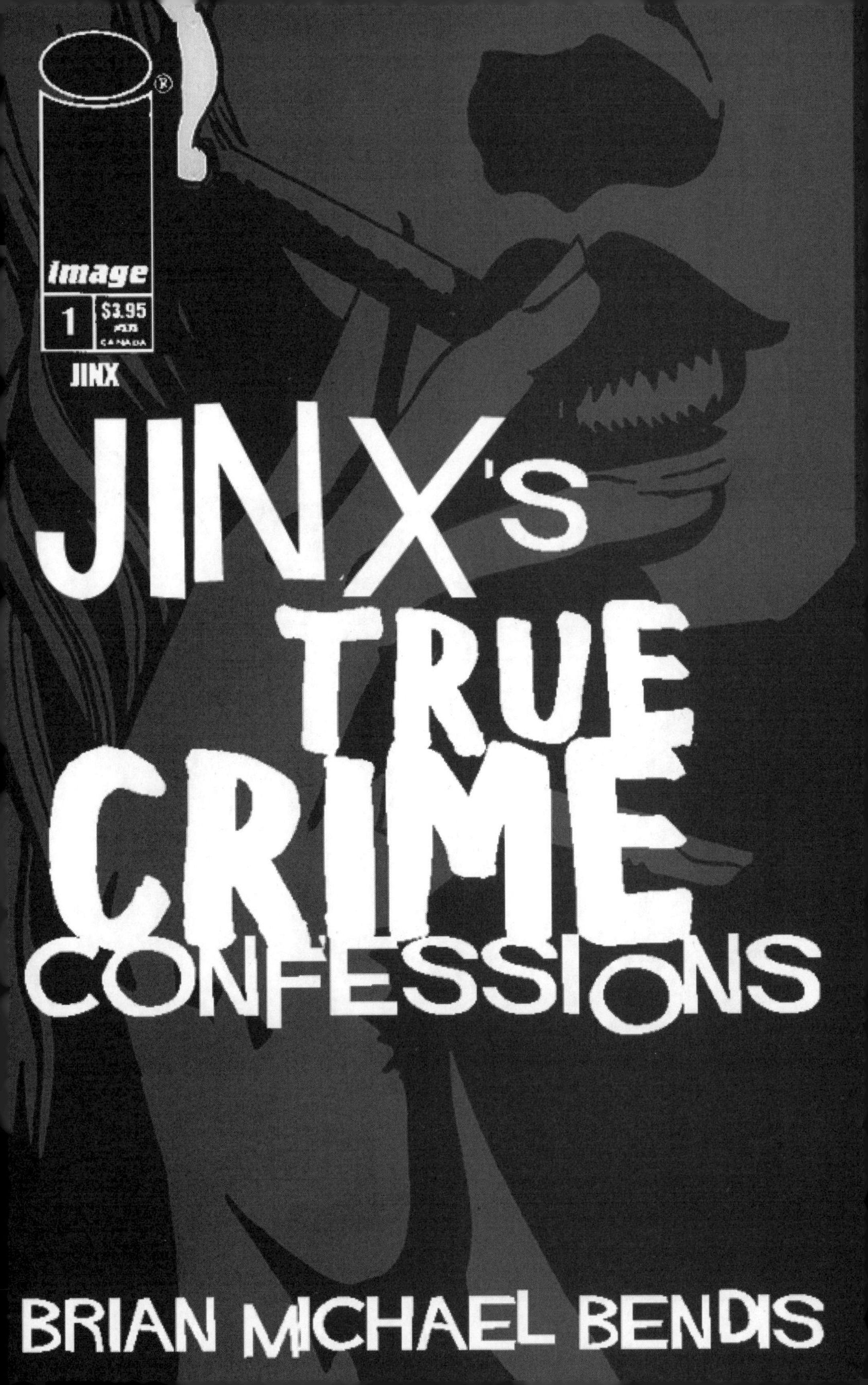
image
1
$3.95
CANADA
JINX
JINX'S
TRUE
CRIME
CONFESSIONS
BRIAN MICHAEL BENDIS

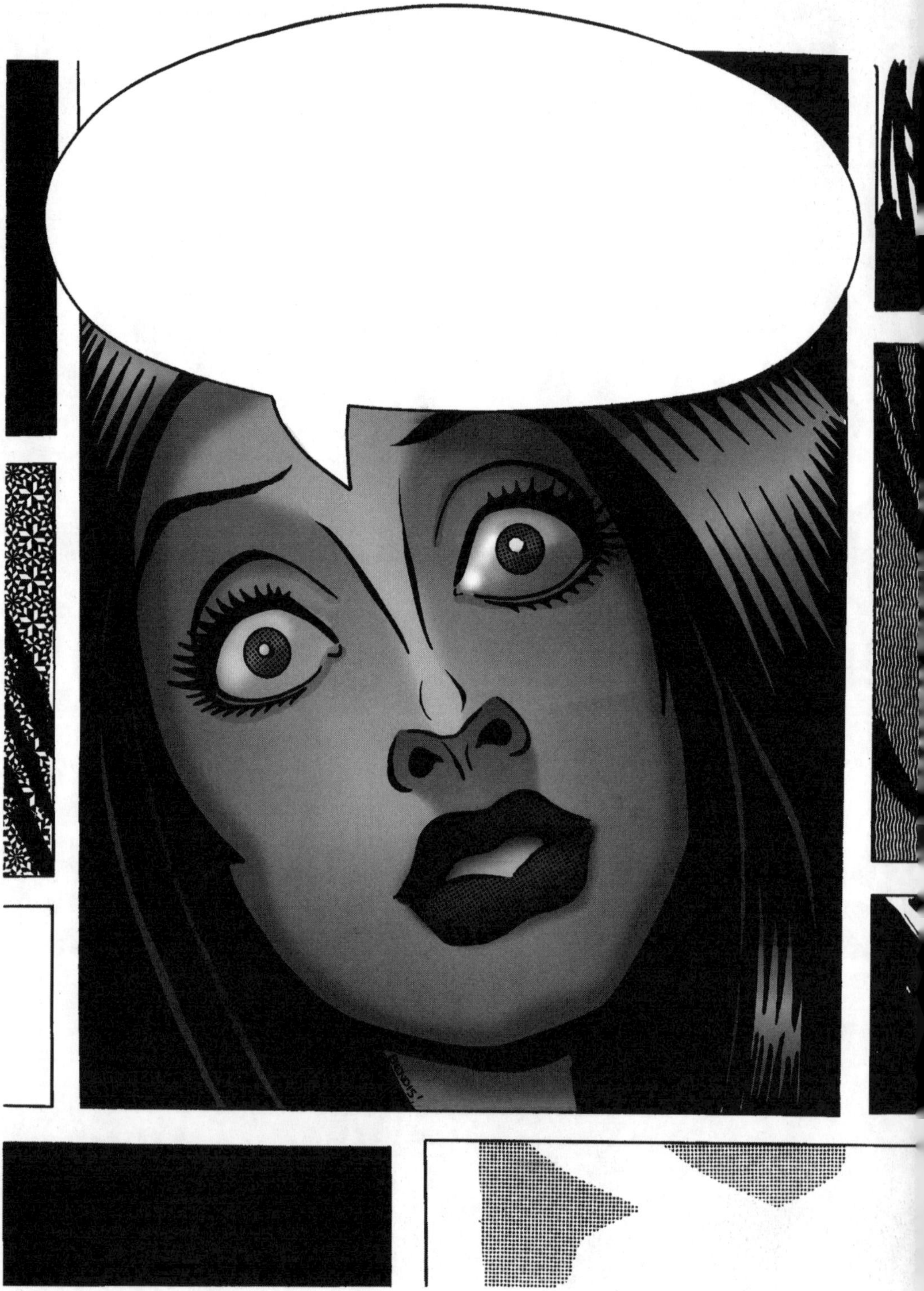

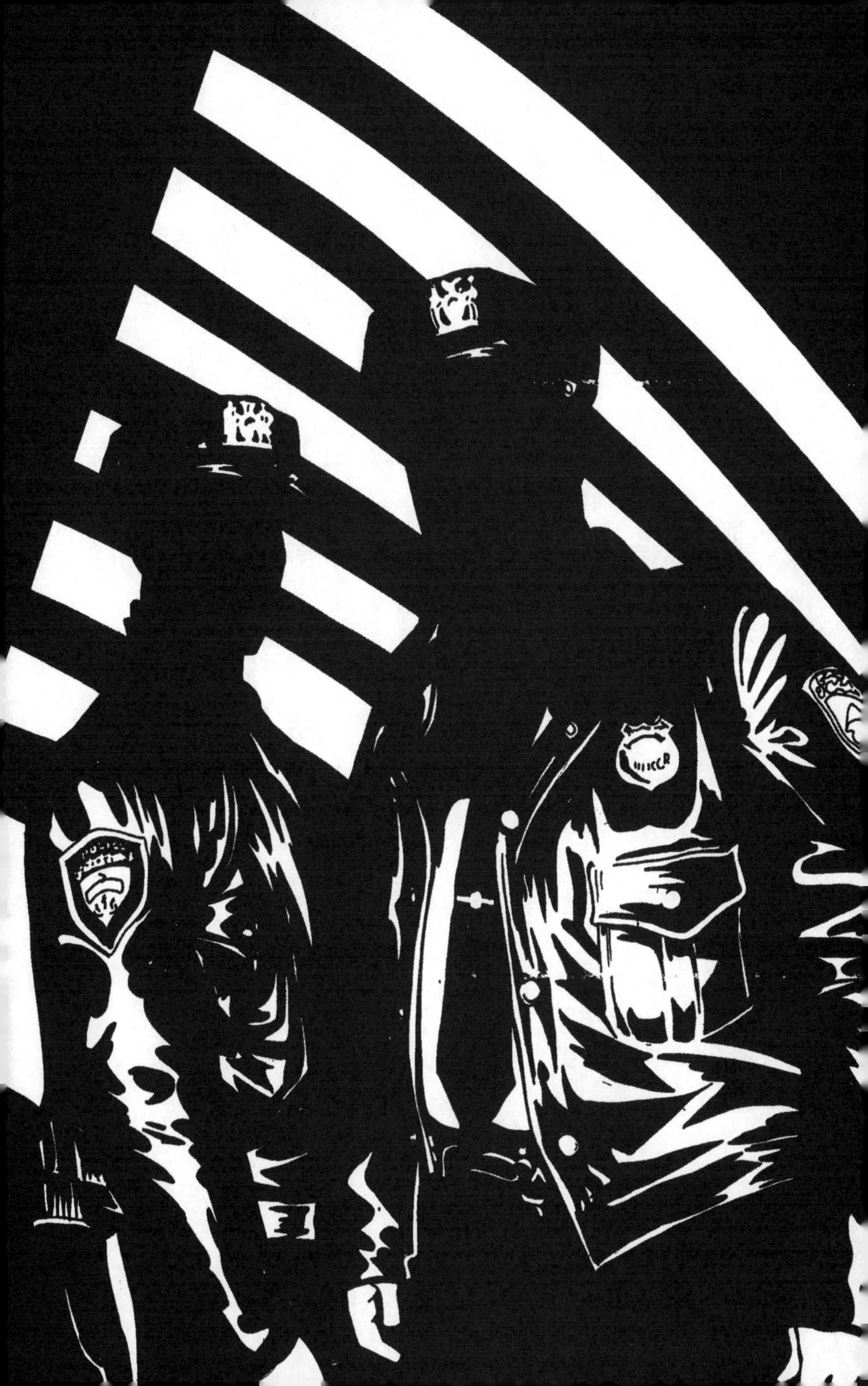

COVER TO LOCAL MAGAZINE. A STORY ON THE INSULAR WORLD OF THE INTERNET.

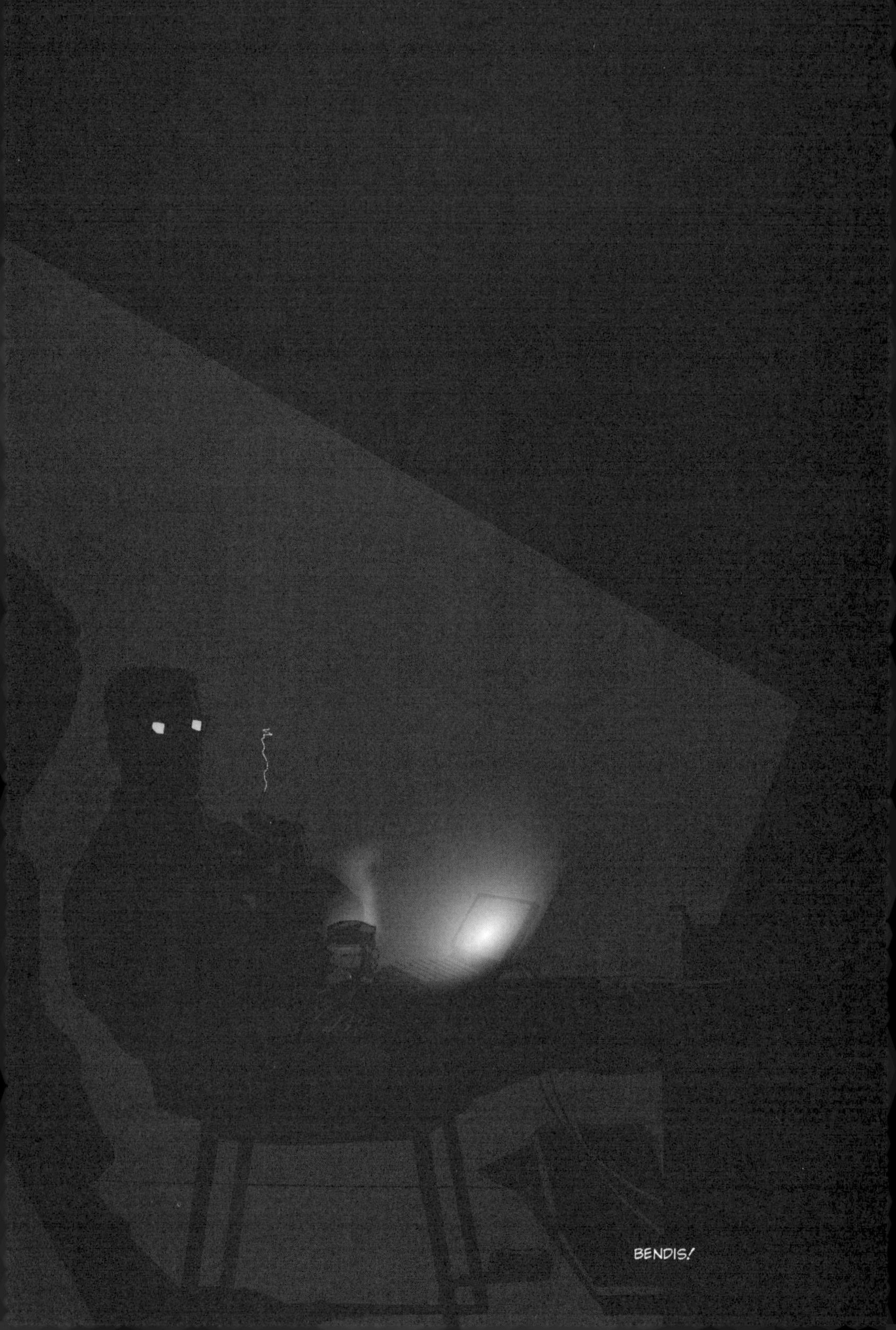
BENDIS!

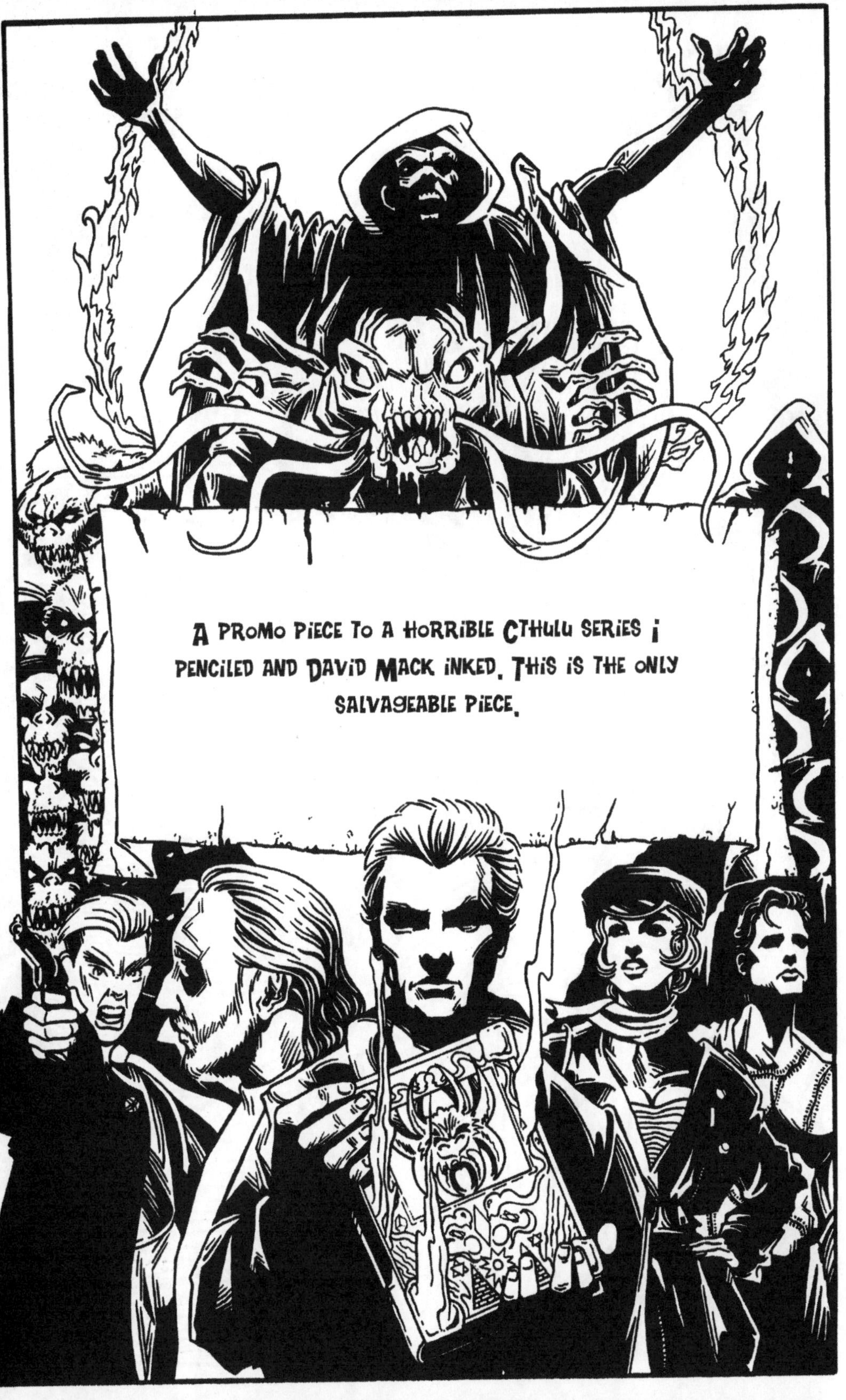
A PROMO PIECE TO A HORRIBLE CTHULU SERIES I PENCILED AND DAVID MACK INKED. THIS IS THE ONLY SALVAGEABLE PIECE.

SPANDEX TIGHTS PIN-UP COPYRIGHT BRIAN GLASS

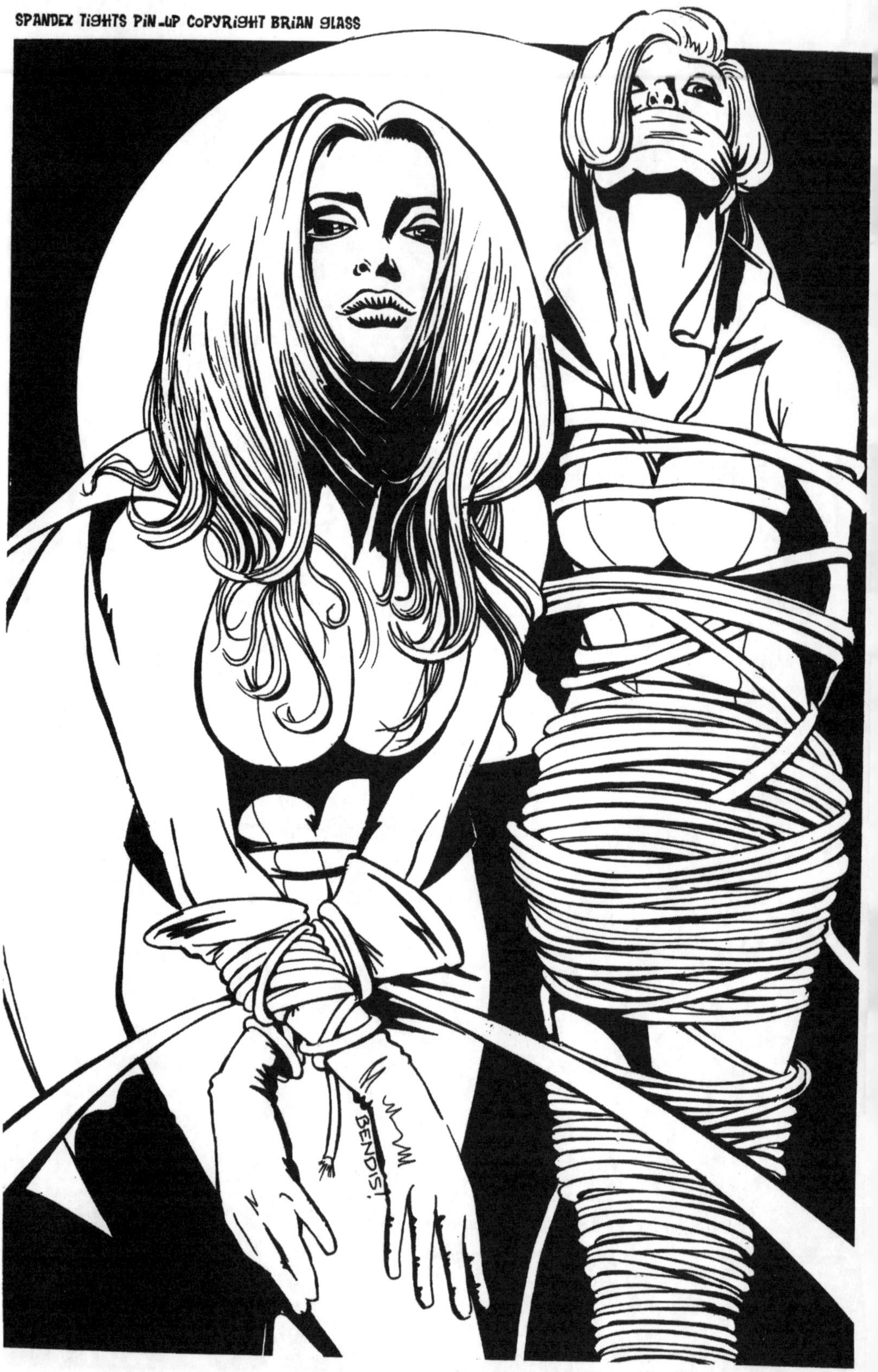
BENDIS!

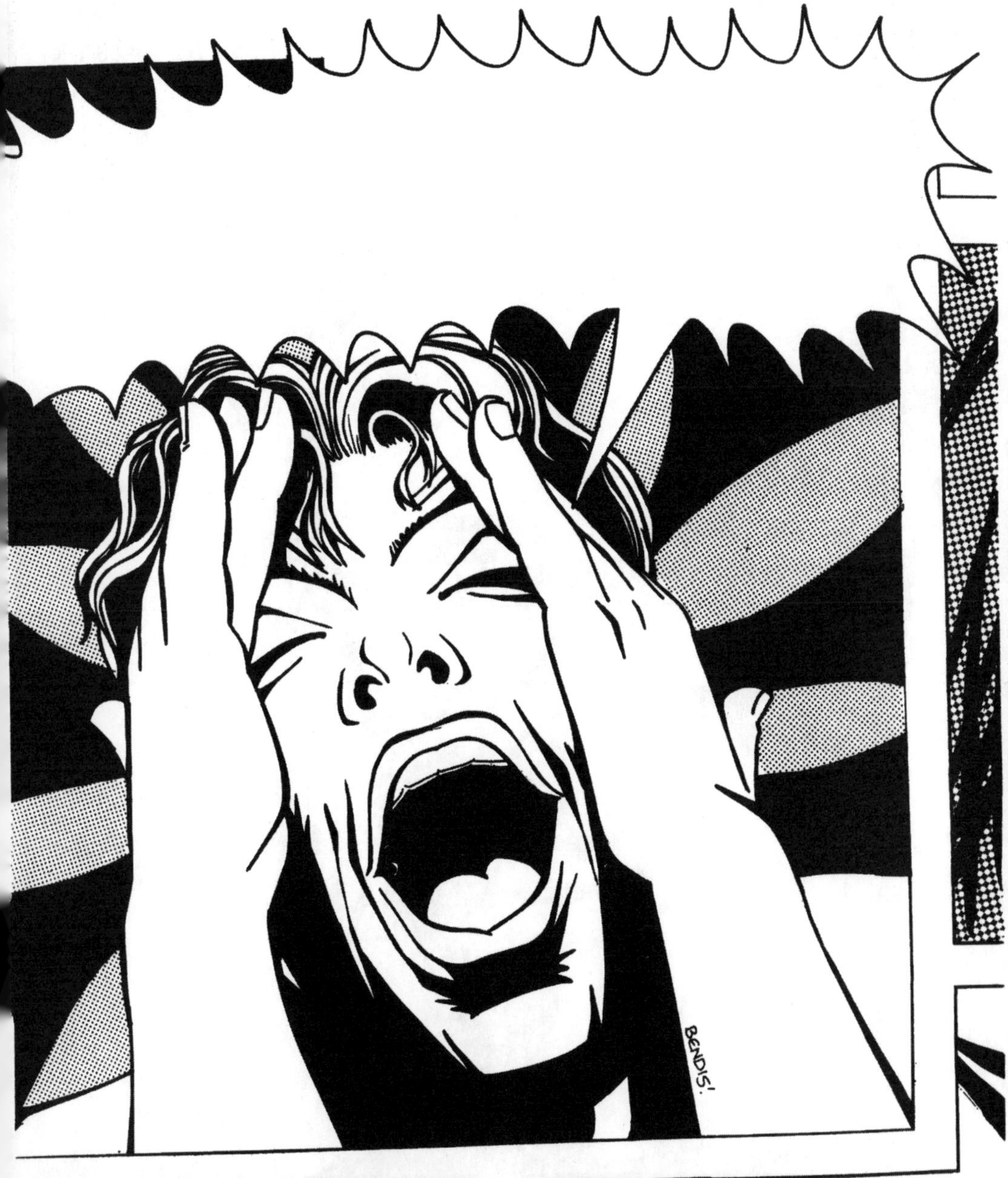
BENDIS!

THESE PORTRAITS WERE SOMETHING I DID FOR MYSELF; I DO THEM WHEN I AM STUDYING THE ARTIST'S WORK. HARD TO EXPLAIN HOW IT HELPS ME UNDERSTAND THEM, BUT IT DOES. I HAVE ABOUT FIFTEEN OF THESE. NO ROOM FOR THE HASSELHOFF THOUGH, SORRY.

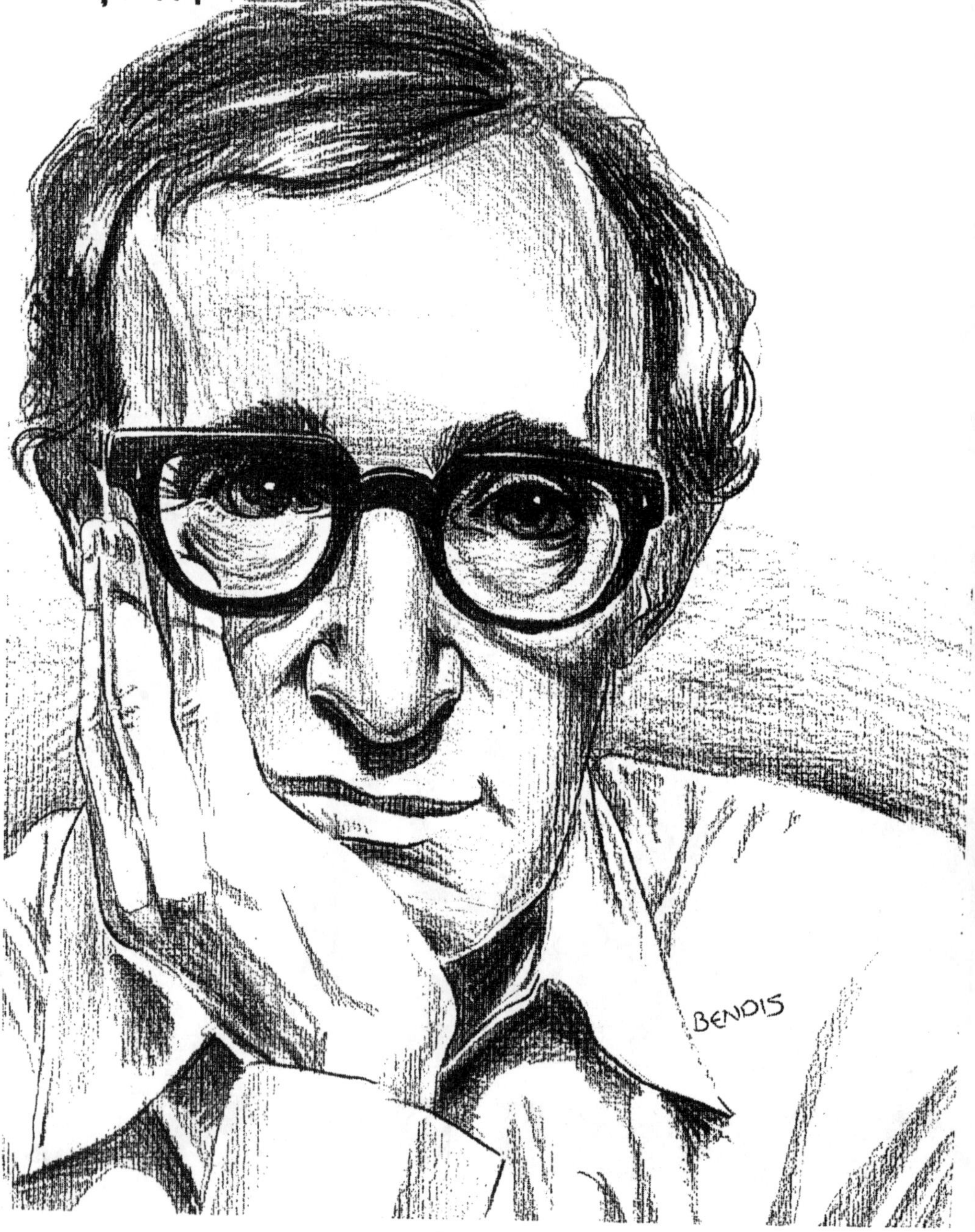
BENDIS

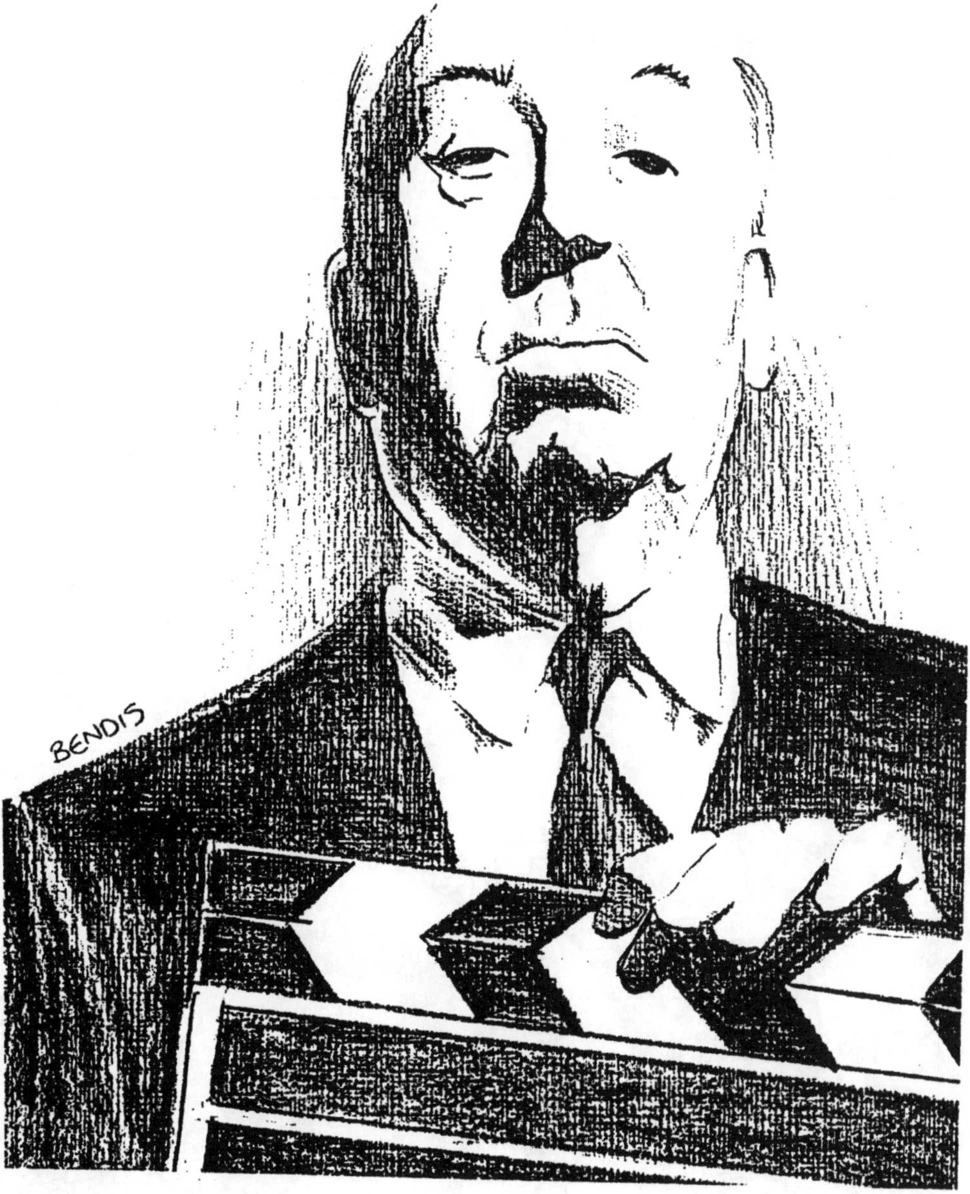
BENDIS

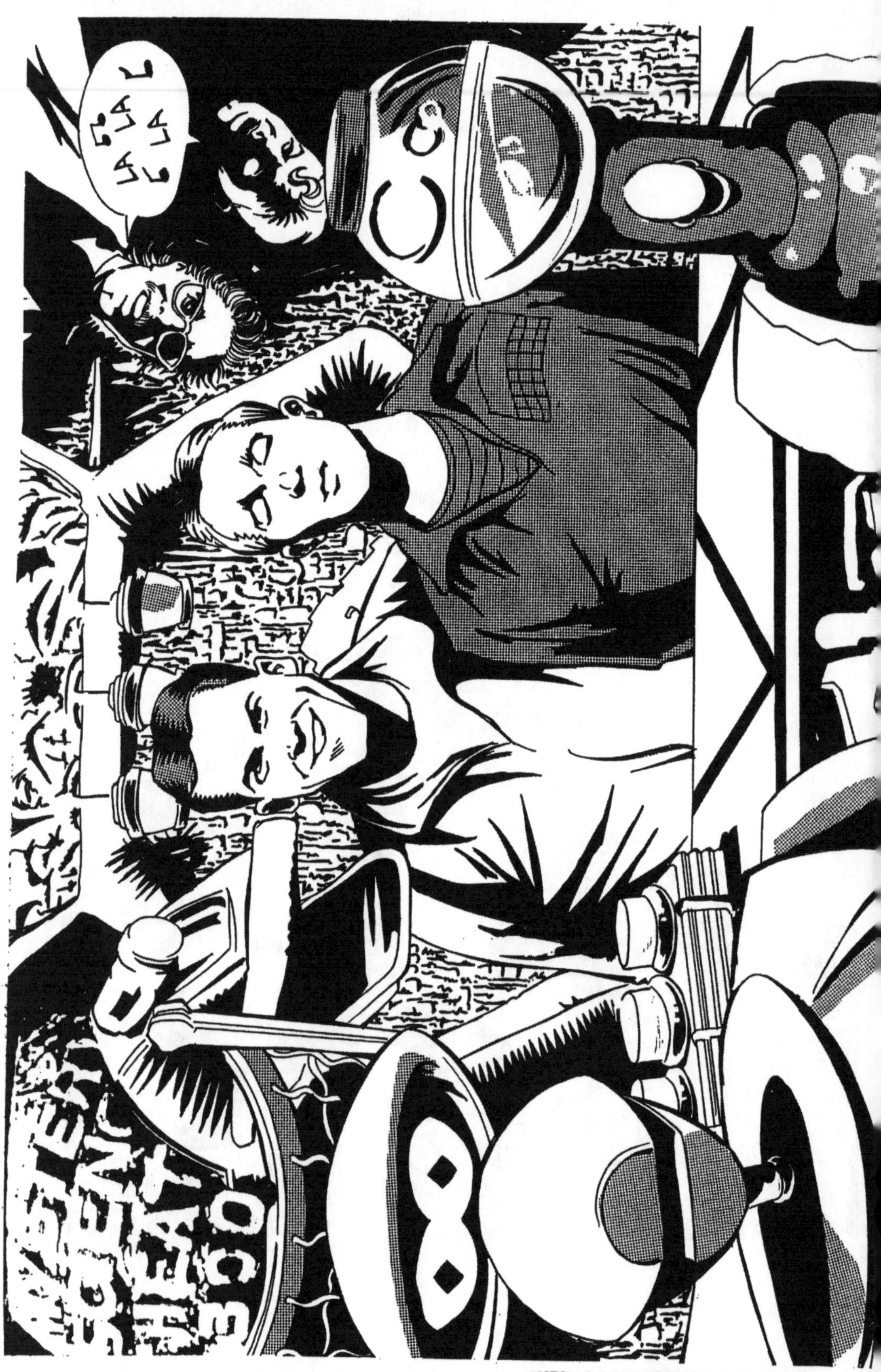
LA LA LA L

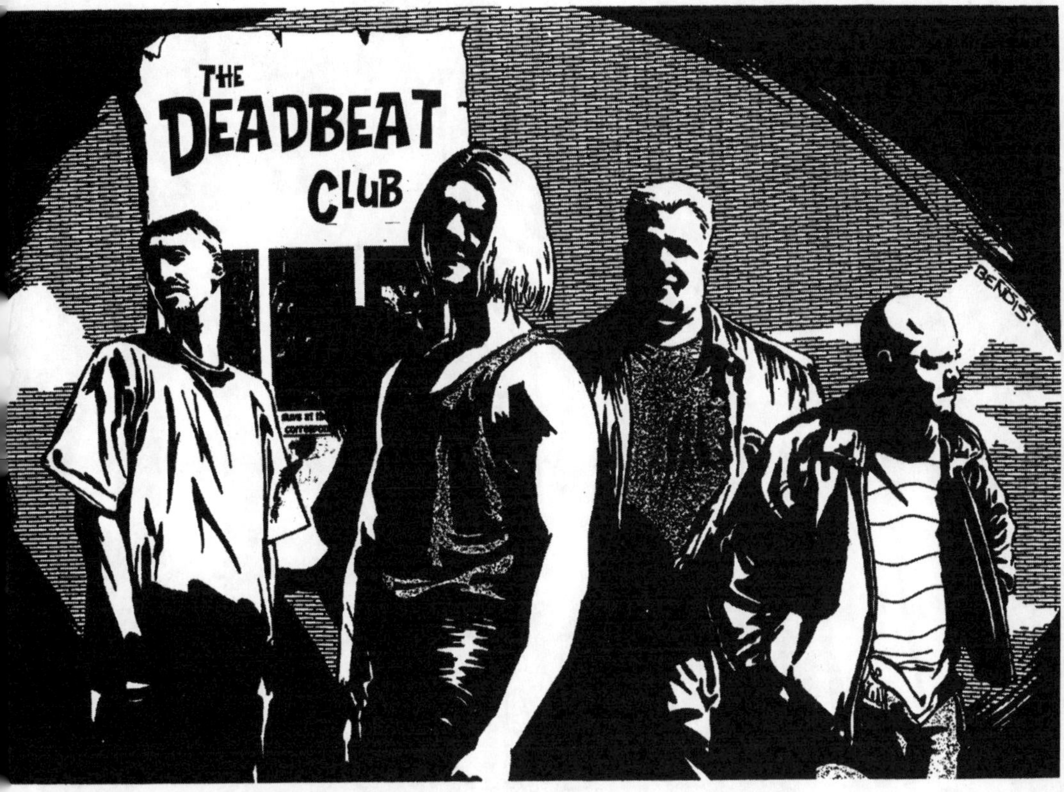
THE DEADBEAT CLUB
BENDIS!

THE DEADBEAT CLUB, A CRIME COMIC I WROTE BUT NEVER DREW--YET, IF I EVER DRAW ANOTHER CRIME COMIC, THIS WOULD PROBABLY BE IT.

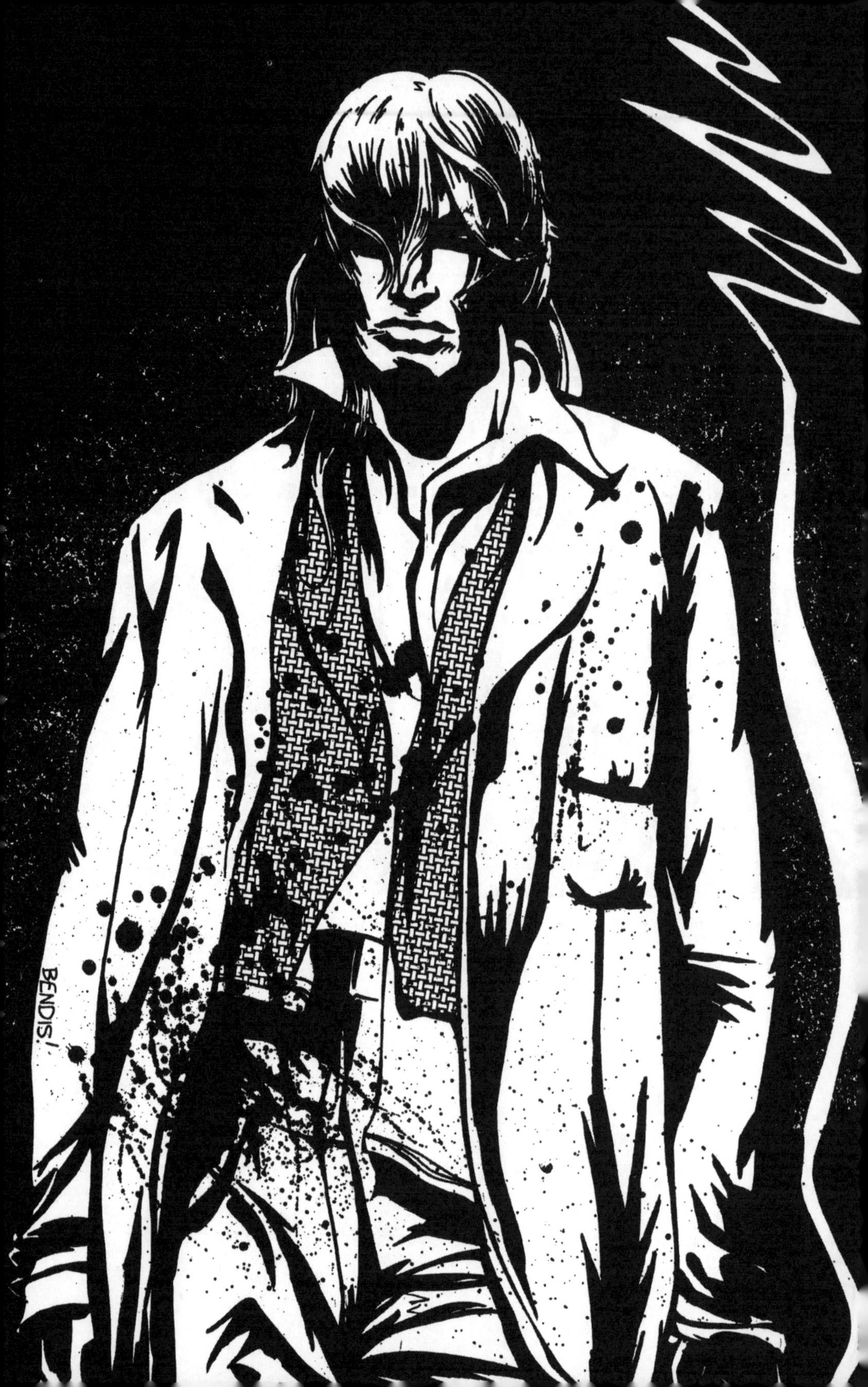
BENDIS!

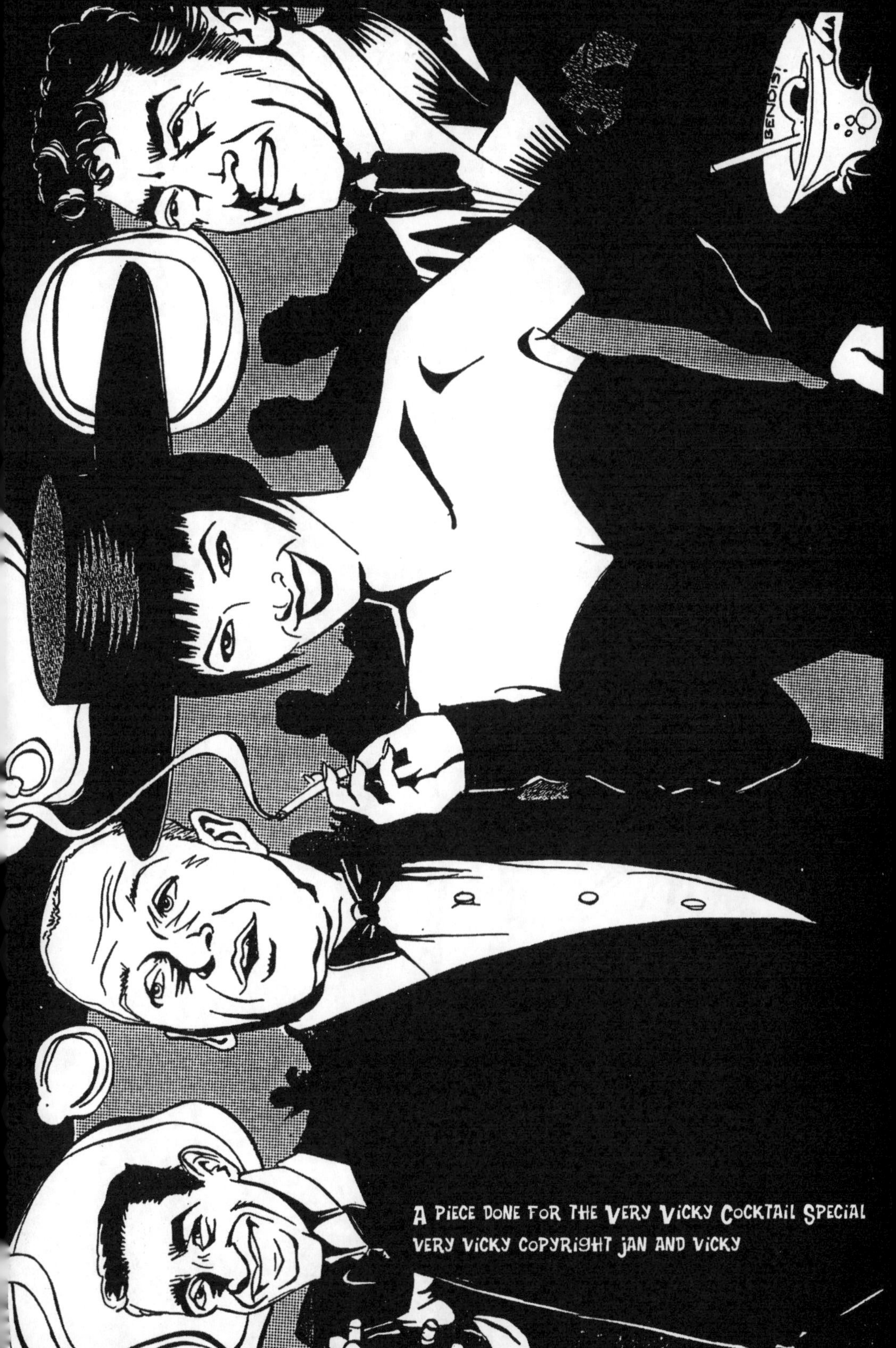
BENDIS!
A PIECE DONE FOR THE VERY VICKY COCKTAIL SPECIAL
VERY VICKY COPYRIGHT JAN AND VICKY

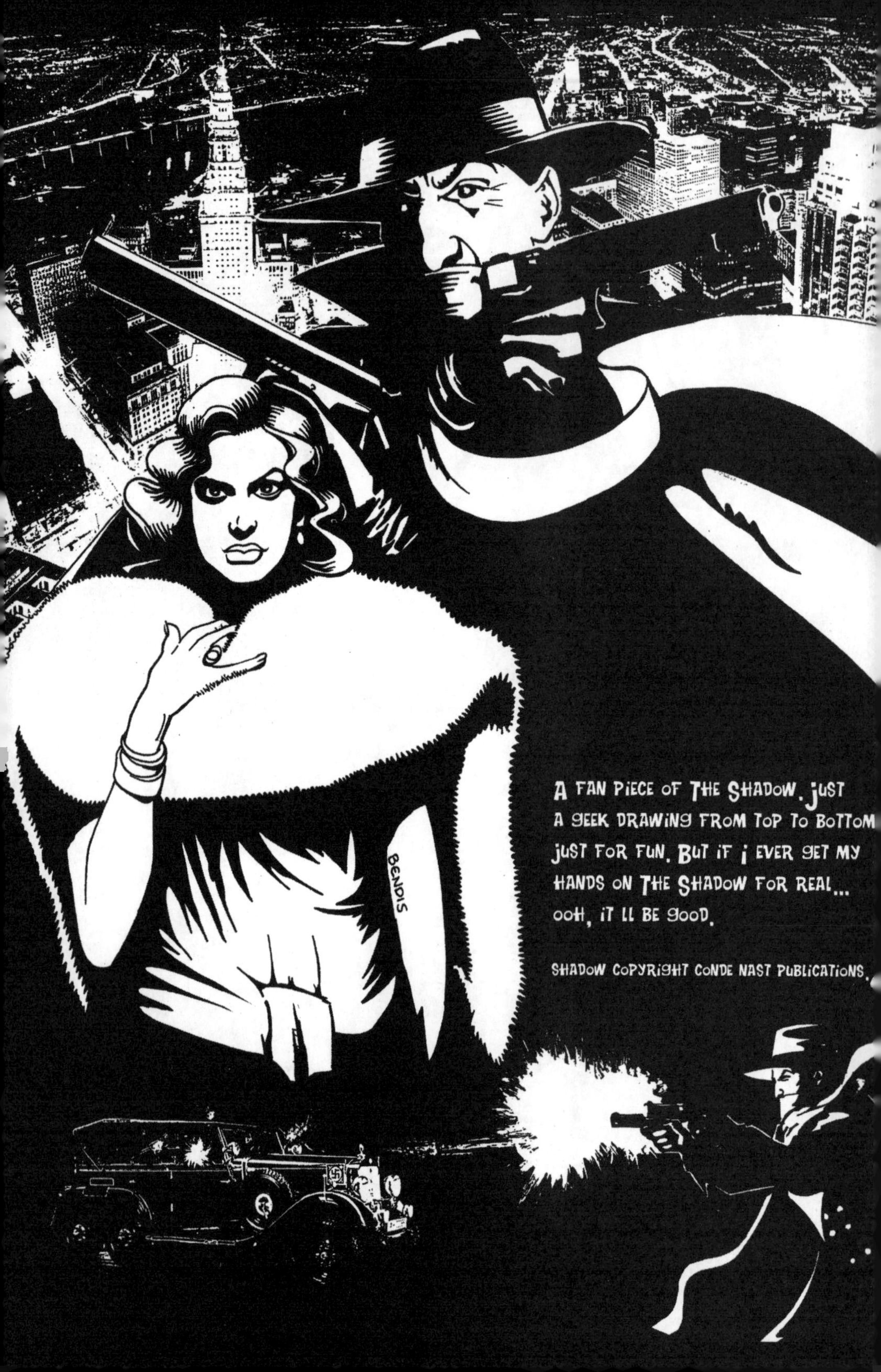
BENDIS
A FAN PIECE OF THE SHADOW. JUST A GEEK DRAWING FROM TOP TO BOTTOM JUST FOR FUN. BUT IF I EVER GET MY HANDS ON THE SHADOW FOR REAL... OOH, IT LL BE GOOD.
SHADOW COPYRIGHT CONDE NAST PUBLICATIONS.

# ESSAYS

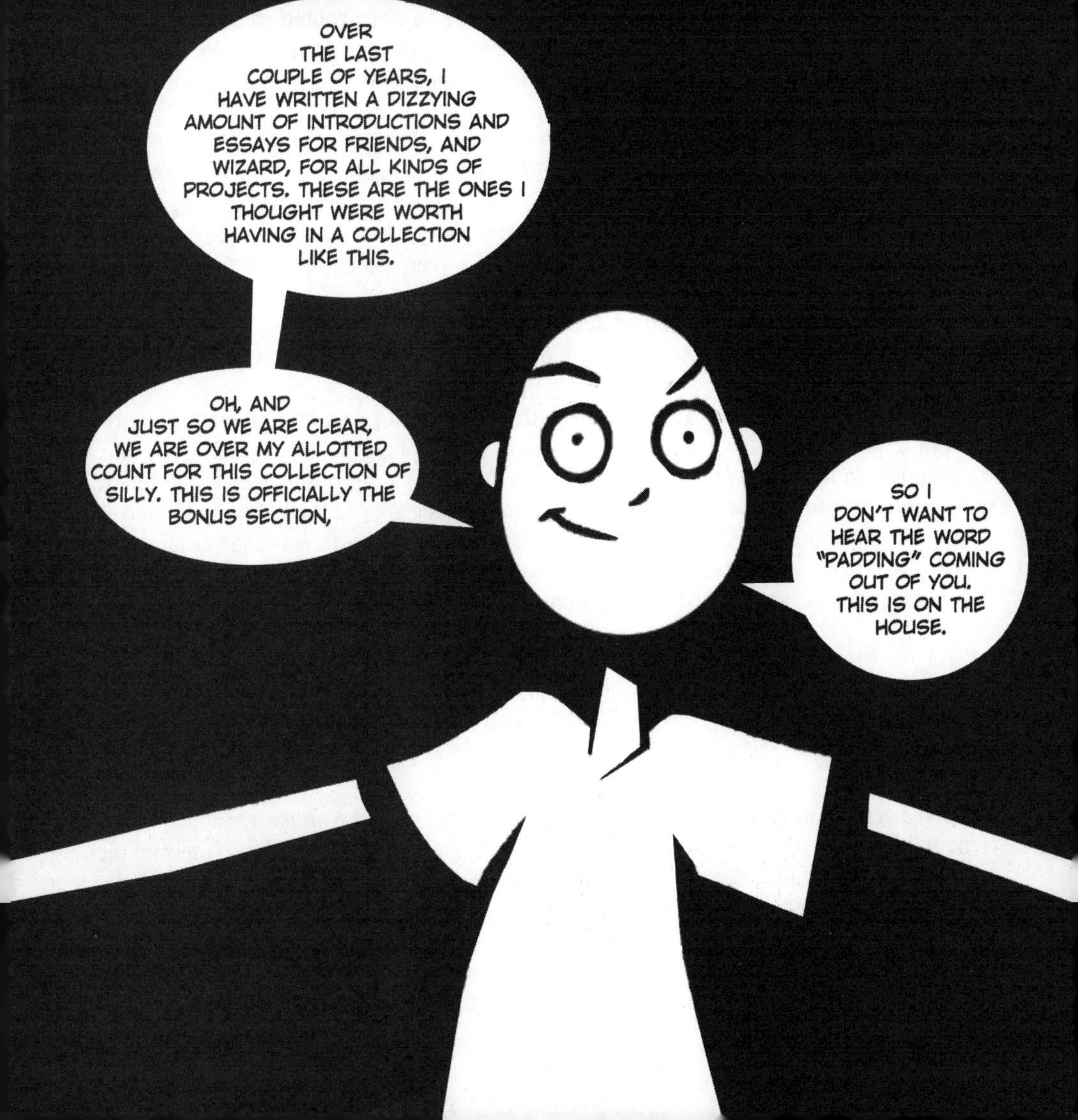
OVER THE LAST COUPLE OF YEARS, I HAVE WRITTEN A DIZZYING AMOUNT OF INTRODUCTIONS AND ESSAYS FOR FRIENDS, AND WIZARD, FOR ALL KINDS OF PROJECTS. THESE ARE THE ONES I THOUGHT WERE WORTH HAVING IN A COLLECTION LIKE THIS.
OH, AND JUST SO WE ARE CLEAR, WE ARE OVER MY ALLOTTED COUNT FOR THIS COLLECTION OF SILLY. THIS IS OFFICIALLY THE BONUS SECTION,
SO I DON'T WANT TO HEAR THE WORD "PADDING" COMING OUT OF YOU. THIS IS ON THE HOUSE.

# KABUKI INTRO

Well, I've known David since we were stationed in Korea together in 1952. Oh, wait, it was Caliber in 1992, it just felt like Korea. Oh, I kid Caliber. I'm sure the wounds will heal one day. They have to eventually, right?

As I write this I realize that the days of our budding friendship have officially become "the good old days." We were both working in independent black-and-white comics, both single, both starving, and no one gave two and a half shits about either of our work. But we showed you!!! Hahahahahaha!!

When I met David, I was fucking up the first half of a graphic novel called *Fire*, and David was elbow deep into his groundbreaking, world changing graphic novel tour de force, *Happy the Clown*. Oh, yes, we can definitely say we knew each other when.

What could a Jew from Cleveland and the most gentile gentile from Kentucky have in common? Aside from mild bi-polarism, we both felt a deep-rooted passion for everything the comic page could do. And not the page itself, anyone can love that. We honestly loved what was going on in-between the borders, what was going on under and over the page, what floated around the comic.

And when you spend all of your day thinking and philosophizing to yourself about this invisible and imaginary fourth dimension of comics that you might have invented inside your rubber cement-addled mind, it's an amazing day when you find someone who totally knows exactly what you're talking about…even if they're from Kentucky.

(And sure I could try to explain what the hell I am talking about with this fourth dimension of comics right here in this intro, but I ain't exactly getting paid by the word.)

But here is the real reason I am friends with Dave: when I was first showing him my work in progress on *Fire*, and I swear to god I'm not plugging, Dave was totally and genuinely in love with my storytelling, or, more pointed, my promise as a storyteller. But he gently tossed out the suggestion that my inking line weight might not be the most appropriate choice for the style of book I was trying to pull off. It was a casual and friendly remark. A suggestion, really. He took a pen and he inked a head right on my scratchy pencils just to illustrate his point (no really shitty pun intended).

Well, this floored me. And it might sound like a miniscule little thing but his comment was so right on the money that it altered and defined my noirish art style forever. I literally don't know how I would have been able to graduate my work to the next level without him.

Soon after this episode, I started *Goldfish* and David started *Kabuki*. I realized that just by being around David, just by talking to him on the phone, just by tricking him into picking me up in his car and taking me to conventions that were totally out of his way, made me a better comics creator.

They say that Eric Clapton is only as good as the company he keeps. That when Clapton is working with Marc Knopfler or George Harrison, his guitar playing is more focused and powerful. That's kind of how I feel about myself when working with David. Now I am not comparing myself to the rock god guitarists of all rock god guitarists (I couldn't get my hands on anywhere near that much heroine if I tried) but I know for a fact that I m a better comic book creator because of my friendship with David.

Oh, yeah, and it goes both ways. I realized that this poor fellow was in desperate need of my voice of reason. Because early on in *Kabuki*'s creation, David had the insane idea that I actually pencil *Kabuki*. Oh, man, how bad would that have sucked!!?? Can you imagine? Well, I know the offer was just a warm extension of our growing friendship, and I know that he would have come to his senses on it as well. (But we do laugh about how quickly our friendship would have ended had I indeed accepted this gig. I was not the gentle collaborator then I have since grown into.)

It also became very clear, very quickly, that David was going to be one of the greats. A true artist. A unique voice. A purposeful and unapologetic storyteller who had so many tricks up his sleeve that sometimes dozens of them would fall into one single painting. David can write and draw and paint in any style he chooses with equal conviction and craftsmanship. Just in this collection alone find a medium he hasn't toyed with.

It's an amazing sight to see. I have been witness to David's creative process in a lot of its forms. I have seen David pencil in a fury of emotion, I have seen him doodle whimsically, I have seen him dribble spit into a Lady Death painting while the brush swirled it into the mix. I have seen David edit out of this intro any number of other things I have seen David do in private.

But watching David create is one of the true joys of my life, and I say that with full conviction. It's an amazing and inspiring thing to behold.

I want to wrap this up because even writing this has made me want to go draw something. But seeing the new pages David created for this edition of *Kabuki* made me think of this little intro that Bill Sienkiewicz wrote to the collection of his work on the X-Men title *New Mutants*. He was talking about how fans were constantly wishing that he would have drawn the mutants in the same style he drew his groundbreaking work on *Moon Knight*— "I liked your old stuff," they said—and how now years later they always ask him to draw in the same style he drew *The New Mutants*. "Draw it in your old style." He laughed in the intro that *The New Mutants* was now his old stuff.

Well, I think the same goes for David. I know you're going to be blown away by the amazing work in this collection, but good news, it's already the old stuff. David has already reinvented himself and his signature character into something you didn't see coming. David has never once given his audience what he thinks they want—he only gives them what he has.

And what he has is some hot lesbian action!! I kid, of course, its not all that hot.

But seriously...congrats David, another masterpiece. It was an honor to watch you create it.

BENDIS!
October, 2001

# AMAZiNG SPiDER-MAN 14 iNTRO

FROM THE WIZARD REPRINT SPECIAL

This is it! This is the shadow every single comic book creator has been chasing for forty years, the long, twisted shadow of the greatest comic book villain ever created, (no, not Rob Liefeld) Norman Osborn!

Oh, pipe down over there with your Joker talk and your Doctor Doom whining, I don't want to hear it! Norman Osborn was the finest villain ever concocted. And my point is extremely well illustrated in a recent issue of *Tangled Web* where comic book scribe Ron Zimmerman fashioned an issue with all the Spider-Man villains sitting around a bar trading war stories. The issue ends with Norman Osborn revealing himself and bragging the ultimate Spider-man villain brag: "I killed the woman he loves." The other villains fall silent. They have nothing to say to top that. And did you notice how I slipped the words Ultimate Spider-Man into that paragraph all subtle like. I know—it's impressive.

"Always put your characters in the place they would least like to be." This is a quote from screenwriter Alvin Sergeant that I have been obsessing over in my own work. It sounds so simple. It is so simple.

And the Green Goblin personifies this for Spider-Man. The character quickly evolves himself into the most dramatic conflict in comic book history. This is the villain that will unmask Peter Parker, torture him and then hurt him—really hurt him. He kills Gwen Stacey. No takebacks. No tricks. Wow! And she stayed dead! And all the while we sympathize with Norman because he knows not what he does. He is trapped by demons he doesn't even know exists. Plus, he is the father of Peter's best and maybe only friend. Wow! This is a great villain!!

And, to think, you can't tell any of that is going to happen at all from this incredibly goofball first appearance.

BENDIS!

# DAREDEViL iSSuE ONE iNTRO

FROM THE WIZARD REPRINT SPECIAL

"There is one shining star in the Marvel galaxy whose origin turns me on perhaps a bit more than some of the others. There is one particular character whose creation was somewhat more of a challenge, somewhat more difficult to work out, and somewhat more satisfying to savor when it was finally completed."

- Stan Lee on Daredevil's origin from *Son of Origins*.

I found this Stan Lee quote while doing my tons of research for the monthly *Daredevil* book and it sort of surprised me. I don't think I ever heard Stan come out and pick a favorite among the dizzying array or creations that bear his name.

But, then again, looking over the first issue of *Daredevil*, I mean, really looking it over, you can tell that Stan had rolled up his sleeves and tried something different. With Spidey and the FF already instant classics, already watershed creations in the history of comics with their precise mixture of real-world problems and super-hero adventure, I am sure Stan felt an eager urge to push the envelope even further.

It seems as though he asked himself—I did it with super heroes; can I do it with pulp heroes?

And do not be fooled, peppy, Daredevil is not a superhero. He is a pulp hero brought to modern day comics. Look at this first issue. Does it look more like Superman or Dick Tracy? More like the FF or The Spirit? (And every time the Daredevil series has thrived creatively in its amazing history, it has been treated by its creative team like a pulp and not a super hero.)

That all said, there is something really charming about the hard sell on the front cover: Remember Spidey? Remember FF? Stan knew he was force-feeding us a pulp hero. He knew he was gift-wrapping it as Spider-Man hoping to trick his new readers into trying something they might not have wanted if you asked them.

And with all great mythologies, this simple premise (a blind man with heightened senses), this perfect character dichotomy (lawyer by day, vigilante by night)--
this is the stuff pop culture legends are made of.

Bendis!
Oct. 2002

# ULTiMATE SPiDER-MAN: A CONFESSiON

So the question is, what qualifies an admitted alternative comics artist and crime fiction writer to get a gig helping to revamp a classic the likes of Spider-Man?

Ok. All right, I am going to confess something to you here, and by doing so I am going to ruin my reputation. For eight long years I have spent every waking moment creating this public persona of a tough-talking, smart-mouthed writer/artist and I am kissing it goodbye.

It was whatever year it was that I was 10 or 11 years old. And man, I was all about the Marvel Comics. You name it! I was immersed. I never read a bad comic. They were all equally perfect.

But my favorite thing to buy was the comic book with the record attached. It was like a read-along. You read the comic and actors and such act it out on the record. I loved them! I remember having a *Star Trek* comic book and record set and thinking in awe: "Wow, how did they ever get William Shatner himself to reprise the role for this record?!?"

My favorite one was an issue of *Fantastic Four* that John Buscema drew where the FF basically relived their origin. I had a couple others, too, but I wanted all my comics to have a record.

So, I took my crappy little Radio Shack tape recorder and my crappy little Cetron sixty-minute audio tapes and I convinced my brother to join me in our own vocal interpretation of my collection of Marvel Comics.

We would take all the toys that we had that actually produced a noise (toy guns, trucks) and create a real theatre of the mind. We would sit there for hours and work on each character's vocal stylings and decide which toy went with which sound effect.

One comic in particular that I remember spending a lot of time on, I mean a lot of time, was the issue of *Amazing Spider-Man* where Peter Parker goes to France for something only Gerry Conway would think of and sees the clone of Gwen Stacey. I don't remember what issue it was, but that's what editor Ralph Macchio gets paid for. He'll insert the exact issue number right about...here...

It would take forever, but we eventually perfected our one-take recording of the entire issue. I was the voice of Peter, Gwen, and Robbie Robertson. My brother would be The Tornado and various henchmen. And all the French people sounded like...well, like 10 year olds doing French accents.

It became a real art form.

I don't know exactly when we stopped making them, but I'm pretty sure it was around the same time my mom came across one of the tapes. She didn't know what it was, popped it in only to hear my brother and I reenacting an intimate scene between Reed Richards and Sue Storm. Basically it was me doing both voices and then kissing my hand for a sound effect, but regardless, it creeped my mom out.

Here is the following interaction between my mom and myself. She is standing in the doorway to my room holding the tape.

"Is this you?"

"Yes?"

"What is this?"

"It's mine!"

"How are you making the kissing noises?"

"With my hand?"

"You're not kissing your brother like that, are you?"

"Oh God, no. Eeww!"

"You know, that's not appropriate."

"Can I have my tape please?"

"Uh…maybe you should go outside and play or something."

So, I think you can clearly see why I was the perfect choice to write the following pages you are about to read.

Ok, not really, but it made me feel better in an odd way.


Brian Michael Bendis
Cleveland, Ohio
October, 2000

P.S. I was relating this story to one of my best friends, John, who isn't in the comics biz, and he told me that when he was that age he and his best friend had a super secret West Coast Avengers Club.

Now that's just weird.

IMAGECOMICS.COM

# MORE GREAT TITLES FROM IMAGE

**A DISTANT SOIL VOL I**
**THE GATHERING**
ISBN: 1-887259-51-2
STAR07382

**AGE OF BRONZE VOL I**
**A THOUSAND SHIPS**
ISBN: 1-58240-2000
STAR13458

**ARIA VOL I**
**THE MAGIC OF ARIA**
ISBN: 1-58240-139-X
STAR11559

**AVIGON**
ISBN: 1-58240-182-9
STAR11946

**BLUNTMAN AND CHRONIC**
1-58240-208-6
STAR13070

**BULLETPROOF MONK**
ISBN: 1-58240-244-2
STAR16331

**CHASING DOGMA**
ISBN: 1-58240-206-X
STAR13071

**CLERKS**
THE COMIC BOOKS
ISBN: 1-58240-209-4
STAR13071

**DARKNESS VOL I**
**COMING OF AGE**
ISBN: 1-58240-032-6
STAR08526

**DAWN VOL II**
**RETURN OF THE GODDESS**
ISBN: 1-58240-242-6
STAR15771

**DELICATE CREATURES** ISBN:
1-58240-225-6
STAR14906

**E.V.E. PROTOMECHA VOL I**
**SINS OF THE DAUGHTER**
ISBN: 1-58240-214-0
STAR13075

**FATHOM VOL I**
ISBN: 1-58240-210-8
STAR15804

**G.I. JOE VOL I**
**REINSTATED**
ISBN: 1-58240-252-3
STAR16642

**GOLDFISH**
**THE DEFINITIVE COLLECTION**
ISBN: 1-58240-195-0
STAR13576

**JINX**
**THE DEFINITIVE COLLECTION**
ISBN: 1-58240-179-9
STAR13039

**KABUKI VOL I**
**CIRCLE OF BLOOD**
ISBN: 1-88727-9-806
STAR12480

**KIN VOL I**
**DESCENT OF MAN**
**ISBN: 1-58240-224-8**
**STAR15032**

**LAZARUS CHURCHYARD**
**THE FINAL CUT**
ISBN: 1-58240-180-2
STAR12720

**LEAVE IT TO CHANCE VOL I**
**SHAMAN'S RAIN**
ISBN: 1-58240-253-1
STAR16641

**LIBERTY MEADOWS VOL I**
**EDEN**
ISBN: 1-58240-260-4
STAR16143

**MAGDALENA VOL I**
**BLOOD DIVINE**
ISBN: 1-58240-215-9
STAR15519

**MAGE:**
**THE HERO DEFINED VOL I**
ISBN: 1-58240-012-1
STAR08160

**NOWHERESVILLE**
ISBN: 1-58240-241-8
STAR15904

**OBERGEIST VOL I**
**THE DIRECTOR'S CUT**
ISBN: 1-58240-243-4
STAR15853

**POWERS VOL I**
**WHO KILLED RETRO GIRL?**
ISBN: 1-58240-223-X
STAR12482

**RISING STARS VOL I**
**BORN IN FIRE**
ISBN: 1-58240-172-1
STAR12207

**SAVAGE DRAGON VOL I**
**BAPTISM OF FIRE**
ISBN: 1-58240-165-9
STAR13080

**TELLOS VOL I**
**RELUCTANT HEROES**
ISBN: 1-58240-186-1
STAR12831

**TOMB RAIDER VOL I**
**SAGA OF THE MEDUSA MASK**
ISBN: 1-58240-164-0
STAR03000

**TORSO**
**THE DEFINITIVE COLLECTION**
ISBN: 1-58240-174-8
STAR12688

**VIOLENT MESSIAHS VOL I**
**THE BOOK OF JOB**
ISBN: 1-58240-236-1
STAR160053

**WITCHBLADE VOL I**
**ORIGINS**
ISBN: 1-887279-65-2
STAR07991

**ZORRO**
**THE COMPLETE ALEX TOTH**
ISBN: 1-58240-090-3
STAR14527

image®
COMICS

## BACKLIST

For The Comic Shop Near You Carrying Comics And Collections From Image Comics, Please Call Toll Free 1-888-Comic Book.

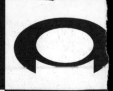